AUTHORITY IN
THE MODERN STATE

AUTHORITY IN THE MODERN STATE

BY
HAROLD J. LASKI

ARCHON BOOKS
1968

LIBRARY OF CONGRESS CATALOG CARD NUMBER: 68-21685
PRINTED IN THE UNITED STATES OF AMERICA

091229

TO
MR. JUSTICE HOLMES
AND
FELIX FRANKFURTER
THE TWO YOUNGEST OF MY FRIENDS

I AM tempted to believe that what we call necessary institutions are often no more than institutions to which we
have grown accustomed, and that in matters of social
constitution the field of possibilities is much more extensive than men living in their various societies are ready
to imagine.

Recollections of de Tocqueville,
Page 101.

PREFACE

THIS volume is in some sort the sequel to a book on the problem of sovereignty which I published in March, 1917. It covers rather broader ground, since its main object is to insist that the problem of sovereignty is only a special case of the problem of authority, and to indicate what I should regard as the main path of approach to its solution. Where, therefore, the previous studies were, in the main, negative and critical, this book is positive and constructive. In the main, the evidence upon which its conclusions are based is French. That is because an earlier study of de Maistre convinced me that it is in France, above all, that the ideals I have tried to depict are set in the clearest and most suggestive light. I had originally intended to follow this volume by a third essay on the political theory of the Conciliar Movement. But it now seems to me more useful to attempt a definitely constructive analysis of politics in the perspective set by the first chapter of this present volume. Accordingly I have planned a full book on the theory of the state which I hope to have ready within a reasonable time.

For so modest a volume this book, like its predecessors, has debts too immense to go without acknowledgement. Among the dead, I would like to emphasise how very much I have learned from Acton and Maitland; their writings have been to me a veritable store-house of inspiration. Among living men, I owe much to Professor Duguit of Bordeaux, to Dr. Figgis, and, in spite of, and perhaps because of, our differences, to Professor Dicey. My old tutor, Mr. Ernest Barker of New College, is the unconscious sponsor of this, as of my earlier book. Indeed, if it has merit of any kind, it is to the teaching of politics in the Modern History School at Oxford that I would ascribe it.

Friends have been generous in their counsel. My colleagues, Dean Pound and Professor McIlwain, have been untiring in their constant encouragement; and from Dean Pound's own writings, soon, one may hope, to be collected in some more permanent form, I learned the value of a pragmatic theory of state-function. My friends of the *New Republic*, particularly Mr. Francis Hackett, and Mr. Herbert Croly, have given me generous assistance. Mr. Graham Wallas has lent me great aid by friendly and suggestive counsel; and I found his "Great Society" an invaluable guide to many difficult paths. To an unknown critic in the London *Times* I owe the debt that keen comment must always create.

But the great obligation of the book is to Mr. Justice Holmes. It goes too deep for words; and I can only emphasise my consciousness that I shall never know how much I have in these years learned from the talks we have had and the letters he has written. They are things that come but once or twice in a lifetime.

One more personal word the reader will perhaps allow me. I began my other book with a sense that it might give pleasure to my friend A. R. Herron. He was killed before I could finish it. This book would have gone to my friend Frank Haldinstein, scholar of Christ Church and captain in the Royal Engineers. But his name, too, has been added to the list on which the Oxford of my generation will, with undying pride, write those of Arthur Heath, of Nowell Sievers, and of A. D. Gillespie—all of them of New College. When I look back on certain magic nights at Oxford and re-read these pages in the light of their memory, I realise how halting they are compared to the things they would have said. But I take it that for them the one justification of this conflict would have been the thought that we who are left are trying in some sort to understand the problems of the state they died to make free. To have known them was an education in liberty.

Lastly, as also firstly, every page of this book has in it the help my wife has given me. But to do more than mention that is unnecessary for either of us.

HAROLD J. LASKI.

April 21, 1918.
Harvard University.

CONTENTS

AUTHORITY IN
THE MODERN STATE

CHAPTER ONE

AUTHORITY IN THE MODERN STATE

I. THE ORIGINS OF THE MODERN STATE

MAN is a community-building animal: it is by reverent contact with Aristotle's fundamental observation that every political discussion must now begin. We start with the one compulsory form of human association—the state—as the centre of analysis. Yet there are few subjects upon which enquiry is so greatly needed as upon the mechanisms by which it lives. Outside our state-context we are, after all, largely unintelligible, must be, as Aristotle so scornfully proclaimed, beasts or gods who defy interpretation. Even in birth we inherit the qualities of unnumbered generations so that a bias is present before ever it has obtained expression. This emphasis upon state-life has become more vital as the scale of existence has become progressively greater. To the unity of interdependence, at least, the world has been reduced, so that, today, the whim of a New York millionaire may well affect the lives of thousands in the cotton-mills of Bombay.[1]

Not that state-history can in any adequate sense be made the biography of great men. We can even less today accept the epic-theory of Carlyle than that so characteristically contributed by Bolingbroke to Voltaire when he found in the interplay of personal fantasy the true source of events. Not, of course, that history will ever be an exact science in the sense that exactness belongs to mathematical enquiry. It is only magnificent sciolists like Machiavelli who dare to look upon history as an endless cycle. For most it will mainly be what Thucydides strove to make of it—the great storehouse of political wisdom. For all history that is not merely annalistic must lead to the formulation of conclusions. It has in it the full materials for a state-philosophy simply because

[1] G. Wallas, "The Great Society," p. 3 f.

the evidence we possess so largely relates to political life. From Aristotle down to our own time the one constant effort has been the determination of the conditions upon which that life should be lived. And, where the effort has been most fruitful, it has been induction from experience. Systems have helped us little enough. The vague ideal of a revolution, the chance phrase of an orator, the incisive induction of some thinker more deeply-seeing than the rest—it is upon these that, for the most part, our creeds have been builded. The sources of our principles are as varied as human experience simply because there has, from the outset, been no large tract of human life with which the state has not concerned itself.

Certainly the state has about it the majesty of history; and it is old enough to make its present substance seem permanent to the mass of men. It has become so integral a part of our lives that the fact of its evolution is no longer easy to remember.[2] It has almost passed beyond the region where criticism may enter by reason of the very greatness of its mission. Aristotle's formula for the expression of its purpose has lent it a great, if specious aid. The realisation of individual virtue in the common good[3] is a conception fine enough, in all conscience, to suffuse with a glamour of which the treachery is too late discovered the processes by which it moves along its way. The conception is yet inadequate because it fails to particularise those upon whom it is intended that benefit shall be conferred. Aristotle himself had certainly what the modern age would regard as an impossibly narrow conception of citizenship;[4] and Plato's virtue is so confined to the special experiences to which it is annexed as to limit to but few the full enjoyment of capacities.[5] The nature of the state, moreover, has become

[2] A book that would do on the grand scale what Mr. Edward Jenks so brilliantly attempted in his "Short History of Politics" is badly needed; but it would need the learning of Lord Acton combined with the large vision of Mr. Graham Wallas to write it.

[3] Cf. T. H. Green, "Collected Works," Vol. II, pp. 550-1.

[4] "Politics," 11, 5. 1264 b.

[5] Cf. the admirable remarks of Mr. Barker in his "Political Thought of Plato and Aristotle," p. 113. I think his argument is even more strongly reinforced when the attempt of the Meno to specialise ἀρετή into a purely functional quality is remembered.

so intimately involved with that of society that we tend, like
Hegel, to speak of it less in terms of logic than of rhapsody.[6]
Yet the very fact that it has a history should surely make
us cautious. The state is no unchanging organisation. It is
hardly today either in purpose or in method what it was to the
Greek philosophers, or to the theologians of the medieval time.
The medieval state is a church; and the differentiation of civil
from religious function is a matter of no slight difficulty.[7] In
the form in which it becomes immediately recognisable to ourselves the modern state is, clearly enough, the offspring of the
Reformation, and it bears upon its body the tragic scars of
that mighty conflict. What it is, it has essentially become by
virtue of the experience it has encountered. Upon its face is
written large the effort of great thinkers to account for the
unique claims it has made upon the loyalties of men. Nor is
their thought less clearly present, even if it be but by implication, in the policy of those who have directed political
destinies.

The modern state, we urge, is the outcome of the religious
struggle of the sixteenth century; or, at least, it is from that
crisis that it derives the qualities today most especially its own.
The notion of a single and universal authority commensurate
with the bounds of social life was utterly destroyed when Luther
appealed to the princes in the interests of religious reform.
External unity was destroyed to be replaced by a system of
separate unities and the weapon of divine right was the instrument he forged to that end.[8] What, virtually, he did was to
assume the sacredness of power, and thus, by implication, the
eternal rightness of its purposes. He builded better than he
knew. The religious disruption synchronised with the full

[6] Cf. "Philosophy of Right" (trans. Dyde), p. 278. The very brilliant
paper of Mr. Bosanquet printed in the *International Crisis*, p. 132 f.,
hardly speaks a different language. Cf. also the amazing citation from
Sir Henry Jones in J. A. Hobson, "Democracy after the War," p. 118.

[7] As Dr. Figgis has very brilliantly shown, "Churches in the Modern
State," Appendix B.

[8] Or perhaps rediscovered. The political theory of the early fathers
never, of course, dissented from the sacredness of secular power. It is only
in the excitement of the investure controversy that its indirect derivation
began to be seriously urged.

realisation of national consciousness in Western Europe, and
the modern state is clearly visible as a territorial society divided
into government and subjects. The great preamble to the
Statute of Appeals[9]—the one statutory example of English
Byzantinism—is no more than official announcement that the
English state permits no question of Henry's complete sovereignty. Government, for the most part, was royal; for over the
free towns of Germany, and the Italian cities, was cast the dubious cloak of imperial suzerainty. Holland had not yet arisen
to suggest the problems of a sovereign republic.

But state and society are not yet equated. That is the work
of the thinkers of the Counter-Reformation. The church might,
as in England, assume a national form; but religious difference
went deep enough to limit state-absorptiveness. France learned
a partial toleration from the misery of civil war; and almost a
century of social and economic confusion was necessary before
Germany took a similar road. Not that this early toleration is
at all complete; it is born too painfully for that. It is, at most,
the sense of the French politiques that the state must not perish
for religion's sake. It admits the impossibility of making men
sacrifice their consciences upon a single altar. The task of conviction was no easy one, and the lesson was only partially learned.
Europe, in what at least the medieval thinkers deemed most
fundamental, had become accustomed to unity of outlook.
Unity of outlook was secured by reference of power to a single
centre. The partition of Western civilisation into a medley of
religious systems developed problems of the first importance.
A man might owe allegiance to Rome in one set of opinions and
to London in another. He might think as Pius V bade him in
matter of transubstantiation, and in those great political questions of 1588 take the fleet into the English channel against the
papally-approved might of Spain. Your Catholic might be a
member of the English state, but there was always, for him a
power outside. For some, it might preside over all indirectly;[10]
for others it might only in its own sphere be supreme. But,
where conflict came, men like Parsons would show that to

[9] 25 H. VIII, c. 19.
[10] As the Jesuits argued. Cf. Figgis, "From Gerson to Grotius" (2d ed.),
p. 203 f.

attack the state was not an onslaught on the fabric of society.[11] Thus, from the outset of its modern history, the problem is raised as to the authority to be possessed by the state. Not Romanists alone doubt its absoluteness. Archbishop Whitgift set the keynote to the temper that is turned into theory. He was by nature inapt to grasp the niceties of political metaphysics, and a Presbyterian theory which, like that of Cartwright, struck at the root of state-omnipotence aroused him to fierce anger.[12] From the threshold of the seventeenth century what the state demands is the whole of man's allegiance lest, in seeking less, it should obtain nothing. James I had at least a logician's mind. Aiming at supreme power for the state he deemed himself to personify, he could not doubt that Presbyterian structure was subversive of his whole position. If the ultimate seat of authority were not with himself, he seemed already on the threshold of anarchy. The only difference between Parliament and the Stuarts was as to the place in which that supreme power resided; and Parliament made the Civil War the proof of its hypothesis. Hobbes only got his volume printed under the Commonwealth because it conveniently applied to any form of despotism.

The medieval worship of unity,[13] in fact, is inherited by the modern state; and what changes in the four centuries of its modern history is simply the place in which the controlling factor of unity is to be found. To the Papacy it seemed clear in medieval times that the power to bind and loose had given it an authority without limit or question. The modern state inherits the papal prerogative. It must, then, govern all; and to govern all there must be no limit to the power of those instruments by which it acts. Catholic and Nonconformist are alike excluded from citizenship simply because they denied, as it deemed, the fulness of state authority. They refuse absorption by its instruments, and the penalty of refusal is exclusion.[14] The

[11] Cf. Prof. McIlwain's brilliant introduction to his edition of the "Political Works of James I" (Harvard University Press, 1918).

[12] Strype, "Life of Whitgift," II, 22 ff.

[13] Cf. my "Problem of Sovereignty," p. 2.

[14] This is what Mr. Seaton, in his admirable book, calls the second stage of religious persecution. "Toleration under the Later Stuarts," p. 6 f.

representatives of the state must be sovereign, and if the Stuarts abuse their prerogative, the result is, not its limitation but its transference to Parliament. Always the stern logic of theory seems to imply that the dominating institution is absolute. Locke, indeed, saw deeper, and argued to a state that thought it had already won its freedom that power must be limited by its service to the purposes it is intended to accomplish.[15] But the accident of foreign rule gave that power a basis in what could, relatively at least to continental fact, be termed popular consent. Thenceforth the sovereignty of Parliament became the fundamental dogma of English constitutionalism. Without, there might be the half articulate control of public opinion; but that, as Rousseau said,[16] was free only at election time. Its control was essentially a reserve-power, driven to action only at moments of decisive crisis. "A supreme, irresistible, uncontrollable authority, in which the *jura summa imperii* or rights of sovereignty reside"[17] is, as Blackstone says, the legal theory which lies at the root of the English State. For practical purposes, that is to say, the sovereignty of the English state means the sovereignty of the King in Parliament.[18]

France travelled more slowly, but, always, it was in the same direction she was travelling. Her earliest political speculation was, as Bodin bears witness, already of a sovereign state; and it is, as he emphasises, a state which boasts a royal organ to declare its sovereign purposes. Bossuet makes it clear that the centralising efforts of her three great ministers had not been vain; and it was not merely Voltaire's acid humor that made him equate the sovereignty of France with the will of Louis XIV. But, sooner or later, abuse involves disruption. The atmosphere of the eighteenth century was not favourable to the retention of a belief in divinities. The profound speculation of Montesquieu, the unanswerable questions of Rousseau, herald a transference of power similar to that of England. The people becomes master in its own house, and the dogma of national

---

[15] Second treatise, Ch. XI, Sec. 14 f.

[16] "Contrat Social," Bk. III, Ch. XV.

[17] Comm. I, 48.

[18] I think this would express, somewhat differently, the point made by Professor Dicey in the famous first chapter of his "Law of the Constitution."

sovereignty becomes the corner stone of the reconstructed edifice.[19] But as in England, the sovereign people is too large for continuous action. Its powers become delegated to the complex of institutions we call government. Thenceforth, for general purposes, it is through this channel that the state-will is expressed. Parliament is the nation, and its sovereignty is there given adequate fulfilment.[20] Only on rare occasions, as in 1830 and in 1848, is there sign of clear dissent from governmental purposes. Only then, that is to say, can we argue a revocation of powers.

Nor is American evolution at all different, though here there are more checks upon the exercise of the governmental power.[21] The people is ultimately sovereign in the sense that, sooner or later, it may, through proper reforms, or, in the last resort, through revolution, get itself obeyed. There is no immediately sovereign body, as in England or in France. Certain limitations upon state and federal government are taken as fundamental and continuous expressions of popular desire; and the rights thus enshrined in the constitution it is the business of the Supreme Court to maintain. Yet, even here, it is, for most purposes, a governmental will that we at each moment encounter. The problem of authority may ultimately resolve itself into a question of what a section of the American people, strong enough to get its will enforced, may desire.[22] But such continuous resolve as the business of state daily requires one hundred million people cannot directly undertake. What here becomes essential is the device of representation. Sovereignty, therefore, in America, as elsewhere, is the acts of government as the people and the Supreme Court acquiesce in their enforcement. The multiplicity of governmental powers demanded by the federal system makes no difference; it is merely a question

[19] Cf. the suggestive brochure of Hauriou, "Du Souveraineté Nationale."

[20] The reader can get a clear idea of this article by comparing the speeches of M. Barthou, March 19, 1909; of M. Ribot, May 14, 1907; of M. Deschonel, May 2d, 1907; and of M. Clémenceau, March 13, 1908—all in the Chamber of Deputies. I have discussed them below in the chapter on administrative syndicalism.

[21] Cf. the interesting remarks of Boutmy, "Studies in Constitutional Law" (trans. Dicey), p. 159 f.

[22] As in the Civil War.

of administrative convenience. The fundamental fact is that when we speak of acts done by America the actor is a government of which the subjects are more or less inert instruments. In that sense American evolution, though superficially different in form is, in substantial character, similar to the development of the European system.

II. STATE AND GOVERNMENT

IT is, then, with a sovereign state that we are today confronted. For its fundamental agents, that is to say, there is claimed a power from which no appeal is to be made. The attributes of sovereignty have been admirably described by Paley. Its power, he says,[23] "may be termed absolute, omnipotent, uncontrollable, arbitrary, despotic, and is alike so in all countries." Limitation of any kind it does not therefore admit; it acts as it deems adequate to its purposes. But the state, of course, may assume a variety of forms. It may, as in the France of the *ancien régime*, be an absolute monarchy. It may, as in the England of the eighteenth century, be a narrow oligarchy, or, as in modern America, its form may be democratic. The substance of the state, however, does not so vary. It is always a territorial society in which there is a distinction between government and subjects. The question of form must, of course, affect the question of substance; but its real reference is, in fact, to the prevailing type of government. That is, in part, a question of those who share in power; in part, also, a question of the basis upon which responsibility is to rest.

Such a definition excludes the equation of state with society. The exclusion is made because there are obviously social relationships which can not be expressed through the state. It may be true that man's nature is determined by the environment in which he lives, but that environment is not merely a state-creation. No one would claim in England, for example, that the Roman Catholic church is a part of the state; but it is yet obvious that it acts upon its members as a social determinant. The family is an institution of society, and no one will doubt that the state may affect it; but it is not merely a part of the state. The state is concerned only with those social relations

---

[23] "Moral and Political Philosophy," Bk. VI, Ch. VI.

that express themselves by means of government.[24] That is not to say that the province of the government may not be wide; and, indeed, as at Geneva under Calvin, there may be almost no element in life with which it may not attempt to concern itself. But immediately it is perceived that there are relationships that in fact escape its purview, it becomes obvious that the state is only a species of a larger genus, and the nature of its especial problems begins to emerge. For churches, trade-unions, and a thousand other associations are all societies. They refuse absorption by the state and thereby raise, sometimes in acute form, the definition of their connexion with it. Churches, certainly, have denied to the state any absolute sovereignty; by which they mean that the canons of their life are not subject to the control of its instruments.[25] Trade-unions have been hardly less defiant. The state, indeed, has rarely hesitated to claim paramount authority, even if, on the occasions of conflict, it has not been overwhelmingly successful.[26] The claim is naturally important; but, manifestly, if it has not, in the event, been able to prove itself, it demands more rigid enquiry.

It makes clear, however, the point upon which insistence must be laid. Whatever power the state may assume, we have always its division into a small number who exert active power, and a larger number who, for the most part, acquiesce in the decisions that are made.[27] Obviously, of course, the fact of acquiescence is vital; for Hume long ago made it a commonplace that ultimate power is always on the side of the governed.[28] The fact of power may be most variously justified. Divine

[24] Mr. Cole, indeed, actually defines the state in terms of government only ("Self-Government in Industry," p. 70 f.), but though this is a result largely true it seems to me, for reasons explained below, the second and not the first state of the process.

[25] Cf. Hansard, 4th Series, Vol. 115, Sep. 2d, 1902, p. 1014. Mr. Perks, "The question whether a Nonconformist will be justified or not in resisting the rate is a matter for each individual conscience, and having settled that question for himself, we will not be likely to be influenced in the slightest degree by the fact that he may lose his right as a citizen."

[26] Cf. my "Problem of Sovereignty," Chs. II-V for some instances.

[27] Cf. Duguit, "L'Etat: Le Droit Objectif," pp. 242-54.

[28] "Essays: of the First Principles of Government" (World's Classics ed., p. 29).

right, utility, or social contract are all methods that have on occasion been used to demonstrate legitimacy. What, in general, we assume is an identity of interest between government and subjects. We lend to government the authority of the state upon the basis of a conviction that its will is a will effecting the purpose for which the state was founded. The state, we broadly say, exists to promote the good life, however variously defined; and we give government the power to act for the promotion of that life. Its acts, then, in our view, are coloured by the motives that lie behind it. It wins our loyalty by the contribution it can make to the achievement of the state-purpose.

We can, then, distinguish between state and government. Rousseau quite clearly grasped this difference. The state, for him, was the collective moral person formed by the whole body of citizens; the government was merely an executive organ by which the state-will could be carried into effect.[29] He realised the clear possibility of disparity of effort. A government that sought to usurp power for selfish ends has not been unknown; and Rousseau therefore reserved sovereignty—for him the ultimate right to do anything—for the state alone.[30] Power was authority that had not yet been dignified by moral attributes; and that alone the government possessed until judgment of its motives had been made.[31] Where he went wrong was in his effort to ascribe a necessarily beneficent will to the state itself—a view that, largely dependent as it was upon his identification of state and society—was in reality no more than an *a priori* assumption.[32] There is no will that is good merely by self-definition; it is actual substantiation in terms of the event that alone can be accepted as valid. To introduce, as he did, a distinction between the "general" will and the "will of all," is, in reality, simply to take refuge in mysticism. A will that fulfils the purpose of the state is, of course, good where the end of the state is, by definition, good also; but that is a question of fact upon which opinions may differ. What Herbert Spencer thought for the good of the state Professor Huxley dismissed as

[29] "Contrat Social," Bk. III, Ch. 1.
[30] *Ibid.*, Bk. III, Ch. X.
[31] Cf. *Ibid.*, Bk. III, Chs. XVI and XVIII.
[32] Cf. the admirable appendix in Professor Maciver's recent volume, "Community," p. 413 f.

administrative nihilism. Numbers, certainly, even to the point
of unanimity, make no difference. They may justify political
action; but they will provide no guaranty of its rightness.
Since Rousseau wrote, moreover, a new complication has been
introduced in the problem of size. In the Greek city-state, in
Geneva, in the republic of Andorra, it was comparatively easy
to discover an effective popular opinion; today, as John
Chipman Gray so admirably said, the real rulers of a society
are undiscoverable. The new Chancellor of the Exchequer
may be dependent upon a permanent official whose very name
is unknown to the vast majority whose destinies he may so
largely shape; and, indeed, the position of the English civil-
servant has been defined as that of a man who has exchanged
dignity for power. Public opinion may be the ultimate controlling factor; but not the least complex of our problems is,
as Mr. Lowell has said,[33] to discover when it is public and when
it is opinion.

Accepted theory tells us that the state is sovereign. It is,
that is to say, the supreme embodiment of power. What its
will has determined it has the right to enforce. Yet in the only
sense in which this is an acceptable theory, it in reality tells us
nothing. The state exists as the most adequate means we have
yet invented for the promotion of an end we deem good. If by
the emphasis of its sovereignty we mean that it must be obeyed,
the thesis is self-evident when its act is in accordance with that
end; but no one, surely, would urge that the state must be
obeyed if the methods it followed were those of Machiavelli's
prince. How are we, save by individual judgment, to tell if the
state-act is in truth the adequate expression of right purpose?
Rousseau resolved the difficulty by making his state call fre-
quent meetings of its citizens and assuming rightness where
moral unanimity was secured.[34] Yet there are few who have
lived through this age of blood and iron who will be willing to
attribute infallibility even to an unanimous people. Nor does
Rousseau meet the difficulty that, in sober fact, the modern
state cannot function save by selecting certain of its members
for the fulfilment of its task; and that selection means that our

[33] "Public Opinion and Popular Government," Part One.
[34] "Contrat Social," Bk. III, Ch. XVIII.

obedience, in reality, goes to a government of which we accept,
for the most part, the decisions. But few who accept on the
ground of high purpose the sovereignty of the state will urge
that government is similarly sovereign. The difference of fundamental moral emphasis may well be vital.

To postulate the sovereignty of the state, therefore, is hardly
helpful unless we know two things. We need, in the first place,
to enquire by what criteria the consent of the state to some
course of governmental action is to be inferred. We need also to
have information as to the coincidence of the action with what
is termed right conduct. But it is surely obvious that these
criteria and this information are, in fact, established by each
one of us. No matter what the influence which constrains us
to refusal or acceptance it is, at bottom, an individual act of
will. The real basis of law, therefore, is somehow in the individual mind. Our attitude to it may be most variously determined. An Irish peasant of the seventies may have gone moon-
lighting less from an opinion that violence alone would teach
the British government its lesson than from a fear of local dis-
approval. But, politically, we can be concerned not with the
hidden motives but with the overt acts of men. In that sense
the basis of the state is clearly a reservoir of individualism because each will is something that ultimately is self-determined.
What determines it to act is a different and far more complex
question; but there is never in the state an *a priori* certainty
that a government act will be obeyed. The possibility of anarchy is theoretically at every moment present. Why it is
rarely operative demands more detailed investigation.

A realistic analysis of the modern state thus suggests that
what we term state-action is, in actual fact, action by government. It is a policy offered to the people for its acceptance.
It becomes state-action when that acceptance is predominantly
operative. The passive resistance of the Nonconformists to
Mr. Balfour's Education Act, for example, was not sufficient to
make the Act void. It was able to be put into operation and
was therefore accepted by the English state. There have, of
course, been periods when this twofold stage of political action
was only partially necessary. The Greek city-state acted not
by means of representative government but, at least in certain

periods of its history, by the voice of its whole citizen-body. It thus fulfilled Rousseau's ideal of a continuous exercise of sovereign power. But that can no longer be the case. The modern state, for good or ill, has outgrown the possibility of government by public meeting, and it is upon some system of representation that reliance must be placed.[35] The representative organ is, directly or indirectly, government. State-action, in such analysis, is simply an act of government which commands general acceptance. This M. Esmein has clearly perceived. "Although", he says,[36] "the legislative power is the true regulator of sovereignty, it is above all by the executive power, that its action is felt by the citizen body." Such a theory has at least the merit of fitting the actual facts. It makes no moral presumptions. It takes account of the fact that the state as a whole may repudiate, as in 1688, the acts of its representatives for reasons that it deems good. It admits, what the situation itself compels us to admit, that the exercise of authority, whether we call it power or sovereignty or what we will, is, in the vast majority of cases, in the hands of government.

In such an aspect, several results are immediately obvious. An adequate theory of the state must examine not so much the claims of authority but their actual validation in terms of practice. Its assumptions are naturally important; but it is rather as an *a priori* index to achievement than as a definitive measure of it that they must be regarded. It is, that is to say, helpful to be told that the object of the state is to secure the good life. But however important may be the knowledge of purpose, much more important is the knowledge of function. The state, for instance, to its members is essentially a great public service corporation; and it is, to put it bluntly, upon dividends that the mind of the public is concentrated. The question we must ask is not what the state set out to do, but what, in historic fact, has been done in its name. In terms of prediction, we do not ask the moral programme of a state: the more fruitful method is

[35] On the comparative value of large and small states of the remarks of Freeman. "Hist. of Federal Government in Greece and Italy" (ed. of 1893), p. 39 ff.

[36] "Eléments du Droit Constitutionnel" (ed. of 1906), p. 22, and cf. Jellinek, "System der Oeffentlichen subjektiven Rechte," p. 28.

by the patient analysis of its practices, to discover their probable result. The problem of authority then becomes clear. We want to know why men obey government. We want the causes that explain the surely striking fact of a voluntary servitude of a large mass of men to a small portion of their number. We want to know also the way in which authority should be organised if the results of the state-purpose are best to be attained. Do we need, for instance, one authority, or many? Is it, as Rousseau conceived, dangerous to divide our power? Must the force at the command of authority be, as the timid Hobbes assumed, without limit of any kind? Is the individual, in other words, absorbed in the state? Does his freedom mean, as Hegel makes it mean, to live the life that authority ordains? Or does freedom mean the recognition that there are certain reserves within the individual mind about which ultimate resistances must be organised? Has man, that is to say, rights against the state? If he belongs to a church, where must his obedience go if there is conflict of authority? Is he interstitial no less than social, and must we protect his denial of complete submergence in his fellowships? To none of these questions can we yet obtain in any sense an adequate response. Yet it is these questions we must answer if we are one day to have a working philosophy of the state.

III. THE NATURE OF OBEDIENCE

ANY political speculation thus involves an enquiry into the nature of obedience to government. It is an enquiry which no political philosopher may yet dare to answer. One day, we may hope, the social psychologist will give us insight enough into the factors of human association to enable us to emphasise the main elements involved; and we as yet can say little more than Hume when he insisted that obedience is necessary to the existence of society. Some things, indeed, we can already vaguely see. Imitation must count for much.[37] The tendency in men—which Mr. Graham Wallas has even dignified into an instinct—to accept leadership is vital.[38] We can hardly ap-

[37] But see an important warning as to its influence in G. Wallas, "The Great Society," Ch. VIII.
[38] Cf. the admirable chapter of Dr. MacDougall, "Social Psychology," Ch. VII, esp. p. 194 f.

prove the account of Sir Henry Maine which makes of it a habit bred into the tissue of the race by countless ages of subservience to the state; though it is no doubt true that to an extent which greatly needs analysis the state is built upon the inertia of men.[39] Macaulay, in an interesting passage,[40] has told us how naturally the Duke of Wellington took for granted the courageous discipline of the soldiers on the ill-fated *Birkenhead;* and, in a less degree, this sense of discipline that results from training must play a large part in ordering life. But it is not the whole answer to the problem.[41]

Political thinkers are, for the most part, divided in their answer (at best provisional) into two schools. The most fundamental, because it is that which has most subtly influenced the results of juridical enquiry, is perhaps the school of Hobbes. In that view, obedience is founded upon fear. Government is able to exert the authority it possesses because it has behind it the ultimate sanction of force. Men obey its dictates because the pain of disobedience makes them cowards. Law is thus the command of government, and we obey the law because the penalties of disobedience are, for most of us, too serious to be endured. The theory does not, perhaps, take the highest view of human nature; but the fear-psychologists, from Thrasymachus to Hobbes, are rarely generous in their outlook. That the theory has an element of truth is, of course, indubitable. But that it is obviously only a partial explanation immediately the history of coercion is studied is surely not less clear. No one can watch the slow rise of toleration into acceptance, can see how dubiously it was proposed, and how suspiciously it was put into operation, without realising that if, ultimately, acceptance came, it can only have been because the attempt to use fear as a method of compulsion proved, in the event, to be worthless. If fear was the real ground of obedience, the early Christians could hardly have survived; and certainly the failure of the Penal Laws against Catholicism in England becomes inexplicable. The fact is that a unity produced by terror is at best but artificial; and where the deepest

[39] H. Maine, "Popular Government," p. 63.

[40] "Life," by Sir G. Trevelyan (Nelson's ed.), 11. 293.

[41] Cf. Mr. Wallas' remarks, "The Great Society," Ch. V.

convictions of men are attacked terror must prove ultimately worthless.[42]

The school of which the name of Rousseau is deservedly the most famous adopted an entirely different attitude. For it, the basis of obedience is consent. Men obey government because the return for their obedience is the "real" freedom it is the object of the state-life to secure. Unless that obedience be general, anarchy is inevitable; acceptance of the government's command is therefore essential that its purposes may be made secure. For Rousseau himself, perhaps, it is the will of the citizen-body alone that must be binding; but it is difficult to see how that will can be directly known in the modern state. And for political purposes it is probable that this is the most fruitful avenue of approach. It needs, indeed, a singularly careful statement. The idea of a social contract itself we have to reject as fiction; and it is perhaps safer not to make use of the term contractual in the determination of state relations. For contract, after all, is a definite legal term to which precise meaning is attached; and to apply it to the vague expectations raised by the acts of government is to shroud ourselves in illusion.[43] But the emphasis of consent is unconnected with such difficulties. It emphasises, what needs continual iteration, that the end of the state is fundamental. It throws into relief the striking fact that while the government of the state must endure, if its own existence is to be possible, its purpose is at each stage subject to examination. Members of the state we all may be, but it must exist not less for our welfare than its own. It is here, perhaps, that we have been led astray by the dangerous analogies of the nineteenth century. When we accept the idea of the state as an organism, what is emphasised is subjection of its parts to the welfare of the whole. But, in sober fact, the welfare of the state means nothing if it does not mean the concrete happiness of its living members. In

[42] Cf. Sir F. Pollock's interesting essay on the Theory of Persecution, "Essays in Jurisprudence and Ethics," esp. p. 175.

[43] This, I think, would equally apply to the school of M. Leon Bourgeois which explains the state as founded upon quasi-contract. Every lawyer knows what quasi-contract is, but in the realm of politics it only serves to give a specious exactness to inexact notions.

that aspect, the concept of an organism is, as Dr. McTaggart has brilliantly insisted,[44] inapplicable. For the individual regards himself as an end not less than he so regards the state; and we are here again confounded by the important fact of a refusal of absorption into the whole that is greater than ourselves. If we are fundamentally Catholics, for instance, we do not the more truly realise ourselves by obeying the Clarendon Code; what we do is to make ourselves different, to destroy ourselves for the state by making for it meaningless the personality that is our contribution to its well-being. And that can only mean that acts which touch us nearly must be dependent for their validity upon the consent they can secure. Legally valid they may well be in the sense that they emanate from the authority that is empowered to enact them. But no student of politics can stop there. A political judgment is not a pronunciation of legal right alone. The law of the British constitution may not give to Englishmen the right of free speech; but that does not mean that an English Prime Minister will not encounter difficulties if he fails to regard that right as real.[45] We must, indeed, discuss the grounds upon which consent may be given or withheld; but that does not disturb the fact that the element of consent is essential to any adequate analysis.

In the theory of obedience, then, the element of consent to policy, however indirect, is of the first importance. We are, in some degree sufficient to prevent rebellion, satisfied with the provision made by government to fulfil the purposes of the state. But the fact of broadening demand is here sufficiently remarkable to merit attention. The state, we have said, exists to promote the good life of its members; government is the mechanism by which that purpose has been translated into the event. But the question of actual translation is always a question of fact. The motive of statesmen, the objective merit of their acts, demand continuous enquiry. No one can survey

[44] See his fine essay on the Conception of Society as an Organism in his "Studies in Hegelian Cosmology."

[45] For a refusal to obey the Defence of the Realm Act on this ground see an interesting note upon the action of the executive council of the Quakers in the London *Nation* for December 8, 1917, and see the report of the trial in New York *Evening Post*, June 24, 1918.

the history of the English state without being impressed with the way in which the basis of its government in consent has been progressively extended. Government, under William the Norman, is the king; the purpose it has in view in his reign is to achieve the thing he wills. The good life of its members, in any abstract ethical sense, the full realisation, for example, of the personality of the conquered Saxon churl, is here in all conscience meaningless enough. Magna Charta limits royal despotism by the controlling factor of baronial interest; yet, here again, to introduce a concept of general welfare is a dangerous anachronism. When the country gentlemen begin to rule, the state is a bigger and finer thing than when its law was a variation upon the selfish aims of William Rufus; but no one, to take a single instance, can read the record of its game laws and enclosure acts, and mistake its devotion to the interests of the squire. With the Industrial Revolution, power passes to the middle classes; but the long record of Combination Acts and of antagonism to such measures as would have given an unpropertied labourer an interest in the state, have a meaning which no honest observer can misunderstand. When Hannah More can tell the women of Shipham in 1801 that the charity dispensed to them is to show them their dependence upon the rich, and comes "of favour and not of right"[46] it is clear that the attitude she represents does not visualise a state in which the concept of the good life has or obtains any general application. The acutest of political observers in nineteenth century England, Walter Bagehot, regarded a "permanent combination" of the working classes as an "evil of the first magnitude," and he did not hesitate to say that the way in which "the electors only selected one or two wealthy men to carry out the schemes of one or two wealthy associations" was "the only way in which our own system could be maintained."[47]   No one, indeed, can read Mr. Bagehot's gloomy prophecies of the probable effects of the Reform Act of 1867

[46] Hammond, "The Town Labourer," p. 229. I know no more vivid illustration of the way in which the state-purpose changes than this brilliant book.

[47] "Collected Works," Vol. V, p. 120. The quotation is from his "English Constitution."

without feeling that for him Government is something that carries out the will of the "higher classes." When a distinguished connection of the English royal family can explain the advent of compulsory military service as "necessary at this time when the people were getting out of hand"[48] it becomes clear that scrutiny must be made of the way in which the purpose of the state gets translated into acts of government.

In such a scrutiny certain obvious facts clearly emerge. No one claims that in the modern state the good life, in any reasonable definition, is realised by any but a small minority of its members. Liberty in the sense of the positive and equal opportunity of self-realisation we have hardly in any genuine sense established. That is not a cause for repining but a simple fact; and it is to be set in the perspective of the remembrance that far larger numbers share in what of good the modern state can secure than at any previous period of history.[49] But whether we consider the patent inequalities in the distribution of wealth, the results of the competitive struggle in industry, the hopeless inadequacies of our educational systems, the one thing by which we must be impressed is the absence of proportion between political purpose and its achievement. We no longer believe that a simple individualism is the panacea for our ills. "The mere conflict of private interests", said Ingram thirty years ago,[50] "will never produce a well-ordered commonwealth of labour"; and on the other hand it is not less clear that the simple formulae of a rigid collectivism offer no real prospect of relief.[51] The truth is that in the processes of politics what, broadly speaking, gets registered is not a will that is at each moment in accord with the state-purpose, but the will of those who in fact operate the machine of government. They are, it is true, selected for that purpose by the electoral body of the state; and it is increasingly obvious that universal adult suffrage, or

[48] Quoted in J. A. Hobson, "Democracy after the War," p. 67.

[49] Even in a gloomy period of English history Francis Place could in his "Improvement of the Working People" record the great change for good that he had observed in his own lifetime.

[50] "History of Political Economy," p. 298.

[51] I mean in the simple sense that would transfer all industrial activities to government.

some close approximation to it, will be the electoral system of every country that shares in the ideals of Western civilisation.

Theoretically, doubtless, the conference of universal suffrage places political power in the hands of that part of the state which has not enjoyed, or at least only partially enjoyed, the benefit of its purposes. Nor is the reason for this hidden from us. It is more than three centuries since Harrington enunciated the law that power goes with the ownership of land;[52] and if we extend that concept, in the light of the Industrial Revolution, to capital in its broadest sense, it is now a commonplace that political power is the handmaid of economic power. In that aspect, it is not difficult to understand why the easy optimism of the reformers of the first half of the nineteenth century has been so largely disappointed.[53] They were not, in fact, attacking the real root of the problem. No political democracy can be real that is not as well the reflection of an economic democracy; for the business of government is so largely industrial in nature as inevitably to be profoundly affected by the views and purposes of those who hold the keys of economic power. That does not necessarily mean that government is consciously perverted to the ends of any class within the state. So to argue is to project into history a malignant teleology from which it is, in no small degree, free. But when power is actually exerted by any section of the community, it is only natural that it should look upon its characteristic views as the equivalent of social good. It is, for example, difficult to believe that John Bright opposed the Factory Acts with a view to his own pocket. It is not less impossible to assert that Dr. Arnold opposes the emancipation of the Jews out of a selfish desire to benefit his own church. But it was then natural even for a humane factory-owner to believe that good conduct consists in maintaining the prosperity of the manufacturing classes, and that whatever, in his judgment, is fatal to that prosperity is mischievous. Dr. Arnold believed the English nation to be by definition Christian; and to admit the Jews to Parliament would thus, in his views, have been a contradiction in

[52] "Works" (ed. cf. 1747), p. 39, cf. Bonav's remarks, "Philosophy of Political Economy," p. 90.

[53] Cf. Mr. Graham Wallas' superb analysis, "Human Nature in Politics," passim.

terms.[54] It has been necessary for Mr. Justice Holmes to remind the Supreme Court of the United States that the Fourteenth Amendment does not enact Mr. Herbert Spencer's Social Statics.[55] The fellow-servant doctrine could never have won acceptance in an industrial democracy.[56] The Osborne decision is naturally to be expected from a group of men whose circumstances and training would have obviously tended to make suspect the methods and purposes of trade-unionism.[57]

This is a truth perhaps somewhat difficult to perceive in our own day because it tends to be obscured by the mechanisms of the democratic powers. But the examination of past history makes it more than clear. No one can analyse the social and political conditions of the ancien régime in France without perceiving that the whole effort of its structure was towards the maintenance of aristocratic interests. Whether we regard the form of the States General, the composition of the Parliaments, the privileges of the nobility, it is, as Acton said, "class government" that they imply, "the negation of the very idea of state and nation."[58] The episcopal opposition to Catholic Emancipation is a similar phenomenon; it is grounded upon the conviction that it was detrimental to the interests of the Established Church.[59] The same problem confronted the authors of the American Constitution. "The most common and durable source of Factions," said Madison,[60] "has been the various and unequal distribution of property. Those who hold and those who are without property have ever formed distinct interests in society. . . . The regulation of these various and interfering interests forms the principal task of modern legislation and involves the spirit of party and faction in the necessary and ordinary operations of government." It does not, generally speaking, seem inaccurate to say that the proc-

[54] Cf. my "Problem of Sovereignty," p. 89.

[55] Lochner v. New York, 198 U. S. 45, 75-6. The whole opinion throws a flood of light upon this question.

[56] Cf. A. Birrell, "Law of Employers' Liability," p. 20.

[57] Cf. Webb, "History of Trade Unionism," Introd. to the 1911 edition, esp. p. XXV.

[58] "Lectures on the French Revolution," p. 41.

[59] Cf. my "Problem of Sovereignty," p. 123 f.

[60] *The Federalist*, No. 10.

esses of politics are a struggle between the possessors of a certain power, and those who desire to share in its exercise. The grounds of exclusion have been very various. Often we meet with suspicion of those unpossessed of property. Sometimes membership of a religious creed is held as a disqualification. The general fact is that, whatever the grounds of exclusion, those who have possession of power are not lightly persuaded to part with it, or to co-operate in its exercise. Admission to rights is the gate most difficult of entrance in the political citadel.

It is yet obvious that if the democratic synthesis be permanent—and it is upon that assumption alone that this analysis is valid—in the matter of rights there can be no differentiation. Government exercises power not in the interests of any party or class within the state but in the interest of the state as a whole. But that is undisguised idealism. In sober fact, government is exerted in the interests of those who control its exercise. That is, indeed, progressively less true. A modern parliament would not dare to debate a Factory Act in the style of 1802. Few modern statesmen would venture to analyse a Reform Bill in the caustic fashion of Bagehot or Robert Lowe. No responsible statesman would now speak of atheists in the style of Edmund Burke.[61] But once the fact is clear that the result of government is in practice different from what theory makes it, the necessary inference is a suspicion of power. What use is the sovereignty of the state if it means the aristocratic privileges of the ancien régime? What use is the sovereignty of the state if if it permits the maintenance of the slums of the modern city? The conclusion, surely, is forced upon us that the state permits a sinister manipulation of its power. It is the habit of government to translate the thoughts and feelings and passions with which it is charged into terms of the event and deem them the achievement of the state-purpose. But so specialised a welfare as that which is achieved is obviously different from the ideal end so vigorously emphasised by philosophy.

Not, indeed, that the record of government is an unrelieved catalogue of perversions. Few would be so malicious or so

[61] Cf. for instance, the second " Letter upon a Regicide Peace." "Works" (World's Classics ed.), Vol. VI, esp. p. 192 f.

stupid as not to believe that there are numerous instances of statesmen who have pursued a general good wider than their private desire because they believed the times demanded it. That, surely, was the case of Sir Robert Peel in 1846. He destroyed, almost consciously, his party in order to achieve an end he thought more splendid than its own fortune; and he did not falter even when his policy involved his political downfall. It would have been simple, to take a different problem, for John Hus at Constance, or for Luther at Worms, to have recanted. In either case the desertion would have been easy— as easy, for example, as Luther's desertion of the peasants some five years later. But the individual action does not destroy, even if it may mitigate, the general tendency. There has been yet no state in history in which the consistent effort has been towards the unique realisation of the common good.

If the state is sovereign, what, in such an aspect, does its sovereignty imply? It is, we are told, an absolute thing; and the most generous of modern German theorists has allowed it only the limitation of its personal grace. But this theory of auto-limitation is in reality meaningless;[62] for to be bound only by one's will is not, in any real sense, to be bound at all. Now sovereignty, we are told,[63] "is that power which is neither temporary, nor delegated nor subject to particular rules which it cannot alter, nor answerable to any other power on earth." What this really means is less formidable than the appearance seems to warrant. It implies only that for the courts the will of a sovereign body, the king in Parliament for example, is beyond discussion. Every judge must accept unquestioningly what fulfils the requirements of the forms of law. But, for the purposes of political philosophy, it is not so abstract and *a priori* a definition we require. What we desire to know is not what has the legal right to prevail, but what does in actual fact prevail and the reasons that explain its dominance. Here, it is clear enough, the legal theory of sovereignty is worthless. Once we are in the realm of actual life it is upon the limitations

[62] The best defense of this theory is in Jellinek, "Recht des mod. Staates," p. 421 f.

[63] Pollock, "History of the Science of Politics," p. 52. I ought to add that Sir F. Pollock is here stating a view in which he does not himself share.

of sovereignty that attention must be concentrated. What
then impresses us is the wide divergence between legal right
and moral right. Legally, an autocratic Czar may shoot down
his subjects before the winter palace at Petrograd; but, morally,
it is condemnation that we utter. Legally, Parliament could
tomorrow re-enact the Clarendon Code; but what stirs us now
is the injustice of its policy. There is, that is to say, a vast
difference between what Dean Pound has admirably called
"Law in books" and "Law in action."[64] It is with the latter
alone that a realistic theory of the state can be concerned.

IV. THE LIMITATIONS OF POWER

In actual life, then, the sovereignty of the state is subject to
limitation. The power it can exert, either directly, or through
its instruments, is never at any moment absolute. Attention
must be ceaselessly paid to the thousand varied influences that
play upon the declaration of its will. Power, that is to say, is
held upon conditions. The members of the state look to it for
certain conduct as alone capable of justification. They think,
in brief, that there are certain principles by which its life must
be regulated. Few would urge that those principles can at any
moment be regarded as unchanging. It is a matter of the
simplest demonstration that moral ideals cannot escape the
categories of evolution. Conduct that would distress one generation is regarded with equanimity by its predecessor. But
that does not alter the vital fact that for authority a way of
life is prescribed. It is not, indeed, laid down in a written
code, though it only lies the more profoundly in our nature
because it is inarticulate. For every statesman knows well
enough that there are certain things he dare not do because the
sense of the public will be against him. That system of conventions is important. It emphasises the conditionality of
power. It means, in other words, that so deep is the expectation of what, broadly speaking, may be termed the right conduct of authority that its antithesis ensures the provocation
of penalties.

This can, perhaps, be more usefully expressed in another
way. Whatever the requirements of legal theory, in actual

[64] 44 *American Law Review*, p. 12.

fact no man surrenders his whole being to the state. He has a sense of right and wrong. If the state, or its instruments, goes too consistently against that sense, he is pricked into antagonism. The state, that is to say, is for him sovereign only where his conscience is not stirred against its performance. Nor is this all. He expects from the state the fulfilment of its purposes. He expects it to make possible for him the attainment of certain goods. Again, the degree of expectation is subject to serious change; an Anglo-Saxon churl will have hopes different from those of an English workman of the twentieth century; Mrs. Proudie will exert a different power in the Barchester of one age than will the wife of her husband's successor. When the realisation of these hopes is keenly enough felt to be essential to the realisation of the purpose of the state we have a political right. It is a right natural in the sense that the given conditions of society at the particular time require its recognition. It is not justified on grounds of history. It is not justified on grounds of any abstract or absolute ethic. It is simply insisted that if, in a given condition of society, power is so exerted as to refuse the recognition of that right, resistance is bound to be encountered. By right, that is to say, we mean a demand that has behind it the burden of the general experience of the state. It is, as T. H. Green said, "a power of which the exercise by the individual or by some body of men is recognised by a society either as itself directly essential to the common good, or as conferred by an authority of which the maintenance is recognised as so essential."[65]

But this, it may be argued, is a claim hardly less theoretic than sovereignty itself. It may not be able to get itself recognised The government may, through malice, or in honesty, doubt its wisdom and oppose it. But a right admits of enforcement. There are, in the first place, the ordinary channels of representative government; in a democratic state, for instance, periodic reference is made to the people for the refreshment of power. At an English general election, for example, ministers are returned to or rejected from office either to perform certain things, or because it is believed that the opposing party will better represent the purpose of the state. The

[65] T. H. Green, "Collected Works," 11, 419.

Labour party in England today is demanding for "every member of the community, in good or bad times alike (and not only to the strong and able, the well-born and the fortunate)," the securing "of all the requisites of healthy life and worthy citizenship."[66]   A large portion of the British state is thus striving to achieve certain things as rights because without them life is not deemed worth the living.   By rights it means the recognition that every member of the state must without distinction possess certain goods, and that the situation implied in that possession is too fundamental to be subject to the whims of authority.   These rights are to be written into the fabric of the state.   They limit what authority can do by making them a minimum below which no member of the state must fall. They are, normally, written into the fabric of the state by the constitutional processes provided by law; and it is perhaps well, as Green has suggested,[67] to emphasise the desirability of achievement by this means.   But the reserve power of revolution always exists.   The American War of Independence is the vindication of a claim to a certain right of self-government;   and in that case territorial conditions made possible the foundation of a new state separate from the old.   The French Revolution is the assertion of a lack of confidence in the holders of power, and the change in the form of the state that the claim to certain rights might be fulfilled.

In the case both of the American and the French Revolution we have the programme upon which the new order was founded: in neither case can it be said that it was in any full sense achieved.   But this does not lessen the significance of the moral that is to be drawn from the study of the problem of rights. Whenever in a state a group of persons large enough to make its presence felt demands the recognition of certain claims, it will not recognise a law which attempts defiance of them; nor will it accept the authority by which that law is enforced.   Recent events have thrown this attitude into striking relief.   The attitude of Ulster before 1914 was a refusal to accept the sovereignty

[66] "Labour and the New Social Order, Report on Reconstruction by the Subcommittee of the British Labour Party" (Reprinted in *The New Republic*, Vol. XIV, No. 172, Part II, p. 4).

[67] "Works," II, 417 f, cf. Barker, "Political Thought from Spencer," p. 60.

of an Act of Parliament which granted self-government to Ireland. The refusal was made in the name of conscience; and whatever be thought of the penumbra of passions and personalties by which it was surrounded the fundamental fact has to be recorded that Parliament and the ministry found themselves jointly powerless in the face of an illegally organised opposition. The women suffragists were able, over a period of eight years, to set at defiance the ordinary rules of law; and few people today seriously doubt that the reason why that defiance was so successfully maintained was the fact of its moral content. Those who refused obedience to the Military Service Act of 1916 were able to prove the powerlessness of the state to force them into subjection. Convinced of the iniquity of war, they claimed the right to be absolved from direct contact with it; and it is highly significant that in America the Quakers should have received express exemption from that contact. That is the tacit admission that where the means taken by the state to achieve its purposes conflicts with the ideals of another group there are occasions when the state will find it wise to forego the claim of paramountcy. And, here again, the real fact involved is that of consent. No state can act in the face of the active opposition of any considerable portion of itself. No state will venture in practice to claim control over certain areas within the competence of other groups. Acts of authority are thus limited by the consciences that purposes different from that of the state can command.

That is to affirm that government dare not range over the whole area of human life. No government, for instance, dare prescribe the life of the Roman Catholic Church. Bismarck made the attempt, and it is doubtful if it will be repeated.[68] Where alone the state can attempt interference with groups other than itself is where the action of the group touches territory over which the state claims jurisdiction. There is no certainty that the state will be successful. There is even no certainty that it merits success. It may, indeed, crush an opponent by brute force. That does not, however, establish right; it is merely the emphasis of physical superiority. The only ground for state-success is where the purpose of the state

[68] Cf. my "Problem of Sovereignty," Ch. V.

is morally superior to that of its opponent. The only ground upon which the individual can give or be asked his support for the state is from the conviction that what it is aiming at is, in each particular action, good. We deny, that is to say, that the general end of the ideal state colours the policy of a given act of a special state. And that denial involves from each member of the state continuous scrutiny of its purpose and its method.

It deserves his allegiance, it should receive it, only where it commands his conscience. Bismarck failed in the Kulturkampf precisely because he could not convince the German Catholics of the moral superiority of his position to that of Rome. It was right that he should have so failed; for the basis of his position was virtually the assertion that the duty of the individual conscience is a blind and impulsive obedience to government. He did not understand that to put a minister in office does not permit the citizen body to cease all interest in affairs of state. On the contrary, because it is in the name of that citizen-body that power is exerted, it is essential that they should have convictions about the goodness or badness of the particular end that power is intended to serve. We can make no distinction, except in possible aspiration, between government and subjects, so long as there is acquiescence by the one in the policy of the other.[69] An act of government becomes a state-act whenever the members of the state do not attempt at least its repudiation.[70] For power is held not for evil but for good, and deflection from the path of right purpose ought to involve the withdrawal of authority for its exercise.

This, clearly enough, must make an important difference to the emphasis we place upon rights. Once we insist upon consent as the most fruitful source of the claim to obedience, there

[69] This amends somewhat the argument of my first book (Ch. I, p. 11). I there argued that we have no right to identify the citizen with the state; but I now think it is better to emphasise the possibility of distinction and to argue for the identity of moral responsibility where there is passive acquiescence. Liebknecht, in such a view, does not share in the responsibility of the German state for the destruction of Belgium.

[70] I say "attempt"; for it is conceivable that the members of a state might desire and aim at, repudiation, but fail because the government was too powerful to be immediately resisted with success.

is cast upon the individual member of the state the duty of scrutinising its policy; for if he ought ultimately at least to protest, and perhaps to disobey, where his conscience is involved, an active interest in politics is the most indispensable condition of citizenship. Nor is that active interest an easy matter. It is scarcely difficult for the son of a political family, brought up, like the younger Pitt, to regard politics as the one adequate pursuit of the mind, to catch the vision of its devious bye-ways. But, for the average voter, there is scarcely the same infallible source of understanding in questions of state, and the opportunity of training is essential. Few would now interpret training to mean the weekly discussions of Harrington's *Oceana;* but it is undeniable that some satisfactory substitute has still to be found. An illiterate man has no real means of performing the functions of citizenship. A man who is exhausted by excessive physical labour is similarly debarred from the opportunity of adequate understanding. If the nervous and mental energies of men are exhausted in the sheer effort of existence, as they so largely are exhausted, it is plain that the most efficacious well-spring of political improvement is poisoned at its source. One of the main evils of the history of government, indeed, has been the tragic fact that over a great period politics has been the concern of a leisured class simply because no other portion of the community has had the time or the strength to devote itself in any full measure to these questions. That is not in any sense to suggest misgovernment; but it is to suggest the impossible narrowness of the source from which the dominating ideas of government have been drawn. It is to suggest that if the state is to be in any real sense representative of the wills and desires of its members, their wills and desires must have some minimum physical basis of material and intellectual adequacy upon which to function.[71] That in turn implies that means must be taken to safeguard the expression of their hopes. Rights are no more than the expression of this minimum and its safeguards in broad terms. The right of free expression, for example, is obviously essential if desires are to be made known. If governments can suppress whatever

[71] Cf. Webb, "Industrial Democracy" (ed. of 1911), pp. 766-84 and the Report of the Subcommittee of the British Labour Party cited above.

they may dislike, as in the lean period of English radicalism,[72] the result is obviously to put a premium upon the maintenance of the *status quo*. The right to freedom of association is simply the recognition that community of purpose involves community of action. The right to education is simply the registration of a claim to understand in civilised terms the ways and means of social life. A power that fails to achieve these things, much more, a power that aims at thwarting them, has abused the trust that has been placed in its hands. Power has thus to be limited by rights because otherwise there is no means, save continual revolution, of achieving the purpose of the state.

And it is important to recognise in full measure the curious limitations of power. Even if we grant, for the purpose of argument, its general disposition to good will, there are two great means by which it may suffer perversion. It may, in the first place, be deliberately misused for selfish ends. There have been periods, for instance, in the history of American states when it is matter of common knowledge that the machine of government was disgracefully exploited. The histories of Tammany Hall, of Mr. Kearney in California, of the Philadelphia gas ring, are all of them infamous enough to need no comment.[73] "Some states," Lord Bryce has written,[74] ". . . have so bad a name that people are surprised when a good act passes." No observer of American politics, indeed, can fail to emphasise as a fundamental fact in the life of the commonwealth the general suspicion of all who are interested by profession in the business of government. A justice of the Supreme Court of the United States has written a vehement denunciation of the influence of high finance upon American political life.[75] Nor is such perversion confined to America alone. The connection of great financial concerns with foreign policy is a problem old enough to have its importance recognised by every fair-minded observer. If a German firm can

[72] Cf. Veitch, "The Genesis of Parliamentary Reform," Chs. IX-XIV—an invaluable book.

[73] Cf. Bryce, "Am. Commonwealth," II, 406-448.

[74] *Ibid.* II, 163.

[75] L. D. Brandeis, "Other People's Money." Mr. Justice Brandeis was not, of course, a member of the Supreme Court when this was written.

use the force of its government in order to coerce a foreign power into granting it a share, dishonestly gained, in spoils of doubtful moral validity,[76] obviously the considerations which affect the foreign policy of a state demand an exact scrutiny. If the Russo-Japanese war can even partially arise from the private ambitions of interested courtiers,[77] measures have obviously to be taken to limit the scope of abuse to which the power of government is subject. Phenomena like Mr. Cecil Rhodes, who deliberately set aside the consideration of nice moral issues,[78] raise problems of the first importance.

But deliberate perversion of power brings with it, in the long run, its own downfall. What is more difficult of enquiry is the devotion of governmental authority to narrow purposes which are deemed good by an irresponsible controlling minority. The Combination Acts are a notable instance of this kind. They reflect, of course, the general tendency of the French Revolution to regard all associations as evil;[79] but they represent also, in more sinister fashion, an entire failure on the part of government to understand the problems of the working-class. The House of Commons refused, both in 1824 and in 1826, to allow the abuse of man-traps and spring-guns to be remedied; and it was only after a long struggle that, in 1836, a prisoner on trial for felony was at last allowed to have the benefit of counsel. "The existence of unjust and foolish laws," says Professor Dicey,[80] "is less remarkable than the grounds upon which these laws were defended. Better, it was argued, that honest men, who had never fired a gun, should be exposed to death by spring-guns or man-traps than that a country gentleman should fail in preserving his game. A prisoner, it was suggested, though he might occasionally, through inability to employ counsel, be convicted of a murder or a theft which he had never committed, had no reason to complain, for the very absence of an advocate turned the

[76] Brailsford, " The War of Steel and Gold," p. 38.

[77] *Ibid.*, p. 52.

[78] As in the Glen-Grey Act for example, Cf. Hobson, "Imperialism" (ed. of 1905), p. 236.

[79] Cf. chapter V. below.

[80] "Law and Public Opinion" (2d edition), p. 88.

judge into a counsel for the prisoner. The plea was notoriously untrue; but had it been founded on fact, it would have implied that injustice to a prisoner could be remedied by neglect of duty on the part of a judge."

The process of administration has been beset by similar difficulties. Everyone knows of the Circumlocution Office immortalised in "Little Dorrit;" and the remarkable experiences of Mr. Edmund Yates in the Post Office are not without their suggestiveness.[81] Sir Henry Taylor explained the evils of the irresponsibility that existed in his day. "By evading decisions wherever they can be evaded," he wrote,[82] "by shifting them on other departments and authorities whenever they can be shifted; by giving decisions on superficial examination,. . . by deferring questions till, as Lord Bacon said, they resolve of themselves; by undertaking nothing for the public good which the public voice does not call for; by conciliating loud and energetic individuals at the expense of such public interest as are dumb and do not attract attention; by sacrificing everywhere what is feeble and obscure to what is influential and cognizable . ·. .the single functionary may . . .reduce his business within his powers, and perhaps obtain for himself the most valuable of all reputations in this line of life, that of a safe man." The complaint of Charles Buller is similar,[83] and the final consequence of the bureaucratic process was given its permanent expression by Carlyle.[84] "The mode of making the service efficient," said a distinguished civil servant of the fifties,[85] "seems never to have entered their minds." The routine of habit, in fact, is impermeable to the normal channels of change; and so important a critic as Sir Charles Trevelyan actually thought that it was the spirit of 1848 which induced England to put its house in order.[86] There

[81] See his amusing "Recollections," Vol. I, pp. 96 f, 106.

[82] "The Statesman," p. 155.

[83] Cf. his character of Mr. Mothercountry in his "Responsible Government in the Colonies."

[84] "Latter Day Pamphlets" (ed. of 1885), p. 47.

[85] "Civil Service Papers," 1854-5, p. 272. He is speaking of the House of Commons.

[86] "Second Report of Commission on Civil Service." Parl. Papers, 1875, Vol. XXIII, p. 100.

has, of course, been vast improvement since that time; but the tendency to which administration is liable is a constant factor in the exercise of authority.

In all this, the argument of deliberate malevolence is as inaccurate as it is obvious and certain that the result is the perversion of the end the state should serve. It is perhaps dangerous, as Burke suggested, to go back too often to the foundations of the state; but it is at least no abstract question upon which we are engaged. If we find that, in the event, authority has certain habits, and that they result in evil, we have to seek means of their effective change, or at least some safeguard against the evil. And it is in events alone that we must search for our truths. It is useless, as Burke rightly saw,[87] to discuss "the abstract right of a man to food or medicine. The question is upon the method of procuring and administering them." If we find that, however good the intention of those who hold the reins of power, that intention is somehow, if not frustrated, at least inadequately realised in the event, we have to examine the elements involved in such translation into practice. All kinds of factors may complicate the problem. If the member of Parliament, for instance, be Sir Pitt Crawley, it is hardly useful to force upon his attention the rights of man. If the member of the House of Lords be a promoted Archdeacon Grantley assuredly he will not grasp the social problem in an adequate perspective.[88]   The fact here is that to many of those who are engaged in the task of government, the problem of authority is either unknown, or is unconsciously set in terms of the *status quo*. That Duke of Newcastle who desired to do what he would with his own, was probably completely unaware that there was a theory of the state involved in his attitude. Queen Victoria's refusal, in 1859, to make Mr. Bright a Privy Councillor on the ground that "it would be impossible to allege any service Mr. Bright has rendered, and if the honour were looked upon as a reward for his systematic attacks upon the institutions of the country, a very erroneous impression might be produced as to the feeling

[87] "Reflections on the French Revolution." "Works" (World's Classics, ed.), Vol. IV, p. 66.

[88] Cf. Mr. Wallas' comment, "The Great Society," p. 332.

which the Queen or her government entertain towards those institutions"[89] is, in reality, an expression of the conviction that the middle class had better know its place, and not meddle with the business of its superiors. The implication surely is that Bright's long attack on institutions only partially democratised was, in the royal opinion, no contribution to social improvement.

In every phase of the general social question the real assumption is the belief for which Burke so strenuously argued. "Property," he said,[90] ". . .never can be safe from the invasions of ability unless it be, out of all proportion, predominant in the representation." It is, as he said, a simple truth that "the same quantity of property which is, by the natural course of things, divided among many, has not the same operation." But that is, in reality, to argue that power goes with the distribution of property, and it supposes power to be rightly used only where it is exerted in the interest of property. In a period of revolution it was perhaps natural for him seriously to over-estimate the dangers to which property is subject. Mr. Gladstone, at least, was less fearful. "There is a saying of Burke's," he told Lord Morley,[91] "from which I must utterly dissent. 'Property is sluggish and inert.' Quite the contrary. Property is vigilant, active, sleepless; and if it ever seems to slumber, be sure that one eye is open." That surely is the lesson of history; for every class which possesses property will claim that it has an abstract right to power. Yet Burke, more than any man of his time, would have thought little enough of so abstract a claim; and he would have insisted that the real test of property, as, therefore, of the power which it controls, is the way in which it functions.

V. THE ATTACK ON THE SECULAR STATE

In our own time it is in general felt that the result of the democratic process is unsatisfactory. The authority that is exerted in the name of the state fails to result in accomplishing that

[89] Trevelyan, "Life of Bright," p. 283.

[90] "Reflection on the French Revolution." "Works" (World's Classics ed.). Vol. IV., p. 55.

[91] Morley, "Life of Gladstone," III, 352.

for which the state exists. It is into the cause of this discrepancy that we are examining. Virtually, the answer that we make is an insistence upon the humanity of men. "A nation or a state," Professor Dicey has written,[92] "means, conceal it how you will, a lot of individual selves with unequal talents and in reality unequal conditions, and each of these selves does—or rather must—think not exclusively but primarily of his own self. The old doctrine of original sin may be totally disconnected from the tale of Eve and her apple, or any other religious tradition or theological dogma, but it represents an undeniable fact which neither a statesman nor a preacher can venture to ignore." Certainly even if we make no assumptions as to the psychological factors involved, it is true enough thus to urge that the system, social, economic, political, under which we live, emphasises drastically the principle of self-interest. In such perspective, the object at which the state aims must be made superior to the private ideals of its constituent parts, except insofar as they coincide with that larger object. And if authority is thus subject to exploitation, it must be subject to limitation also. It can act without restraint only where its end is in fact coincident with its ideal object. Its policy, that is to say, is only sovereign where it is serving the sovereign purpose.

That raises an immediate difficulty. Upon the rightness of its policy it is clear that doubt may exist. On the theory of taxation, for example, there is a clear line of distinction in England between the Liberal and Conservative parties. Broadly speaking, Liberalism stands for direct, Conservatism for indirect taxation.[93] In such a difference there is no ground for repudiation of government action in terms of revolution. The special tax involved might, indeed, well have such consequence; resistance to a head-tax on Roman Catholics, for example, is an argument not difficult to justify. The point at which resistance becomes an expedient factor is not a matter for definition or prophecy; it will vary with the circumstances of each age. All we can say is that at times in the history of a state there may well come a point where the maintenance of

[92] "Law and Public Opinion" (2d ed.), p. LXXX.
[93] Cf. Jèze, etc., "Problemes de Politique et Finances de Guerre," p. 27.

order seems to some group of men worthless as an end compared to achieving, by other than constitutional means, some good deemed greater than peace. That is the reservoir of anarchy of which resistance to oppression is the most fertile source of supply. It is not in any sense a denial that the large purpose of the state is supreme. It rather insists on its supremacy and denies that character to governmental acts on the ground that they do not achieve that end in any adequate fashion. Nor is it necessarily an arid persistence on behalf of some abstract theorem remotely capable of realisation. It is not for such things that revolutions have been made. Most men who have taken part in practical politics will admit that a theoretic preference for an abstract system does not involve their immediate effort after the destruction of an existing government which, on all reasonable showing, suits the conditions of its age.[94]

It is this perhaps that best sets the background for the constructive answer to our questions. What, in actual fact, are the social forces over which the power of the state ought not to be extended? What are the limits to its authority? In what way ought its power to be organised? There are two obvious kinds of limitation to be discussed. Both are connected with the fundamental problem of liberty. Its definition is perhaps the subtlest question the political philosopher has to confront. The truth, of course, is that the meaning of liberty will vary with every age. Each generation will have certain things it prizes as supremely good and will demand that these, above all, should be free. The permanent elements of liberty we shall hardly know until some inspired investigator gives us that history of which Acton dreamed. To our own generation it seems almost certain that the insistence upon absence of restraint is in no sense adequate. A liberty to enslave one's self becomes immediately self-contradictory; and Mr. Justice Holmes has finely insisted, in one of the most significant of his opinions, upon the intimate connection of liberty with equality.[95] Nor does Mill really aid us much in his distinction

[94] Cf. Gwynne and Tuckwell, "Life of Sir C. Dilke," I, 177.

[95] See his dissent in Coppage *v* Kansas, 236 U. S., I, 26-7. The best defence I know of the idea of liberty as absence of restraint is in Seeley's "Introduction to Political Science," 101 f.

between self-regarding and other-regarding qualities; for the fact is that we can have no information as to the social relevance of any act until we consider its consequences.[96] "When we speak of freedom as something to be highly prized," said T. H. Green,[97] "we mean a positive power of doing or enjoying something worth doing or enjoying, and that, too, something that we do or enjoy in common with others." That is more valuable than the negative conception because it insists on what, in this age, we feel to be fundamental in liberty—the power of adding something to the quality of the common life. But it does not, of course—though Green had elsewhere answered that question[98]—tell us what it is worth while to do or to enjoy; and here again, acute difference of opinion is possible. It was as a historian that Acton approached the problem, and his answer had a connotation not to be misunderstood. "By liberty," he said,[99] "I mean the assurance that every man shall be protected in doing what he believes his duty against the influence of authority and majority, custom and opinion." To a practical statesman that will seem perhaps a counsel of perfection; and, certainly, it is a counsel that, at every stage, will encounter acute difficulties of practical operation.

It yet sets, in the background of Green's conception, the idea we need of the internal limitation upon the action of the state. It insists upon the greatest truth to which history bears witness that the only real security for social well-being is the free exercise of men's minds. Otherwise, assuredly, we have contracted ourselves to slavery. The only permanent safeguard of democratic government is that the unchanging and ultimate sanction of intellectual decision should be the conscience. We have here, that is to say, a realm within which the state can have no rights and where it is well that it should have none. No state, in truth, is ever firmly grounded that has not in such fashion won the consent of its members to

[96] Cf. Prof. Dicey's comment. "Law and Public Opinion," p. XXVIII.
[97] "Works," III, 371.
[98] In the "Prolegomena to Ethics."
[99] "History of Freedom," p. 3.

action. The greatest contribution that a citizen can make to
the state is certainly this, that he should allow his mind freely
to exercise itself upon its problems. Where the conscience of
the individual is concerned the state must abate its demands;
for no mind is in truth free once a penalty is attached to thought.
Nor will consent so won be real consent. It is patent to the
world that the inexhaustible well-spring of democratic resource,
as against any other form of government, is that no other
system can be certain of itself. The methods by which an
autocracy must secure consent are today, or should be, tolerably
well-known; and while they may seem at times to have the
efficacy of poison, they result always in death or violent remedy.

Freedom of thought, then, the modern state must regard
as absolute; and that means freedom of thought whether on
the part of the individual or of a social group. Nothing is
more stupid than for the state to regard the individual and itself as the only entities of which account must be taken, or
to suggest that other groups live by its good pleasure. That
is to make the easy mistake of thinking that the activities of
man in his relation to government exhaust his nature. It is
a fatal error. The societies of men are spontaneous. They
may well conflict with the state; but they will only ultimately
suffer suppression if the need they supply is, in some equally
adequate form, answered by the state itself. And it is tolerably
clear that there are many such interests the state cannot serve.
The growth of religious difference, for example, makes the
state-adoption of any religious system a matter of doubtful
expediency; and that means, as has been before insisted, that
the internal relations of churches will in fact deny state-inter-
ference. A society like the Presbyterian Church, which recog-
nises only the headship of Christ, will resist to the uttermost
any external attempt at the definition of its life; and experience
seems to suggest that the state will lose far more than it can
gain by the effort. Where the fellowship is economic in nature
the problem is, indeed, far more complex; for the modern
state is at every turn an economic organisation. But, even
here, the impossibility of absorption is shown by the tragic
history of such things as the Combination Acts. The state
may well exact responsibility for the thought such fellowships

may have where it seeks translation into action; but it will establish its exaction only where the individual, himself judging between conflicting claims, is driven to feel that the effort of the state is more valid than the other.

That is to say that for the state there are found subjects of social rights and duties. They are not the creation of the state; the state is simply an organisation existing for the realisation of an end. The subjects of those rights are sometimes individual human beings; sometimes they take the form of fellowships of men. Those fellowships possess a personality into the nature of which it is not here necessary to examine.[100] The fundamental fact for the state is that they present an activity that is unified and must be treated as involving the possession of rights. But the individual stands above and outside them. The only way the state can truly prosper is by sweeping into itself the active assistance of his mind and conscience; and it will succeed in that effort only insofar as it respects them. Whatever, therefore, concerns the conscience of man, whatever brings its activity into operation, must, for the state, be sacred ground. That this involves difficulties in practice is unquestionable. But if the action of the vital agency of government arouses such conscientious opposition as to be incapable of application, it seems, to say the least, possible that it needs re-examination in terms of its moral character. If a measure has so wrought upon the natural political inertia of men as to prick them into insurgency, it has probably interpreted with maleficent purpose the end of the state. Even where the opposition is small, it is probable that more is gained by the possession of that energy of character which is willing to offer challenge than by destroying it.[101] A state which oppresses those who are antagonised by the way in which govern-

[100] The bibliography of the subject is enormous. Its most fruitful treatment seems to me the two volumes of Léon Michoud, "Theorie de la Personnalité Morale," with which I am largely in agreement. I have tried to indicate the nature of the problem in an article in the *Harvard Law Review* for February, 1916.

[101] I should like to refer to Prof. G. Murray's really noble introduction to Mrs. Hobhouse's "I appeal to Caesar," with which I am in glad agreement.

ment interprets its purposes is bound to drift slowly into despotism.

It is asserted that such an attitude is impractical. A man may think as he pleases; but opposition to government is the coronation of anarchy. It is, to say the least, uncertain whether the assertion is so formidable as it appears. Disorder may be better than injustice. It was assuredly better for England that the Civil War asserted the impossibility of the Stuart claims than that humble obedience should be offered to them. Every government is a *de facto* government except insofar as the rightness of its effort makes it *de jure*. A man has, above all, to be true to himself; for, once the fatal step is taken of humbling himself, against his inner promptings, before the demands of authority the way to acquiescence is easy. Nor must we be misled by the effort at confusion that is implied in the division of the state into minority and majority. The lever of public opinion is a weapon too easily brought into use. We rarely analyse it into its constituent parts. We rarely estimate how far a majority-opinion is in fact active consent, and how far it is in reality no more than the inert acquiescence that prefers slumber to challenge. In a problem like religious education, for example, the amount of conscientious and instructed opinion on either side is small; and the real truth is that a bill like Mr. Balfour's measure of 1903 wins acceptance rather because the mass of men is uninterested in the technical problems involved than because the particular solution of the church of England makes to them some transcendent appeal. When Sir Frederick Smith can stigmatise the Welsh Disestablishment Act as "a bill which has shocked the conscience of every Christian community in Europe,"[102] he must be aware that the phrase is no more than vulgar rhetoric, and that in fact any estimate of the Act's popularity it is impossible in that fashion to make. In the process of government the importance of this inert factor can hardly be too greatly emphasised. It needs some vivid action to stimulate to resistance a body of men large enough to make its presence felt in the state. We probably tend seriously to underrate the effort that is needed to embark upon

[102] Cf. Mr. Chesterton's "Poems" (1914) for the comment on this remark.

such resistance. Certainly the remark may be hazarded that it is never aroused without deep causes to which attention must be paid.

The assumption here made is that every individual is above all a moral being and that the greatest contribution he can make to the state is the effort of his moral faculties. That is in reality an assistance to society. A state in which the consciences of men are alert and energetic will hardly embark upon the path that may lead, for example, to the invasion of Belgium. A government which knows the existence of those consciences will hardly allow its mind to wander in the direction of such wrong. It is when there has been systematic training in effortless acquiescence, that there is the easiest opportunity for injustice. It is in such case that the state, perhaps even civilisation, may feel the nemesis of that docility. In that sense, by preventing the senses of men from being so sodden as to mistake legality for moral right, we have the surest safeguard against disaster. The active conscience of the members of a state acts as a self-operating check against perversion from its purposes.

But conscience is not a thing which reacts instinctively to any set of circumstances. It needs instruction. It has to be trained into the fine perception of the complex issues by which it will be confronted. The mind with which it interacts needs nourishment to be energetic. Here, indeed, is the significance for the state of Socrates' great plea that virtue is knowledge. An untutored people can never be great in any save the rudest arts of civilisation. Here, again, we have the elements upon which to base a limitation of state-power. No state can through its instruments deny education to its members. It must provide them, that is to say, with means at least adequate to a full perception of life; for, otherwise, the purpose of the state is at one stroke negatived for them. Even Adam Smith put education among those activities it was well for the state to undertake;[103] and Mr. Graham Wallas has wisely insisted that the growing interest of the workers in the fruits of learning is one of the surest tests we have of progress.[104] That does

[103] "Wealth of Nations" (Everyman's ed.), II, 269.
[104] "The Great Society," p. 302.

not condemn the state to any particular system. It does not even suggest that there is a radical wrong in giving one man the advantage of a classical training while his brother is sent to a technical institute. It merely suggests that the provision of some agreed minimum of what is adequate to the purpose of citizenship is essential and that no state is satisfactorily organised where this condition does not obtain. It is the more urgent because political problems are so vast that no state, least of all a democracy, can hope to deal with them unless each member is sufficiently articulate to transfer the judgment of his experience to the increase of the common store. "An autocratic sultan," it has been happily remarked,[105] "may govern without science if his whim is law. A plutocratic party may choose to ignore science if it is heedless whether its pretended solutions of social problems. . .ultimately succeed or fail. But a democratic society must base its solutions upon the widest possible induction open to its members. That is not less American experience.[106] Indeed, it may be claimed that the recent experience of the whole world has very strikingly demonstrated the need of associating the active assistance of men with the policy of the state; and it has been found that such assistance is more active the more highly it is trained. That is, in fact, to emphasise that by neglect of its resources the state has wasted the opportunity of their richest increase; and that, surely, must involve the erection of safeguards against the continuance of such neglect.

We are indicating avenues of possible approach rather than detailing the exact use to which they shall be put; and it is perhaps better to analyse the general bearing of this attitude than to catalogue its constituent factors.[107] It is an attitude which primarily suggests that the study of social life will in, any scientific perspective, suggest some minimum rule of social conduct.[108] Immediately the interdependence of men is real-

[105] "Report of the Sub-Committee of the British Labour Party," last paragraph.

[106] Cf. "The Report of the President's Mediation Committee to the President of the United States" (1918), p. 21.

[107] This will be attempted in a later work on the principles of politics.

[108] Cf. Duguit, "L'Etat Le Droit Objectif," Ch. II.

ised there is ethically involved the notion of a minimum equality. That is not to say that all men are born equal. It is
simply to say that the unity involved in the mere concept
of social purpose must prevent the unnecessary degradation
of any individual. Nor is it for one moment to suggest that
this rule of conduct is an unchangeable thing. The needs of
each age, no less than its potentialities, are, of necessity, different; and with every age our rule of conduct will therefore vary.

Nor are we, like Adam Smith, suggesting the existence of
"natural laws of justice independent of all positive institution;"[109] for that, in truth, is to put ourselves outside the realm
of scientific speculation. The body of principles which can admit of an immutable and inflexible application to politics would
be so generalised in character as to be of little practical worth.[110]
The life of politics, as of the law, lies in its functioning. Theft
may be bad and punishable by law; but we cannot apply the
criminal code until we near the penumbra which surrounds the
case. And that penumbra may well make the principle inapplicable. What we do is to deposit hypotheses that have come to
us from the facts of life; we declare that their application will
enrich the content of the social life. These hypotheses are not
the mere whims of chance opinion. We cannot, at least in politics, where decision is necessary, take refuge in a scepticism
which, logically followed, makes conduct impossible. We urge
that the argument for one principle can in fact be better than
another. It is today, for example, broadly believed that the
case for factory acts is stronger than the case for industrial
laissez-faire. The governmental regulation of factory-condi-
tions has by now become a part of our rule of political conduct.
That has not been universally the case. But our experience has
grown with time and we today think in other terms than the
early nineteenth century. When the hypothesis that sums up
such a general experience becomes generally enough accepted

---

[109] "Theory of Moral Sentiments" (ed. of 1759), p. 549. A theory of natural law independent of change is defended by one of the most brilliant of
the younger school of philosophical jurists, Professor M. R. Cohen, in an
article, "Jus Naturale Redivivum," in the *Philosophical Review* Vol. XXV,
p. 761.

[110] Cf. Mr. Justice Holmes in Lochner *v.* New York, 198 U. S. 45, 76.

it gets written into the code of principles that we in general regard as beyond the realm of ordinary discussion. The problem here is not very different from the growth in the law of torts of liability without fault. We have penal statutes which directly conflict with the older concept of that category. The statutes aim, for social reasons, at securing the mass of men against certain dangers. Workmen's Compensation, for example, throws the burden on the employer in the belief that it is more socially advantageous for the burden so to fall. What is here done is to withdraw an area of social action from the ordinary concepts of law by making it statutory. It places a statutory clause—the provision, in certain cases, for accident—as one of the conditions a master must observe if he wishes to engage in business.[111] Workmen's compensation is thus simply a regulation of experience. It is a principle withdrawn for the general good from the operation of industrial competition. The general rule of conduct is in nowise different save that its substance is perhaps more fundamental.

That is the sense, for example, in which a real value may be attached to the Bill of Rights in an American constitution. Misinterpreted as it often may be,[112] perverted as it certainly has been, it yet testifies to the vital character of a solid body of social rules. To write into the body of a constitution not immediately accessible to amendment principles which are the result of social experience is to put them beyond the reach of ordinary mischance. Nobody who has at all examined the character of American political life can doubt that this vague well-spring of idealism has not only had, but still potentially possesses, a profound influence. The constitutional provisions against an established church, for instance, are of course derived from a bitter experience of Anglican persecution. They have undoubtedly prevented the growth of the social status connected in England with the official religion, which still leaves a deep mark

[111] Cf. my paper on the "Basis of Vicarious Liability" in 26 *Yale Law Journal* 105 and Cf. Pound, 25 *International Journal of Ethics*, p. 1.

[112] For the way in which the Fourteenth Amendment has been misinterpreted, for example Cf. Collins, ''The Fourteenth Amendment and the States.''

upon English life.[113]   The way in which every state constitutionally insists upon the subordination of the military to the civil
power is the safeguard against the aggression involved breeding
into the mind of a people the thought that the army is a thing
apart, not subject to the rules of justice.   No one can doubt that
Magna Charta means to an Englishman something that is not
easily to be over-emphasised; sufficient, indeed, to make it
possible for a distinguished judge to insist that only the specific
declaration of Parliament can secure its annullment.[114]   The
psychologic background of provisions such as these is an immense preventive against the abuse of authority.   They give
to doctrines the arms which make possible resistance to oppression.   They sanction the effort of legisative idealism.   They
represent, however vaguely, the moral desperation of a people.
"A poetical adage" may not, as Bentham sneeringly said,[115]
"be a reason;" but it is likely, if it have root in experience to
provide one; and he himself goes on to explain to what vast
results a simple phrase like "mother-country" may give
rise.

Obviously, of course, such an attitude as this is in the closest
relation to the modern revival of natural law.[116]   We are well
enough able now to see the main source of the discredit into
which it fell during the nineteenth century.   It had tended, in
the previous age, to regard the problems of law as far too simple
and their solutions as accordingly at hand.   It shared the discredit which the dissatisfaction with the French Revolution
inflicted upon an optimistic outlook.   It was too highly abstract
and too little careful of the forms of law.   It over-emphasised
the degree to which reason is finally operative in the determination of an adequate ideal.   In the result, as Dean Pound has

[113] For the remains of its influence in Oxford Cf. Dicey, "Law and Public Opinion," 479-83.

[114] Rex *v.* Halliday (1917).   A. C. 261, 294.   Cf. my comment in 31
Harvard Law Review, 296.

[115] "Theory of Legislation" (translated by C. M. Atkinson), Vol. I, p. 92.

[116] On this cf. the great essay of Saleilles, "Ecole historique et droit
naturel" in *Revue Trimestrielle de droit civil* 1902, I. 80-112. Charmont "La
Renaissance du Droit Naturel."

shown,[117] the pessimism of the historical school triumphed over what seemed as more than a metaphysical miasma. But, in fact, the effort made by the theorists of natural law enshrined a truth of which too great neglect is possible.

That truth consists in the realisation that one of the great mainsprings of human effort is the realisation of a good greater than that which is actually existent. The eighteenth-century theorists made the error of regarding that good as unchangeable. The facts, of course, proved too strong for so rigid an outlook. But this insistence upon idealism in law is not open to the same difficulty if, with Stammler, we regard the ideal of natural law as continually changing in content.[118] We have, as he has pointed out,[119] a twofold problem. We must know the relation of law and morals. That is, of course, the ordinary problem investigated by the legal philosophers. It is not, however, the crux of the question. We need to understand how a legal rule is to be made just in the special conditions it is to confront. That is a purely functional problem. It is clear, for instance, that into the idea of justice arbitrary control cannot enter;[120] but it is not less clear that opinion may differ as to what is arbitrary control. Professor Dicey, for example, has attacked the French system of administrative law as fatal in practice to the triumph of objective principles;[121] and Maxime Leroy has expressed his discontent with the English rule of law.[122] What surely, we can alone admit as dogmatic is the fact that justice is somehow to be attained yet, granted the fact of institutional evolution it is clear that the content of justice is bound to vary. The balance of forces in a community is subject to sufficient

[117] "The End of Law," 30 *Harvard Law Review*, p. 221. I owe my whole understanding of the background of this problem to the really noble edifice Dean Pound has erected in these papers.

[118] See above all his "Lehre von dem richtigen Rechte" and his "Wirthschafts und Recht" (2nd ed.), 119. "Lehre von clem richtigen Rechte," pp. 13 ff. 120 *Ibid* pp. 208-9.

[119] "Lehre von dem richtigen Rechte." pp. 13ff.

[120] *Ibid* pp. 208-9.

[121] "Law of the Constitution," Chap. XII.

[122] Libres Entretiens 4me series, p. 368. I have tried to deal with this question in some detail below.

variation to make the conflict of ideals inevitable. A process of internecine selection secures the triumph of some attitude.

This theory of internal limitation upon the action of authority is essentially a pragmatic one. It admits that any system which failed in practice to secure what is largely termed the end of social life would be inadequate. It is sufficiently alive to the importance of stability to seek to place the fundamental notions of each age beyond the temptation of malicious enterprise. It is such notions that we have termed rights. It is such notions we have denied the power, at least in theory, of government to traverse. For we say that their realisation is essential to the end of the state; and government is itself only a means to that end. The state, in fact, must limit its instruments by the law of its own being. Sovereignty, in such an aspect, can never belong to the government if we term it the supreme power to do what is thought necessary. Government, it is clear, will have a power to will. But that will may come into conflict with other wills; and the test of the allegiance it should win is the degree in which it is thought to be more in harmony than its antagonists with the end of social life.

And this, it is clear also, envisages a pluralistic conception of society. It denies the oneness of society and the state. It insists that nothing is known of the state-purpose until it is declared; and it refuses, for obvious reasons, to make *a priori* observations about its content. It sees man as a being who wishes to realise himself as a member of society. It refers back each action upon which judgment is to be passed to the conscience of the individual. It insists that the supreme arbiter of the event is the totality of such consciences. It does not deny that the individual is influenced by the thousand associations with which he is in contact; but it is unable to perceive that he is absorbed by them. It sees society as one only in purpose; but it urges that this purpose has in fact been differently interpreted and is capable of realisation by more than a single method. In such an analysis the state is only one among many forms of human association. It is not necessarily any more in harmony with the end of society than a church or a trade-union, or a freemasons' lodge. They have, it is true, relations which the state controls; but that does not make them inferior to the state. The assumption of inferiority, indeed, is a fallacy that comes from comparing different immediate purposes. Moral inferiority in purpose as between a church and state there can hardly be; legal inferiority is either an illegitimate postulation of Austinian sovereignty, or else the result of a false identification of state and society. The confusion becomes apparent when we emphasise the content of the state. When we insist that the state is a society of governors and governed, it is obvious that its superiority can have logical reference only to the sphere that it has marked out for its own and then only to the extent to which that sphere is not successfully challenged.[123]

Here, indeed, is the source of a serious confusion in the recent developments of the neo-Hegelian theory of the state.[124] "Will not force," said Green,[125] "is the basis of the state." That, in a sense, is true enough; but it obscures the real problem of discovering upon what will, in actual fact, the policy of the state is based. The search is perhaps an endless one. Certainly we must, in its course, bear in mind Green's own caution that "the idea of a common good which the state fulfils has never been the sole influence actuating those who have been agents" in its life.[126] They can never realise it, as he thinks, except in some imperfect form. Here, surely, is a fundamental point. For even if it be true that we are watching in the state the slow process of a growing good which, despite error and wrong, will somehow be realised, the growing good cannot, by sheer assumption, necessarily be said to be situate in one set of men rather than another. That, surely, is a matter for examination. Few would now be found to urge

[123] For an interesting suggestion that the state has the right to insist upon fair dealing in the internal life of other societies cf. Professor Sabine's review of my book in the *Philosophical Review* for January, 1918.

[124] Particularly in Prof. Bosanquet's very brilliant volume on the "Philosophical Theory of the State." I may perhaps be allowed to say that criticism does not preclude the recognition that this book is, with the single exception of Green's "Principles of Political Obligation," the greatest contribution made by an Englishman to political philosophy since Mill.

[125] "Works" II, 426 f.

[126] *Ibid.* 434.

that the administration which ruled England after the peace of 1815 had a conception of good denied, for instance, to Francis Place and the radicals.

The state is based upon will; but the wills from which its will is eventually formed struggle amongst each other for survival. The idea of a "general" will that is necessarily good emerging from that struggle seems, on the whole, to contribute but little to our understanding of the event. A will is "good" if it is a good will; but it is difficult to see why any character should be affixed to it until we have had time to watch it in actual operation. That was the merit of Green's attitude. He did not for one moment deny that in the transition from theoretic purpose to practical realisation a significant transformation may occur. The lofty splendour of Mr. Bradley's "My Station and its Duties" may well suffer translation into the station of the Anglican catechism. It is, indeed, the inherent defect of idealism that it never enables us to come to grips with facts. It incurably tends to blur them over. It thinks so largely in terms of a beneficent teleology as to soften the distinction between political opposites. It beatifies the *status quo* by regarding each element as an integral part of a process which it insists on viewing as a totality. But, in the heat and stress of social life, we cannot afford such long-period value. We may well enough regard the lean years after 1815 as the necessary prelude to the great reforms of the thirties. But that does not make them the less lean. We may urge that society is in fact one and indivisible; but the dweller in a city-slum cannot, in the nature of things, transgress the unseen barrier which, for him, is far more real than the philosophic bonds perceived by the abstract observer. He is surely to be pardoned if, for example, he regards class distinctions as real when he sees the tenacity with which privileges he does not share are defended. He may well insist that if they are relatively necessary to the construction of the whole, it is against that whole that he is then in open revolt.

The method of realism has at least the merit of a greater simplicity. It would not regard the South African war as necessarily good because the Union of South Africa Act has been a superb triumph. It is interested in judgments upon the links of a chain not less than in the chain itself. Theoretically, it can perceive how every act may move in unity down the endless stream of time. Practically, it insists that the fact of discontinuity is vital. It perceives at least two such basic centres of discontinuous action. There is the individual mind. There is the mind, that is to say, of man considered in reference to personal self-realisation without involving in that process the self-realisation of others. There is the group-mind also. There is the mind, that is to say, of a number of men who, actuated by some common purpose, are capable of a unified activity. From both of these, in their myriad forms there of course proceed acts of will. If a "general will" meant anything, it would only mean the totality of those wills insofar as they realised the general social purpose. But no one knows immediately where that purpose is, by some individual act, about to be realised. The assumption that it is so realised must be a generalisation not from purposes but from results. An Act of Parliament may differently affect different men. Because it means well to them all, because it achieves good as a majority of legislators conceive it, does not mean that in fact it is therefore good. The realist interpretation of politics does not, for one moment, insist upon a divergent interest between the desires that have secured historic fulfilment and the desires that would have secured the social good. But it does deny the idealist contention that there is any necessary relevance between them.

From that twilight world it is surely better to emerge. Let us judge an institution not by its purposes but by its achievement in the terms of those purposes. Let us judge, for example, the Roman Catholic Church not as the earthly embodiment of the body of Christ but by what it has made of that body in the history of its earthly form. If we remember St. Francis we must not forget the Inquisition; if we insist upon the wrong of Hus' condemnation, we must not neglect the splendid ideals of the Cardinal of Cusa. We have to remember, in brief, that the realisation of the Kingdom of God involves the holding of property, the making of contracts, the appointment of officers, the determination of dogma. The fact that the Pope is the vicar of Christ does not exclude scrutiny into the details of his election.   And our judgment upon the state must be in similar terms.   The step is easy from talk of state to talk of community, but it is an illegitimate step.   The state may have the noblest purpose.   The objective at which its power aims may be unquestionable.   But it, too, at every moment, is acting by agents who are also mortal men.   The basis of scrutiny becomes at once pragmatic.   The test of allegiance to established institutions becomes immediately the achievement for which they are responsible.   The foundation of our judgment must incessantly be sought in the interpretation of historic experience.   We know, at least in general terms, the aim of the state.   We can measure, again at least in general terms, the degree of its divergence from the ideal end.   That is why no method is at all adequate which seeks the equation of the ideal and the real.   That is why the first lesson of our experience of power is the need of its limitation by the instructed judgment of free minds.

VI. THE DIVISION OF POWER

But, after all, this is an internal limitation.   It seeks its root less in any formal constitution than in the effort to secure in the state the expression of a certain spirit.   It is in no sense a full safeguard against the dangers by which the state is consistently confronted.   We have also to erect a more positive and external limitation upon authority.   Not, indeed, that such machinery alone would be in any sense an adequate thing.   No system of government has been yet devised not capable of perversion by maleficent men.   It cannot be too emphatically insisted that important as may be the policy of any government, the character of those who operate it is hardly less fundamental.   A single instance will perhaps suffice in demonstration.   No one denies that the massive ability of Bismarck puts him in the first rank of statesmen during the nineteenth century.   But it is not less obvious that he consciously acted upon a system of political principles in which the ordinary canons of ethics played no part.   When he embarked upon his campaign against socialism the method of which he availed himself was the deliberate application of principles in which he did not believe and to which he had formerly announced his opposition;   and it is clear that those principles became different by reason of the spirit he infused into their application. Half the difficulty of democratic government consists in the choice of leaders; and in a quasi-democracy where, as in Germany, leadership is imposed from above, ideas that may in one context be admirable, will, in their new atmosphere, serve only as a dangerous soporific. Few things have been more easy than for an able and energetic government, which was willing to pay the price, to bribe a whole people into slavery. Here is a matter where rules of any kind are simply inapplicable. There are a thousand elements in the problem; and no student of political psychology can avoid the admission that we have hardly approached even the beginnings of a satisfactory solution.[127]

When the choice of governors has been made, the question yet remains of confining them to the business for which they have been chosen. We have so to arrange the machinery of the state as to secure not merely the most efficient safeguard against its perversion from theoretic purpose, but also to obtain the fullest promotion of that end. Here is the real hinterland of political enquiry; for the one obvious method by which the past sought refuge from the dangers of authority has proved in fact delusive. That method was the separation of powers. It was from the time of Aristotle conceived that the elements of public business admit of a natural classification into legislative, executive, and judicial.[128] The danger of combining the two latter was forcibly insisted upon by Bodin;[129] and Locke seems to have been the first to point out the value of their active and general separation.[130] But it was Montesquieu who, basing his attitude upon a mistaken interpretation of the English constitution, first urged that the separation of powers is the secret of liberty.[131] Supported by his immense authority, the idea was everywhere propagated with eagerness; and in France and America especially its truth was accepted with

[127] I have, of course, to deal with this problem in a later volume on the theory of politics.
[128] "Politics," IV, 14, 1297b.
[129] "De la Republique," I. X.
[130] "Second treatise," Secs. 143-6.
[131] "Esprit des Lois," Bk XI, Chap. 6.

enthusiasm. The constitutions of the Revolutionary assem-
blies wrote the principle into the fabric of the French state.[132]
In America the constitutions both of the federation and its
constituent parts unhesitatingly adopted it. Madison insisted that the "accumulation of all powers . . . . in
the same hands . . . . may justly be pronounced the
very definition of tyranny,"[133] and the Supreme Court of the
United States asserted such separation to be "one of the chief
merits of the American system."[134]

It is in fact a paper merit for the simple reason that in practice it is largely unworkable. Cromwell discovered that to
his cost;[135] and there has been no state in which methods have
not been used to break down the theoretic barriers. In France
the judiciary has largely been regarded as a delegate of the
sovereign governmental power. In America the development
of the standing-committee in Congress provided a simple system of communication between the cabinet and the legislature.
In Massachusetts, even before the war of independence, the
powerful "Junto" of Boston practically made itself an executive committee.[136] The truth is that the business of government does not admit any exact division into categories. It
has been found increasingly necessary to bestow judicial powers
upon English government departments.[137] The system of provisional orders may depend upon a genial fiction of generous
delegation; but if the work of the Local Government Board
is not, in this particular, legislation, there is nothing that is
worthy of that name. "The work of a taxing department
today," the chairman of the Board of Customs told a recent
Royal Commission,[138] "is an absolutely different thing from

[132] Cf. Duguit, "La Séparation des Pouvoirs" and Esmein's classic
discussion. "Eléments du Droit Constitutionnel" (3rd ed.). pp. 358 f. The
most general treatment is that of Saint-Girans, "Essai sur la séparation des
pouvoirs" (1884).

[133] *The Federalist*, No. 46.

[134] Kilbourne *v.* Thompson, 103 U. S., 188.

[135] Cf. Esmein's analysis, *Revue de Droit Public*, 1899, p. 8 f.

[136] Harlow. "Legislative Methods in the Period before 1825," p. 25 f.

[137] Cf. Prof. Dicey's "Comment," 31 *Law Quarterly Review*, p. 150.

[138] "Fourth Report of the Royal Commission on the Civil Service," 1914,
Cd. 7338, p. 28.

what it was twenty or even ten years ago. In those days Parliament, when it fixed a tax, settled every detail, leaving to the department only the administration of the tax on the lines laid down by Parliament. The tendency of Parliament nowadays . . . . is to lay down only principles, leaving matters of difficulty to the discretion of the department. I think it fair to say that a department like mine nowadays exercises powers which are often judicial and which sometimes get very near being legislative." Nor must Professor Dicey's insistence on the value of judicial legislation be forgotten.[139]

No one, moreover, who has watched at all carefully the development of the English cabinet in recent years can mistake the evident tendency of the executive—a tendency of course strengthened by the fact of war—to escape from Parliamentary control.[140] It is not less significant that both Insurance and Development Acts have given quasi-legislative and fully judicial powers to commissions who are expressly excepted from the ordinary rules of law.[141] This evolution, whether or no it be well-advised, surely bears testimony to the breakdown of traditional theory. The business of government cannot in fact be hampered by the search after the exact branch into which any particular act should fall. And it may even be urged that recent American history bears testimony to the further conclusion that the breakdown of the doctrine has nowhere proved unpopular. Certainly an external observer sees no sign of lament over the Presidential control of Congress;[142] and there has been, in recent years, a clear tendency in England to look for the active sovereignty of the state outside of Parliament. We have in fact come to believe that the loss in formal independence may well be compensated by a gain in the efficiency of government.

The theory yet contains an important truth of which perhaps too little notice has been taken in our time. We have

[139] "Law and Public Opinion" (2d ed.), pp. 483 f.

[140] See the very interesting debate in Hansard, Fifth Series, Vol. 92, p. 1363 f.

[141] Cf. Dicey, "Law and Public Opinion" (2d ed.), pp. XXXIX-XLIV,

[142] Cf. my note in *The New Republic* on the "Future of the Presidency" in the issue of September 29, 1917.

become so accustomed to representative government as to realise only with difficulty the real basis of its successful operation. It presupposes an educated and alert electorate which is continually anxious for the results of that system. It ought not to involve, as it has within recent years so largely involved, a divorce between the business of government and the knowledge of its processes. Aristotle's definition of citizenship as the "sharing in the administration of justice and offices"[143] implies the understanding of some sense now lost—that active participation in affairs of state will alone cause adequate performance even of the humblest civic function. Power, that is to say, which is largely concentrated at a single political centre will produce a race of men who do not display interest in its consequences. In some sort that is a fact that lies at the root of our problems. And it is important simply because the liberty of a state depends so largely upon the situation of power. We realise this, for example, in our awareness of the danger of star-chamber methods; we look with suspicion upon executive justice.[144] We insist that the independence of the judiciary is fundamental to liberty. It is only within recent years that the French courts have been able to free themselves from a narrow worship of governmental power. The supposed deviation of its activities from a theoretic sovereignty made government intolerably careless of its ways and means.[145] The simple rule that no man shall be judge in his own cause stands as one of the few really fundamental truths of political science. And the emphasis upon division of powers leads to the perception of what is becoming more and more obvious as the facts of social life become more widely known. We are beginning to see that authority should go where it can be most wisely exercised for social purposes. That is to say that there is no natural control inherent in the state. It is to suggest, for example, that it may be wise to put certain avenues of social effort out-

---

[143] "Politics," III, 1, 1275 a.

[144] Cf. Pound, "Address to the New Hampshire Bar Association," June 30, 1917.

[145] Cf. Duguit, "Les Transformation du Droit Public," Ch. VII. In this respect at least Professor Dicey's strictures upon administrative law seem to me unanswerable.

side the control of the state legislature. It is to argue that, conceivably, industrial enterprise is better settled by those who are engaged in it, than by the representatives of certain geographical areas with no necessarily expert knowledge of the problems involved.

It is thus no rigid classification of power upon which insistence is laid. Power is regarded simply as the right to will acts of general reference, and the suggestion is made that it should be conferred where it is probable that it can be most usefully exerted. In this aspect it becomes not unlikely that we have in the past, over-emphasised the necessity for its concentration at a single point in the social structure. We have been so concerned, particularly as lawyers, in demonstrating the paramountcy of the state, that we have taken too little regard of the life lived outside its categories. We ought rather to seek a different perspective. What is alone essential is the fullest achievement of the general social purpose. What is at once then evident is the necessity of organising authority with a view solely to that end.

Such an organisation implies a conception of society as basically federal in nature. In that sense the paramount character of the state is *ipso facto* denied. For if it is once clear that there are regions into which the state cannot usefully enter, it is obvious that there are realms over which its authority ought not to be exerted. That is to foreshadow a division, not of powers, but of power upon the basis of functions. It is to picture a society in which authority is not hierarchical but co-ordinate. Nor is the basis of its definition in any sense matter of *a priori* definition. It must change as social necessity may demand. It must have in constant view the possibility of innovation not less vast, for example, than that produced by the Industrial Revolution, or that which seems involved in the more recent experience of war.

To insist upon the federal nature of society is less paradoxical than may at first sight appear. Thirty years ago, indeed, Seeley pointed out that the difference between federal and unitary states was valuable only "as marking conveniently a great difference which may exist .   .   .   .   in respect of the importance of local government;"[146] and, indeed, the difference here between England and the United States is hardly greater than the difference between England and France. What is true here of the state is, of course, even more accurate of society as a whole; and once we regard the state merely as one of its constituent parts, however fundamental, what becomes obvious is the fact that its dominion must be strictly relevant to the problem of what purposes it can best fulfil. Indeed, much of the problem has been greatly obscured by thinking of federalism not in terms of a division of functions upon some rough basis of useful performance but in terms of territorial contiguity. Such a reference is, of course, intelligible enough. Everyone understands why so vast an area as the United States involves some system of decentralisation. The attempt to govern territories so diverse as Arizona and New York by uniform methods would be fraught with disaster. The facts geographically refuse such reduction to unity. The problems of government are in each case so diverse that their local study and solution alone proves efficacious.

The same necessity has been increasingly apparent in the relations between Great Britain and her daughter-nations. It has become obvious that the complex of interests we call Canada and Australia can be better governed from Ottawa or from ·Melbourne than where, as in the first part of the nineteenth century, commands radiated outwards from a single centre at Whitehall. "Government from Downing Street" came to have a sinister import simply because the interests involved were not less real and self-sufficing than the interests of the empire to which they belonged. The conference of self-government was bound to follow immediately the truth became apparent that the possession of kindred interests by a group of men will sooner or later involve the self-management of those interests. The reasons are manifold enough. Downing Street was, in the first sixty years of the nineteenth century, literally unable to cope with the complex problems that confronted it; and the attempt to construct, as notably in the colonial administration of Lord

---

[146] "Introduction to Political Science," p. 95. The whole lecture is most instructive.

Grey,[147] an uniform and equal policy for things that were neither equal nor uniform was bound to result only in constant and dangerous irritation. Nor was it for long conceivable that community like Australia would be content to leave the centre of its ultimate political power, in any sense save that of legal dignity, outside the chief residence of its economic interests.

It is, indeed, argued that within these territories unity is bound in some sort to develop.[148] In the United States, at least, this has in no sense been the case. What, in truth, may be urged is that the original distribution of power has not fitted the development of nearly a hundred and fifty years. But it is surely true in America that what is developing is less complete unity, as in France, as the emergence of new administrative areas. It is probable that the historic system of state-government has, in many cases, broken down; but that has not involved the disappearance of the fundamental idea. It would be clearly impossible to force such conflicting interests as those of agriculture and industry into a kind of Hegelian harmony by the over-simple device of legislating from Washington.[149] Nor is this less true of Canada. No observer of its conditions can fail to note the way in which, commercially, the wheat-producing territory of the West is developing a system antithetic to that of the industrial East; and it is at least not improbable that the West is destined to swing over the balance of political power exactly as in the United States.[150] But in both countries the real need is not for less local government, but for more. In both countries one of the real sources of danger has been to develop a kind of local stagnation by regarding Ottawa and Washington as reserve powers which could be brought to bear upon a recalcitrant community. What is at least as evident is the failure of recent centralisation to solve the administrative problems involved. It is continually found that they are in fact not simple and general, but specialised and local; and the

[147] Cf. his two curious volumes, the "Colonial Policy of Lord John Russell's administration" (London, 1853).

[148] As Prof. Dicey argues, "Law of the Constitution" (8th ed.—), p. LXXVI.

[149] Cf. my "Problem of Sovereignty," Appendix B.

[150] Cf. F. J. Turner, *American Historical Review*, Vol. XVI, p. 217.

spectacle of a harassed official at Washington trying to adjust the thousand varying strands the size of America involves, is not more exhilarating than to see how the Congress permits of dangerous manipulation in the interests of locality.[151]

There is, in fact, a fundamental principle involved in such an attitude upon which too much insistence can hardly be laid. It is the truth that in administration there is a point at which, for every increased attribute, an obvious diminution of efficiency results. Where a government department is overloaded with work what it will tend to do is to pay attention not to the particular circumstances of the special problem involved, but to its general ruling in broad cases of the kind. There is bound to be delay and the price of delay in such matters it is difficult to overestimate. Groups, in fact, must be treated as independent units living, however minutely, a corporate life that gives birth to special considerations. The official at London can hardly enter so closely into the unique penumbra of a Manchester enquiry as fully to satisfy it. What he will do is to look up the records of his department and apply some rule laid down for similar conditions at Liverpool. This has been strikingly illustrated in our own day by the reports of the British Commissions on industrial unrest. The attempt, as the commissioners for the North West discovered,[152] "to regulate every petty detail of the industrial machinery of the area from offices at Whitehall imposes upon the men who are asked to work it an impossible task. The trenches of industrial warfare are in Lancashire . . . . it is not a business proposition to try and command the great industrial army of these areas with a staff 200 miles from the base . . . . there is overcentralisation and . . . . this is a cause of unrest. . . . . It should be considered whether it would be possible not only to leave employers and workmen to settle more matters themselves, but to arrange that high officials . . . . should live in the area and be within close touch . . . . at the earliest possible moment." Hardly less suggestive was the conclusion of the American Commission which had the same problem in view. Here, indeed, the industrial control was

[151] Cf. Beard, "American Government and Politics," p. 269 f.

[152] Report ("Bulletin 237 of the U. S. Bureau of Labour"), p. 49. Cf. p. 77, 110, 118, 185, 214.

private and not public in nature; but it was again insisted that "distant ownership . . . . creates barriers against the opportunity of understanding the labour aspects, the human problems of the industry, and solidarity of interest among the various owners checks the views of any one liberal owner from prevailing against the autocratic policy of the majority."[153] In a still larger industry the same difficulty is noted. "The element of distance, creating managerial aloofness, thus played a very important part. For the employees, the labour policy of 'the company' was what local officials in towns distant from the executive offices made it, and not what the general officers in San Francisco might have wished it to be; distance insulated the general offices from intimate knowledge of industrial relations of the Company. The bonds of confidence and co-operation between company and employees were therefore tenuous. Moreover, the fact that the company, despite its bigness, was part of a national system, qualified all solutions of labour difficulties by consideration, on the part of the company, of the bearing of such solution however intrinsically irrelevant, upon other parts of the country."[154]

This, is, in fact, the inherent vice of centralised authority. It is so baffled by the very vastness of its business as necessarily to be narrow and despotic and over-formal in character. It tends to substitute for a real effort to grapple with special problems an attempt to apply wide generalisations that are in fact irrelevant. It involves the decay of local energy by taking real power from its hands. It puts real responsibility in a situation where, from its very flavour of generality, an unreal responsibility is postulated. It prevents the saving grace of experiment. It invites the congestion of business. And all this is the more inevitable where, as in the modern democratic state, the responsibility for administration lies not in the hands of the civil service but in the statesmen who hold office. What is thereby engendered is an attempt not so much to provide solutions as to evade them. In a great strike, for example, government arbitration will not mean so much a genuine effort after justice as the purchase of a solution on any terms. That is in

[153] Report of the President's Commission, p. 4.
[154] *Ibid.*, p. 10.

the nature of things inevitable. Where basic industries are concerned the government knows full well the unpopularity that will attend it if there is any interference with the normal process of consumption. In industry as a whole, the government is, from the nature of things, interested in the maintenance of order and it knows well enough that the maintenance of order is in inverse ratio to the duration of the strike. What it is driven thus to do is to seek the manipulation of disharmony that its credit may be thereby least injured. And, at the worst, it may suffer itself to be used for the purpose of one of the contending parties. Where picketing, for instance, is concerned, the knowledge that government stands for a certain theory of order, necessarily operates to minimise the strength of the men.[155]

It is noteworthy in this connection that the most highly centralised of modern states should have realised the inadequacy of its system. The most striking development of France in recent years is towards an increase of administrative decentralisation. The causes of this change are profound. Very largely, it is due to the increasing dissatisfaction of the civil service with Parliamentary control;[156] and that has heralded the commencement of an effort at the conference of responsibility outside the traditional categories. The decentralisation of higher education is particularly interesting in view of its success.[157] The erection of certain public services into autonomous establishments with separate budgets has not excluded governmental control; but it has, by the association in their operation of non-governmental interests, involved a real change in the atmosphere of their functioning.[158] Nor is it at all doubtful that the revivification of local life after the war is one of the first problems by which the new France will seek the renewal of its former richness.[158a]

[155] Cf. the remarks of Mr. Cole, "World of Labour," Ch. IX.

[156] Cf. Chapter V below.

[157] Hauriou, "Principes de Droit Public" (1916), pp. 745 f.

[158] Cf. Hauriou, "Précis de Droit Administratif," p. 342 f (ed. Cf. 1914), and Michoud, "Théorie de la Personnalite Morale," Vol. II, Ch. VII, esp. Secs. 247-54.

[158a] Cf. the interesting essay of Lachapelle, "L'Oeuvre de Demain" (1917).

Such decentralisation is fundamental enough; for it can hardly be too earnestly insisted that to place the real centre of political responsibility outside the sphere in which its consequences are to operate is to breed not only inefficiency but indifference. The only way to make municipal life, for example, an adequate thing is to set city striving against city in a consistent conflict of progressive improvement. A man's pride in being a citizen of London or New York can only be made real by giving to London and New York the full responsibility of self-government. The only way in which a new and needed interest in the problems of such areas can be achieved is by giving to those who handle them the full power of effective achievement. What, in despite of trammels, an able man can in this particular accomplish Mr. Chamberlain demonstrated in the case of Birmingham. And it is surely evident that by such a process we do much to relieve the congestion of public business which today stifles the public departments. Nor need we fear parochialism. That, in truth, is the offspring of a time when distance had not been annihilated by the improvement of transportation. It is possible today to go from Manchester to Liverpool in less than the time in which London itself can be traversed. When neighbouring example is thus contiguous a narrowly local sense is but a figment of pessimistic imagination. And with such a change what we open up is one of the fundamental sources of training in the business of government. When the last word has been said about "vestry-narrowness," or the pettiness of local affairs, it is surely evident that, in truth, the real guarantee of adequacy in national affairs is the proper performance of public functions in a smaller sphere. That has been one of the great advantages of the federal system in the United States. Mr. Roosevelt and Mr. Hughes in New York, Mr. Wilson in New Jersey, proved their fitness for high national office by service of a kind that demonstrated their ability to handle public issues. And it is at least not impossible that one day a similar qualification will be demanded as the basis of membership in the House of Commons. It seems, to say the least, not unlikely that the trained servant of a municipality will prove a fitter member of that Chamber than a young and freshly innocent peer whose triumphs have before been confined to the debating societies of Oxford and Cambridge.

VII. THE ORGANISATION OF POWER

THIS at least indicates, even while it does not touch, the real heart of the problem. Its crux is the position of the state relative to that of other groups within society. What we have thus far denied is the claim of the state to represent in any dominant and exclusive fashion the will of society as a whole. It is true that it does in fact absorb the vital part of social power; but it is yet in no way obvious that it ought to do so. It is in no way obvious immediately it is admitted that each individual himself is in fact a centre of diverse and possibly conflicting loyalties, and that in any sane political ethic, the real direction of his allegiance ought to point to where, as he thinks the social end is most likely to be achieved. Clearly there are many forms of association competing for his allegiance. Clearly, also, the vast part of them express the effort of men to achieve the broad aim of social existence. Labour associations aim at the control of production because they believe that with its passage into their hands the life of the masses will be richer and more full. Religious associations are the expression of a conviction that to accept certain dogmas is to secure induction into the Kingdom of Heaven. The state, as we have seen, is in reality the reflexion of what a dominant group or class in a community believes to be political good. And, in the main, it is reasonably clear that political good is today for the most part defined in economic terms. It mirrors within itself, that is to say, the economic structure of society. It is relatively unimportant in what fashion we organise the institutions of the state. Practically they will reflect the prevailing economic system; practically also, they will protect it. The opinion of the state, at least in its legislative expression, will largely reproduce the opinion of those who hold the keys of economic power. There is, indeed, no part of the community of which economic power is unable to influence the opinions. Not that it will be an absolute control that is exerted by it. The English statute-book bears striking testimony to the results of the conflict between the holders of economic power and those who

desire its possession; and, often enough, there has been generous co-operation behind the effected change. But the fundamental truth remains that the simple weapons of politics are
alone powerless to effect any basic redistribution of economic
strength.

That is to say that the political organisation of a state may
well disguise its true character. The liberal and conservative
parties in England, the republican and democratic parties
in the United States, do not the less represent a capitalist
control of politics because they are national parties. Mr.
Osborne's dislike of a labour party with a political programme
did not prove a general truth that the historic lines of party-
division in England represent a satisfactory alignment of economic power to the working-man. It did not prove that
there was in fact a possible harmony of interest between trade-
unions of which the dominant purpose was the control of industry in the interests of democratization and employers who
deny the utility of such control. It is true that the labour
party has entered politics; and it has been argued with some
plausibility[159] that it ought by the slow conversion of the electorate to its creed to arrive by a slow evolution at the control
of the processes of the state. But that analysis is, in fact,
entirely unreal. It mistakes the important truth that the
interests to which the House of Commons attends is, in reality,
the interests of consumers as those are capable of being harmonised with the demands of the prevalent economic system.
The interest of the constituencies of the House of Commons
is predominantly in the regular functioning of economic processes. They want a proper postal service, or railway system,
exactly as the citizens of a municipality will look to the town-
council for gas and tramways and electricity. With the internal
organisation of industrial affairs they will not concern themselves save as disharmony will force them to the recognition
of their importance. Sometimes, indeed, a sudden fit of humanitarianism, as in the Trade-Boards Act, will result in legis-

[159] By Mr. A. E. Zimmern in *The New Republic*, September 15, 1917.
Cf. Mr. Croly's article in the same issue, and the editorial comment on
Mr. Zimmern's letter. Mr. Zimmern's rejoinder is to be found in an arti-
cle on "Freedom and Unity" in the *Round Table* for December, 1917.

lative control. But, primarily, it is in regularity of industrial service that the House of Commons and government are above all interested. And, as a careful observer has pointed out, this is predominantly true of local government.[160]

When, therefore, the functions of the state undergo close scrutiny, it is found that the aspect upon which they concentrate their work is the use by the community of industrial resources. It is not interested in the processes of production as such; it concerns itself in securing due provision from industry for the needs of society. It deals with men in the capacity that is common to them all. It regards them as the users of certain goods. It is uninterested in men as engaged in any function save that of consumption except, of course, insofar as the performance of their duties hinders the achievement of its own basic effort. Clearly, for instance, the state, through its government, would be vitally interested in a railway strike; for it is vitally interested in securing to the members of the state the uninterrupted use of railway facilities. But an analysis of the part played by the government in settlements of industrial disputes can hardly fail to suggest that the primary concern of the state is not in the cause of the dislocation, but in the dislocation itself.[160a] Causes are important only insofar as they seem to imply a renewal of disturbance. In that aspect the relation of the state to a member of the railway unions is very different from its relation to the ordinary member of the public. For its main concern with the trade unionist is to get him back to work; whereas that at which he aims is some redistribution of economic power within a group only the results of whose functionings concern the state as a whole.

That is why it is impossible to regard the state as capable, in any general view, of absorbing the whole loyalty of an individual. It can only secure his loyalty insofar as he does not think that, in the given situation, the railway union has in fact a superior claim. It is just as possible, for instance, for

[160] Cole, "Self-Government|in Industry," p. 77. With much of Mr. Cole's chapter on the state I should find myself in admiring agreement, though with certain changes of fundamental emphasis.

[160a] This is avowedly the motive underlying the Canadian Industrial Disputes Investigation Act.

a man to make the decision that, balanced against the industrial
dislocation, the end of a railway strike is worth the cost, as
it is to conclude that the sacrifices of a great war are worth
the great price they involve if the result safeguards the liberty
of nations.   At a stroke, in brief, the hierarchical structure of
society is demolished.   We have, instead, a series of co-ordinate
groups the purposes of which may well be antithetic.   What
has happened in the history of the state is, on the contrary,
the assertion that it enjoys a unique position for its power.   It
claims the right to judge between conflicting associations and
to interpose its will between them.   It claims that the rights
of societies other than itself are, in fact, within its gift; and
their existence is conditioned by its graciousness.   The fear
of group-persons in English-history is at least as old as Richard
of Devizes;[161] and Blackstone only put into legal form the contempt that Hobbes had poured upon them.[162]   "With us in
England," he said,[163] "the king's consent is absolutely necessary
to the creation of any corporation"; and the Combination
Acts are the proud vindication of the state's claim to exclusive-
ness.   But here, as elsewhere, life in fact overflows the narrow
categories in which the dogmas of state-sovereignty would
enshrine it.   The truth is more and more apparent that these
groups live a life of their own, and exist to support purposes
that the state itself fails to fulfil.   From this it was that Maitland drew the obvious conclusion.   "Some would warn us,"
he wrote in a famous sentence,[164] "that in the future, the less
we say about a supralegal, suprajural plenitude of power concentrated in a single point at Westminster—concentrated in
one single organ of an increasingly complex commonwealth—
the better for that vision may be the days that are coming."

[161] Richard of Devizes' "Chronicle 416." Cf. Stubbs' "Const. Hist." (6th
ed.), I, 455.

[162] On the early history of the English corporation cf my paper in the
Harvard Law Review, Vol. XXX, p. 561.

[163] Com. I, 472.

[164] Introduction to his translation of Gierke's "Political Theories of the
Middle Age," p. XLIII.   On some of the difficulties that the "Concession"
theory must encounter cf. my paper on the "Personality of Associations,"
in the *Harvard Law Review*, Vol. XXX, p. 404.

It is no more than that vision we are seeking to translate into the event.

If, then, we view the state as primarily a body of consumers whose will, over the course of history, has been largely controlled by groups within itself, it clearly follows that the producer who does not share in the ownership of means of production must safeguard his special interest in his personal function in such fashion as will prevent its subordination to the purposes of government. So, too, and in another sphere, a Roman Catholic must arm himself lest his interest in his church be unjustly attacked by a state that has made with some alien religious body an alliance for reciprocal assistance.[165] The main value of his church, indeed, must for him consist in the fact that because it is a church it gives him a guarantee he could not otherwise possess against the invasion of a religious interest. For the individual is lost in a big world unless there are fellowships to guard him; and even those associations may well prove powerless unless they deny that their rights are state-derived. Excommunication, for example, would not seem to him a sentence open to the revision of a state-court.[166] This is in no sense a denial of membership of the state. It is merely an insistence that the aspect in which he is related to his church is an aspect different from his relation to the state. The spheres of each are, in his own mind, distinct; the powers of each are then divided in the light of that separation. In the Presbyterian Church, again, no denial is made of the supremacy of the state in civil matters; but, said Chalmers, "in things ecclesiastical we decide all.[167] " Here, again, the emphasis is upon co-ordinate function. What is essentially denied is the derivation of church rights from the grace of the state.

The position of trade-unionism is in the closest relation to this attitude. It is held that the purpose of that movement emphasises an aspect of the worker's life which is different

[165] Or, as in France, the non-Catholics may have to aim to prevent the state from becoming a branch of the Roman Catholic Church.

[166] Cf. the very interesting opinions in St. Vincent's Parish v. Murphy, 83 Nebraska 630, and Parish of the Immaculate Conception v. Murphy, 89 Nebraska, 524.

[167] Cf. my "Problem of Sovereignty," p. 39.

from the aspect emphasised by the state. The trade-union is concerned with the business of production; the state is, above all, concerned with the general regularity of the supply for consumption. What, then, the trade-union is compelled to deny is the subordination of the function he fulfils as a producer to his interest in the supply of his needs. It is, in any case, painfully clear that the state does not in any full sense secure that supply. It ensures production; but the distribution of the product is weighted in the interest of those who wield economic power. That is the main reason why the worker sees in the productive process a lever that will react upon the state itself. True political democracy is, as he realises, the offspring of true industrial democracy. If he were to admit the paramount character of the consumptive process no strike would ever occur. But, obviously, the judgment is constantly made, and that in industries of basic importance, that the attainment of a new equilibrium in industrial relations is worth the heavy price invariably paid for it. The worker, that is to say, is no more inclined than the Roman Catholic to admit the supremacy of the context in which the state is placed. He refuses to regard it as in any permanently valid sense the sovereign representative of the community. He bases his refusal upon the belief that the results of its functioning bear witness to a grave maladjustment. It is used to support a *status quo* with which he is dissatisfied. He might even urge that the new equilibrium at which he is aiming is worth more to the community than the fulfilment of what the state at present regards as its duties in the consumptive process.

Here, immediately, a division of power is implied. The business of consumption, it is suggested, is proper material for the authority of the state. It is immediately a matter where the interests of men in their capacity of consumers may be taken as substantially equal; at least in the sense that there are certain goods a minimum supply of which is, for each individual, essential to social existence. But somewhere between production and consumption a line must be drawn. The interests of men in production are rarely equal because the share of its results suffers widely varying distribution. There is a broad distinction, for example, between the interest of the owner of capital and the interest of the unpropertied worker. There is at present, also, a distinction, which the sectionalism of trade-unions makes unfortunately manifest, between skilled and unskilled labour.[168] There is a clash of interest, at least in certain trades, between the male and female labour employed.[169] It is probable, indeed, that sectional antagonism within the labour movement is capable of removal by wise activity; and certainly the great English amalgamations of recent years, most notably that of the transport workers, point increasingly in this direction.

But between the interest of capital and that of labour it is difficult to see any permanent basis of reconciliation. They want antithetic things. When the utmost that a capitalism can concede is measured, it still falls short of what labour demands; for the ultimate object of labour activity is democratic self-government in industry, the determination, that is to say, of the methods to be employed at each stage of the productive process, the settlement of tasks and hours and wages by the men themselves. It involves, therefore, the disappearance of a super-imposed hierarchical control. It takes the trade-union as the single cell from which an entirely new industrial order is to be evolved. In such an aspect, the suspicion of labour towards a state that is predominantly capitalist in character is inevitable. For whether the state, through its instruments, seeks, by maintaining order, to prevent the possibility of redistribution; whether it attempts to discover some possible basis of temporary reconciliation; what always emerges from either synthesis is the determination of labour to use the equilibrium so created as the foundation of a new effort towards its ultimate objective. The method of which use is made may vary but the purpose is unchanging.

Labour, therefore, could admit the complete sovereignty of the state only if it could be assumed that the state were on its side. The only thing of which it can in this context be certain is that the power of the state will be predominantly exerted

[168] Cf. Cole, "World of Labour," Chs. VII and VIII. What is said here of over-lapping is even more true of the United States than of England.

[169] On the general problem cf. Webb, "The Restoration of Trade Union Conditions" (1917).

against its interest. For the social order of the modern state
is not a labour order but a capitalist, and upon the broad truth
of Harrington's hypothesis it must follow that the main power
is capitalist also. That will imply a refusal on labour's part to
accept the authority of the state as final save where it is satisfied with its purposes. It means that it will endeavor so to
organise the process of production as to hand over the chief
authority therein to the trade-unions which express its interests. It means, in short, the conquest of productive control
by labour; and when that control has been conquered it is
not likely that it will be easily surrendered.[170]

What, on the contrary, is possible is that some adjustment
will be slowly made between the groups which represent the
interests of producers and the state, in all its constituent local
parts, as representing the consumer. We do not admit, that
is to say, the attitude of the anarchist who denies, like William
Godwin, the need for authority at all,[171] or the attitude of the
syndicalist who emphasises only the producer's interest. The
case against syndicalism Mr. Graham Wallas has felicitously
expressed in a single sentence. "It proved to be more important", he has written,[172] "that under syndicalism men loved
each other less as citizens than that they loved each other more
as gild-brothers." We cannot, in fact risk the possibility of
disorganisation upon the basis of narrow selfishness. However
the productive process is in the future arranged within itself
provision must be made for some central authority not less
representative of production as a whole than the state would
represent consumption. There is postulated therein two bodies
similar in character to a national legislature. Over-great pressure of consumer on producer is avoided by giving to the producers as a whole a legislature where the laws of production
would be considered. The legislature of the consumers would
decide upon the problems of supply. Joint questions, in such

---

[170] I am not here, of course, concerned to point out the steps by which this
control is to be achieved; but I have indicated in the next section some of
the more obvious directions along which it is moving.

[171] A reprint of his "Political Justice" is an urgent need.

[172] "The Great Society," p. 328. See the whole passage from p. 324
onwards.

a synthesis, are obviously matter for joint adjustment. Nor
is the central authority within either division to be envisaged
as uniquely sovereign. Certain functional delimitations, the
cotton-trade, the mining-industry, the railways, shipping,
immediately suggest themselves. From the consumer's standpoint, municipalities, counties, even whole areas like the North
of England, may have group-demands to be settled by group-
action. A balance of internal powers would functionally be
sought. Arrangements would require a system of collective
contracts upon the basis of collective bargaining. Law, as
now, would be matter for the courts. The judiciary could settle
a dispute between a bootmakers' gild and the authorities of
an orphan asylum in Manchester as well in one system as
another. Probably, indeed, a special system of industrial
courts would be developed. Probably, also, just as in the
United States a court of special and pre-eminent dignity de-
cides controversies between the separate states, disputes between a producers' authority and a consumers' would need a
special tribunal. That is why, as M. Duguit has pointed
out,[173] jurisprudence will occupy an important place in the
federalist society towards which we are moving.[174]

VIII. THE SIGNIFICANCE OF FREEDOM

So complex a division of powers as this seems at first sight con-
fusing to one accustomed to the ordinary theory of state-sovereignty. It is not difficult to urge that co-ordination implies
the possibility of conflict and to insist that only by an hierachi-
cal structure of authority can the danger of disturbance be mini-
mised. Yet it is, to say the least, tolerably clear that disturbance is not avoided by the conference of supreme power on the
state. The rejection of that claim to sovereignty, moreover,
involves an attitude to politics which has at least some merit.
There is a sense in which the vastest problem by which we are
faced is the very scale of the life we are attempting to live. Its
bigness tends to obscure the merits of real freedom. And, indeed,

[173] "Le Droit Social, le Droit Individuel," p. 157.
[174] On the whole of this Cf. Cole, "Self-Government in Industry,"
Ch. III, and Paul-Boncour, "Le Fédéralisme Economique," pp. 372-423.

there is industrially abroad a certain suspicion of liberty against which safeguards must be erected.   The individual suffers absorption by the immensity of the forces with which he is in contact.   That is true not less of the House of Commons, of Congress, of the French chamber, than it is of an industry which has largely suffered depersonalisation.   There are few signs of that energy of the soul which Aristotle thought the secret of happiness.   There is little work that offers the opportunity of conscious and systematic thought.   Responsibility tends to coagulate at a few centres of social life; so that the work of most is the simple commission of orders it is rarely their business to reflect upon.   We are clearly tending to be overawed by our institutions; and we can perceive, in a way different from the perspective set by Lecky and Sir Henry Maine, a genuine danger lest we lose hold of that chiefest source of happiness. Clerks and teachers and tenders of machines, for each of whom there is prescribed a routine that fills the most eager hours of life, dare not be asked for the effort upon which new thought is founded.   An expert in the science of factory management has even assumed that for the purpose of productivity a man "who more nearly resembles in his mental make-up the ox than any other type"[175] is desirable.   Happiness in work, which can alone be fruitful of advance in thought, is, as Mr. Wallas has noted,[176] a phrase for most practically without meaning.   The problem to-day, as the problem at the time of the French Revolution, is the restoration of man to his place at the centre of social life.

That is, indeed, the real significance of freedom.   It alone enables the individuality of men to become manifest.   But individuality is bound to suffer eclipse if power is unduly centred at some single point within the body politic.   To divide it upon the basis of the functions it is to perform is the only guaranty for the preservation of freedom.   We too little remember that the appearances of politics have obscured the emergence in our time of new and sinister forces of compulsion.   The pursuit

[175] Taylor, "Principles of Scientific Management," p. 59.   Mr. Hoxie has noted this authoritarian tendency throughout the "efficiency" school. "Scientific Management and Labour" passim.

[176] "The Great Society," pp. 345, 363 ff.   A very thorough collection of data upon this subject would be invaluable.

of an ideal of efficiency, for which, in part at least the New World is responsible, has led men to make a fetish of centralisation. They have not seen that the essence of free government is the democratization of responsibility. They have not realised that no man can make his life a thing worthy of himself without the possession of responsibility. It is useless to respond that men are uninterested in politics. They are interested in anything which nearly touches their lives, provided only that they have a share in its application.

They can develop that control only by preventing the concentration of power. In a society so great as ours, some system of representation is inevitable; and it is only by dividing functions that we can prevent those representatives from absorbing the life-blood of the body-politic; exactly as in France decentralisation alone can cure the dangerous overprominence of Paris. To divide industrial power from political control is to prevent the use of the latter influence against the forces of change. It removes the main lever by which the worker is prevented from the attainment of self-expression. It makes the chief well-spring of progress not the chance humanitarianism the spectacle of an under-paid employment may create, but the earnest and continuous effort of the worker. It thereby gives to him a training in the business of government which otherwise is painfully lacking. For, after all, the one sphere in which the worker is genuinely articulate is the sphere of production. To admit the trade-union to an effective place in government, to insist that it is fundamental in the direction of production, is to make the worker count in the world. He may be then also a tender of machines; but where his trade-union is making decisions in which his own will is a part he is something more than a tender of machines. His very experience on this side of government will make him more valuable in his quality as citizen. He will see the consumptive process more realistically because its details have been illuminated for him in trade-union activity. The very divisions of society will hinge upon the different aspects of his own life. It is upon him that the basis of the state must then be founded.

It has been urged that no society could endure in such a synthesis. Unless, so we are told, there is within it some unique

centre of power, a conflict of authorities may well prove its destruction. A state cannot live unless it possess the absolute and
undivided allegiance of its members. To depict, therefore, a
community in which allegiance is co-operative seems, in such
perspective, to destroy its efficient life. But we have already
in fact discussed this question. We have already shown that
no man's allegiance is, in fact, unique. He is a point towards
which a thousand associations converge; what, then, we ask
is that where conflict comes, we have assurance that he follow
the path of his instructed conscience. Once grant the individual
rights against the state, and it follows that the state must win
his loyalty by the splendor of its effort. What, mainly, is needed
is some source of guarantee against perversion of the state-power.
Partly, that is needed in the relation of churches to the state;
partly, also, and today, primarily, it is needed if the certainty of
industrial progress is to be secured. For we have seen that the
state-will tends inevitably to become confused with that of government. Government is in the hands, for the most part, of
those who wield economic power. The dangers of authority
become intensified if the supreme power be collected and concentrated in an institution which cannot be relied upon uniquely
to fulfil its theoretic purposes. That is why the main safeguard
against economic oppression is to prevent the state from throw-
ing the balance of its weight into the side of established order.
It is to prevent it from crying peace where in fact the true issue
is war. For, important as may be the process of consumption,
it is in nowise clear that the state treats equally those who are
benefited by the process. It is by no means certain that the
standard of life of the worker is not better safeguarded by his
trade-union than by the state.

Yet of one thing we must beware. It is not difficult to project a wanton idealism into our view of the trade-unions. It is
not difficult, when they are contrasted with the policy, for example, of the National Manufacturers' Association of the
United States, to regard them as little short of perfect. We have
ceaselessly to remember that the retention of economic anti-
quarianism by the trade-unions is at least as possible as its reten-
tions by the manufacturer. The attitude of the Lancashire
cotton-operatives to child labour, the attitude of the Pearl but-

ton makers to apprenticeship,[177] are instances of this kind. It is at least possible that we shall have more and more to evolve bills of rights in which the fundamental nations of social justice are put beyond the reach of peradventure. The Lancashire cotton-operatives, indeed, might be voted down in a gild-parliament on a question of child-labour; but it is important that they should be *a priori* prevented from getting into the frame of mind where the interest of the citizen in education can be sacrificed to a demand for cheap labour.

From one difficulty, indeed, we may at the outset free our minds. "A state," writes Mr. Zimmern,[178] "in which the majority of the citizens, or even a substantial minority, doubted to which external authority their supreme allegiance was due would soon cease to be a state at all." This, surely, evades the point at issue. A state in which a "substantial minority" of the citizens did not feel, in a crisis, the call of allegiance would probably be embarking upon a policy at least open to the gravest doubt. It cannot be too emphatically insisted that the real merit of democratic government as opposed to any other form is exactly this dependence upon consent. The very difficulty which caused the breakdown of the policy of international socialism in 1914 was its failure to give to its recognised representatives in the belligerent countries the authority needed to make the German state halt before its policy of aggression. It was precisely because the authority of the German state is paramount that those who manipulate its destinies can without serious question pervert it from the path of right conduct. The safeguard of the English state is the knowledge that there is without its instruments a critical opinion capable of organised expression. Nor is there reason to fear that a state where dissent may organise itself is less capable of unified defence than an autocratically-controlled régime. For a democratic community has its heart in the business that it undertakes. It fights, not with mechanical obstinacy, but the intensity of a conviction derived from the process of free thought. Its victory may be delayed; but unless the odds are overwhelmingly

---

[177] Cf. Webb, "Industrial Democracy," Ch. X.

[178] Letter to *The New Republic*, September 15, 1917.

against it, the spirit it can infuse into its purpose is bound, in the end, to give it victory.[179]

There are at least two directions in which the danger of over-concentrating the power of the state has received a striking emphasis in the last few years. The necessities of war have immensely increased the area of state-control. Social needs broke down the quasi-anarchy of a competitive industrial system, and its place has been taken by two separate forms of management. On the one hand we have the continued management of industry by private enterprise, with, however, a rigid supervision exerted by the state. The danger here is obviously immense. The need of the state in war-time has been increasing productivity and the whole orientation of control has been towards that end. So, even if rules have been laid down, profits taxed, priority of supply enforced, still the situation has in reality involved a state-guarantee of the continuance of the present industrial régime. That has meant an immense increase of centralisation. It has changed at a stroke the whole and elaborate system of safeguards by which labour had sought protection against the dehumanising forces of capitalism.[180] It does not seem doubtful that this change has been in a high degree beneficial. But it has had two grave results. On the one hand there is the problem of giving to the trade-unions safeguards that shall, in the new synthesis, be equal to the power of the old. On the other there has taken place an immense concentration of capital not merely in industry itself, but in finance also. Nothing will be easier in the years that lie ahead either for the owners of capital to demand the continuance of government control, or to insist that naturalisation upon the basis of adequate compensation is alone a fair return for its services. In either case we have a guarantee of interest made a fundamental charge upon the resources of the state. That burden, without a time-limit, may well prove a fundamental obstacle to the democratisation of control.

Nor is the alternative of complete state-management more inviting. Indeed, it may without exaggeration be suggested

[179] As is forcibly pointed out by my critic in the *London Times* of May 17, 1917.

[180] Cf. Webb, "The Restoration of Trade Union Conditions," passim.

that the evils such a régime would imply are hardly less great than those of the present system. For to surrender to government officials not merely political but also industrial administration is to create a bureaucracy more powerful than the world has ever seen. It is to apotheosise the potent vices of a government department. It is to make certain a kind of paternalism which, perhaps above all other systems, would prevent the advent of the kind of individual freedom we desire. After all, we have had no light experience of the state. Municipally it certainly is no less efficient than private industry; but, humanly speaking, there is little or no evidence that its administration is more democratic. The attitude of the London County Council to its carmen is hardly encouraging.[181] The Holt Report on the postal service must give pause to every observer who occupies himself with the consideration of these problems.[182] The long story of grievances in the French civil service is a record that no believer in state-absorptiveness can contemplate with equanimity.[183] The permanent official is no more blessed with an immediate appreciation of that hunger to determine the rule of his own life which is the source of democratic aspiration than the private employer. Nor can anyone examine his record in the present war and feel confident that he has any real contribution to offer. On the contrary, the one complaint of which we on all hands hear is lack of confidence in him from those whose confidence is essential to the right conduct of industry.[184] The centralisation state-management would imply would mean the transference of all power to a class of guardians within the state whose main object, even more than today would, at all costs, be the maintenance of regularity of supply. There would, inevitably, be an effort to play off group against group, to purchase office by favour, to

[181] Cf. Cole, "Labour in Wartime," p. 160 ff.

[182] So far as France is concerned cf. Beaubois, "La Crise Postale et les Monopoles L'Etat," and the note on the American post-office in *The New Republic*, Vol. XIII, p. 167.

[183] Cf. Chap. V below.

[184] Cf. the Reports of Mr. Lloyd-George's "Commissions on Industrial Unrest" (American Bureau of Labour edition), pp. 77-8, 88-9,110-12, 25, 119, 162, 217.

lack inventiveness, by which in every age a bureaucracy is distinguished. Then, as now, the trade-unions would be compelled to fight against an established order for the opportunity of industrial self-expression; and the fight against a state is notoriously more difficult than the fight against private capital. Inevitably, moreover, the public character of the state as employer lends it a factitious popular support against which it is difficult to make headway. And, indeed, government, even less than private enterprise, is hardly prepared to tolerate democratisation of control.

Nor is it prepared to tolerate a democratic judgment. We here touch a vital element in modern government. Our state is a sovereign state, and about the acts of its agents the cloak of its supremacy is cast. In nothing, indeed, has the falsity of such an outlook been more strikingly manifest than in the doctrine of its irresponsibility. We place governmental acts in a different category from private acts. If A harms B the courts always lie open for remedy; but if A be government, it is with problems of a different kind that we become immediately concerned.

The explanation is probably simple. To sue the king in his own courts has about it an air of unreason; for, at least in theory, he is present there, and to sue him is to ask him to be judge in his own cause. When the doctrine of his legal infallibility becomes added thereto we have all the materials for an evasion of justice. For, to the courts, there is no such thing as the English state. There is a king, and the state can shrink behind the personality he will lend for its protection. It does not matter that since the eighteenth century he has been no more than the shadow of a great name. The old form is preserved, and it lends its content to the government by which he has been replaced. An action for breach of contract, indeed, can, by the disagreeable formality of a Petition of Right be instituted; but into the category of tort the concept of liability has not yet entered. Miss Bainbridge may be run over by the mail-van of the Postmaster-General; but the irresponsibility of the state prevents an action against anyone but the humble driver of the van.[185] The Lords of Admiralty may

[185] Bainbridge v. Postmaster-General (1906), I, K. B. 178.

infringe a patent but they remain inaccessible to justice.[186] Sir Claude Macdonald may dismiss an official whom he has, as Her Majesty's Commissioner for the Niger Protectorate engaged for a definite period of years before its expiration; but the ample cloak of state authority is cast about him.[187] "The maxim that 'the king can do no wrong'," said a strong court,[188] "applies to personal as well as political wrongs, and not only to wrongs done personally by the sovereign (if such a thing could be supposed possible), but to injuries done by one subject to another by authority of the sovereign. For from the maxim that the king can do no wrong it follows, as a necessary consequence, that the king cannot allow wrong to be done; for to authorize a wrong to be done is to do a wrong; and as the wrongful act done becomes in law the act of those who authorize it to be done, it follows that the petition of right which complains of a tortious or wrongful act done by the Crown or by servants of the Crown discloses no right to redress, for as in law no such wrong can be done no such right can arise . . . ." So when the Sultan of Johore puts off his sultanship and makes an offer of marriage to Miss Mighell in the guise of an Albert Baker, his sovereignty prevents recovery of damages for breach of promise.[189] The whole thing is a positive stumbling block in the path of administrative moralisation.

Nor is this irresponsibility confined to England. Many of the local jurisdictions of the United States expressly limit themselves from being sued in their own courts even though, as the Supreme Court has said,[190] "it is difficult to see on what solid foundation of principle the exemption from liability to suit rests." In France it is only painfully, and after long hesitation, that a category of state-responsibility is being evolved.[191] We have not taken to heart the great words of Maitland that "it is a wholesome sight to see the 'Crown' sued and answer-

[186] Feather v. Regina, 6 B & S, 257.

[187] Dunn v. the Queen (1896), I, Q. B. C. A., 116.

[188] Feather v. Regina, 6, B. & S., 257.

[189] Mighell v. Sultan of Johore (1894), I, Q. B., 149.

[190] U. S. v. Lee, 106 U. S., 196, 206.

[191] Cf. Duguit, "Transformations du Droit Public," Ch. VII.

ing for its torts."[192]   It is true that an increasing tendency is apparent to provide statutory remedy for wrongful acts.[193] Where government dissolves into a dock company the cloak of sovereignty may well suffer withdrawal.[194] But the essential thesis that a state act—which in practice means a governmental act—gives rise to no liability remains untouched. It is the price we pay for refusing to look facts in the face. The state in this context is a group of officials who may act not less harmfully than a private individual. It is difficult to see why their acts should be excused where harm is caused. And that the more in an age that has witnessed the immense growth of administrative law.[195]

Upon its dangers, indeed, too much insistence can hardly be laid. The most striking change in the political organisation of the last half-century is the rapidity with which, by the sheer pressure of events, the state has been driven to assume a positive character. We talk less and less in the restrained terms of Benthamite individualism. The absence of governmental interference has ceased to seem an ultimate ideal. There is everywhere almost anxiety for the extension of governmental functions. It is probably inevitable that such an evolution should involve a change in the judicial process. The administrative departments, in the conduct of public business, find it essential to assume duties of a judicial character. Where, for example, great problems like those involved in government insurance are concerned, there is undoubtedly a great convenience in leaving their interpretation to the officials who are to administer the act. They have gained in its application an expert character to which no purely judicial body can pretend; and their opinion has a weight which no community can afford to neglect. The business of the state, in fact, is so much like private business that, as Professor Dicey has emphasised,[196]

[192] "Collected Papers," III, 263.

[193] Cf. Mr. Maguire's very able paper in *Harvard Law Review*, Vol. 30, pp. 20 ff., and see especially Canadian Revised Statutes (1906), C. 140, Sec. 20, for an interesting example of legal remedy for injury by negligence on public works.

[194] Mersey Docks *v.* Gibbs, 11, H. C. L. C., 686.

[195] Cf. E. Barker in the *Political Quarterly* for May, 1914, esp. pp. 125 f.

[196] *Law Quarterly Review*, Vol. 31, p. 150.

its officials need "that freedom of action necessarily possessed by every private person in the management of his own personal concerns." So much is at least tolerably clear. But history suggests that the relation of such executive justice to the slow infiltration of a bureaucratic régime is perilously close; and the development of such administrative law needs at each step to be closely scrutinised in the interests of public liberty.[197]

The famous Arlidge case in England[198] is a striking example of what the seventeenth century would have termed Star-chamber methods. It was there decided by the highest English tribunal that when a government department assumes quasi-judicial functions the absence of express enactment in the enabling statute means that the department is free to embark upon what procedural practice may seem best to it; nor will the courts enquire if such practice results, or can by its nature result, in justice. In such an attitude it is clear that what Professor Dicey has taught us to understand as the rule of law [199] becomes largely obsolete. If, as in the Zadig case,[200] the Secretary of State for Home Affairs may make regulations of any kind without any judicial tests of fairness or reasonableness being involved, it is clear that a fundamental safeguard upon English liberties has disappeared. Immediately administrative action can escape the review of the Courts it is clear that the position of a public official has become privileged in a sense from which the administrative law of France and Germany is only beginning to escape.

Nor is it likely that these issues have become significant merely in relation to abnormal conditions. American administrative law, in the sense of a law different in content from a mere law of public offices, goes back to the Ju Toy case,[201] where a majority of the Supreme Court, perhaps somewhat doubtfully,

[197] Cf. Pound, "Address to the New Hampshire Bar Association," June 30, 1917.

[198] (1915) A. C. 120, and see Dean Pound's comment in the address cited above.

[199] "The Law of the Constitution" (8th ed.), p. 179 f.

[200] R. v. Halliday (1917). A. C. 226. Cf. especially the dissenting opinion of Lord Shaw and the comment in 31 *Harvard Law Review*, 296.

[201] U. S. v. Ju Toy, 198 U. S. 253.

held the courts powerless, in view of the Chinese exclusion Act of 1894, to review a decision of the Secretary of Commerce and Labour. But no one would object to action by a government department so long as assurance could be had of absolute fairness in the methods by which a decision was reached; it was exactly the absence of that fairness which constituted the source of grievance and disquiet in the Arlidge case. A recent decision of the Supreme Court,[202] very strikingly comparable with the issue in the English case, suggests that the Supreme Court will be careful of those safeguards as, indeed, the due process clause obviously demands it must be careful. The Public Service Commission of New York ordered a gas company, after a hearing in which witnesses were cross-examined, testimony introduced and the case argued, to provide gas service for a certain district. The company believed that, relative to the expenditure required, a sufficient return would not be had. It therefore appealed on the ground that the order of the commission "was illegal and void in that it deprived the Gas Company of its property without due process of law and denied to it the equal protection of the laws in violation of the Fourteenth Amendment to the Constitution of the United States . . . . "and, after the requisite intermediate stages, the issue came before the Supreme Court on this single ground of error. Mr. Justice Clarke upheld the action of the Public Service Commission. He admitted, for the Court, that the finding of an expert commission is final and will not be discussed again by the courts. Such, of course, has been the general practice of the Supreme Court;[203] and, so far, the decision in no sense differs from the bearing of the opinion rendered in the Arlidge case by the House of Lords.

But there is, at this point, a significant departure. "This court," says Clarke J.[204] "will nevertheless enter upon such an examination of the record as may be necessary to determine whether the federal constitutional right claimed has been denied, as, in this case, whether there was such a want of hearing, or

[202] New York v. McCall et al, 38 Sup. Ct. Rep. 122.
[203] Baltimore & Ohio R.R. Co. v. Pitcairn Coal Co., 215 U. S. 481; Interstate Commerce Commission v. Union Pacific R.R. Co., 222 U. S. 541.
[204] New York v. McCall et al, 38 Sup. Ct. Rep. 122, 124.

such arbitrary or capricious action on the part of the Commission as to violate the due process clause of the constitution." No one, it may be suggested, who studies the history of the due-process clause can deny that, on occasion, it has been sadly perverted from its orginal purposes. But here at least, and in the perspective here outlined, its value must be obvious even to those who are suspicious of the rigidity of a written constitution. The Supreme Court, as the learned judge points out, does not purpose to go into issues probably better settled by the administrative tribunal; but it does, and rightly, purpose to examine into the fundamental question of whether the means taken by that tribunal to attain its end were such as were, on the plain face of things, adequate to the securing of justice.

That, of a certainty, is a safeguard to which the courts will more and more be driven with the expansion of administrative law. Under the Defence of the Realm Consideration Act, for instance, the Home Secretary may issue a regulation which prohibits publication of any book or pamphlet relating to the conduct of the war on the terms of peace without its previous submission to the censor who may prohibit such publication without the assignment of[205] cause. That is to say that the merest and irresponsible caprice of a junior clerk of determined nature might be actually the occasion of suppressing a vital contribution to the understanding of the war. So ridiculous a proceeding is at least prevented by the system of the Supreme Court. In the first place, and above all, a due publicity is secured. It would have to be shown to the Supreme Court that the methods taken to secure the decision were such as to warrant it; and in so vital a thing as freedom of speech one may feel tolerably certain that the methods would be subject to closest scrutiny. It has been the habit of past years to sneer rather elaborately at Bills of Rights.[206] It may yet be suggested that with the great increase of state activity that is clearly foreshadowed there was never a time when they were so greatly needed. Here, as elsewhere, the human needs the satisfaction

[205] Regulation 51. Cf. *London Nation*, December 8, 1917.

[206] A habit unfortunately intensified by Professor Ritchie's "Natural Rights," which, dismissing them historically, was held to dismiss them politically also.

of which history has demonstrated to be essential must be put beyond the control of any organ of the state; that, and no more than that, is what we mean today by natural rights.[207] Governmental power is a thing which needs at every stage the most careful regard; and it is only by judicial control in terms of those rights that the path of administration will become also the path of justice . The problem of responsibility can be approached with profit from another angle. The purpose and the character of government as a trust leads us to regard it as in reality an institution for translating purposes into the event without regard to the fact that the men who operate those purposes give to them a personality of their own. The belief in the reality of corporate persons, indeed, only slowly makes its way into the general body of Anglo-American law. Its progress is at every stage impeded by the general refusal of the courts to recognize the corporate character of the trust. It is nearly thirteen years since Maitland demonstrated with all his profound scholarship, and even more than his wonted charm, that the trust has, above all things, served historically as a screen to promote the growth of institutions which, for a variety of reasons, have found inadvisable the path of corporate adventure.[208] Especially true of the state, this may perhaps receive its simplest illustration in the case of charitable trusts. "A trust," said Bacon there centuries ago,[209] "is the binding of the conscience of one to the purpose of another"—a fit enough description of the process of government. But we have failed to see how that purpose must take account of the categories of time and space. In its legal perspective, the doctrine is most largely a supposed deference to the rights of propriety; and it has paid but little attention to the admirable remark of John Stuart Mill[210] that no man ought to exercise the rights of property long after his death.

This tendency to regard as adequate and all-excusing the purpose enshrined in the trust without at the same time em-

[207] W. Wallace, "Lectures & Essays," 213 ff.

[208] "Collected Papers," III, 321 f.

[209] "Reading on the Statute of Uses," p. 9.

[210] Essay on "Corporations and Church Property" in Vol. I of his "Dissertations and Discussions."

phasising the life that trust engenders has received an interesting illustration in a recent American decision.[211]   A fireman who was engaged in extinguishing a hospital fire was injured through the defective condition of the hospital fire escape. He sued the hospital for damages, and relief was denied on the ground that the doctrine of *respondeat superior* does not apply to charitable institutions.   The basis of the decision seems to be the opinion[212] that the funds of a charity are not provided to liquidate the damages caused in its defective administration; and the funds are therefore not applicable to the redemption of the torts committed by the agents or servants of the charity.[213]   This doctrine, indeed, is not worked out with entire consistency in other parts of the law, since a charitable institution, like the state, is liable in an action for breach of contract. Nor is it an universal doctrine, since it is not applied by the English courts.[214]   It in reality involves a whole series of assumptions.   It starts out from the belief that a charitable institution is in a different position from other institutions in the fact that its purpose is not one of profit.   But this is entirely to ignore the administrative aspect of the problem.   To fulfil the purpose of a charity involves all the usual features of an ordinary corporate enterprise.   It acts by agents and servants.   It harms and benefits third parties exactly as they are harmed or benefited by other institutions.   Where fault is involved it is difficult to see why the exception should be maintained.   It is small comfort to an injured fireman to know that even if he has to compensate himself for his injuries, he is maintaining the strict purpose of the founder of the charity.

[211] Loeffler *v.* Trustees of Sheppard and Enoch Pratt Hospital (1917) 100 Abl. 301.

[212] The result of the case could be justified on the ground that there is no liability for an injury sustained by a licensee when the injury is brought about by a condition of the premises.

[213] Overholser *v.* National Home for Disabled Soldiers, 68 Ohio St. 236; McDonald *v.* Mass. General Hospital, 120 Mass. 432; Jensen *v.* Maine Eye and Ear Infirmary, 107 Me. 408; Downes *v.* Harper Hospital, 101 Mich. 555.

[214] Duncan *v.* Findlater (1839) 6 Cl. & Fin. 894 was decided in American fashion, but since Mersey Docks Trustees *v.* Gibbs, (1866) I H. L. 93 the rule has happily been the other way.

To him the case appears simply one of injury and he suffers not less, but, in the present state of the law, actually more, from the sheerly fortuitous fact that his accident has occurred not at a factory but at a hospital. The thing of which the law ought to take account is surely the balance of interests involved; and the hospital is far more likely to look to the condition of its ladders if it pays the penalty of its negligence than if it saves a certain percentage of its income.

It would, in fact, be an intolerable situation if the only protection afforded the public against the torts of charities were that of the pockets of agents and servants.[215]   Those who founded the charity intended it to be operated; and they, or their representatives must, logically enough, pay the cost of its operation from the funds provided for that purpose. There are, indeed, some signs that the courts are beginning to appreciate this. Relief has been granted to a claimant against the Salvation Army which negligently allowed one of its vans to run wild.[216]   The inadequate protection of dangerous machinery has suffered its due and necessary penalty.[217]   The injury which resulted from the employment of an unskilful nurse has not gone unrequited.[218]

Not, indeed, that any of these decisions really touch the central issue that is raised. We have, in fact, a twofold problem. We have, in the first place, to inquire whether the creation of a charitable trust does not involve the creation of a corporate person exactly in the manner of a business enterprise; in the second place the question is raised as to whether there is any ground for the exclusion of a charity from the ordinary rules of vicarious liability. The answer to the first question is clearly an affirmative one. The Salvation Army, an orphan asylum, a great hospital, are just as much persons to those who have dealings with them as a private individual or a railway company. Differentiation, if it is to be made, cannot be made on the ground of character. If it is, the courts will go as fatally wrong in the results of litigation as did the

---

[215] Cf. *Yale Law Journal* Vol. 26, p. 124 ff.
[216] Hordern *v.* Salvation Army, 199 N. Y. 233.
[217] McMerney *v.* St. Luke's Hospital, 122 Minn. 10.
[218] St. Paul's Sanitarium *v.* Williamson, 164 S. W. 36.

House of Lords in the great Free Church of Scotland case.[219] It was the insistence of the Lords upon the nature of the church as a pendant to a set of doctrines which made them fail to see that more important was the life those doctrines called into being.[220] The life of the Salvation Army is, in precisely similar fashion, more important than the doctrines that it teaches; and we must legally judge its life by what in fact it is, and not by the theories it proclaims.

Herein is found the answer to our second inquiry. The only reason why a charity should not be liable for fault is its public character. But that, surely, is no adequate reason at all. It is probably a simple analogy from the irresponsibility of that greatest of modern charities the state. It is the merest justice that if the public seeks benefit, if men seek to benefit the public, due care should be taken not to harm those interests, not directly public, which are met in the process. A charity's personality will suffer no less detriment if it is allowed to be irresponsible than a private enterprise. A hospital, for instance, ought to be forced to take as much care in the selection of its nurses as a banker in the choice of his cashiers. We have found that the enforcement of liability is the only adequate means to this latter end, and it is difficult to see why the same is not true of every other sphere. French law has not hesitated to hold a county asylum liable for the arson of an escaped lunatic; and we may thence be sure that the prefect of the department concerned is not a second time guilty of negligence.[221] The whole problem is another illustration of the vital need of insisting as much on the processes of institutions as on their purposes. A negligently administered charity may aim at inducting us all into the kingdom of heaven, but it is socially essential to make it adequately careful of the means employed.[222]

The argument, surely, is applicable to the state; for upon

[219] See the report of Mr. (now Lord) Haldane's speech in the special report by Orr and the comment of Dr. Figgis, "Churches in the Modern State," 19 ff.

[220] Cf. *Canadian Law Times*, Vol. 36, p. 140 ff.

[221] Sirey, 1908, III, 98 with a note by M. Hauriou

[222] This and the preceding paragraphs are practically reproductions of some notes of mine in the *Harvard Law Review* for January and February, 1918, and I am indebted to its editors for leave to make use of them.

a vaster theatre it is yet similar functions that its agents perform. For what, after all, is here contended is the not unreasonable thesis that service in governmental functions does not make men cease to be human. Public enterprise is not less liable to error than private; and its responsibility should on that account be not the less strictly enforced. Nor do we perhaps sufficiently realise the possible ramifications of an exclusion of the state from due responsibility. It begins as a legal exclusion; but, sooner or later, that legal category will pass over into the moral sphere. The fact of achievement will become more important than the method by which attainment is reached. Once an end is set up as in itself great enough to set its exponents beyond the reach of law the real safeguards of liberty are overthrown. Irresponsibility becomes equated with the dangerous explanation of public policy; and that, as is historically clear, is the first step towards an acceptance of *raison d'etat*. The forms of protection the law has slowly evolved may be inadequate as the realisation of ideal morality; but they are none the less forms of protection. They represent rules of conduct which have behind them the sanction of social experience; and in that sense it is in a high degree dangerous to exclude any category of men from subjection to them. For the release of the state from the trammels of law means in practice the release of its officials from the obligations to which other men are usefully subject. Sooner or later that release operates as an excuse for despotism. It breeds the worst evils of bureaucracy. It makes those so released impatient of criticism and resentful of inquiry. It is fatal to the real essence of democratic government which involves the conversion of the mass of men to the realisation that some special programme is coincident with right. It neglects, as Dr. Figgis has so well said,[223] "that care for the gradual education of character, which is more important than any given measures, is always so easy to ignore or thrust aside in the enthusiasm of a great cause, and is yet at the basis of all true liberty, whether religious or civil."

For the assumption of an unique concern in government for ideal good is as easy as it is certainly fatal. Nothing is more

[223] "From Gerson to Grotius," p. 95.

simple in the heat and stress of political life than to assume the equation of one's desire with what ought to be the ultimate object of state-endeavour; yet nothing is at the same time more certain than that the equation is a false one. We need not accept Lord Acton's dictum that great statesmen have been almost always bad men to admit that the conference of un-limited authority is at every point attended with danger. The real guarantee of freedom is publicity; and publicity, to be adequate, involves subjection to the control of general rules of right and wrong. That is why the action of the state cannot be put upon a different footing from individual action. The controlling factors of good conduct are thereby loosed. Men who in the ordinary processes of everyday life are gentle and tender and kindly, become in their corporate aspect different beings. But the inference therefrom is not that we should judge that aspect differently; rather does it involve the in-ference that it is our business the more sternly to apply what standards time has painfully evolved.

Herein, also, we may discover another reason for the division of power. The only way in which men can become accustomed to the meaning and content of political processes is by acquain-tance with them. Mr. Graham Wallas has noted[224] the dis-appearance with the advent of machinery of the "essentially political trades," like tailoring and shoemaking, where pro-duction went on under conditions that made possible the organisation of thought. The modern factory has destroyed— for good or ill—that possibility; and that distinction clearly must transfer the centre of social importance outside the fac-tory in each man's daily life. But that, in turn involves making the groups to which he belongs politically real in the only sense of the word that today has meaning. His groups, that is to say, must become responsible groups; yet responsi-bility can only come where some social function is definitely entrusted to the group for fulfilment. It is in the performance of such tasks that the personality of men obtains its realisa-tion. It is in such tasks that their leisure can be made in a full sense rich and creative. That is not the case today. Everyone who has engaged in public work is sooner or later driven to

[224] "The Great Society," p. 299.

admit that the great barrier to which he finds himself opposed is indifference. To the comfortable classes he is liable to seem an "agitator"; to the mass of toiling men he commits the last sin of interference. Here, perhaps, there is a sense in which Rousseau's paradox becomes pregnant with new meaning and it may in the end be true that men must be forced to be free. Certain at least it is that the temptations to leave alone the real problems by which we are confronted is almost insuperable. We make every provision to maintain the *status quo*. Nothing is more simple in the great society than to be lost amongst one's neighbours; nothing is more dangerous to the attainment of the social end. For if the good life is one day to be achieved by the majority of men and women it is only by the preservation of individuality that it can be done; and individuality, in any generous perspective, does not mean the rich and intense life of a few able men.

That is why, at every stage in the social process, we are concerned to throw the business of judgment upon the individual mind. That does not, it ought to be insisted, mean inefficient government. It does not mean that we shall not trust the expert; but it does mean the clear conviction that a judgment upon the expert is to be a democratic judgment. We have had too much experience of the gospel of efficiency to place any reliance that is final upon what promise it may contain. The great danger to which it is ceaselessly exposed is the eager desire of achievement and a resultant carelessness about the methods of its programme. It sacrifices independence to the machine much in the way that party discipline aiming, above all, at victory at the polls, sacrifices conviction, with its possibility of discoveries, to uniformity of outlook. It becomes at once impatient of the exceptional man who cannot be reduced within its categories; but, sooner or later, it becomes impatient also of the average man. For it cannot respect, over any length of time, the slowness with which his mind moves, the curiously intricate avenues along which he travels. It may be true that in any group of men oligarchical government is bound, in the end, and in some degree, to develop;[225] or, at

[225] This is the thesis of Professor Michel's well-known book on political parties; but I feel that he has only discussed half the problem.

least, we need not deny the patent virtues of a man who can guide his fellows. But that is not to say that the leaders are shepherds whom the flock is inthinkingly to follow. It means that safeguards must be erected lest the mass of men become mere units in a sheepfold. It means the insistence that liberty consists above all in the full opportunity for active citizenship wherever there are men with the will to think upon political problems. It means that a democratic society must reject the sovereign state as by definition inconsistent with democracy.

IX. THE DIRECTION OF EVENTS

Such, at least, seems the direction in which the modern state is moving. We stand on the threshold of one of those critical periods in the history of mankind when the most fundamental notions present themselves for analysis. In England, in France, and in America, it is already possible vaguely to discern the character of that dissatisfaction from which a new synthesis is ultimately born. The period when a sovereign state was a necessary article of faith seems, on the whole, to be passing away. Society is freed from the control of any special religious organisation; and the birth of scientific theology in the nineteenth century seems destined to complete that process of disintegration which began with the advent of Luther. It is in social and not in religious theory, that is to say, that we shall search for the sources of new insight. The moral dogmas we shall adopt seem likely to remain unconnected with any special church or school of religious doctrine. It was primarily to prevent such danger that the sovereign state came into being. With the general acceptance of Darwinism the success of its mission seems achieved. For the state itself, not less than the church is subject to the laws of evolution. It survives in any given form only so long as that form with adequacy summarises a general social experience. It has here been urged that it is no longer adequate. The form of organisation it involves is neither politically useful nor morally sufficient. The time has come for new discoveries.

No one who has observed the course of English politics since the triumph of socialised liberalism in 1906 can have any doubts upon this head. It was an epoch which began with immense promise; and, at its close, it seemed likely to end in something but little short of disaster. It began with a gigantic effort to make the categories of state-life more socially inclusive than at any previous period. It ended in a drift towards bureaucratic control from which thinkers of the most diverse schools drew back in distressed scepticism. The state had already begun to overload its instruments with business. The exigencies of government had so strengthened party-control as virtually to destroy the independence of the private member; or, at least, to leave him a pitiful Friday afternoon in which to spread his curtailed wings. No one could doubt that the state would long retain its positive character without some system of decentralisation being devised. For the pressure on Whithall had involved the growth of a new bureaucracy which gave rise to a doubt whether the régime it involved was compatible with individual freedom.[226] Parliamentary democracy had broken down; sovereignty had patently suffered transference from the House of Commons. With both women and trade-unionists alike sources of new loyalty other than the state could be detected; and in Ulster there was a striking determination to deny the finality of a government decision. Moral and economic dissatisfactions were on all hands evident. It was to the foundations of the state that men were going back. They looked upon their handiwork and did not pronounce it good. The great demand of the time was for religious and social innovation; and the benevolent feudalism of the Insurance Act proved, in the event, in no sense due response to the new desires that sought expression. Labour was declaring that the state was essentially a middle-class institution—a difference indeed from the optimistic days when Macaulay could claim that the middle classes were "the natural representatives of the human race." The state-regulation of Germany seemed less and less applicable to the sturdy individualism of the English mind. The one great object of enquiry was from what sources new discoveries in government were to be had. We

[226] Cf. Prof. Ramsay Muir's "Peers and Bureaucrats," and the interesting but grossly exaggerated volume of E. S. P. Haynes: "The Decline of Liberty in England."

had evolved the great society, as Mr. Wallas has pointed out,[227] without planning institutions at all adequate to its scale of life.

That some real progress lay concealed beneath the appearance of this chaos it would be difficult to deny. Yet what emerges, in a perspective that the events of the last four years seem now to have made final, is essentially a bankruptcy in liberal ideas. Nor is it possible to make a claim of greater profit for Conservatism. It was doubtless overburdened by the weight it had to carry in the support of an obsolete second chamber; but on every essential political problem it had nothing acceptable to contribute. Lord Hugh Cecil, indeed, had realised that *laissez-faire* was not without its merits; but its scope was limited by him to fields too narrow and specialised in character to be attractive to the mass of men. The state, in fact, had come to the parting of the ways; but to none of its fundamental difficulties could it offer any comprehensive solution. Ireland, the second chamber, education, poverty, agriculture, the position of women—about all of these there was a plethora of debate; but about all of them the policy of statesmen was to prevent a half-response in the hope that, despite them, a new equilibrium would emerge. And, behind all and beyond all, there loomed the gigantic problem of a labouring class growing ever more self-conscious and ever more determined to control its own destinies. It repudiated the solution of social welfare implied in such a measure as the Insurance Act. Its strikes revealed a more fierce hostility to the forces of capital than had been manifest since the early years of the Holy Alliance. In the famous Dublin Transport Workers' strike it showed a solidarity unique in labour history. The Labour Party seemed to it hardly more instinct with hope than the traditional political forces of the country. It was in workshop and factory that the new ideas were being forged. They showed a striking renaissance of that attitude which, as in Owen and Thompson and Hodgskin,[228] believed that the diversion of labour power into political rather than into economic

[227] "The Great Society," Chap. I. In a paper published in the Smith College studies on the "Problem of Administrative Areas," I have tried to note the significance of this.

[228] Cf. Prof. Foxwell's classic introduction to Menger's "Right to the Whole Produce of Labour."

fields was mistaken. Its influence was securing the reconstruction of social history.[229] It was insisting upon the need of new and wider educational ideals. It was demanding a complete revision of the distribution of wealth. It was thinking out new categories in the productive process. It rejected state-arbitration of its difficulties with capital. It looked with grave suspicion on the use of the army in the maintenance of social order. It emphatically underlined such differentiation of treatment as that meted out to Sir Edward Carson, on the one hand, and to that significant portent Mr. Larkin, on the other. It was, of course, like all renaissances, the work of a minority. But it was a minority that had caught the vision of a life that might be made more splendid and more spiritual than the old. It had realised that the basis of its ideal must be the conquest of economic power. It was upon that mission it had embarked.

Professor Dicey, whose interpretation is the more valuable from his hostility to these ideas, has suggested that the two outstanding characteristics of the time are irreverence for law and a new belief in natural rights. The reason of this surely lies in the general truth that parliamentary government had reached the zenith of its achievement. The complexity of social problems had made them too vast for discussion by debate in the House of Commons to be a sufficient test of legislation. No single legislative assembly in the world had stood the test of the nineteenth century well enough to make men hopeful. Everywhere the tendency had been more and more towards the development of an invisible bureaucracy, until the state itself had seemed, in the last analysis, no more than what the French, in an intranslatable phrase, call a *syndicat des fonctionnaires*—a *syndicat*, moreover, which, as John Stuart Mill saw,[230] is largely controlled by men without understanding of working class ideals. And in this context it is of the first importance to realise that the movement for social reform was less perhaps a genuine effort towards the reconstruction that had become essential than towards a discovery of the minimum conditions of change necessary to the maintenance of the present society.

[229] As in Mr. Tawney's "Agrarian Revolution in the Sixteenth Century," and Mr. and Mrs. Hammond's studies of town and village labour.

[230] "Representative Government,"Ch.III (Everyman's edition),p.209-10.

But the fact has been that the theoretic purpose of the state did not find adequate fulfilment either in governments or legislatures. We were simply forced to the realisation that majority-rule could not be the last word on our problems. So long as political power was divorced from economic power the jury of the nation was in reality packed. Wherein representative government had been supremely successful was in the securing of general political rights in which rich and poor alike have been interested. But once the transference has been made from political rights to economic interests the basic sectionalism of society has been apparent to anyone with the patience to observe the facts. Wherever economic freedom is to be secured, certainly legislative experience does not give us the right to expect it from that quarter. Men and women resented a state of which the law neither expressed nor fully attempted to express the need for translating their desires into effective political terms. They resented and resisted it; that is the real root of lawlessness. The Osborne decision of the House of Lords,[231] for example, destroyed at a stroke the confidence of labour in that judicial tribunal. Everyone knew that the political activity of the trade-unions was an integral part of their functions; everyone knew also that manufacturers' associations did virtually the same thing in virtually the same way. Yet the House of Lords tried politically to strangle the unions within the four corners of an outworn doctrine. The understanding of obvious trade-union implications was at every point absent from its enquiry. But if the highest tribunal of the state can so misinterpret the challenge of its age, lawlessness and the revival of natural rights are not difficult to understand. They are, historically, the perennial symptoms of discontent. They make their appearance at every transitional epoch. They are the invariable heralds of a new time.

England shows her temper only in vague hints and chaotic practical demands; the more logical structure of the French mind makes possible a sharper contrast between opposing attitudes. The one certain thing in the France that came into being with the close of the Dreyfus controversy was a revolt against the centralised state.[232] That revolt was evident in at

[231] (1910) A. C. 87.
[232] This is worked out in detail in Chapter V below.

least three general aspects. The contempt for politics was in France more widely spread than in any other European country. Distrust of the chamber, suspicion of statesmen, a doubt if the struggle was more than the exchange of one faction for another, are everywhere presented to us. There is no more creative literature in the last generation than that in which men like Duguit, Leroy and Paul-Boncour have depicted for us the fall of the sovereign state through parliamentary incompetence. Nor does the trade-union movement emphasise any dissimilar lesson. It lacks the sober and practical caution of English labour. It is frankly idealist and, on the whole, as frankly revolutionary. Those who have most clearly outlined its aims, men like Pelloutier and Griffuellies, those who have analysed its rules and customs like Leroy,[233] point always to the capture of economic power by the proletariat and the emergence of a new society created in federalist terms. Even more striking is the revolt of the civil service. Here the state is attacked at the very root of its sovereignty; and where the bureaucracy joins hands with the worker the path lies open for a new synthesis. Proudhon has displaced Marx as the guiding genius of French labour; and it is above all his federalism that is the source of the new inspiration.[234]

Even those who reject this attitude are largely sceptical of the future of the older ideals. Some have frankly taken refuge in a royalist and aristocratic solution;[235] some, like M. Brunetière, have urged that only a religious revival can restore France to a satisfactory condition. The coalition of the Left dissolved when the separation of church and state had been effected; and it cannot be said that M. Jaurès' presence in the Chamber concealed his frank sympathy with a proletarian revolution. M. Esmein stood out as the solitary political thinker of distinction in France who had not renounced the ancient ways. The strikes before which the state was largely powerless; the endless proposals for decentralisation and proportional repre-

[233] His "La Coutume Ouvrière" is one of the fundamental books of our time.

[234] For the revival of interest in Proudhon Cf. Pirou in the "Revue d'Histoire des Doctrines Sociales et Economiques," 1912, p. 161, and the books there cited.

[235] Cf. Chapter II below.

sentation; the growing tendency of the Council of State to deny in practice the theory of national sovereignty promulgated by the Revolution; the attempt of sociologists like Durkheim to penetrate through the artificial classification of rights by the state to rights derived from a solidarity based on group-needs and group-services;[236] all these, surely, herald, as in England, the transition to a new equilibrium. France, like England, has had her period of lawlessness and a revival of natural rights. But she has wisely rejected the over-simple formulæ of Rousseau as an attempted analysis of social relationships. Rather, as in 1789, she is setting Europe the example of a new perspective in political organisation. The discipline of technical co-ordination, with the liberty it implies, is replacing the authoritarian hierarchy of the Napoleonic state.[237] Nor is this the idle hypothesis of theorists. On the contrary it represents the sober analysis of everyday life drawn from men peroccupied with the practice of law and industry. That is the real basis of its promise and importance.

Generalisations about America are notoriously dangerous; for it is tempting to deny that, in the European sense, there is yet any such thing in America as the state. Rather is the observer confronted by a series of systems of economic interests so varied in character and, at times, so baffling, as to make inquiry almost impossible.[238] It is only within the last generation that America has emerged from the uncritical individualism of a pioneer civilisation. It is little more than a decade since she began directly to influence the course of world-politics. Yet even in a civilisation so new and rich in promise it is difficult not to feel that a critical era is approaching. The old party-divisions have become largely meaningless. The attempt to project a new political synthesis athwart the old formulæ failed to command support enough to be successful. Yet, even in America, that point of economic organisation has been reached where the emergence of a proletariat presents the

[236] See especially the second edition of his "Division du travail Social." It badly needs translation into English.

[237] Cf. Leroy, "Les Transformation de la Puissance Publique," p. 286.

[238] Mr. Herbert Croly's "Progressive Democracy" is by far the best recent analysis.

basic social problems. A political democracy confronts the
most powerful economic autocracy the world has ever seen. The
separation of powers has broken down. The relation between
executive and legislature cries to heaven for readjustment.
The decline of Congress has become a commonplace. The constituent states of the republic have largely lost their ancient
meaning. New administrative areas are being evolved. A
patent unrest everywhere demands enquiry. Labour is becoming organised and demanding recognition. The men who, like
Mark Hanna and Mr. Root, could stand on a platform of simple conservatism are already obsolete. The political literature
of America in the last fifteen years is almost entirely a literature
of protest. Political experimentation, particularly in the West,
is almost feverishly pursued. Discontent with old ideas was
never more bitter. The economic background of the decisions
of the Supreme Court was never more critically examined;
and, indeed, anyone who analyses the change from the narrow
individualism of Brewer and Peckham to the liberalising scepticism of Mr. Justice Holmes and the passionate rejection of
the present order which underlies the attitude of Mr. Justice
Brandeis, can hardly doubt the advent of a new time.

What, in a sense, is being born is a realisation of the state;
but it is a realisation that is fundamentally different from anything that Europe has thus far known. For it starts out from
an unqualified acceptance of political democracy and the basic
European struggle of the last hundred years is thus omitted.
So that it is bound to make a difference to the United States
that its critical epoch should have arrived when Europe also
confronts a new development. American economic history
will doubtless repeat on a vaster scale the labour tragedies of
the old world and think out new expedients for their intensi-
fication. But there are certain elements in the American problem which at once complicate and simplify the issue. Granted
its corrupt politics, the withdrawal of much of its ability from
governmental life, its exuberant optimism, and a traditional
faith in the efficacy of its orthodox political mechanisms that
may well prove disastrous, there are yet two aspects in which
the basis of its life provides opportunities instinct with profound
and hopeful significance. It can never be forgotten that America

was born in revolution. In the midst of its gravest material-
ism that origin has preserved an idealist faith. It has made the
thought of equality of opportunity and the belief in natural
rights conceptions that in all their vagueness are yet living
entities no man may dare to neglect. When the dissatisfaction
with economic organisation becomes, as it is rapidly becoming,
acute enough to take political form, it is upon these elements
that it will fasten. Americans, in the last analysis, believe in
democratic government with a fierce intensity that cannot be
denied. They may often deceive themselves about its forms.
They may often, and very obviously, suffer an almost ludicrous
perversion of its expression. The effort of their workers may
be baffled by the countless nationalities which have yet to
complete the process of Americanisation. Their trade-unions
may be as yet for the most part in a commercial stage. Yet,
from the confused chaos of it all, one clear thread may be
seized.

It is towards a new orientation of ideals that America is moving Exactly as in England and France challenge has been
issued to theories of organisation that have outlived their usefulness. That was the real meaning of the Progressive Movement. It symbolised a dissatisfaction with the attitude that
interpreted happiness in terms of the volume of trade. The
things upon which interest become concentrated are the fundamental elements. It is the perversion of political power to
economic ends that above all receives analysis. The economists
demand a re-valuation of motives.[239] "Why should the masses,"
asks an able recent inquirer,[240] "seemingly endowed with the
power to determine the future, have permitted the development
of a system which has stripped them of ownership, initiative
and power?" and his answer is virtually a sober indictment
of capitalism. "The fundamental division of powers in the
United States," says President Hadley,[241] "is between voters

[239] This is the work that has been performed by Mr. Veblen with something like genius in his "Theory of the Leisure Class;" the "Instinct of Work-
manship;" the "Theory of Business Enterprise;" and the great book on
"Imperial Germany and the Industrial Revolution."

[240] W. H. Hamilton, the Price-System and Social Policy. *Journal of
Political Economy*, Vol. XXVI, p. 31.

[241] Quoted in Hamilton, op. cit. p. 37.

on the one hand and the owners of property on the other. The forces of democracy on the one side . . . . are set over against the forces of property on the other side. . . . Democracy was complete as far as it went, but constitutionally it was bound to stop short at social democracy." It is against this condition that the liberal forces of American life are slowly aligning themselves. A law that is subservient to the interests of the *status quo* is overwhelmingly unpopular; the use of the injunction in labour disputes, for example, has actually been a presidential issue.[242] The Clayton Act, with all its defects, is yet a wedge that organised labour can one day use to good purpose.[243] Things like Mr. Justice Holmes' dissent in *Coppage v. Kansas*[244] deposit a solid sentiment of determination that will not easily pass away. The lawlessness that is complained of in American labour is essentially the insistance that the life of the workers has outgrown the categories in which traditional authority would have confined it. The basis of a new claim of rights is in America autocthonous. Nor is it possible to doubt that only concessions large enough to amount to the admission of its substance can prevent it from being made. In either case, we have the materials for a vast change in the historic outlines of American federalism.

It is thus upon the fact that ours is an age of vital transition that the evidence seems clearly to concentrate. The two characteristic notes of change are present in the dissatisfaction with the working of law, on the one hand, and the reassertion of natural rights upon the other. The validity of the acts of the legal sovereign everywhere suffers denial unless its judgement secures a widespread approval; or, as with the South Wales Mines in England and the Railroad Brotherhoods in the United States, an organised attempt may successfully be made to coerce the action of government in a particular direction. Violence, as with the militant suffragists in England may well come to be regarded as a normal weapon of political controversy; nor have

[242] Cf. Groat, "The Attitude of American Courts in Labour Cases," passim.

[243] Its defect is that it still leaves American trade unions at the mercy of the common law doctrine, Cf. conspiracy. The act is, U. S. Statutes, 1913-4, C. 321.

[244] 236 U. S. 1, 26.

those who suffered imprisonment for their acts regarded the penalty as other than a privilege. In such an aspect, the sovereignty of the state, in the only sense in which that sovereignty can be regarded as a working hypothesis, no longer commands anything more than a partial and spasmodic acceptance. For it is clearly understood that it in practice means governmental sovereignty; and the need for the limitation of governmental powers is perceived by men of every shade of opinion. Nor is the reassertion of rights less significant. It involves in its very conception a limitation upon the sovereignty of the state. It insists that there are certain things the state must secure and maintain for all its members, and a state that can not secure such rights as are deemed needful by a minority as important, for example, as organised labour, will sooner or later suffer a change in form and substance. The basis of law in opinion is more clear than at any previous time; and the way in which that opinion is fostered outside the categories of the normal political life until its weight is great enough to make heedless resistance impossible is a fact of which every observer must take account.

X. CONCLUSION

It is difficult to see how such potentialities at any point harmonise with the traditional theory of the state. The lawyer may still manipulate that theory for the purposes of judicial enquiry; but, beyond that narrow usefulness, its day seems to have departed. We have been taught that the state is sovereign; yet it is in practice obvious that its will is operated only by a portion of its members and that to this portion the possession of sovereignty is denied. It is urged that the state aims at the good life; and, again in practice, it is clear that the realisation of its purpose is so inadequate as to render at best dubious the value of such hypotheses. It is insisted that the state can be bound only by its own consent; yet, in practice also, and unless we wish merely to play upon words, it is clear that throughout its recent history groups other than itself have compelled its adoption of a policy to which it was opposed. The books tell us that it is irresponsible; yet, in practice also, what mainly confronts us, especially in France, is the growth of a state-responsibility which, however reluctantly conceded, is still responsibility. We are told that sovereignty is indivisible; yet, unless again we wish merely to play upon words, the fact of its broad partition is on every hand obvious. Nor is the notion of the state as fundamentally representative of society in any sort more acceptable. It is true where it fufills the broad objects of a social life that is now conceived in ethical terms; but, more and more, men are coming to doubt whether the result of the state process is, invariably or even normally, the achievement of what such an ethical perspective must demand. It is rather towards another attitude that men are turning. It is rather of other categories they are beginning to make use. For the orthodox theory of the state has proved largely without basis in the event. It may be true as a dream; and it is doubtless undeniable that dreams are often enough capable of realisation. But it is for those who cherish the dream to give proof of its relation to the facts.

The basis upon which we proceed is the simple truth that men and institutions are possessed of power. It is clearly perceived that, in itself, power is neither good nor bad; its use alone affords material for judgment upon its ethical content. It is held that its concentration at any special point within society increases the possibility of its perversion to dubious purpose. That has involved the increasing insistence that our general notions of right and wrong be put beyond the reach of danger. The state, in a word, is to be subject to law; and that is no more impossible in a political democracy than when, for state, Bracton could use the name of King. The interdependence of political and economic structure is, moreover, not less potent than in the past; and it is thus sheer anachronism to regard as adequate an industrial order in which power is not in democratic fashion distributed.

The individual, that is to say, is to become increasingly the centre of social importance. Otherwise, in so vast a world, his claims may well suffer neglect. After all it was for his happiness that the state, at least in philosophic interpretation, existed from its origins; for if the good life does not bring happiness to humble men and women it is without meaning. So that it is upon the happiness he is able to attain that our judgment of its processes must be founded. It is in this context obvious that such judgment could not in our time be an

optimistic one. The merely material conditions of happiness
are today achieved for too few of us to give any right to satisfaction. Freedom, in the sense that it has been here maintained,
is alone real, is a good attained only by a small part of society.
Nor have we evidence that such limitation is inherent in the
nature of things. On the contrary, the evidence we possess
points so emphatically in the opposite direction as to justify
the assumption of its inadequacy. Yet, without that general
freedom, the state is a meaningless thing. The problem of
authority becomes, above all, the duty so to organise its character and its processes as to make it, in the widest aspect, the
servant of right and of freedom. But to make it the servant
of freedom is already to limit its powers.

The emphasis upon freedom is made because it is believed
that only in such fashion can the ethical significance of personality obtain its due recognition. For the harmony we need
between rulers and subjects it is not upon outward law but
inward spirit that reliance must be placed. The social order
of the present time tends more and more to destroy the personal will of each member of the state by asking from him a
passive acquiescence in its policy on the ground of generous
purpose. It is here argued that such uniformity is the negation
of freedom. It is neither active nor vital. It in reality denies
perhaps the ability and certainly the justice of the mind that
tries to fathom the motives of government. It is thus the
death of spontaneity; and to destroy spontaneity is to prevent
the advent of liberalism. We have thus to deny that right and
wrong are state-created dogmas which shift with the interest
of those who control the state. We do not, like Lord Acton,
postulate an unchanging content of goodness; for the very
essence of this theory is the acceptance of the fact of evolution. But it is denied that right is what is subjectively so
deemed by government. A certain objectivity, to be established by argument and experience, is made inherent in it.
The one thing in which we can have confidence as a means of
progress is the logic of reason. We thus insist, on the contrary,
that the mind of each man, in all the aspects conferred upon
him by his character as a social and a solitary being, pass
judgment upon the state; and we ask for his condemnation of

its policy where he feels it in conflict with the right.

That, surely, is the only environment in which the plant of liberty can flourish. It implies, from the very nature of things, insistence that the allegiance of man to the state is secondary to his allegiance to what he may conceive his duty to society as a whole. It is, as a secondary allegiance, competing in the sense that the need for safeguards demands the erection of alternative loyalties which may, in any given synthesis, oppose their wills to that of the state. In the ordinary acceptance of the term, such an attitude denies the validity of any sovereign power save that of right; and it urges that the discovery of right is, on all fundamental questions, a search, upon which the separate members of the state must individually engage. We ask, in fact, from each the best thought he can offer to the interpretation of life. For we have proceeded far enough in its understanding to realise its complexity. We know that no solution can be permanent or adequate that is not in each detail based upon the widest possible experience. But we know also that such experience must be free and capable of influence if it is to receive its due respect. The slavery of inertia is a weed that grows everywhere in wanton luxuriance; and we are, above all, concerned to make provision against its intrusion.

In the external relationships of the state it is clear that the Machiavellian epoch is drawing to a close   The application of ethical standards to the foreign policy of nations is a demand that has secured the acceptance of all who are concerned for the future of civilisation. Yet it is assuredly not less clear that the internal life of the state requires a similar moralisation. We realise now the danger of a state that makes power the supreme good and is careless of the purpose for which it is exerted. We have sacrificed the youth of half the world to maintain our liberty against its encroachments. Surely the freedom we win must remain unmeaning unless it is made consistently effective in every sphere of social life. This generation, at least, can never forget the ghostly legions by which it is encompassed. It ought also ceaselessly to remember that it is by those legions its effort will be judged. They will measure our achievement in terms of their supreme devotion. They will accept no recompense save the conquest of their dreams.

CHAPTER TWO

BONALD[1]

I. THE IMPLICATION OF THEOCRACY

THE theocratic system seems to have found an eutha-
nasia the more tragic in that it proceeds unobserved.
It shares therein the fate of half a hundred political
systems which have failed to base themselves upon the fact
of evolution. For no theory can now hope for survival which
is not based upon the changing necessities of social life. The
obvious generalisation that the creation of dogma carries with
it, in grim Hegelian fashion, its own negation, confronts the
observer at every stage of the historic process. And of theocracy
this has been the case in a peculiar degree. The claims of its
representatives have grown as their acceptance has become the
more impossible. It was at the very nadir of his fortunes that
Hildebrand made claim to the lordship of the world. It was
when Garibaldi and his redshirts were thundering at the gate
that Pius IX registered his infallibility. The garment has been
the more royally displayed that the shrunken body may be the
better concealed.

Yet two great truths theocracy has enshrined; and, of a
certainty, no estimate of its character would be just which did
not take account of their value. More, perhaps, than any
similar system of ideas theocracy has understood the worth of
dogma. It has seen that the secret of existence is the preservation of identity. It has realised the chaos of instability. Nor
is this all. Its believers have grasped, perhaps more fully
than any thinkers save the doctrinaire liberals of the nine-

[1] On Bonald the best descriptive account of that of Moulinié (Pari
1916) which is, however, weak in its criticism. There are famous essays
by Sainte-Beuve in his "Causeries," Vol. IV, and by Faguet in his "Politiques
et Moralistes," Vol. I. See also Bourget, "Etudes et Portraits," Vol. III,
Montesquieu, "Le réalisme de Bonald."

teenth century, the difference between the essence of a political system and the accidental principles which arise from the method of its application. They have ceaselessly insisted on the importance of securing beyond peradventure the fundamental notions of their age. They did, indeed, go mistakenly further. They did take the fatal step of arguing that an ideal to be true must be unchanging. Of the relativity of ideas they had no notion; or, if they dimly seized its importance, they denied its philosophic rightness. For they deemed it the business of speculation to search for absolutes. They had no patience with anything save the eternal. If, in the result, a changing civilisation has been compelled to desert their standards, that does not mean the total error of the ideals for which they fought. On the contrary, that of which the historian must take constant account is not merely the sharpness of their vision, but the accuracy of their prophecy. Again and again they cast a vivid light upon the conditions of their time. The fact of their failure is not proof of their ineptitude. On the contrary, they brought powerful support to a theory of politics for which, on other grounds, strong and insistent justification can still be made. What in brief they suggested was the apotheosis of authority. Liberty to them was error. They tried to find its falsity in the divinity of its antithesis. It is rather in the emphasis of their application than its source that modern criticism tends to begin its attack. And at least one powerful school of political enquiry has rejected its premises rather than its conclusions. In that sense it is still a living influence at the present time.

The source of its curious revivification in the nineteenth century is in no sense difficult to discover. They who returned from exile in 1814 believed that their experience was the final condemnation of liberal principles. They had seen the triumph of anarchy in the name of freedom. They had been the victims of an egalitarianism for which history afforded no precedent even if it offered an ample justification. The institutions they had inherited had been ruthlessly overthrown. The ideals they had cherished were cast aside in an unpitying contempt. Tradition had been butchered that Reason might have its Paris holiday; and to tradition they were united by every tie of kinship and of interest. Their exile had been the breeder of hate rather than of understanding; and it was in a spirit of revenge that they returned. The age which the twenty-five full years of revolution had turned into antiquity became for them the *Saturnia regna* of an earlier time. That for which their kin had paid with blood became hallowed because it had been the cause of suffering. They came not to amend but to restore. As they had forgiven nothing, so they had failed to learn the lesson of their banishment. They deified the past; and in that vision of enchantment they discovered a little easily the principles of a theocracy.

This was in a particular degree true of the Roman Church.[2] No institution had had a more singular history in the period of revolutionary misfortune. The States-General, at the outset of its deliberations had been in no sense an anti-clerical assembly. The mass of the people was passionately catholic; and their confidence in the clergy is proved by the fact that the cahiers of the Third Estate had been largely entrusted to their hands. They had ample opportunity to win for themselves the urgent confidence of those in whose hands would lie the destinies of the coming revolution. The idea of a separation between Church and State was, in 1789, present in the mind of no single practical statesman. The Church was responsible for its own misfortunes. To the popular dislike of Ultramontanism it gave ground for action. Its support of the extreme reactionists earned for it the distrust and anger of moderate men; while the hatred which the upper clergy earned no less than they received was thereby extended to the mass of its members. From the outset the clergy seemed to threaten the Revolution; and when the Revolution created a Republic their Roman allegiance threatened its unity. The onset of war and its early disasters gave an opportunity to the enemies of the Church of which they did not fail to make good use. Suspicion turned to intolerance, and from intolerance was born an implacable persecution.

[2] On the character of the Roman church at the time of the Restoration see the essay on Lamennais below. Even allowing for its anti-clerical bias M. Debidour's "L'Eglise et L'Etat en France de 1789-1870" is easily the best treatment.

Yet the ills of the Church under the Convention and the Assembly would have given no grounds for the ultramontane passions of the Restoration. What secured their onset was the calculated policy of Napoleon. True to the principles which have made the name of Erastus the mistaken symbol of oppression, he saw in the church no more than an admirable political weapon. He declared himself a Gallican; and his absorptive temper made of Gallicanism a doctrine to which no self-respecting member of the church could give adherence. It is, indeed, possible that before the Napoleonic era the declaration of 1682 probably represented the normal clerical attitude. But when the principles of 1682 resulted in a papal captivity and the Organic Articles the temper of the church was bound to change.

It became evident to most that a trust in Rome was not incompatible with a faith in France; and the transition from compatibility to dependence was almost fatally easy. There is something of poetic justice in the fact that a nominal application of its own principles should thus have taught the French clergy their inherent error. When Louis XVIII came back to Versailles the church which accompanied him had new principles to maintain and new standards to enforce. The tenets of a royalist faith they had always upheld; and of his support they were from the outset assured. But they had learned from a better experience that only (so they deemed) an exclusive and ultramontane church was certain of security. They did not perceive that Napoleon had only attempted the enforcement of the very principles they were themselves to preach. They did not know that they, like him, were encompassing the imprisonment of the mind, and that they, like him, were to fail because their task was from the outset impossible. The mind of man may demand the ease of dogma, but it so demands only that it may destroy. The church made the fatal error of their persecutor and assumed that in unity alone can strength be discovered. They came back to enshrine in law the uniqueness of their sovereignty and they only fashioned thereby the instrument of a second Revolution.

They had learned nothing in their exile save to brood upon their misfortune. It was patent to them that what had occured was the fruit of human wickedness. That of which they had need was a political organisation whereby the errors from which they had suffered might become but a hideous memory. They needed a political theory which ensured the permanent satisfaction of their demands. Their life was based upon their traditions. It was from their traditions that they drew their claims. So it was that they erected their history into a philosophy that they might destroy the category of time.

II. THE BASIS OF TRADITIONALISM

TAINE has refused the title of philosophers to the Traditionalists of the Restoration; and in the sense that it was their business rather to refute than to make enquiry there can be no doubt that he was right. Their fate, indeed, has been in every way somewhat curious. The literary effectiveness of De Maistre, the skill with which he presents his pessimism, the acuteness of his reflections—all these have combined to give his work the permanence that is undoubtedly its historic due.[3] The tragic interest of Lamennais' life would of itself be sufficient to arouse increasing speculation; but he becomes of even greater importance from the fact that the most vital aspect of nineteenth century Catholicism is in a special sense his creation. The conciliatory spirit of Ballanche gives to all his speculation a singular charm that is absent from the work of his compeers.

Bonald has been less fortunate; and, in truth, it is but within recent times that the value of his uncritical and uninspired dogmatism has been fully understood.[4] The rebirth of a sceptical suspicion of the worth of the Republic tended, inevitably, to send men back to him whom De Maistre signalled as his master,[5] and from whom, in the early days of his fame, Lamennais was proud to receive high commendation.[6]

Bonald, indeed, lacks all the stigmata of popularity. His

[3] I have discussed the political theory of De Maistre in the last chapter of my "Problem of Sovereignty."

[4] The real understanding of Bonald probably dates from Comte, Cf. "Politique Positive" III, 605.

[5] Cf. the very interesting correspondence in Vol. XII. of De Maistre's collected works and "Principe Constitutif." p. 493.

[6] Boutard, "Lamennais," I, 154.

life was the ordinary career of an emigrant noble. Not even the fear of the guillotine came to give it a touch of momentary excitement. He wrote badly, even harshly, with all the ruthless, pettifogging logic of the medieval scholastics.[7] He lacked even the supreme merit of brevity. He was totally out of accord with the spirit of his time. All for which it came to stand he branded as the utmost sin; all for which he cared was lost at the barricades of 1830. The monarchy for which he cherished so passionate an affection destroyed itself by acting on his principles. He urged nothing that history, if it did not falsify, at any rate failed to respect. He did not, like De Maistre, die before the course of events had proved the impossibility of his ideals. He did not, like Lamennais, find in the events of his age the basis of a better philosophy. He belonged always to the eighteenth century, not, indeed, in the essentials of its intellectual attitude, but in its dogmatic and inflexible spirit.[8] Once he had arrived at his principles, he did no more than devote himself to their elaboration. He never examined his time. He was satisfied to search the past and to misread it that the justice of his claims might be made manifest. A single event— and it is impossible to understand his attitude save on the assumption that to him the Revolution was no more than a point in time—served as the basis of everything he thought and felt and dared so greatly to hope. He is the prophet of an outworn gospel, so that his very watchwords have been almost forgotten. That which he so solemnly preached is, for the most part, that against which a democratic society has been most solemnly warned. Yet he is hardly to blame for his conclusions. He did no more than sum up with remorseless logic the result of the reaction of authoritarian temper with egalitarian revolution.

He represents the amazement of the aristocracy at the challenge of a people whose existence it had forgotten. He put its case vigorously, bluntly, sincerely. He failed completely to understand that the principles of the *Ancien Régime* could ever return. He could regard the Revolution only as a hateful episode, and he tried to explain why it was essentially a warning and an example. It is perhaps a little difficult to explain

[7] Cf. Sainte-Beuve, "Causeries," IV, 330.

[8] As M. Faguet, in his brilliant study, so strikingly points out.

his influence. He said only what the *émigrés* desired to hear.
But he wrote the epitaph of Bourbon Kingship and it was
assumed that between his philosophy and the creed of Rousseau
there was no alternative. For thirty-five years he reiterated
his principles under half a hundred forms. The principles of
philology, the marital relation, the theory of knowledge—from
the analysis of all these he constructed his tremendous sociology.
When the last criticism has been made, there remains something almost of splendour in the courage and the determination
with which he applied himself to his task. If, in the light of
modern change, all that he has written reads like a bitter defence of special creation by one who has sadly encountered the
Darwinian hypothesis, much may be pardoned to one who
loved his ideals so greatly. And, as with De Maistre, it may
even be suggested that he the better served human freedom
when he threw the implications of his attitude into a relief so
striking and so logical.

Nor is this all. The basis of his philosophy must be interpreted from the angle of its chronological significance. He
began to write, as Sainte-Beuve[9] has pointed out, on the morrow of the Terror. He had been a witness of its tragedies;
and because so many of its victims were of his order, it was
inevitable that it should have bitten deeply into his soul. It
was then natural for him to translate that bitterness into political terms. He could see in the Revolution no more than the
coronation of anarchy. It had shattered the temple of political
science and he must lay his hand to its restoration. And it
was no less natural that he should start from a disbelief in
man and in reason. It was for their redintegration that the
Revolution had been effected. The individualism of the eighteenth century had been traitorous to every rational principle
of social order. It had dared to proclaim the rights of man,
and it had embodied its principles in a Declaration. It had
declared the sovereignty of reason and the Directory was to
prescribe a confidence in faith. So he came to hold that the
very foundations of such an attitude were conceived in sin.
The Rights of Man meant the execution of the King; the
Sovereignty of Reason meant the persecution of the Catholic

[9] Sainte-Beuve, op. cit., p. 324.

Church. Equality wrote its formulæ in letters of blood, and the blood was the blood of his friends. An attitude to his age other than that of hate was thus impossible. That he should have undertaken a polemic against the eighteenth century was logically the result of his humanity. To the rights of man he would oppose the rights of God.[10] To the sovereignty of reason he would oppose the sovereignty of faith. Since the eighteenth century had created a new philosophy, he would go back to its precursors that he might uproot its errors. Everything for which the Revolution stood he would ceaselessly denounce, so that he does not even spare the generous intelligence of Madame de Stael.[11] He sought a universal formula against Revolution and he outlined a theodicy that he might apply it. He never, like De Maistre, admitted the relativity of history. He never, like De Maistre, allowed an influence to the God-directed exertions of great men on the one hand, or to the cumulative effect of minute causes on the other.[12] The diminution of universality seemed to him the admission of weakness. The eighteenth century must not be spared but slain. Every dogma for which it had argued he denounced with remorseless hate. He erected, in fact, the negation of its principles into an alchemically mingled compound of antagonisms he chose to call a philosophy.

He deserted the eighteenth century; and that he might the better refute its canons of truth he went back to that which is most alien to its spirit. The seventeenth century in France is the very embodiment of his temper. A centralisation which culminated in the unquestioning promulgation of divinely-ordained monarchy was the very synthesis for which he was contending. The theories of Bossuet were but those of a De Bonald who had not yet encountered the Revolution. They enabled him to take firm hold of the theory of Divine Right—a theory which, through Suarez and Bellarmin, took him back to the great days of scholastic authority. It is, indeed, vital to judge him in this context. For De Bonald was the last representative of that great tradition. His very method was the

---

[10] "Legislation Primitive," p. 93.

[11] Cf. his "Considerations."

[12] "Principe Générateur," p. 15.

dialectic parrying of text with counter-text. He wrote, as he said,[13] not as an orator but as a logician. The Revolution gave him his premises, and from the seventeenth century he drew his conclusions. The neat geometrical arrangement of his material and his pride in a sort of mathematical logic[14] send him back to the days when men slew truth with a syllogism. The writers whom he loved were to him a constant and enduring influence, so that he seems sometimes almost to have expected that the name of Bossuet would spring from cold print to the eager confirmation of the living tongue. He felt those dead who had thought as he thought as part of a living society, and it was thus that when he went to their ideas for confirmation that he felt the justification of contemporary history. And since the thought of the reformers and the ideologues were absent from their pages, he could not but feel for his opponents the impulsive hatred of strangeness.[15] The Revolution was due to the rejection of the natural laws he had discovered in his teachers.[16] And it was simply for the restoration of their activity that he was concerned. He did not see that thus to deal with man in no more than his medieval context was to shut himself off from a vital human experience and to demean man into an abstraction. "Man," he said,[17] "is the same everywhere," and it was upon the basis of that mistaken generalisation that he began his work. The "incontestable authority" he granted to history in political judgment became the authority of medieval history, just as his religious text of truth became the axioms of the medieval church.[18] But no theory could hope for acceptance of which the inductions were based on so factitious and arbitrary a disdain of men.

III. THE POLITICAL THEORY OF BONALD

It would be possible to reconstruct the political theory of Bo-

[13] "Théorie du Pouvoir," I, 3.

[14] Cf. "Théorie du Pouvoir," I, i, 3, p. 146. "Essai sur l'ordre social," p. 282.

[15] "Observations sur Condorcet," p. 309.

[16] "Théorie du Pouvoir," Bk. III, IV, p. 153.

[17] "Théorie du Pouvoir," I, III, p. 146.

[18] "Théorie du Pouvoir," p. 289.

nald by asserting the antithesis of every doctrine for which the eighteenth century stood sponsor. As it asserted the individuality of man, and emphasised the importance of his unique separatism, so Bonald urged that only in his social context is man at all significant. As it had deserted the ways of God, so he proclaimed that only by treading in his path could salvation be attained. As it was fascinated by the theory of a social contract, so did he find in that theory the head and centre of political disaster. The eighteenth century is essentially an age of the sceptics; and Bonald, as a consequence, constructed a philosophy that begins and ends with God. There is nothing of perverseness in all this. It is the natural reaction of a stern temper from the experiences of an alien ideal. He asserted the primacy of God because he did, in fact, believe that all science must begin in this fashion.[19] God, for him, was essentially the directing force of the world and he has not ceased to govern his creation.[20] Indeed Bonald almost overwhelms us with the varied arguments which are intended to demonstrate the necessity of a belief in Divinity. Powerful arguments they are not; and of them it is perhaps best to say that they above all demonstrate his inability to pursue metaphysical enquiry. They are frequently confused and, more rarely, contradictory. But to this he would have doubtless replied that in any case he made entire abstraction of philosophy.

He made abstraction of philosophy because it was basically individualist.[21] It spoke not in the name of God, but of reason; and reason, as the Revolution had taught him, had done nothing save provoke a vain and fruitless debate. Reason meant the Convention and the Directory; Reason had executed the fine flower of the French nation. It was clearly the destruction of stability; and he significantly comments that in the stable theocracy of the Jews as in the unchanging Spartan kingdom the philosopher had found no place. For them tradition had been enough, and yet on the basis of that

[19] "Essai sur l'odre social," p. 282.
[20] "Théorie du Pouvoir religieux," I, i, Ch. 3. Cf. I, 1, VII, note on p. 177, and I, 1, p. 132.
[21] "Théorie du Pouvoir," II, VI, V, 356, 357.

ancestralism his age condemned they had enjoyed a prosperous history. Nor was this all. There was no unity in philosophy. Pythagoras, and Thales, Zeno and Epicurus, Bacon and Descartes are all in fundamental disagreement. What message does philosophy bring that philosophy does not also contradict? So that therein there is no authoritative utterance. But he who speaks in the name of God speaks a language that is common to all.[22]

He is thus without interest in individual thought. The only important thought is that of society, and the thought of society is the reflexion of the mind of God.[23] So that when he is concerned to examine man as a social being he is, in fact, occupied with the relation of man to his creator. If he can discover the laws by which God has created the world, and by which he continues to govern it, his problem is solved. All he has then to do is to deduce the consequences of those laws. His method of enquiry is what might have been expected from one in whom the authoritarian temper had been schooled into rigidity by the subtle hardness of the Oratorians. Like a good medievalist, he uses his texts as cannon to provide a continuous fire against the enemy. The unreality of his atmosphere at the outset clings throughout to his conclusions. He does, indeed, make use of history; and an admiring critic has therein sought to discover an exponent of political realism.[24] But the history is no more than a philosophy teaching by arbitrarily selected examples. He sought only for that which would prove the danger of variety; and the only history for which he cared was that which illustrated its misfortunes. He wanted no more than a stick wherewith to beat the philosophers of the Revolution. His fundamental starting-point makes clear his whole direction. The dependence of the world upon God makes the desertion of his laws the zenith of social treason. The Revolution committed that sin; and he had thus no other task than to enounce the rules which will give ground for his accusing hate.

[22] "Théorie du Pouvoir religieux," I, II, 9.

[23] "Théorie du Pouvoir religieux," I, II, 9.

[24] Montesquieu, "Le réalisme de Bonald;" and cf. M. Bourget, "Etudes et Portraits," Vol. III, pp. 23 ff.

He has, of course, to justify the ways of God to man.[25]   He
achieves this end in his own grim fashion by preventing the
escape of the world from the influence of natural law.[26]   His
God has desired man's happiness, and the laws he has laid down
are the expression of his will to that end.   But the will of God
is unchangeable, so that the universe is governed by an iron
law.   Here, of course, Bonald departs in striking fashion from
the attitude of the eighteenth century.   He has none of the
flexibility of Montesquieu.[27]   God may create and he may
destroy; but all that he accomplishes he must achieve on the
basis of his preliminary definitions.   So that the nature of
man, for instance, is independent of God.   He could not create
a soulless humanity.   The logic of contradiction is an universal principle, in order that the authority of Bonald's deductions
may be maintained.   Miracles, as a consequence, are outside
the realm of possibility;   and though Bonald allowed them
later in his thought a grudging entrance into life, he seems
always to have resented their occurrence.[28]   It is true that
too-zealous Christians have based a scheme of existence upon
them.   But the true philosopher "is freed by thought from the
restriction of space and time;"[29]   and while Bonald admits that
miracles are not metaphysically inconceivable, he yet denies
that God will so constantly intervene in the affairs of men as
to attempt the abrogation of his own ideas.   It is sufficient
that he has organised the universe.   The business of men is to
discover the method of its organisation that they may apply
its principles to their governance.[30]

Bonald has, perhaps wisely, nowhere given us any consistent
account of these natural laws.   They result, of course, in optimism, since, as the work of God, they must be perfect.   History then becomes a progress towards their realisation, and the
problem of the statesman is mainly shifted to their application.   Bonald, indeed, has the simplest of formulæ for that so-

[25] Cf. "Essai sur l'ordre social," p. 35.
[26] *Ibid.*, p. 70.
[27] Nor even of Bossuet. Cf. the "Politique," VII, art. VI, prop. V. and VI.
[28] "Essai sur l'ordre social," p. 67.
[29] *Ibid.*
[30] "Essae sur l'ordre social," p. 110.

lution. The means of enquiry are reason and tradition. The study of nature will give each man the opportunity of their acquaintance. He will at once observe, for example, that the rights of a father over his children, of a master over his servants, partake of the order of nature. They are necessary to life, and what is necessary is divine. So, too, in politics, the prince's search for necessary governmental relations will result in their immediate discovery. And it is important to emphasise that what he means by discovery is essentially a declaration. Man does not make laws; he only declares them. The obvious test of the rightness of his policy is whether the state over which he presides is in revolution or at peace. If it is in revolution the prince has clearly embarked upon a policy that is contrary to natural law. The meeting of the States-General in 1789 is an example of such error. It resulted in revolution. Its members endeavoured to make law, instead of remaining content with its promulgation. They broke, that is to say, with tradition; and Bonald would doubtless have urged that the execution of Louis was the penalty of attempted innovation.

But God has gone further.[31] He has been even more generous to men in his gift of the means of perception. Language is a method whereby the understanding of divine law may be made apparent. It was given to the first men that they might communicate the truths they discovered. And the further gift of writing committed to a permanence more objective than memory the secrets of each age. It made possible, for instance, in the Bible the positive enshrinement of moral and political truth. Nor are these divine laws few in number. The truths of logic and of mathematics are of this order. And those of politics are so important as to require especial means for their enforcement. They clearly involve, for instance, an absolute and hereditary monarchy; yet many people, as history shows and as Bonald in his exile at Heidleberg can not forget, have lived in a republic. Such nations, indeed, have paid the penalty for their defiance. It is the habit of nature to exact her compensations. Inevitably, since without such application society cannot exist in its normal form. A return to what is good has thus the continuous assurance of victory.

[31] Cf. the "Dissertation sur la pensée de l'homme."

Thus even in the midst of these gloomy dogmas, De Bonald can find ground for hope. Revolution is God's medicine to bring men back to his ways. That is, at any rate, one method of interpreting the significance of the Restoration.

The source of this philosophy is obvious.[32] *Non est potestas niso a deo* might well serve as its watchword; and it is under the shadow of Bossuet that it has been conceived. He hardly, indeed, admits the latter's influence. But from the standpoint of one who hated the eighteenth century a return to the ideals of Bossuet was inevitable. Nor is it difficult to understand how a profound Catholic, impregnated with an hereditary loyalty to an unfortunate house, should have let his fancy roam to the zenith of its fortunes. Odd sentences of the New Testament might well serve to set the Divine seal on that retrospective adventure, and the pain of exile would do the rest. If it was objected that in this annexation of God he was grounding his system in intolerance, he might well reply that the alternative to intolerance is intellectual anarchy.[33] The forces of social cohesion cannot have fair play if men think as they will. Given his God as the creator of necessary law, it was inevitable that he should cease to regard the world as self-determining. Nor was it less inevitable that the experience of Bonald should colour his interpretation of that law. All political philosophies are the reaction of temperament upon its chronological perspective. If God has made the world power must come from him, and power in any legitimate form Bonald could hardly concede to men for whom he had so profound a hate. So that he could admit legitimacy only to the house with which he had associated his fortunes, and he was then willing to identify the legitimate with the divine. *Per me reges regnant et legum conditores justa decerunt* received a new beauty when applied to the House of Bourbon. But to have admitted its application to Napoleon would have been a self-condemnation to perpetual exile.

IV. THE ATTACK ON THE INDIVIDUAL

His God is clearly one who will restore an order that he loves. Bonald has been terrified at the results of individualism; and

[32] Cf. "Romans," XIII, 1, with Théorie de Pouvoir, I, II, p. 135.
[33] "Oeuvres," X, 258.

authority is the chart by which he is to find the haven of relief from its burdens. It is perhaps for this reason that the God he depicts is so much more stern and far off than that of his masters. With both Bossuet and Aquinas God is one who continually influences the course of life; but they had not, like Bonald, lived in a time of revolution.[34] Change to him has become the synonym of evil and he binds his God to act but seldom that the rightness of a static organisation may be manifest. And since it is individualism that he is concerned to combat he must elevate the value of society. It is necessary to the existence of man. It is true that a certain individualism results from the relation of God with him whom he created in his own image; yet that very relation leads man to contact with his fellows that they may in common fulfil the principles of their origin.

And, indeed, man cannot live alone. All that he is he owes to society and only as a member of it is he intelligible. His theory of language is used to confirm this attitude.[35] For an individual who stood without society could not inherit the means of grasping the laws governing the universe by which he is confronted. The only real being is the social being.[36] The only man who has the opportunity to develop his powers is a member of a group. Bonald is thus able, and with much force, to make short shrift with Rousseau's state of nature. To picture a world without organisation is, for him, to misinterpret the whole meaning of creation. It is to picture a world without law, and the one thing that can be posited is the existence of law. He points out acutely that when Rousseau urged men to live according to nature, he did, in fact, make tacit acceptance of principles inherent in its order. But it is difficult to understand how principles of this kind can be discovered and maintained in the ungenial terrors of savage existence.[37] For the attainment of the life Rousseau desired a social existence is essential; and its at-

[34] Cf. "De. Reg. Prin." III, VII, and Bossuet, "Politique," VII, 6, V and VI.

[35] "Législation Primitive." I, 156. This theory of language has been effectively criticised by M. Ferraz in the first volume of his "Histoire de Philosophie."

[36] "Législation Primitive," II, 170.

[37] "Théorie du Pouvoir," II, IV, V, p. 329-30.

tainment would be undesirable unless the primary fact of society were at the outset admitted.

For Bonald, indeed,—and here he differed radically from Aquinas—society is prior to the individual. The latter derives his meaning simply from his social context, where to Aquinas the function of society is not to create but to perfect the life of man. But for Bonald this is too narrow a conception. His society is in a real sense a person.[38] It is not a mere algebraic bracket, linking men together into an artificial unity. It is one, and indivisible.[39] It is organic, and, like an organism, it has a will whereby to make manifest its desires.[40] Society is thus rendered independent of individuals. It exists of and in itself and they do no more than contribute to the richness of a life from which they in turn draw nourishment.[41] The general will of this society, moreover, is the divine will conscious of those necessary laws upon which he lays such striking emphasis. But will must be directed that it may become manifest in action; and it is to the monarch that he confines its direction that it may take form in legislation. The social will so expressed, moreover, is superior in its claim to all other. It is further freed from the embarrassment of superiority, since than society there can be no higher being. Nor will it act unwisely. "The general will of society," he wrote, "is necessarily conservative in character."[42] That is to say it is conservative when it is freed from the dangerous influence of individual or national wills which in their search for substantive form take shape in revolutions. If it is somewhat mystical, it is none the less an intelligible attitude. That it derives from Rousseau it is certainly difficult to doubt; but whereas Rousseau drew from it the principle of national sovereignity the whole point of Bonald's conception is to urge cause against that principle. For national sovereignty is, in its essence, an individualist doctrine; and it is from the organic character of society that

[38] *Ibid.*, I, 1, p. 28.
[39] *Ibid.*, II, IV, V, p. 329-30.
[40] *Ibid.*, II, IV, p. 128.
[41] *Ibid.*, I, ii, passim.
[42] "Essai sur l'ordre social," p. 33.

Bonald is anxious to deduce the *a priori* impossibility of that attitude.

He has made the individual but a link in a chain. Society as a whole is thus the real founder of civilisation. Great men are no longer entitled to credit for their discovery since it is by reason of their social gifts that they have attained to greatness. They could not have worked without the instrument of language that their thought might receive expression; and the object of language was social enrichment. So that for him a great man is no more than the reflexion of his time, a servant of its needs. It is therefrom that he should draw his inspiration. Insofar as he follows the path of his own fortune he deserts both his genius and his function.

It is impossible not to feel that he has in mind those daring spirits of the Revolution whose ability might so easily have been deflected into channels less tragic in their consequence. But they followed the call of their ambition and he is accordingly tempted even further in the direction of their control. He does not merely limit individuality. He insists upon its socially dangerous character. Wherever he sees the exercise of personality he urges that it is the root of crime. For, at the outset, he has the material for its condemnation. He has insisted upon the supremacy of society. He has reduced men to no more than unimportant functions of its power. Thereby he has the right to attack all which might in some sort detract from its omnipotence.

He equates individualism with anarchy, and he makes some misuse of history to demonstrate the truth of his attitude. The Reformation to him is no more than the idle pride of a monk engaged in the defence of his order.[44] Luther called to his aid all the evil passions and avid interests alike of men and princes. He cast a torch into a sea of oil and the result was the ghastly conflagration of the sixteenth century. Here was the influence of individual talent refusing to take its stand on the firm basis of tradition. Luther sought out novelty; and society paid the penalty for the passion of his misinterpreted conclusions. So

[43] Cf. Mauduit, "Les Conceptions Politiques et Sociales de Bonald," p. 83.

[44] "Théorie du Pouvoir," II, v, vi, 283-4.

with Calvin[45] and with Henry VIII.[46]   In each case we have a man determined to give the freest play to his self-will; and in each case a reign of terror is the consequence.   For they put their trust in an opinion to which age had failed to give the sanction of traditional affection.   They urged a cause based on no more than reason.   It was inevitable that men should arise to contradict their conclusions and to sacrifice the blood of others in the pursuit of proof.   They made a fatal error. They did not attempt the preservation of what had been proved by time.   They attempted to examine and of this the social consequence is dispersion.   But of dispersion the eldest child is anarchy.

This, too, is the cause of that ceaseless multiplication of Protestant opinion he deemed so vast an evil.[47]   For what in truth Luther achieved was to make each man the sole judge alike of belief and practice.   But that is to preach a mental equality which can only result in the degradation of principle. Little by little each will pare away from the body of accepted tradition that which he cannot accept until atheism is the result.[48]   Between catholicism and atheism he sees no half-way house.[49]   To reject the one is to embrace the other.   To reject the one is to replace divine invention by the fiendish ingenuity of men.[50]   For those who once question the fundamental dogmas fail entirely to perceive that the principles of social religion have been established for all time.   Critically to estimate their validity by the degree of their personal inacceptability is to strike a fatal blow at the root of morality.   For no blow can be struck at the foundations of religious order which does not react on the political structure.[51]   Political and religious strife always develop along parallel lines.   So, for example, the real source of the French Revolution is to be found in the teaching of Calvin.   To urge the priesthood of believers in the

[45] *Ibid.*, II, i, IV, 38.
[46] *Ibid.*, 292.
[47] *Ibid.*, 296.
[48] *Ibid.*, 350.
[49] *Ibid.*, 353 f.
[50] *Ibid.*, 177.
[51] *Ibid.*, 306, 340.

sixteenth century is to send Louis XVI to the scaffold in the eighteenth. So closely is religion embedded in the framework of society that he who develops religious change is bound to seek political change also that the structure may be altered to meet his religious needs. So the supposed constitution which limited Louis' power was no more, in sober truth, than an attempt at the provision of opportunity for Calvinist growth. It thus is the destruction of that unity which alone makes possible the continuance of social order.

Nor is this all. The grandchild of reform is philosophy and from its impassioned curiosity has been born the most deadly error. Philosophy—so Bonald urges—has no function save that of destruction.[52] Its guides are self-interest and passion. It dethrones God to replace him by nature, and each of her devotees interprets differently her meaning. Religion becomes unnecessary. The people dethrone power to crown law. The old love of one's neighbour is removed to give place to some philanthropy he can hardly bring himself to describe.[53] The philosopher dispenses with the Atonement; and man thus being by definition good society is reduced from the necessary condition of existence to no more than a business association. It is asked to justify itself by the terms of its contractual institution. Yet the very sceptics who thus remorselessly examine are refused by their own logic. A contract supposes power for otherwise its enforcement is impossible.[54] But a contract cannot constitute that which would be its own negation. A contract involves the ideal of equality between the contracting parties; but that very equality is born of power.[55] Those who would make the possession of power dependent upon its useful exercise forget its origin. Power comes from God, and he alone can set conditions to its use. If men could so limit it, it would no longer be itself. Its identity would be destroyed. It would be sheerly arbitrary in character—the creature of popular whim and fantasy. But the power which is instituted by God is in essence different. It assures man freedom for it has been insti-

[52] *Ibid.*, 22.
[53] *Ibid.*,335.
[54] "Principe Constitutif," p. 450.
[55] "Essai sur l'ordre social," p. 99.

tuted upon the basis of the fundamental principles of the universe.

And a further consequence must be drawn. If the true sovereign of the universe is God then everyone, no less the sovereign than his subjects, have duties towards him.[56] He has set the rhythm of Life and they must make possible the fulfilment of its motif. Their right thus becomes no more than the right to fulfil their duty, the right to act in accordance with the will of God. In such an aspect the folly of those who would draw up a *Declaration of the Rights of Man* is self-evident. For while they affirm the equality of men's rights they affirm no less the right to property. But what becomes of property where some men, equal in the theoretic possession of rights, are yet without the means of subsistence? Clearly the denial of the rhythm Bonald has postulated creates a deadly rhythm of its own. The acceptance of individualism crushes into atoms the very basis of society. By making the social question something to be resolved by reason, instead of admitting that it is from the outset dependent on God, and is thus justified without the need of social response, it leaves open a path for every method of anarchic destruction.[57] No one, he urges, dare accept the claim of science to make men better by making them intellectually enlightened. On the contrary, the result of increasing knowledge is the desire of domination. The individual seeks rather for means to satisfy his faculty of self-absorption than to accomplish social good. To proclaim the existence of rights is to make of each man a potential tyrant. The philosopher who proclaims the advent of liberty only ensures the régime of anarchy. For to question is to destroy. To question is to satisfy one's whim and though such caprice has not made the world, it may yet destroy it. And when caprice has been identified with individuality the transition to traditionalism has been made. For each man then contributes his own restlessness to the disturbance of the social fabric. The logical result of the eighteenth century is thus obviously the horrors of the Revolution.

It is, of course, obvious that the source of this criticism is

[56] "Essai analytique," p. 57.
[57] "Théorie du Pouvoir," iv, v, 356.

the famous polemic by Bossuet against the Reformation.[58] "Those who create revolt in the name of freedom become themselves tyrants." So it was Bossuet wrote, and his words might be the text of Bonald's examination. Urging as he does the unity of society, he denies the validity of all enquiry, political no less than religious, on the ground that it destroys that unity. He searches out each pretext of the eighteenth century for the denial of the dogmas of the *ancien régime*, and erects their negations into new dogmas. Fundamentally he attacks that individualism which Comte, in a fit of temper,[59] once dismissed abruptly as the disease of the Western world. Without unity of opinion and belief there cannot be hope of social survival. The very fact of the Revolution is the evidence of this truth. To insist on the value of the individual, to erect into a system, as Rousseau did, his right to self-development is to misinterpret the organic nature of society. An organism presupposes nervous co-ordination, and of that co-ordination freedom of belief is the main antagonist. So there must be but one religion in France; for the very existence of other confessions secretes the germ of social disaster. And this is for him the more true in the case of Protestant dogma, since its basis is the primacy of the individual. It thus becomes the business of the statesman to ward off the danger of anarchy. He must insist on the necessity of uniformity. "Unless" he wrote in a tremendous sentence, "unless we have a religious and political unity, man cannot discover truth, nor can society hope for salvation."[60]

V. IMPLICATIONS OF THE ATTACK

A CURIOUS trinitarianism pervades the whole speculation of Bonald, and it is upon its basis that he erected his social philosophy.[61] For the number *three* he seems to have cherished a peculiar weakness, so that, like the devotees of the beast in Revelations, he is everywhere able to discover the operation of

[58] Cf. Bossuet, "Hist. des Variations," Bk I, pp. 316, 340, 419, etc.
[59] "Politique Positive," iii, 614.
[60] "Essai sur l'ordre social," p. 33.
[61] Cf. Faguet, *op. cit.*, i, p.

a threefold cause. For some abstract reason the source of which remains strangely obscure, he believed that from a belief that the cause is to the means, as the means is to the effect, the mind can solve all political questions. The business of society, whether domestic or political or religious, becomes then the realisation of that relationship. Perfection is simplified into its permanent attainment.[62a]

He had no difficulty in deciphering its details.[62a] Domestic society is clearly composed of three elements. The father is the cause, the mother the means, the child is the effect. Since the father is the cause, he must clearly have power, for, otherwise, the division of it would destroy its efficacy. Nor can that power be abrogated. In the eyes of its parents, for example, a child is always a minor. That is why primitive society gave to the head of the family the power of life and death. That is why the woman taken in adultery may be slain without mercy by her husband. The wife, indeed, does no more than receive from her husband the power of reproduction. Her one duty is to obey him. As she is midway between child and man, so she partakes of the nature of both. To the one she issues commands, to the other she offers submission. The child itself has no function save to obey. Were it otherwise the unity of family power would clearly be destroyed. Nor is this unfair to the child who, in receiving from his parents the gift of language owes to them his most precious possession. For without them thought would thus have been impossible, and his obedience is the price he pays for so unique a privilege.[63]

The function of domestic society he regards as simply reproductive. Man may be mortal, but the society to which he belongs is imperishable. He thus owes to it the duty of reproduction and it is for that purpose the family has been established. Bonald has thus the greater reason for denying the importance of the individual. It is only as a member of the family-group that he is entitled to consideration. It is essentially that group which is the real unit of society. Only from it does social function spring. Man himself is only an incident

[62] "Principe Constitutif," p. 441 f.
[63] *Ibid.*, p. 445.

in a succession of births so vast as to make him infinitesimal in comparison.

If the family is thus the social unit one can clearly discern therein two types. The ordinary family does no more than guard its daily interests. The care of its needs exhausts its time and its capacities. It has no more to do than to maintain itself in existence, without being a burden upon its fellow-men. It is important only from the point of view of population. It is the broad base upon which a finer and more complex structure may be made to rest. The noble family is different. The credentials of birth demonstrate that it has passed the stage of the worker's inevitable inertia. It is occupied with the defence of society, the student of its problems, the resolver of its doubts. It may thus rightly demand the privileges that come from this self-sacrifice. It has leaped beyond the toilsome and narrowing cares of daily existence. It alone is really fitted to deal with the great problems of men. There is nothing sordid or meagre in the subject of its contemplation. It thinks on a higher plane of life. It is accustomed to that objectivity of attitude which alone makes possible a social existence.[64]

The argument is as old as Aristotle, and no better than when he made it. What in truth he was attempting was the discovery of a basis for the family organisation of the *ancien régime*. His *"famille ordinaire"* is no more than the peasant-family of eighteenth century France and because it was then powerless he strives to demonstrate that it is in fact actually unfitted for political faculties. It was with a similar purpose that the *"famille noble"* should have the typical attributes of a family such as his own. The army and the magistracy were recruited from its ranks; what more natural than to assume that they are so recruited because their capacity fits them for that type of labour? He insists on the value of an hereditary nobility merely to ensure the permanence of that order and where he argues for its indispensability he means no more than that he could not wish it otherwise. So, too, is to be understood his contempt for property and age. He rejects the latter as a classification of service "because it is necessary to choose use-

[64] Cf. what is said below of M. Bourget's reconstruction of these arguments.

ful men,"[65] and utility depends on class and not on maturity; moreover an indiscriminate choice would result in disorder.[66] He rejects property because it will open the path to indiscriminate ambition. He is, in fact, looking back on the Revolution and fearing the advent of the middle class. So, too, may be explained his insistence on the superiority of the agricultural family.[67] Industry is the enemy of order. It is the captains of industry who continuously insist on the value of independence. It is commerce which has been the parent of wars and of the mad doctrine of liberty. From it has sprung that yearning for luxury which is the mother of decay. It gives rise to a superabundance of population. It results in the dispersion of family unity. With agriculture all is different. The soil nourishes those to whom it gives birth. Almost in the manner of the Physiocrats, but without their glowing discrimination, he paints a picture of the serene joys of agricultural existence.[68] He insists on its solidarity. It unifies by the nature of the occupation it affords. It makes no distinction between master and servant. It permits of ancestralism and of a common toil. It achieves a kinship with nature and the production of all that men truly require for their satisfaction.[69] He shows no small contempt for the industrialism of Adam Smith,[70] and, at least by implication, the idealising reforms of Saint-Simon. The division of labour is the coronation of individualism and he will have none of it. He loves too deeply the solid conservatism of the French peasantry to be willing to depart from their ways. For, after all, it was they who supported the king and the church. It was from the cities that sprang disturbing thoughts. It was business men who had quarrelled with the old economic order and erected their impatience into a vicious philosophy. He could compare Paris with Brittany and he could hardly doubt the reason for their distinction. Paris was industrial and in Paris had been born the wildest theories of social organisation.

[65] "Théorie du Pouvoir," V, vii.
[66] "Principe Constitutif," Ch. IX.
[67] Pensées Diverses, p. 6.
[68] La famille Agricole et Industrielle."
[69] Cf. "Mélanges," p. 441.
[70] *Ibid.*, p. 505.

But in Brittany men inherited the ideas of their fathers and to question had become not less than to sin.

The union of families is the State; and it was here, perhaps most vividly, that Bonald showed in his narrow traditionalism the influence of the Revolution. "When God wished to punish France," he once wrote in an amazing sentence,[71] "he withdrew the Bourbons from its governance." His whole effort, in fact, is simply the attempt to discover a political structure which should obviate the possibility of their expulsion. He desires the construction of a static society on the principles of the *ancien régime*. He thus makes the object of the state essentially conservation. Just as the family provides society with its members, so does the state aim at the preservation of peace between them. But to that end it has need of an instrument. It has to prevent the conflict of individual wills from resulting in the destruction of the body politic. It has to see to it that a continuous progress is made towards the realisation of those necessary relations that are the declaration of the will of God. It is not easy to mistake their nature; for all Bonald has really attempted in their statement is to idealise that which the Revolution came to deny. If he has succeeded in concealing his particularism in a fine cloud of apparent abstractions, that does not hide the fact that it is a particular problem he has in mind. The "constituted" society upon which he lays so much emphasis may be one in which "necessary relationships" are observed; but what Bonald means by "necessary relationship" is simply an obedience to his prejudices. A "non-constituted society" is but one that has striven to work out its own political salvation, and in the process has discovered that there are truths of which even the great Bossuet did not dream.

He is at any rate right in the assertion that society is given and that since it is given it must be organised. For whatever society is, an inchoate and discrete mass it is not. The fundamental question of politics is thus a problem in the method of

[71] "Pensées Diverses," p. 172.

organisation. What is the nature of sovereignty? Why should one man rule over another? Bonald sees clearly enough that the problem of sovereignty is not merely a question of power but also that, in some sort, it is a question where only the arguments of reason can apply. For him all theories of sovereignty reduce themselves, in the main, to two types. Men rule either by virtue of divine right or from the authority of a social contract. Bonald, of course, has no choice in such an alternative. Society is the creation of God. *Omnis potestas est a deo;* and we may cease the vanity of argument. Power is a social institution and the divinity of social institutions is simply obvious. He has no patience with the theory of a social contract.[72] It is obvious to him that the idea not merely most repugnant but in truth most inconceivable to men is that of their subjection to equals. It is contrary to human psychology. Only where some are in the position of inferiors is there a willingness to accept so hard but so necessary a fact. Nor does he believe that a social contract can arise before there is power; for a contract implies the idea of organisation and to organisation power is already essential. That a social contract is impossible once the existence of power has been admitted is of course obvious; for once it is present there is no longer that equality of status which permits of its institution on valid terms.[73]

He urges the necessity of power because he is convinced of its naturalness. It arises in society just as in a crowd it is always the custom for some one man to take charge. He has no confidence in the disposition of a mass of men. It lacks direction and wisdom. It cries out for a leader. It can only be transformed into a society when someone has given it functions to perform, orders to obey.[74] Until then it will be found always to be unhappy and in confusion. He urges that the primary desire of a people is for safety and that it is their habit to seek for the leader who is most likely to secure it. The crowd without a leader is like a child without its parent. It lacks the *raison d'être* of its existence.[75] It has none of the elements of

[72] "Principe Contitutif," p. 449.
[73] *Ibid.* p. 450.
[74] "Demonstr. Phil.," p. 108-9.
[75] "Pensées Diverses," p. 12.

self-preservation.   Power is thus the offspring of necessity. There must be some master of men in order that men may be saved.

It cannot be denied that there is much of truth in such an attitude. But Bonald could not, of course, fail to realise that he has done no more than push his enquiry back rather than solve it. If all that society required was leadership, the usurpation of Napoleon would be justified. The problem clearly has been that of the organisation of power. The need is to discover the seat of an authority which must be postulated as essential to existence.

Bonald's answer to this question has in it but little originality. His theory of political organisation is little more than a restatement of Bossuet's, but of a Bossuet whom the Revolution has made a little plaintive and almost tragically unreal. He starts out from two fundamental principles. Princes are the ministers of God.[76] They are the ministers of God, no doubt, that their position may be unassailable by a bourgeoisie which has listened to the blasphemies of Rousseau. And it is because they are the ministers of God that their interests are at one with those of the people. For the welfare of the state is essentially an unity, which transcends the welfare of particular members. Here, clearly, he has the opportunity to slay the obvious facts of social life with the amazing abstractness of his passion for the trinity. Since the cause is to the means as the means is to the effect that relationship must be discovered in political society, and, desiring its presence, he has no difficulty in finding it. King, minister, subject—these are the obvious triad which gives supreme power to the prince.[77] It gives supreme power; and, for its maintenance, there is clearly required hereditary kingship on the one hand, and hereditary nobility on the other. They are required because they are naturally good. They are naturally good because they have been tested by the experience of time. They are good because without them there would be anarchy. The absolutism of the crown is essential, in fact, to the unity of the state.[78] Society,

[76] "Observations sur l'ouvrage de Madame de Stael," p. 128.
[77] "Legislation Primitive," Bk. II, Ch. iv, p. 228.
[78] "Théorie du Pouvoir," Vol. I, Bk. i, Ch. ii.

like an organism, is one, and, being one, it can have only a single head. One man must therefore dominate lest all men should be destroyed.

He can therefore reject that division of powers which Montesquieu had postulated as the safeguard of liberty.[79] He can reject it for the good reason that he does not believe in liberty. He will, indeed, accept Montesquieu's dictum that power is the general will of the state; but he argues that the will of the state must necessarily be single, and that it can aim at no more than self-preservation. So to limit it is to obviate the danger that the fascinating questions discussed by Montesquieu should fall within the purview of his thought. He realised clearly enough that Montesquieu was entirely out of sympathy with the *ancien régime* and that his speculations tended to its dissolution. He believed that the separation of powers was the dogma most hostile to the unification of sovereignty. He saw that once men were prepared to parcel it out the result must inevitably be an implicitly federalised state. But such a political organisation tended to the republicanism which his experience of the Revolution led him to identify with impiety. To separate powers was to confound them. To separate powers was to give a handle to every dissident element in the state. When Louis XVI summoned the States-General he committed exactly this error; and he paid the penalty with his life. What Montesquieu thus attempted was, in his eyes, the provision of a permanent basis for royal execution and he was compelled to reject his philosophy.

The fundamental tenet in his creed is thus the nature he ascribes to sovereign power. He was a worshipper of its unity because the experience of its opposite had been fatal to the ideas he most deeply cherished. It can never be too greatly emphasised that the thought of Bonald was virtually completed in 1796. There is nothing in his last work which is not, at least impliedly, in his first. Neither the history of the Napoleonic adventure—after all, the practical expression of his attitude—nor the tragic misapprehensions of Charles X in any wise altered his outlook. He cared for nothing save stability. He naturally admired the environment of his time, and he

[79] "Théorie du Pouvoir," Bk VI, Ch. III, p. 411.

sought the conditions of its permanence. He conceived that an unified absolutism would achieve that end because under Louis XIV his ideals had found a full expression. He believed that there is no remedy for disorder save uniformity of thought. Men had to be kept in subjection because the price of their freedom was too immense. It is, of course, a common enough attitude. We have ourselves, for the most part, done no more than transfer from king to state his erstwhile divinity. The king's need has become *raison d'état* and we have simply multiplied the basis of sovereignty.[80] Bonald would have urged the inherent error of such a policy on the ground that it was unworkable. He saw in the free expression of opinion the conditions of misfortune. Where men begin to question he could not doubt that they begin also to destroy. For they question essentially that they may reconstruct, and the method implies a period of disturbance. Toleration is thus the negation of order.[81] Sovereignty cannot be dispersed simply because it cannot then be exercised. To disperse it is to make it fallible; and the possibility of error is the excuse for anarchy.

This, indeed, is his generalisation from the experience of the eighteenth century. When it questioned traditional institutions it overthrew them.[82] Little by little it exacted from the crown the instruments of power. The admission to political privilege of the Hugenots in 1788 was the destruction of religious uniformity. The summons of the States-General two years later gave to the unrealised welter of accumulated grievance the power which translated it into action. For the States-General was a human institution; and where its advice was neglected, its pride stirred it to compulsion. Where before order had been possible, the doubt Louis had cast on his right to the full exercise of his sovereign power meant that jealous men would usurp it. To him, in fact, every event in the Revolution is the logical result of that single error. Once loosen the strict bonds of power and there is no check to the passions of

---

[80] Cf. the interesting little work of M. Léon de Montesquieu, "Raison d'Etat." This is, of course, the whole basis of M. Duguit's theories. See especially his "Transformations du Droit Public."

[81] "Théorie du P. Religieux," Bk. VI, Ch. II.

[82] Cf. "Pensées Diverses," p. 33.

men. Here, clearly, he feels like De Maistre, that the executioner is the corner-stone of society. And he emphasises the virtues of tradition exactly for this purpose. Men cannot venerate what is new, because where they understand they are sceptical. But veneration is the corollary of obedience. The unity of power has behind it all the overmastering sense of antiquity. It is the one dogma of government which has survived. It is the one dogma which has received the continuous respect of men. Moreover, it alone is the basis of solidarity. The very fact that there is only one elevation to which none save the sovereign can pretend creates a common bond of interest between men. It sets outside the range of ambitious exertion the hopes which may inspire social discontent. It keeps society ordered neatly in ranks and stations by urging men to fulfil the duties to which their class and birth traditionally call them. It suggests that necessary interdependence of function which keeps the minds of men from straying into dangerous paths. Its very neatness suggests to the majority a disharmony in novelty of outlook. It is thus a guarantee of social peace. The king wills; and his command is binding upon every element in the body politic. There is thus generated a perception of equality which has all the advantages and none of the inherent dangers which a pluralistic sovereignty possesses.

To say that the king is absolute sovereign is not, of course, to postulate an arbitrary tyrant. Here, again, the origin of his thought is the speculation of Bossuet. Just as the latter was endeavouring to find a justification for the absorptiveness of Louis XIV, so was Bonald attempting to show that absolutism is not an excuse for the accusation of arbitrary power. Arbitrary power was, for him, a power exercised independently of the necessary laws of social organisation. It was the power of one who, like Napoleon, sought his own good and failed to make it coincident with the good of France. Absolute power is exercised for the benefit of the people. It is the instrument by which laws in conformity with the will of God are promulgated. Here, obviously, is a defence against their degeneration into tyranny. For if the object of absolute power is no more than the translation into legislative terms of the will of God, the function of the king is not creative but declaratory. He is thus in no sense omnipotent. He is limited by the laws of his being. And he finds the laws it is his duty to declare not by any inherent revelation, but by the research of reason on the one hand, and by a selection among existing institutions on the other.[83] The king will continually exercise his mind on the problem of political organisation. He will search out among the achievements of men those which have the better contributed to social improvement. Here is a source of the wisdom by which such a political order may find its justification. For since this is an order of reason the people may themselves discover the wisdom of its enactments. Nor does Bonald, on the whole, have any fear that absolutism may degenerate. A wise ruler, he urges, will immediately preceive the harmony of interest between himself and his subjects, and his policy will of necessity adjust itself to the enrichment of their common purpose. He insists, moreover, on the importance of realising that the universe is teleological. There is behind it the mighty and beneficent purpose of its maker. To that all institutions and all men are, in the end, subordinate. So that ultimately good may be expected even from bad institutions. Social defect is self-curative by the inspiration it affords to a reaction from its errors. Nor does the king stand alone. It must never be forgotten that there exists the ministerial body through which the king acts. He has the benefit of their advice and of their criticism. They can warn him of impending dangers. They can urge him against unwise courses. Society has thus given itself an admirable and self-regulating check against kingly error.[84]

Not that, in any case, kingly error would justify deposition.[85] The good Bonald glows with passionate indignation at the mere thought of its possibility. If our king is a bad king we must endure him. An attitude of hopeful resignation is alone possible to Christians. For to admit the rectitude of deposition is to admit the justice of social scepticism. It is to admit a virtue to that which destroys. It is to give to jealous men the

[83] "Essai sur l'ordre social," p. 65.
[84] "Principe Constitutif," Ch. X, p. 465.
[85] "Théorie du Pouvoir," Bk. I, Ch. IX. Cf. Bossuet, *op. cit.*, Bk. VI, 1 and 2.
[86] "Principe Constitutif," Ch. XI, p. 468.

hope of a share in power by enabling them to misrepresent motive and achievement for their own base purposes. The institution of kingship is divine, and to allow men to question it is to allow them to doubt the work of God. It is this which makes him insist also on the necessity of hereditary monarchy. Where the succession to the throne is at the outset guaranteed, we have an assurance of stability. We have that foreknowledge of events which is a safeguard against interested schemers. Not only is primogeniture natural—how otherwise could it be of so marvellous an antiquity—but it is a vital assurance of continuity in national life. To deny it is to admit the roots of division within the state. He reasonably points to Poland as an instance of the paralysis which results from an elective system.[86] There, power has been in fact divided and the fate of Poland is the measure of its error. There is no surety for existence without integration. To establish beforehand the natural order of events is clearly to minimise the dangers of transition.

The whole purpose of these elaborate safeguards is obvious enough. Bonald has been impressed by the diverse aims the will of man can encompass, and he searches the means to minimise the disharmony of their interplay. That which he most greatly fears is the influence of unorthodox opinion.[87] He regarded democracy as *per se* an effort after political defiance which seeks to transfer power to itself. But the weapon of democracy is discussion and from discussion is born intellectual perversity. "Avec des mots," he wrote,[88] "on pervertira la raison des peuples;" and propaganda he thus did not hesitate to brand as sin. He denied,[89] indeed, that the influence of the press can secure the passage of great measures. For not only do they consistently misinterpret a public opinion that they do not understand, but they serve only to darken counsel and so to hinder action. A censorship of the press is thus a necessity that power may have adequate protection.[90] Only in this way can men of evil disposition be prevented from attacking every

[87] "De la liberté de la presse," p. 3.
[88] *Ibid.*, p. 13.
[89] *Ibid.*, p. 16.
[90] *Ibid.*, p. 29.

necessary institution of society. "Ces jeunes anonymes," he wrote scornfully,[91] . . . . exploitent à leur profit, et comme une industrie ou une proprieté patrimoniale la religion, le gouvernement, les lois, l'administration." They erect their private opinion into the will of the state and are thus the very harbingers of revolution. Control of opinion is then no more than the paternal regard of the Crown for the welfare of its subjects. It has had brilliant results and antagonism to it he ascribes to the insensate pride of malicious spirits. Nor does he doubt[92] that all liberty is in fact simply the concession of instituted power which may set the terms of reason to its benevolence. To him[93] the whole demand for the right of discussion under the Restoration was simply the inevitable consequence of that representative government instituted by the Charter of 1814. For, as he urges,[94] the result of that measure is to inaugurate a rivalry between royalty and the populace for power. It is an endeavour of the other to usurp what it has no right to retain. It has a tragic outcome. It results in the creation of two powers and hence of two societies. They cannot live in tranquillity within the same state, and the disturbance from which France suffers is the effect of their collision. He looks back regretfully[95] to the times of the Grand Monarch when unity of political outlook was the first law of life. He mentions[96] with the tenderness of affectionate agreement the custom of the Roman Senate which was wont to banish those philosophers whose theories threatened the harmony of the state. They realised the fundamental truth he is here concerned to inculcate[97] that society perishes not by the absence of truth—that is at the basis of social existence—but by the presence of error. The nourishment of man is his ideas, and to allow him free access to a food that has not been examined is to run the risk of social poisoning.[98] "Un écrit dangereux," he declared with

[91] *Ibid.*, p. 44.
[92] *Ibid.*, p. 61.
[93] *Ibid.*, p. 117.
[94] *Ibid.*, p. 137.
[95] *Ibid.*, p. 142.
[96] *Ibid.*, p. 143.
[97] *Ibid.*, p. 148.
[98] *Ibid.*, p. 156.

passion,[99] "est une declaration de guerre à toute l'Europe;" and it was no more than an obvious duty to suppress it.

Freedom is thus a dangerous chimera and remedies against its pursuit must be found. It is for a return to the ancient ways that he is most deeply concerned. The misfortunes of France have come because her king abandoned the natural path of royalty.[100] They bowed before the erection of a system and the consequence is their submission to its continuous examination. Such an endeavor to reduce to written form the elements of social life seems to him profoundly erroneous. Popularisation he always held as a grave danger for it prevented the unification of opinion. To write out the basis of government is to defeat the end for which it was made. Trouble is the eldest child of knowledge. He puts his trust rather in a decent mystery which alone makes possible an adequate veneration. To write the constitution is to tempt the passions of men. It is to suggest that there are limits to the royal power. It is to tell the people that certain rights are theirs by nature and they will have no sense of proportion in their demands. For royalty he demands an invisibility and an omnipresence.[101] In business and pleasure alike the ways of kings must be mysterious and hidden. Bonald even blames lightly the action of Louis XIV in appearing publicly at the fêtes of Versailles; while he is certain that the raillery of Marie-Antoinette made the pleasures of the Court insupportable to the mass of men. The king must try[102] adequately to mirror the divinity of which he is an image. He must be simple, severe, dignified. His nobility must cease[103] that vain pursuit of titles which incites jealousy without invoking respect. It must instead set itself to the creation of a reverence for the solemn fact of power.[104] Unless that is done, the destroying angel of envy will cast its baneful influence over France. But to this end one means alone is at all adequate and effective.

[99] *Ibid.*, p. 157.
[100] "De la Justice Divine," p. 132.
[101] *Ibid.*, p. 145.
[102] *Ibid.*
[103] *Ibid.*, p. 149.
[104] *Ibid.*, p. 150.

VI. THE RELIGIOUS ASPECT OF THE STATE

RELIGIOUS passion was the supreme influence of Bonald's life. Only in its acceptance could he see that elevation of heart and loftiness of spirit which are the basic conditions of progress.[105] The people that respects religion is a happy people, for it is certain to respect authority. Religion he believed to be essential to the intellectual satisfaction of man, for otherwise its universality was inexplicable.[106] Only by reason of the assumptions it makes can the world be understood. Even Rousseau admitted it to be essential;[107] and Bonald seeks no further justification. When the devil admits the worth of right, good men have no more duty than its translation into action.

Religion for him was the basis of political stability. It helps the statesman by its insistence on moral ideas. It gives birth to a standard of conduct. It gives a definite context to the vague ideas of right and wrong which results in a test of action. It creates justice by its emphasis on the necessity of applying its standard to the facts of life. This *a priori* test, indeed, he deems the most valuable preservative of the social order. For when one deals in a mystic absolute the time for discussion has passed. We cannot waste our time in argument against the decrees of God; and it is their support that Bonald brings to his ideal of the state. He brings it because his order is divinely ordained and he desires the sanction of God for his canons of political wisdom. He does not, of course, lack texts to prove his point; but his scholasticism is more profound than the superficial casuistry of quotation. He is satisfied that no good man can be without religion. He looks upon religion as the sole sanction of moral activity. Clearly, therefore, he must make religion interchangeable with politics. What in society man above all needs is that which will enable him to bear the burden of life. His troubles are so vast and so manifold, that consolation is essential if he is to find them supportable. Only religion can assuage his cares. It softens the disharmonies of social existence by directing the interests of men rather to the life that is to come than to the life that is. It gives to politics

[105] *Ibid.*, p. 155.

[106] "Théorie du Pouvoir," I, VI.

[107] *Ibid.*, I, IV.

the basis of a necessary mythopoiesis. It acts, in fact, as a social chloroform to dull the hearts of men against the pain of truth. It is the justification of the present by its reference to a divine past. So is it a preventive against discontent.

Religion, of course, means the Roman Catholic religion. Protestantism, by its very definition, is fatal to these mighty purposes. It is out of accord with the realities of sovereignty. Lutheran ideals beget oligarchy, and Calvinism the government of Geneva. Each, in fact, destroys the unity which is the essence of a monarchic system. Such forms of faith are for him comparable only to that pleasant feeling of internal satisfaction which Rousseau mistook for religion. Its true basis is the fundamental fact of sacrifice.[108] Its true basis is the tacit acceptance of your environment even though that acceptance give pain. Religion is thus pre-eminently social, for the necessity of sacrifice is born from the fact of society.

The object of religion is clearly to repress the evil and individualist passions of men, to make them capable thereby of social existence. Only the Catholic faith can do this at all adequately because only the Catholic faith is truly one. It insists on the repression of the individual will. It has only a single sovereign, since that which the pope commands is at once universal law. Obedience to his command is the basis of membership of his church. So that Catholicism does not follow the fatal path of Luther and of Calvin. It forbids man to think for himself. It prescribes the belief he may alone accept. It thus secures within itself the constant exercise of that general will of which the operation is the condition of social permanence. Religion, for Bonald, is thus a training in social conduct. It is the great defender of society. By teaching men resignation, by preventing them from following the will o' the wisp of their private intellectual whim, it safeguards the maintenance of principle. It thus interacts with the state. There is very clearly a joint relation between two institutions so obviously complementary in character. Civilised society, indeed, is simply religion in its political aspect. It is religion considered in its human emphasis.

If that is true, then Bonald cannot doubt that religion must

[108] "Théorie du Pouvoir," II, Bk. I, Ch. II, p. 22.

be the guiding factor in the state.[109]   Religion has given to the
state the assistance which makes its life possible.   Religion
must then be restored to its erstwhile sovereignty over men.
The chief cause of political decay is the contempt which evil
men have poured upon it for their own base purposes.   The
obvious policy of enlightened government is to restore it to
the fullness of its power.[110]   Such a restoration would posit as
axiomatic the principles of his faith.   Education would minister to its needs.   It would preach the gospel of duty and therein
find the sanction of tradition.   It is Catholicism alone, in fact,
which has the sure proof of excellence which comes from antiquity.   It alone has preached an unchanging social doctrine.
To ensure its dominance is to give to France the religion most
in accord with her history.   Tradition associates French glory
with Catholic success and its rehabilitation would give to the
throne the proud weight of its incomparable power.

He would go even further.   He would not permit the existence of more than one religion in a country.   So to do is to
destroy the fundamental unity which Catholicism predicates.
Without identity of belief the gate is open for civil war; but
where men think alike the tragedy of dissident action is impossible.   Intolerance is thus essential to his outlook, and, like
Lamennais in the earlier phase of his thought, he saw no distinction between toleration and indifference.   To allow the
preaching of other faiths was for him only to proclaim that
you are uncertain of the truth about your own.   Men tolerate
only where they do not love.   Those who have firm hold of
Catholic truth know that its alternative is unthinkable.   For
once Protestantism is given a foothold, it treads the primrose
path to anarchy.   Men cease then to believe in the necessity
of sacrifice, and the vaunting pride of jealous ambition strikes
a fatal blow at the solidarity of the political fabric.   Only intolerance, in fact, makes possible the "philosophie de nous"
with which he proposed to replace the egocentric creed of Voltaire and of Rousseau.[111]   In this aspect, of course, nothing was
less wise than the Edict of Nantes, nothing more politic than

[109] "Leg. Prim.," II, 115.
[110] *Ibid.*, i, 180.
[111] "Oeuvres," XII, 65.

its reversal. For the edict split the French state into two irreconcilable halves and destroyed the unity of power. Richelieu's attention was diverted from the necessities of foreign war simply because he could not depend on the support of the people. The seed of opposition had been planted and La Rochelle was its harvesting.

He has thus a simple and mechanical view of the interaction between religion and politics. "Quand il (le pouvoir) manque d'un côté" he wrote,[112] "il en faut d'avantage d'un autre." Relax the bonds of religious discipline and he did not doubt that the result would be written in the records of crime. And religion is the real basis of all because it gives the sentiment to men upon which their fortitude is founded. It bids them do their duty, where, otherwise, they would not hesitate to act from motives of self-interest. It thus draws men's minds to the great end. It insists on their social context. It points to unity as the plain object of their endeavour. It is favourable to monarchy by that very reason. But unity is always in danger of attack from malicious ambition. That is why liberty of thought, no less in politics than in religion, must be restrained.[113] The really intelligent man is he who knows that what he preaches is so supremely important that he will permit no divergence from his opinion. Enlightenment for him is only the subjective aspect of intolerance, and Bonald did not doubt that he was enlightened. And because he thought government as necessary as food,[114] he welcomed religion as a means of stimulation where the appetite might otherwise be lacking. The Catholic religion became in this aspect the more vital since it alone insisted that the source of nourishment must be single. So convinced was he of the virtue of the unity it so rigidly prescribed that he found the sovereign safeguard of civilisation in the return of Protestants to the Catholic fold.[115] Otherwise, it was clear, the power of the world would continue to be divided. But power was to be compared to a seamless tunic which cannot be torn asunder.[116]

[112] "Pensées Diverses," p. 33.
[113] "Oeuvres," X, 258.
[114] "Pensées Diverses," p. 12.
[115] "Oeuvres," X, 296.
[116] "Oeuvres," XI, 121.

Very clearly, what he was eager to discover was the sovereign remedy against thought. He welcomed the Catholic religion simply because it rendered all speculation a superfluity. It asked men only to believe and it named faith the proudest of the virtues. He genuinely feared the declaration of principles founded upon intelligent enquiry. To give privileges was to admit rights and to admit rights was to extend them. So that once reason was set to work there was an end to the stability of the state. The religion that made of reason an unnecessary luxury was thus naturally in accord with his temper. "Le seul allié," he wrote,[117] "dont la France ait le désir et le besoin (est) le pouvoir." But, for Bonald, to put one's trust in God was to accept the existing world as necessarily perfect because it was the divine handiwork. To preach Catholicism was thus to steel men's hearts against thought and, as a consequence, to turn them away from revolution. Wisdom and religion became thus politically interchangeable terms. The only charter necessary to a well-constructed state was the charter of religious enthusiasm. It makes a people prosperous and happy, above all, it makes them contented and peaceful. The one object of the state must then be its promotion. The government which has not learned this lesson is already doomed, and has become the accomplice in its own destruction.[118] But a state that is wedded to religion has discovered the secret of permanence. It has destroyed all doubt of itself. It has attached to its existence the emotion of necessity. It has woven itself into the stuff of other men's lives.

VII. CRITICISMS

To such an attitude the Revolution of 1830 supplied the only possible answer. But it supplied an answer which, apart from its possibility, was at the same time decisive. For it showed clearly enough that whatever the Revolution of 1789 had failed to achieve, it had at any rate made men out of temper with despotism. The monarchy of the Restoration had not concealed its sympathy with Bonald's ideas. The spasmodic attempts it had made after the pale ghost of an attenuated lib-

[117] "La Justice Divine," p. XIII.
[118] *Ibid.*, 22.

eralism did not in any way destroy its essential continuity with the *ancien régime*. It even butchered the Charter to make a theocratic holiday and the men of Paris turned once more lightly to their barricades. For it is useless to answer unreason with reason. A spiritual prejudice can only be eradicated by the spectacle of passionate events. That which it attacks is the very basis of all that cannot be harmonised with its dogma and to the protests of the spirit the spirit alone can fling its ringing reply.

The detailed criticism of Bonald's ideas, in fact, would be an useless task. What he represents is not a system but an attitude. What he represents is the intellectualism of vivid emotions realised in a fashion peculiarly intimate and keen. He could never change his principles, and, indeed, he made proud boast that the world of politics is a changeless world which knows neither spring nor autumn.[119] His temperament was too unyielding to permit him the understanding of political philosophy. His mind was tragically inflexible. One who could see the Revolution and the Restoration unmoved was assuredly not created for the tasks of statesmanship. Sainte-Beuve, in an illuminating passage;[120] has compared him to a Roman of the ancient time, and the analogy explains much. For what fundamentally interested Bonald was character and by character he meant the strength to accept a given environment. His life was an unceasing protest against any effort after change. The meaning of intellectual or moral aspiration was unknown to him. All he could do was to postulate his principles and he attained them by the hypostatisation of his public passions. The man who could honestly believe that the exile of the Bourbon was God's punishment[121] on France for its national sin was assuredly unfitted to cope with the practical questions of so sensitive a time. He did not realise that the Revolution had marked an epoch in the history of man. Because he was able to blot it out of his thought and go back to the golden days of Louis XIV he imagined that others, too would forget. That they would choose to remember seems never

119 "Pensées Diverses," p. 29.
120 "Causeries," IV, 330.
121 "Pensées," p. 172.

to have entered his mind. That Rousseau might in fact have been more than a poetic will o' the wisp who spent fine phrases on inadequate thought he would not for one moment contemplate. The Revolution attacked the fundamental prejudices of his heart—religion and kingship—and all with which it was connected he came to regard as tainted at its source. He had, in any case, a narrow and unyielding mind. His letters reveal the courteous pedant who goes through life like a footman at a court function. For it must be admitted that there is something of the servitor in Bonald's nature. Honest, incorruptible, earnest—all these he may have been. No one can doubt that he felt deeply and had pondered much on the fundamental questions. But he was too easily content with the life he found to have the courage to examine its rectitude. He mistook his country estate for the Garden of Eden and the Revolution seemed to him little less than the expulsion from Paradise. He had been schooled severely by church and state. The pupil of the Oratorians and the royal guard never forgot the training he had received. Everything he wrote was conceived in full dress and wears the air of having been written in the ante-room of a royal levée. He has none of the light touch of de Maistre so that his words, if they are sharp, are not yet winged.[122] There are few instances in the history of political ideas of so able a man being so completely deceived as to the character of his age. He differs from de Maistre in that the latter, as his pessimism revealed, was essentially hurling a protest at a thing for which he could feel nothing save hate. But Bonald is optimistic, and if he does not spare the Revolution he has no doubt whatever of the curative effect of his remedies.

His simplicity, in fact, is the sole cause of his charm. That he was proposing the bitterness of despotism to a people which had enjoyed the fruit of liberty he seems in nowise to have realised. It did not in the least move him that the men he attacked should have written books which commanded the profound respect of able men. He had so childlike a faith in the nobility of his cause that he did not hesitate to ascribe disagreement to malicious egoism. He did not see that his king and his God could no longer exert the old fascination.

[122] Sainte-Beuve, "Causeries," IV, 330.

He did not see that a dynasty which had mounted the scaffold lost thereon the secret of its superiority, that a Pope who had suffered imprisonment thereby proclaimed his desertion by the God of whom he was the appointed vicar. The old watchwords had lost their magic. They had been dulled into argument and they could not justify themselves by debate. Whatever it had failed to achieve, the Revolution had taught men the splendour of speculation. It had become an impossible task to preach that thought was disease.

It is true that Bonald had the past on his side. It is true that the experiment against which he so passionately inveighed had all the danger of novelty. But because he clung so tenaciously to his traditions he shut himself off from the future. What in hard fact he was demanding was simply that the system which satisfied his emotions should be the accepted method of government. What he entirely failed to perceive was the still more indubitable fact that the majority of thinking men in France were dissatisfied with that system. It seems never to have entered his mind that there might have been cause for the Revolution. If Taine condemned it no less wholeheartedly, he had at any rate adventured some sort of examination.[123] It is not necessary to etherealise the Revolution like Michelet to perceive how inevitably it is the consequence of the system for which Bonald stood sponsor. He saw that system given a second trial; and he did not in the least understand how tragically it repeated its old errors. The simple truth is that with the march of mind absolute government is necessarily anachronistic. The will of man is an individual will; and it sweeps into the general will only to the point where the degree of fusion makes possible a social existence. But even while it accepts it questions and by its doubts it dissolves. So that, in any final analysis, democratic government is the only practical government simply because it is only in a democracy that an individual will can safeguard its reserves.[124]

[123] I say "some sort" because after M. Aulard's relentless examination in his "Taine, Historien de la Révolution Française" it is impossible to have any confidence in Taine's authority.

[124] This has been brilliantly asserted in Lord Morley's "Notes on Politics and History."

No man, in fact, will live a life ordered for him from without unless the state of which he is part has accepted a swine-philosophy. It has beatified order at the expense of thought. It has endeavoured to give men the minimum basis of material satisfaction and dignified their acquiescence by the name of citizenship. But that is not merely a stunted ideal; it is also an impossible experience. A state may have every perquisite of sovereign power. It is yet the clear lesson no less of history than of philosophy that the basis of sovereignty is the opinion of men. That was why, in the end, even the emperor of the great Roman kingdom came to depend upon the chance whim of his obscure soldiery. That was why, also, the word of an unknown monk commanded a respect and exerted an influence which shook to its foundations the proud edifice of papal power. Continuous order is the expression less of peace than of death. The *Pax Romana* was less the measure of civilisation than of sterility; and there came a time when men exercised their right to pick and choose among its benefits. What every unique sovereignty will sooner or later attempt is the control of mind. Yet it is equally certain that sooner or later it will exert its effort after control by the material pacification of men. But liberty has her compensations; and the result of that very pacification is the stimulus to intellectual effort. The men who have been fed into peace are nourished into examination. The offspring of food is revolution.

Bonald made the mistake which has been fatal to every system of politics thus far in history: he took no account of the progress of mind. He assumed an abstract man and confounded him with men.[125] It is a mistake as easy as it is disastrous; for every abstract creation becomes its creator's Frankenstein. Men somehow refuse to accept the categories in which philosophers would chain them. Their world, whether for good or evil, is a dynamic world; and they accept no moment in history as its apogee. But the result of such kinesis is clearly to make every political ideal adequate only for the moment when it is formulated, insofar as it is a system which claims a practical application. And because men are various they move in varied

[125] That is to say that the effort to depict him as a realist is without basis in fact.

direction. Their effort is different and their interpretations of life refuse reduction to a single scheme. The result is to demand a system of government of which the essential condition is the distribution of power. Political good refuses the swaddling-clothes of finality and becomes a shifting conception. It can not be hegelianised into a permanent compromise. It asks the validation of men and actions in terms of historical experience. For whatever history is not, the ancients were right when they insisted that it is philosophy by example. And since each age has different memories, there is no constancy of form or substance possible over, at any rate, long periods of time. Everything that is systematised becomes a category that is capable of decay. The peasant of Norman England who saw himself bound to the soil assuredly did not dream that one day there would be an England wherein the law would know neither bond nor slave; yet we who analyse the course of those events in which he played a part recognise the inevitability of the process. The king's will is law only so far as men will consent to its exercise. The king's will is law in the France of the *ancien régime*; but those men who in the summer days of 1789 gathered in the tennis-court of Versailles knew how lightly a monistic sovereignty is founded. Bonald may have been right in his contempt for all who were not of his order; he may have ground for his worship of Bourbon kings. The church in which alone he believed salvation to be found may in fact have possessed an exclusive right to its conference. Yet the world believed none of these things, and because it disbelieved, his theory of the state was no more than the emptiest of dreams. His social philosophy drew its importance from the fact that it summed up a vital epoch in the history of government. It explains, even if it does not justify, the effort of the Revolution. It makes intelligible the watchwords and the achievement of the nineteenth century. It shows why men had ceased to be satisfied with the formulæ of absolutism. For it is at war with every permanent reality of human life.

VIII. THE REVIVAL OF TRADITIONALISM

THE dead still speak, as M. de Vogué has aptly reminded us;[126]

[126] His "Les Morts qui Parlent," indeed, is nothing so much as a hymn in praise of tradition. Cf. M. Bourget's essay in "Etudes et Portraits" Vol. III.

and the doctrines of Bonald have found a curious revivification in our time.[127] The age when it was permissible to adore the Revolution passed away with the Franco-German war; and with its scientific interpretation a decisive challenge was flung at the pretensions of democracy. The authoritarian tradition, in fact, is far from dead; and it is only within the most recent times that the Third Republic has won the secure confidence of the French people. Even today its claims are rejected by thinkers of no light significance. To them it represents an intellectual attitude not merely distasteful, but even out of accord with the facts of social life. They look upon the Revolution as the starting point of the democratic adventure. They accept the enquiries of M. Taine as authentic history,[128] and they have not hesitated to condemn the fundamental dogmas for which it stands. The idea of national sovereignty appears to them a flagrant mistake, and as a consequence, they have been driven back to the *ancien régime*. It is in the idealisation of its political formulæ that they search the avenue of social salvation. They deny the validity of the democratic state. For them, it results in a partition of power which is wasteful. It makes pretence to an egalitarianism fundamentally incapable of realisation. It allies itself to a febrile nationalism which is no more than the momentary confidence born of a premature faith in the possibilities of science. The things they believe essential to the right ordering of society-religion, unity of power inequality, the mysticism of faith—all these they rightly perceive are out of accord with the traditions of democratic régime.[129] The transformation of the modern state thus seems to them fraught with the gravest dangers to its welfare. It is the spirit, at any rate, of Bonald; and few things have a more curious interest than this renewed enthusiasm for his dogmas.

Historically, indeed, the bond of intellectual filiation is logical and clear. The traditionalist and ultramontane schools

[127] M. M. Bourget and Salamon have edited a selection of his works with a preface by the former. Cf. also L. Dimier, "Les Maîtres de la Contre-Révolution" and the two laborious articles by C. Marechal in the "Annales de Philosophie Chrétienne" for 1910 and 1911.

[128] Cf. M. Bourget's study, "Etude et Portraits," III, 82-113.

[129] Cf. the very able and suggestive analysis of their attitude by D. Powdi, "Traditionalisme et Démoratie."

exercised upon Combe the profoundest influence; and positivism, accordingly, had nò sympathy with democracy.   He believed in the value of integrated organisation; and it was from that starting-point that he began his assault upon individualism. He was impressed, like Bonald, with the inequalities of men; and in the distribution of power he saw its dissolution.   Liberty seemed to him the most fatal of errors, and the yearning for it no more than a disease of the Western mind.   He equated liberty with anarchy, and the Declaration of Rights he dismissed as private metaphysics.   He desired a science of experimental politics amd its criteria of good were to be based upon the *status quo*.[130]   When there was added to his quasi-scientific contempt for individualism, his worship of order and of unity the materials for the modern protest were already prepared.   But to his analysis the illusions of the Franco-German war added the pessimism of Taine and the subtle pyrrhonisms of Renan.[131] The corner-stones of that edifice the nineteenth century had so patently erected seemed thus to be overthrown.   It then seemed legitimate to go back to an era untroubled by the necessity of accepting democracy as axiomatic.

It is this restoration which modern traditionalism has effected; and if the assault has been confined to a small group of thinkers it is impossible to deny the ability with which it has been made. Historical circumstances, moreover, have helped it much.   The last twenty-five years have seen a steady decline in the vitality of parliamentary government.[132]   The struggle against the church, the development of a labour party hostile to the state, the patent deficiencies of the civil administration, the relation between the army and the fanatic clericals have all combined

[130] Cf. the remarkable essay of M. Faguet in the third volume of his "Politiques et Moralistes." The historically, but not intellectually, important volume of M. Maurras—"L'Avenir de l'Intelligence"—is useful in this connexion.

[131] On the anti-democratic theories of Renan, M. G. Strauss' "La Politique de Renan" is of great importance.

[132] Works like Ostrogorski's "Democracy and the Organisation of Political Parties," Wallas' "Human Nature in Politics," Michel's "Political Parties" and Walter Lippmann's "Preface to Politics" show this attitude very remarkably.   Cf. also M. Charles Benoist, "La Crise de l'Etat Moderne," Vol. i.

to throw the most unworthy characteristics of a bourgeois democracy into its ugliest perspective. Even the stoutest defenders of the Republic have been eager for the adoption of new methods, for the discovery of a more effective synthesis. In the result, it has not been difficult to construct a case against the accepted axioms of democratic government. The science which overthrew the antiquated theology of the *ancien régime* erected no adequate system in its place. The political methods of modern government were found to be worthless instruments so long as they were not based upon the simultaneous possession of economic power.[133] The spread of popular education achieved far less than had been predicted for it. In the consequent disillusion protest was inevitable. Nothing was easier, and nothing was more natural, than to reject the political theory of the Revolution. But where the protest failed was in its inability to understand—as Bonald failed to understand—that the true course was rather to utilise the experience of the nineteenth century and to temper it by logical innovation than to dismiss the experience of a hundred years. The disillusion was less disgust than dissatisfaction; and it was not difficult to perceive that to the majority of men the cure for democratic failure was more democracy. However ugly might be the perversion of its forms it still, for most, at any rate, wore an aspect more politically acceptable than that of any other system. The distress which gave rise to renewed enquiry was born rather from a realisation of the eventual certainties of democracy, an impatience with its hesitations, than from any thoroughgoing rejection of its postulates. But those who denied its adequacy had at the least a superficial basis for their attack.

It is perhaps not surprising that it is from men of letters rather than from students of politics that the assault has mainly come; and they have therein finely maintained the great French tradition of making criticism a commentary upon life. What is fundamentally important in their attitude has been best represented by Brunetière and Bourget. M. Brunetière, indeed, is less a political than a moral analyst, and

---

[133] This is really the starting-point of the syndicalist attack on the state. See, above all, the very brilliant articles of M. E. Berth in the "Mouvement Socialiste" for 1907-8.

less an analyst than a superb master of intellectual controversy; and it is rather with the moral implications than with the political structure of democracy that he has been concerned. He represents essentially the reaction against the scientific movement of the nineteenth century, and what he has brilliantly performed is the relentless examination of its claims. But he has never forgotten that science and democracy are twin sisters; and his criticism of the one has been, in fact, a veiled assault upon the other. M. Bourget seems almost a reincarnation of Bonald—of a Bonald, indeed, who has read his Comte and his Darwin, and emulated the literary charm of Joseph de Maistre. He has occupied himself with the political foundations of the modern state, and he has attempted to undermine them by means which Bonald would assuredly not have rejected. Nor has able assistance been wanting to their enquiry. With every virtue except moderation and clearsightedness M. Maurras seems to have been endowed; and his ruthless polemic has given birth to a school of thought which is doing nothing so much as the reinterpretation of the *ancien régime* in terms of modern life.[134] M. Barrés has lent the support of his delicate nationalism to the reaction; and what his work has lacked in vigour and power has been more than compensated by the clearness and sincerity of its expression.[135] The conversion of M. Lemaître to this school is only the most striking of many similar changes.[136] It is hardly too much to say that the protagonists of the reaction remain unequalled in France for the power with which their cause has been advocated.

Complete unity of purpose, indeed, the traditionalists cannot be said to possess. They are agreed rather upon what they deny than upon their affirmations. The pagan eclecticism of

[134] The important work of M. Maurras is scattered over "L'Action Française." But see his "Enquête Sur La Monarchie" (1909), his "Dilemme de Marc Sagnier" and his "Trois Idées Politiques." An interesting criticism is that of Descoqs, "A Travers l'Oeuvre de M. Maurras."

[135] Cf. his "L'Ennemi des Lois" and his "Scènes et Doctrines du Nationalism" especially the preface. There is a brilliant critique of his work in M. Parodi's volume.

[136] Cf. Maurras, "Enquête," 427 ff.

M. Maurras can hardly live in permanent comfort with the strict religious orthodoxy of M. Bourget; nor has the religious doctrine of either any necessary or coherent connexion with the positivist Catholicism of Brunetière. But a school of thought they have been able to create, and the hypotheses for which they stand are a logical and adequate whole. They derive, indeed, a certain factitious interest from the political life of modern France. They are so passionately in antagonism to its fundamental outlines as to demand, almost of necessity, a careful examination. Their ideas are the ideas of men who have not hesitated to hold themselves aloof from a world with which they feel no sympathy. There is a certain self-satisfaction in the completeness of their paradoxes which makes them again and again willing to make a holocaust of truth that their logic may have her victories. But therein they are no more than true to the traditions they represent. They elevate their desires into principles in the approved fashion of Bonald. They follow their master in making their dissatisfaction with the age the foundation of their system. Every theory of the state, indeed, must in some degree be the expression of private thought. But it has been in a special degree true of traditionalism that it has, albeit unconsciously, apotheosised the subjective attitude. Its doctrines have been singularly more personal than those of any other school. Insofar as that has been the case, traditionalism has been, inevitably, a narrow and transient expression of discontent. It has resulted in an unreality which is entirely inadequate for the purpose of practical politics. But a weakness for the unreal and the impractical is perhaps one of the indulgences permitted to the upholders of the theocratic system.

IX. THE TRADITIONALISM OF M. BRUNETIÈRE

THE starting-point of Brunetière's attitude[137] seems to have been his dissatisfaction with the naturalism of the later nineteenth century.[138] In art and in letters alike, he found that the

---

[137] On Brunetière's work generally see Parodi, *op. cit.* 31-71, and the powerful essay by V. Guiraud, "Les Maitres de l'Heure," 59-141.

[138] Cf. "Le Roman Naturaliste" passim.

standards of authority evolved in the classical period of French literature were no longer accepted. This absence of traditional criteria seemed to him to result in dangerous consequences to social life. Not only were the naturalists pessimistic in their general philosophy, but they had surrendered all interest in, and all effort after, moral judgment. They became purely individualist in outlook, and they proclaimed the worth of experience for its own sake, without reference to its moral character. Their æsthetic was entirely subjective, and they seemed to claim, at whatever cost, the right to cultivate to the full their own personality. They trod, in fact, the primrose path to anarchy. Nor was this all. They did not hesitate to affirm that scientific progress had justified their pretensions. They were doing no more than to claim for art and for literature their right to the fullest enquiry. In rigidly scientific fashion, they were accumulating observations upon life. They were largely indifferent to the consequence of their examination; for it was not the business of the scientist to concern himself with practice. It seemed to Brunetière in the most dangerous sense immoral and unrealistic thus to disregard the reaction of enquiry upon life. It showed an absence of social feeling, a failure to understand that it is the bonds, rather than the interstices of existence that must be emphasised. The lesson of the naturalists would loose the chains of social cohesion. The overthrow of this critical anarchism was the business of every thinker concerned for the welfare of the state.

But an examination of the basis of naturalism led him, obviously, to the discussion of its historical foundations.[139] He could not hope to understand its origins without going back to the eighteenth century. It was here, essentially, that the root of the trouble was to be found. Voltaire, Diderot, the Encyclopédists, these were the first men who had not hesitated to peer into every nook and cranny of the social fabric. For antiquity they had less a sense of reverence than of distaste. They had taught men to be dissatisfied with their condition, and they had overthrown the traditional foundations of society. He could not but compare the confusion of the eighteenth century

[139] Cf. "Etudes Critiques," 4th series—the essays on Montesquieu, Voltaire, Rousseau.

with the meticulous sense of order so characteristic of the seventeenth century. He liked its air of neatness. He liked its confidence in objective standards of conduct. He was charmed by its *a priori* lack of discontent. The authoritarianism of Bossuet, in particular, took fast hold of his affections.[140] He began to trace back to its influence all that was effective for good in the moral life of France. Unity, faith, authority, order—these were the watchwords he evolved from his researches. Their absence from the creations of naturalism was the cause of its maleficent influence. It was clearly his task to erect an objective system of critical enquiry of which these should be the essential principles.

But more than this was demanded. Some part, at any rate, of scientific achievement, Brunetière was compelled to admit, and since naturalism threw around itself the cloak of scientific enquiry, it was vital to set limits to the domain of science. Here, indeed, he was confronted by the difficulty that while he was anxious to oppose man and nature, art and science, he was himself the urgent defender of the doctrine of evolution in the forms of literature.[141] It was clearly necessary to escape that conclusion, or, at the least, to bend it to his purposes. It was here, perhaps, that Brunetière made his most brilliant effort.[142] The causes of variation are unknown. Change is simply a fact—for which no reason can be ascribed. Aristotle, Molière, Darwin—we can postulate no adequate cause for their emergence.[143] They are simply given us; and their effort is the starting-point of each new direction evolution may take. What Brunetière did was to deny the applicability of causation

[140] The posthumous volume on Bossuet edited by M. Guiraud is decisive testimony on this point.

[141] Cf. "L'Evolution de la poésie lyrique" and "L'Evolution des genres" and "La Doctrine evolutive" in the sixth series of "Etudes Critiques."

[142] What follows is in reality a summary of his four volumes, the "Discours de Combat" and the "Sur Les Chemin de Croyance." The fundamental articles are "La Renaissance de l'idéalisme," "L'Art et la morale, Le besoin de croire" in the first, "L'Idée de solidarité" in the second, "La Renaissance du paganisme, l'action sociale du Christianisme, l'Evolution du concept de science" in the third, volume of the "Discours." See also his "Après le procès" in *Revue des Deux Mondes* for 1898.

[143] Cf. "Génie dans l'art" in *Revue des Deux Mondes* for 1884.

to this field. *Ignorabimus* he wrote large over the entrance to it. But immediately that admission is made there is room for a system of ethics which, above all, has objective standards of conduct. When we postulate the impossibility of knowing the causes of variation, there is need of the dogmas of Christianity. It seems, at least to the outsider, an amazingly scholastic syllogism; but, after all, the syllogism was the invention of the scholastics. For variation is caused by chance, and chance is only the name the eighteenth century coined for Providence. Evolution makes us a mosaic of ancestral virtue and ancestral vice—and that is essentially the doctrine of original sin. Here is the basis of the Christian teaching, and we accept it because its main achievement is to promise salvation at the cost merely of repressing the evil influence of our natural origin. We have to cease, in fact, to follow the reckless will-o'-the-wisp of individual desire. The main need of life is discipline, and we require discipline that social life may be possible. The worth of any doctrine thus consists in its social utility which Brunetière equates with its morality. But the demands of discipline are clearly order and unity; and order and unity can only be acquired by the recognition of the worth of tradition.[144] For tradition is the soul of a nation, the deposit of those traditions whereby its life has been guided. More, it is even a national protector, for it acts as a safeguard against the revolt of inconsistency. To accept tradition is to accept something which gives to life an objective logic, a guarantee against divergent aims and contradictory desires. Because we need discipline we must have tradition. But tradition is the twin-sister of religion and gains therefrom the adequate sanction of self-sacrifice. The one religion which rightly insists upon their worth is Catholicism, and it was the liberal wing of the Catholic party to which, accordingly, Brunetière offered his support.[145]

There is not an element in this doctrine which Bonald would have failed to recognise. Its insistence on discipline as the safeguard against moral anarchy is only a more pleasing form

[144] "Les Ennemis de l'Ami Française" in the first series of the "Discours."

[145] Cf. "Tradition et Développement" in the "Annales de Phil. Chr." for 1906.

of the emphasis laid by the earlier thinker on self-sacrifice. And Brunetière in essence rejected Protestantism for exactly the same reason as Bonald—that its foundations already imply anarchy. It was for that reason that he denied the fundamental formula of Descartes, exactly as Bonald, a century before, had urged the worthlessness of metaphysics. Both thinkers agreed that faith was the primary need—the willingness to leap into the dark hinterland of mental action beyond the limits justified by rationalist logic. And, like Bonald, this attitude led him to turn to the church as the best instrument of moral unity.[146] It would provide, in his view, the objective criterion of conduct by the enunciation of its dogmas. He even believed that freedom of thought would thereby be assisted, since the thinker, having at his disposal an infallible test of good, would have the assured means of right thought. It would thus bring peace to men's souls, a refuge from the tortures of uncertainty which drove the nineteenth century into an acceptance of moral indifferentism. Here lay the supreme merit of orthodoxy, that it gave life the integration of doctrinal consistency. That, indeed, was the virtue de Maistre and Bonald had claimed for their theories. They had been confronted by an age of disruption, and they had found in infallible unity the only relief from doubt. They had urged, as Brunetière urged, that without the sanctions of authority, the individual soul is cast chartless on an unending ocean. It was because he cared so deeply for right and wrong that he was willing to enchain the reason of man; but he made the mistake of his predecessors and identified his private theory of right conduct with the public needs of his age.

His whole work, indeed, is a protest against democracy simply because he has so overwhelming a sense of the dangers of moral error. He deems the fabric of society so fragile that he offers worship to the forces which, at whatever cost, have prevented its overthrow. It is a philosophy that is unwilling to take risks. It refuses all experiment of which the results are not merely predetermined, but are also pronounced good by a tribunal which faith has accepted as infallible. But such a theory can only end by taking things as they are as the ideal;

[146] Cf. "Après une visite au Vatican" in "Questions Actuelles."

for anything else would be out of accord with tradition, above all, out of accord with the oldest of traditions which is his own tribunal of enquiry. It matters, perhaps, but little that the progress of psychological science should run directly counter to Brunetière's ideas. What is mainly of importance is the realisation that the political implications of his thought are the exclusion of liberty on the one hand, and of equality on the other. It involves the exclusion of liberty because it insists that men shall think only in directions pronounced good by external enquiry. It thus takes no account of freedom of conscience. Its standard of morals has reference only to the general need. It sacrifices the individual to its sense of absorptiveness. It involves the exclusion of equality because the infallibility it confers upon its tribunal must inevitably be extended to the men who operate it.

We declare, in fact, the divine right of Rome, and the only equality men can then enjoy is the equality of intellectual servitude. It thus does more than release men from thought. It is determinist in that its fundamental principles are already known, and, as with Bonald, the only business of the thinker is deduction. It demands the unity of power; and, thereby, it asks from each of us exactly what the modern world has proclaimed its most priceless heritage. It is basically a static philosophy. It puts the mind of men into leading-strings and makes of Rome their driver. But it has been the whole lesson of experience that the development of Roman doctrine is, for the most part, a development forced from without; and by universalising the dominion of Rome Brunetière was, in effect, erecting a barrier against intellectual advance.[147] That the price of order can be too high seems never to have crossed his mind. Nor did he occupy himself with the problem of how order was to be attained. Like Bonald, he seems to have taken it for granted that there would be no period of transition from the anarchy of which he complained to the unity he exalted. He seemed satisfied that principles are accepted by the mere fact of their enunciation.

But, after all, the first fundamental truth is the existence of difference, and to ignore it is to avoid the central problem.

[147] As he himself realised. Cf. "Discours," 3rd series, p. 229.

What Brunetière did was to repeat the error of his predecessor and so to dislike his age as to misinterpret the conditions of action. He failed to understand that the problem in moral as in political life is a problem of guarantees. All that men are willing to sacrifice to society is the lowest and not the highest common factor of their intimate beliefs. For they are not simply members of a herd; they are something more. They are individuals who are interested passionately in themselves as an end, and no social philosophy can be adequate which neglects that egocentric element. That, indeed, is merely to say that no social philosophy can be other than pluralistic. Ragged and disjointed as a consequence it may be; and continually out of accord with venerable tradition. But this, after all, is a ragged and disjointed world, and it continually is guilty of unhistorical innovation. Sovereignty, in fact, has necessarily to be distributed in order that the purposes of men may be achieved. The test of their achievement, whether moral or intellectual, or political, is not an immediate reference to a permanent and external canon, but the consequences of action in the elucidation and enrichment of life. It is this, after all, which makes the loyalties of men so diversified; for they are bundles of conflicting aims.[148] It is this too, at bottom, which gives to the loose sovereignty of the democratic state its ultimate justification: that alone of all governmental conceptions it admits the adequate realisation of personality. A theory which would sacrifice them to its cross-section of logic is at once forced and unnatural. It has value, maybe, insofar as it throws light on the tendencies of the time; but it is out of harmony with its inevitable direction.

X. THE TRADITIONALISM OF M. BOURGET

The work of M. Bourget is little else than an assault upon the foundations of the nineteenth century.[149] It is from an analysis

[148] Cf. Mr. Lippman's note in *The New Republic* for April 14, 1917, and my "Problem of Sovereignty," passim.

[149] It is very difficult to particularise. But no one who reads "L'Etape" and "Un Divorce" with the three volumes of "Etudes et Portraits" can mistake the direction. There is a very clever attack on M. Bourget in Jules Sageret's "Les Grands Convertis." See also V. Guiraud, *op. cit.*, and Parodi *op. cit.*

of what he believes to be its character that he has come to the acceptance of traditionalist doctrine. Brought up in the school of Renan and Taine,[150] he has all their quasi-scientific precision of statement and of temper. His starting-point has been the disillusion they suffered after the events of 1870. They came to believe that democracy was a political deception, and it was upon the basis of their pessimism that Bourget has erected his theory of aristocratic Catholicism. Its resemblance to the ideas of Bonald is little less than startling; and, indeed, it is important that M. Bourget should retain for him so striking and peculiar an affection.[151] For him Bonald remains one of the great masters of political science, and no one has been more responsible for the resuscitation of the earlier thinker. It is Bonald, alone, moreover, who has surpassed him in his contempt for the eighteenth century. To them both the Revolution is the crystallisation of moral and political error. The Declaration of the Rights of Man they both dismiss as a puerile exercise in metaphysics.[152] Both are contemptuous alike of logic and the attempt to deduce a theory of politics from the abstract conceptions of individualism. For M. Bourget has no confidence in reason. For him it is an instrument of destruction, and he goes back to instinct, tradition, prejudice, for the real sources of events. He is uninterested in the idealism of the Revolution. It seems to him so contrary to the facts it encounters that he can have no patience with its trifling. When he has described the facts he has seen, he believes that he has been given the vision of actual society, and it is in his personal inductions that he has placed his confidence. M. Bourget, indeed, differs from his predecessor in that he is able to clothe his doctrines in a form of singular literary charm. He has at his command the specious terminology of modern science,[153] so that, often enough, what is in truth no more than a plea can appear in the guise of a statement. He never wanders far from reality, even if his realism is essentially selective. His work is a powerful polemic against the democratic state. Just as Bonald composed his attack in

---

[150] Cf. "Lettre Autobiographique."
[151] Cf. "Etudes," III, 23 ff.
[152] Cf. "Etudes," III, the essay on Le Péril Primaire.
[153] Cf. the curious first essay in the first volume of the "Etudes."

terms of the Revolution, so does M. Bourget express his attitude in terms of parliamentary government.[154]   But the real defect of Bonald's teaching was its completely subjective character. He built a state on the power of his own order, and deemed that he had thereby rendered service to the ideal.   M. Bourget, indeed, is less selfish; for his satisfaction with the bourgeoisie to which, by truth, he belongs, goes no further than the admission that it has its place in any scheme of political construction. But not less than Bonald, his argument is at the service of his desires; and he has the less excuse than the earlier thinker simply because he did not write under the shadow of 1789.

   No one, in fact, can study the work of Bourget without being convinced that the recognition of certain temperamental characteristics is fundamental to the understanding of his attitude.[155]   If M. Bourget is not a snob, it is at any rate upon the life of a leisured and cultivated aristocracy that he lavishes his affections.   There is no virtue with which he is not prepared to endow it.   Delicacy of taste, beauty of person, fineness of perception, clarity of insight—into the hereditary possession of these, his aristocracy comes by the simple fact of birth.   It alone is capable of cultivating all that is rich and delicate in life. Nothing is more bitter than Bourget's contempt for those who would seek to usurp the functions of an aristocracy.   His plebeians are always devoid of the qualities which can make them acceptable as other than obedient subjects.   They always end miserably when they seek to raise themselves above their class. For, by the mere fact of birth they are excluded from the full understanding of elegance and refinement.   The ordinary affairs of commerce and agriculture—for these they are hereditarily endowed.   But for the larger spheres of life, social, political, intellectual, they have no aptitude.   Thus the real tragedy of life is the exclusion of the men of talent from their rightful place in the world.

   It must, indeed, be confessed that the refinements of M. Bourget's aristocracy are a little exotic.   Most of his aristocrats are

[154] Cf. especially the "Crise du Parliamentarisme" in Vol. II of "Pages de Critique."

[155] On all this the earlier pages of M. Sageret's book are both apt and amusing.

a little weary, and they have drained the cup of life to the dregs. So that they have need of that which will enable them to maintain existence in its proper perspective. It is thus that they come to adopt the Catholic religion—as a kind of perfume for the soul. It is thus, too, that they possess themselves of the moral superiority which distinguishes their mind from that of the vulgar herd. For they wear their religion as a beautiful garment, and they have none of the intense realisation of its presence by which the lower classes deface it. Their acceptance of religion is largely a result of their world-weariness on the one hand, and their recognition of its social utility on the other. They accept it elegantly, in the spirit of an academician awarding a prize of virtue. They do not trouble themselves with dogmas. They do not, as German peasants have attempted, undermine its social character. They recognise its function in the promotion of social well-being, and they accept it out of duty to the position they occupy.

For the fundamental fact in their character is the uniqueness of their position. M. Bourget has continually insisted that the virtues he extols in the aristocracy are peculiar to that class. They form an *élite*, a caste. Study the world of politics or of industry, and those qualities are notably absent. And their absence is the more notable since the one object of the bourgeoisie is their cultivation. The simple fact is that nowhere is there present outside the aristocracy the *milieu* appropriate to their development. And since it is clear that these are the qualities demanded of a governing race, it is obvious that the aristocracy, reinforced, he will admit, by the upper class of the bourgeoisie, ought to have charge of government. They alone have the faculties which will take from the business of politics its modern uncleanliness. A class-stratification of society, at once formal and fairly rigid, he deems essential to its well-being. It is true, of course, that this class does not rule today. It is true also that its qualities are devoted to any save political ends; but that, after all, is the fault of the system to which we submit. Such superior beings cannot be expected to ask the suffrages of the mob, or to mingle with the modern politician. It is true, indeed, that men may

[156] "Etudes," III, 264.

be met who, though not of the aristocracy by birth, seem to partake of its quality. They, however, are exceptional; and the race from which they spring is rapidly exhausted by the effort it expends in the production of such imitations. We cannot erect a theory upon the chance fact of their occasional emergence. That would be to consider man as an individual and to give him rights in virtue of his own personality. But that is a doubly false conception. Social rights M. Bourget denies; it is upon social duties that he lays his emphasis. It is the duty of the aristocrat to accept luxury and refinement just as it is the duty of the peasant to accept his lot to toil. They accept it, because as individuals they are unimportant. The main need is to promote the solidarity of society and that is effected by the expression of its needs in terms of the family. Now of that the individual is but part and his personal tastes are thus insignificant. The fundamental fact, indeed, upon which Bourget's system of ideas is founded is the denial of an individual régime. For immediately we admit its claims we remove the basis of a horizontal social structure. We cast confusion into the state. Birth becomes unimportant. Culture is a matter of purchase and sale. Competition becomes the order of the day and an inelegant dynamic is the basis of the state. But that is the basic error of which the nineteenth century has been guilty.

It is clear enough—it is also unimportant—that such an attitude is out of accord with the current of thought in our time. But when M. Bourget left his romances to restate his social theories in a more formal guise it was upon the basis of these sentiments that he wrote. Nor did he fail to claim for his doctrine the benison of science. The fundamental virtue of Bonald, he pointed out, was his realism. He based his theories on the facts of social experience and his tremendous inductions have thus the validation of life. Such a method M. Bourget deemed finely experimentalist in temper. He compared it to the discoveries of Le Play, and, indeed, the researches of the latter have long been annexed by the traditionalists.[157] What M. Bourget did not understand was the simple truth that the im-

[157] M. Léon de Montesquieu has, indeed, edited an anthology of Le Play's writings on this principle.

portant contribution, both of Bonald and of himself, is not the facts collected, but the interpretation that is based on those facts. Bonald may emphasise the excesses of the Revolution just as M. Bourget himself insists on the deficiencies of parliamentary democracy. But the problem does not end there. There is a side to the Revolution which is not outrageous just as there is a side to parliamentary government which is not deficient. Where the scientific temper is not evident in the work of either critic is in the modification of his observations be facts which, however unwelcome, are still important. The experimentalist method, if it is to be valid, must consist in an accurate report of the experiment.

Nor is there more ground for satisfaction in the results of the enquiry, which, also, are for M. Bourget in accord with the discoveries of science. They are summed up in a plea for religion, for aristocracy, and for monarchy. That is to say that M. Bourget finds the real need of the nineteenth century to consist in the destruction of its own achievement. Nor is he at all uncomfortable in his denial of the Revolutionary assumptions. It is so easy to take its watchword as an abstraction instead of as a programme, that M. Bourget considers it refuted by the mere statement of the difficulties it encounters. Liberty he identifies with anarchy. He cannot understand the enthusiasm for its attainment. He seems to regard it as no more than the product of the uncritical enthusiasm of the eighteenth century for individualist doctrine. But individualism in only an endeavour to escape from the consequences of the social bond, and he is thus happy in his right to dismiss it. It is hostile to order and security. It shatters the exercise of legitimate authority. Nor is he less confident about the folly of equality.[158] This is obviously out of accord with the facts of every day life. But the mistake of M. Bourget is to think that equality is the expression of anything save an opportunity for the full development of personality. The study of his own master, Taine, should have taught him that obvious lesson. To proclaim that men are born equal is not in the least to proclaim, as M. Bourget would have us believe, that they are born identical. Equality so defined it is, of course, easy

[158] "Etudes," III, 140 ff.

to scatter to the winds; and where it is absent there is no real ground for fraternity. Brotherhood is born of similarity of function, and where there are the barriers of class, there is no ground for its existence. So that when the Revolution has been thus dismissed, it is at last possible to attempt the reconstruction of a France which has been untrue to herself.

To M. Bourget, indeed, the whole problem is as simple as an algebraic equation, with the consequence that his work has all the specious exactitude characteristic of Taine. The life of a nation is its tradition. That has in it elements of truth. But M. Bourget would use the tradition of France as a dogma and he will not allow the nineteenth century to form any part of it. For him, indeed, tradition is not a living thing, but a series of dead, inert principles to the logic of which the national life must be chained. The tradition of France is monarchical, regional, catholic, aristocratic.[159] So at least it is if one neglects its history since the Revolution. But that M. Bourget will do without difficulty because the nineteenth century has been a century of novel experiment and he is dissatisfied with its results. Disorder, individualism, scepticism, corruption, these have resulted from the adoption of the Revolutionary ideals; and M. Bourget is unsparing in his denunciation of their source.[160] Disorder is bad because only in stability can security be found. Individualism is contrary to the obvious structure of society. Scepticism is evil because the nature of the social bond demands the sanction of religion if it is to operate at all adequately. Corruption is the clear consequence of the method a democratic society must evolve for its governance. It is the natural result of a parliamentary régime and to him this is the head and centre of disaster. Legislation is passed in haste to suit the transient whim of the electorate. The most sacred rights of society are lightly violated. Promises are wantonly made and as wantonly broken. Personalities replace principles, and national institutions are dishonourably perverted to private ends. Party spirit replaces public spirit. The only fruit of universal suffrage is the pathetic manipula-

---

[159] Cf. his letter to M. Maurras in the "Enquête," and the latter's comment.

[160] "Pages de Doctrine," Vol. II, 52 ff.

tion of the electorate. The pretended establishment of self-government brings with it only the erection of a sinister oligarchy the more dangerous because it is invisible. The elective system fails to pick out those who can best serve the interests of the state. Argument is stifled by the development of a colossal bureaucratic machine. Within the chamber, talk has replaced action. The purely idle belief in equality has resulted in the withdrawal of the most capable from public life. The vital elements of the state, in short, are poisoned at their source. Heroic remedies are essential if so terrible a malady is to be counteracted.

It is, of course, undeniable that there has been a decline in the parliamentary life of democracies in the last quarter of a century. That has been true not merely of France but of every country in the old world and the new. But where Bourget's criticism is erroneous is in his suggestion that it is the root idea of democracy which is mistaken. The real truth is rather that we are working with a machinery adapted to deal with a civilisation immensely less complex than our own. It is only in our time that the full fruit of the Industrial Revolution has been gathered. Only since 1870 has it been fundamentally necessary for the state to relate itself to industrial problems. The decline in the parliamentary life of France is the decline that is natural to an organisation hampered by a multitude of unnecessary business. France has had to deal with constitutional problems, the Separation, the problem of administrative efficiency, a vast revolution in foreign policy, a new era in the history of labour. The whole centre of her life has been readjusted at the very moment when the mechanism of government has been most inadequate. But there is certainly not perceptible a decline in the quality of French life. Rather does the outsider see a gain in solidity and effectiveness. Her political thought has never been richer.[161] Her economic ideas have rarely been so profuse. Her literary achievements have been immense. The condition of her people has been vastly improved. And beyond the traditionalist group of which M. Bourget is so

[161] It is hardly necessary to mention names. But the work of Duguit, of Geny, of Paul-Boncour, of Leroy and of Hauriou constitutes an achievement of which any nation might well be proud.

effective a sponsor, it does not seem that there have been any doubts of democracy.

Certain new truths, indeed, France has been compelled to learn. We have too long regarded the discovery of representative government as a panacea, and nothing is today so greatly needed as new methods of administration. It is undeniable that what is vaguely termed the general will of society does not find complete expression either in governments or in legislatures; we are simply forced to the realisation that majority government cannot be the last word on our problems.[162] The real crux of the democratic difficulty is the fact that political power is divined from economic power. Wherein representative government has been supremely successful is in the securing of general political rights in which rich and poor alike have been interested; but once the transition has been made from political rights to economic interest the basic sectionalism of society has been apparent to anyone who has had the patience to observe the facts. What has happened is simply a growing consciousness on the part of the workers that the concepts of democracy are as applicable to industry as to politics, and we have lived in the time of criticism and unrest which is naturally symptomatic of the search for a new synthesis.[163] But the orientation of the problem is as different as possible from that which M. Bourget has given it. He is so obsessed by the political vices of democracy that he has neglected altogether their real source. He has failed entirely to see that capitalism on the one hand and the present form of parliamentary government on the other are nothing so much as historic categories which disappear when they have served their purposes. In the result the solution he suggests reads less like an answer to our questions than an interesting survival from an ancient time.

He demands a monarchy.[164] One of the follies of democracy

[162] Cf. Berth's articles cited above. Æ's "National Being" is an important landmark in this connection. Cf. *The New Republic*, Vol. X, p. 270 and the first chapter of my "Problem of Sovereignty."

[163] Of which M. Paul-Boncour in his "Fédéralisme Economique" (1901) has brilliantly sketched the outlines. Cf. also Maxime Leroy's 'Transformations de la Puissance Publique."

[164] On all this M. Maurras' "Enquête" is fundamental.

is its distribution of power of which the only consequence is
its nullification. But M. Bourget has only to study history to
see that the distribution of power is only the expression of certain social facts which are inherent in the nature of society.
It may be true, as he says, that monarchy unifies that power;
but that is exactly why monarchy is more and more rejected
as a form of active government by intelligent men.   It may
stand as the symbol of the national soul; but it stands as the
symbol of the national soul only in its antiquarian moments.
The self-interest of monarchy may demand, as M. Bourget
claims, that it serve the national well-being.   But the test here
must be historical and it is precisely because of its failure so
to validate itself that the monarchical solution has been rejected.   Supple it may be; but there are other forms of government no less capable of elasticity.   M. Bourget, indeed,
would urge that if the monarch be deceived error, after all, is
inherent in all human endeavour.   He suggests that the very
elevation of the monarch's position, his dynastic interests,
will make his evasion of error the more essential as his responsibility is the greater.   He finds in the monarchy the power of
selection in which democracy has so signally failed.   For what
is here necessary is continuity which implies the removal of
certain families from the mass of the people that they may serve
the state.   The corollary of his monarchy, in fact, is aristocracy—not, indeed, closed to external access.   The man of the
people will be permitted to ascend above his station, but he
must demonstrate his right and not assume it.   Here he goes
back to the ideal of the *ancien régime* and finds in a hierarchy
of classes to each of which its functions are attached the true
method of social distribution.   Of course it goes without saying
that the members of his aristocracy will be rightly chosen.   In
mind and attitude, in taste and in desire, they will have all
that goes to the making of a brilliant civilisation.   Such qualities it must possess since, otherwise, it will prove unacceptable.

Criticism of such demands is as unnecessary as criticism of
Bonald's ideas.   Nor is it easy to have sympathy with Bourget's plea for a restoration of the Catholic system.   It is, of
course, true that Catholicism is social and orderly and mystic.
It would assist his political schemes in that it has no room for

divergent belief. It acts as the consolidation of faith. It ex-
alts the heart over the head; and Bourget, like Bonald, has
no doubt that what comes from the Catholic heart is noble.
He demands the Catholic religion as a safeguard against the
disruptiveness of rationalism.[165] It will provide men with a
sanction of self-sacrifice. Its hierarchical organisation makes
it well fitted to stand sponsor for the monarchical idea. It is
zealous for authority, it has continuity, it has discipline. For
the purpose of protecting his antiquarian state he could hardly
have chosen better. But the very choice is simultaneously
demonstrative of M. Bourget's failure to understand his age.
The glamour of the theocracy he postulates no longer haunts
the minds of men. The worship of unity is dead. The oneness
we seek is the oneness of effort and not of purpose. We are
not willing to set conditions to men's dreams. We are not de-
sirous of returning to the orthodoxy of medieval time. Toleration has been the parent of liberalism, and liberalism has effectively destroyed conceptions of society which leave no room for
its innumerable variations of form and desire. With the power
that monarchy implies we cannot trust any man in so complex
a civilisation. We cannot mark off class from class in face of
the social and biological evidence we possess. M. Bourget has
to account for the structure of American society and the transformation of the English aristocracy before we can accept his
static theories.[166] The invitation he issues to intolerance an
age which finds its surest guarantee of progress in the freedom
of the mind dare not for a moment consider. Loisy in France,
Tyrell in England, stand out as the achievements of a democracy which has rejected the moral guarantees a rigid Catholicism has proffered.[167] It is otherwhere we shall search for new
hopes.

XI. THE SIGNIFICANCE OF VARIETY

So we are led to the rejection of unity. And it is worth while
to emphasise the grounds upon which we reject it. That for

[165] Cf. "Pages de Critique," Vol. II, p. 110 ff.

[166] The illogical character of his "Outre-Mer" is one of the strangest of
M. Bourget's many inconsistencies; for the aristocracy he found there
is barely fifty years old.

[167] Cf. the essay on Lamennais below.

which we are concerned is the preservation of individuality. It is fifty years since John Stuart Mill pointed out its relation to human improvement.[168] Certainly if there is one truth to which all history bears witness it is that unity is the parent of identity. But it is almost an equal commonplace that where men seek the ease and sloth of uniformity they are, in fact, if unconsciously, attaining the bitterness of stagnation. That was the error of the Eastern world. It was the secret which the great thinkers of Greece taught us by their example to avoid.

It is particularly important at this hour to prevent so grave a disaster. Democracy has made termendous progress in this generation. But the destruction of social and political privilege has a fatal tendency to extend itself into the sphere of mind. It is, indeed, difficult for a state at once to accept difference of opinion and to be effective as a striking unit. But that, after all, is the price we pay for our achievement of freedom. Nor is it unessential to insist upon its worth. "Mankind," says Mill in a famous sentence,[169] "speedily become unable to conceive diversity when they have been for some time unaccustomed to see it." To establish the singleness of political sovereignty is certainly to assist in its suppression. Political reality is never at bottom single, and there is no right purpose in its coercion to unity. Let the mind once bow itself to that yoke, and truth, at a bound, is sacrificed to comfort. Thus to submit to the pressure of a peace that must inevitably be temporary is, indeed, the subtlest form of self-indulgence. Thought is by nature revolutionary, and to the consequence of a great idea it is obvious we can set no limit. But, after all, thought is the one weapon of tried utility in a difficult and complex world. If it is to be effective we must place power in its hands; for to withdraw from it the means of active exertion is to blunt its effort after good. Therein, it is clear, the distribution of sovereignty is involved. Yet the forces that make against our progress are so great that it is hardly less than treason to our heritage thus to deprive ourselves of what service thought may render. Nothing, at any rate, is so certain to make our corporate life devoid of its richness and its elevation.

[168] "Liberty," Chapter III.
[169] *Ibid.* (Everyman's ed.), p. 131.

CHAPTER THREE

LAMENNAIS

I. THE PROBLEM OF LAMENNAIS

THE enigma of Lamennais remains still a problem for those who seek to probe the secret of the human mind.[1] The winds of controversy that so sorely swept his troubled life even yet are far from stilled. To many, he remains the arch-apostate of the nineteenth century; and to them, his abandonment of beliefs for which he had at one time so stoutly fought is, without exception, the greatest treason of which we have evidence.[2] He did not, like Newman, live to receive the homage of his friends, even while he retained the respect of those who rejected his philosophic outlook. He did not, like Tyrrell, create in his death a reformation of which, even now, the consequence can be but dimly conceived. It was by hard and tortuous thought that he abandoned the beliefs of his youth; and those on whose affection his life had been founded, left him to an end of which the proud courage could not conceal the lonely despair.[3]

There is a sense, indeed, in which his career is little less than the mirror of his age. For the course of his life represents not merely the reaction of Catholicism from the destructive assault of the French Revolution, but also the dawning perception in the minds of able men that when due rejection of its errors has been achieved, it still embodied political truth which is fundamental to the creative understanding of modern life.[4] The high-priest of the Catholic reaction, it was his fortune, partly, no

---

[1] I have appended to this essay a critical note on the more important discussions of Lamennais.

[2] Cf. Guillon, "Histoire de la Nouvelle Hérésie du XIX me siècle," and the work of Lamennais' friend, Gerbet, "Réflexions, sur la chute de M. de Lamennais" (1838). Lacordaire's "Notice sur le rétablissment en France de l'ordre des Frères Prêcheurs," p. 68 f. is in the same tone.

[3] Cf. the comment of the Duchesse de Dino, ". . . . et l'abbé de Lamennais qui meurt comme un pauvre chien aveugle." Chronique, Vol. IV, p. 159. (3 March 1854).

[4] The paper below on Royer-Collard endeavours to illustrate this thesis.

doubt, by what he wrote, but, above all, by what he was and what he symbolised, to forge the mightiest weapon in its undoing. By an intellectual evolution of which it is difficult to deny the logic,[5] he came to argue that all for which in his earlier days he had stood as so passionately the protagonist, was out of accord with the need of his time. Little enough is left now of the great edifice he so laboriously constructed. Pages, indeed, there are in his work of which Renan said[6] that no more brilliant anthology exists than that which could be gathered from it. But his books are no longer read;[7] for they were written essentially for a series of specific situations and the great work he dreamed of writing he did not live to complete.

Yet he remains as the champion of two mighty causes which still battle for the empire of the mind. The eternal struggle between order and liberty has received no more arresting embodiment than in his own febrile and tormented soul. The memory that remains not even the dull weight of time can, in the result, deprive of its fascination. He strove to answer problems of which we are still searching the solution. If we now state them differently, their fundamental content has in no sense been altered. That he wrote in an age before theology had been made scientific[8] has in no wise disturbed the basic principles of his plea. That he did not grasp the true basis of the democratic faith hardly weakens the argument he made on its behalf. He stood at the parting between two worlds. He strove to arrest the onset of forces he was at the last driven to recognise as irresistible. It is the dramatic quality of his challenge to those whom he had so splendidly led which gives him in the nineteenth century a place at once exceptional and important. He dare not be forgotten so long as men are willing to examine the principles upon which their life is founded. For few have faced so courageously the difficulties of existence. None has suffered more nobly in the effort to confound them.

[5] Cf. Janet, "Philosophie de Lamennais," p. 56 f.

[6] "Essais de Morale et de critique." M. Maréchal has edited such an anthology for his strictly ultramontane years.

[7] Most of them are now unprocurable except by accident.

[8] Renan has emphasised the significance of his lack of a critical spirit. "Essais de Morale et de Critique," p. 154.

II. THE CHURCH IN THE NAPOLEONIC AGE

HE had grown to manhood in the most complex and troubled age the church had known since the cataclysm of the sixteenth century. If the papacy had refused to make of itself the unquestioning instrument of Napoleon's purpose, it could not withstand the fury of his onset. He had proclaimed himself the protector of the ideas of 1682,[9] and the principles of clerical nationalism were invoked to justify an Erastian régime. Napoleon, in fact, looked upon the church as no more than an effective political weapon,[10] and thereby he gave to ultramontanism a new reason for existence. A church which lay at the heel of a military adventurer must search out afresh the foundations of its being. The localism upon which it had built so much seemed, in the result, likely to prove fatal to its sense of tradition and of personality. It was not unnatural that those who were attached to it by the closest of personal ties should turn from the old Gallican theories to principles which seemed to give it a wider basis for its claim to freedom. Sons of France its priests might be: but, above all, they were citizens of a religious society. To own allegiance to one who persecuted their church was to admit that the ecclesiastical power was inferior to the secular. But that involved the betrayal of a fundamental tradition. It seemed, too, to suggest that the events of which Napoleon was the symbol had won from them an adherence that was logically impossible.[11] They dare not reconcile themselves with the Revolution.[12] Many of them it had sent to the scaffold; many were in exile. Of those who remained in France not the least part had refused to take oaths which seemed to them the denial of their faith. For them, the church was itself a state, and they would not bargain over the nature of their citizenship with an organisation hostile to its purposes. And of that revolution, Napoleon was the heir. If he had restored a clerical order, it was clear that he did not love it. The Pope

[9] Nielsen, "History of the Papacy in the XIXth Century," I, 317.

[10] *Ibid.*, I, 223 f.

[11] Cf. the speech of Pius VI printed in Theiner's "Documents," I, p. 1 f.

[12] In this aspect it is important to remember that the Concordat of 1801 was in truth an ultramontane victory and was generally so regarded. Cf. Debidour, "L'Eglise et L'Etat," p. 210 f.

was a prisoner in his hands. Many of the cardinals were in captivity; and those who stood by his purposes were no more than the weak creatures of his defiant ambition.[13] What, above all, Napoleon taught the church was the impossibility of remaining a function of the state. It must work out again the principles of its freedom. It must re-establish its separateness that it might regain its purity. A church could not claim catholicity if it became the instrument of a single and jealous power. Nor did Napoleon render it the homage of an unique affection. To Jew and Catholic, to Protestant and Mohammedan he proffered his goodwill indifferently. But in the credo of the Roman Church such toleration found no place. A new synthesis was required if it was to be true to its ancient heritage.

So it was that men began to turn their minds to the task of its reconstruction. In that mission which was in truth the most tragic of exiles, De Maistre was forging the new weapons of a regenerated papacy.[14] Bonald had already asserted in his tremendous, if tedious syllogisms, the old dogmas of the ancient conflict between Rome and an earlier empire. The new ultramontanism, indeed, was no more than a different aspect of the old. Nor was what it preached absent from the hearts of thousands, even if the iron hand of Napoleon's crafty minister stifled it at the utterance.[15] But de Maistre and Bonald were concerned less with the church than with the state. If each adopted the theocratic solution it was not because they realised, *a priori*, that the starting-point of inquiry must be the rightness of ecclesiastical control. They approached the problem as statesmen, and their establishment of the papal sovereignty was, for them, less a principle than an induction. It was from the tremendous experience of an age so full as to make the previous generation already antiquity that they went back to Rome as to the parent of all social order. They urged the necessity of an ultramontane policy rather as an effective supplement to other means than as itself the basis of all things. Loy-

[13] Though Maury, of course, had great talents.

[14] I have discussed De Maistre's solution of the problem of the Revolution in the previous volume of these studies.

[15] For Fouché's work as censor see D'Haussonville, "L'Eglise Romaine et le premier Empire," passim.

alty to, and passion for its splendor they of course in no sense lacked. But what was needed was a philosopher who should speak in the name of the Church, and deny the principles of the Revolution solely as the servant of its claims. If Bonald and de Maistre served that end, it was the accident of good fortune rather than of design. But it was in the name of the Church that Lamennais came to do battle with the Revolution, to deny its principles and to refute its purposes. He came to vindicate the church from the trammels of state-control. For secular politics he had no interest. It was religion alone which held his allegiance. With the state, with Napoleon, he in no conscious sense concerned himself,[16] save insofar as they affected the subject of his enquiry. How to regain for the church her ancient sway over the minds of men,—this and this only was his problem. It was in the answer he made that he created the Roman Church of the nineteenth century.

He was a child of the Breton country, and his family inherited the simple loyalties of that primitive race.[17] But Lamennais, from the outset, was different. His temperament was morose, and the fits of nervous anger to which he was liable account, in some sort, for the solitude of his childhood. Books and the sea were his main companions, and to the end of his life he retained a passionate affection for the wild coast of Brittany. Away from it, indeed, he was never really happy, and once, in Paris, he compared himself to those exiles who sat down in ancient days by Babylonian waters.[18] He read much and widely; and it is difficult to doubt that his early acquaintance with Rousseau and Voltaire must in some degree have influenced his mind.[19] His own theories on education, indeed, show distinct traces of the influence of *Emile*;[20] but the pressure of events must have effaced the early impression of such disturbing thoughts. It was to his family that priests fled from the persecutions of the Jacobins, and in their house that they

[16] Note, however, the eulogistic passage in the "Réflexions sur l'Etat de l'Eglise," p. 21.

[17] Lamennais's ancestry has been copiously studied by M. Maréchal in his "La famille de Lamennais" (1913).

[18] Spuller, "Lamennais," p. 27.

[19] Cf. Duine, "Notes de Lamennais" (1907).

[20] "Correspondance" (ed. Forgues), i, 61.

celebrated, at dead of night a mass the more sweet because it was surrounded by danger.[21] It is not difficult to understand how firm an impression such scenes should have imprinted on his mind; nor can one hesitate to trace to them the secret of his hatred for the Revolution and its works.

But though he was deeply attached to the Catholic faith, he did not shrink from questioning it; and it was not until the age of twenty-two that he made his first communion.[22] That the erosion of his doubts was mainly the work of his brother it is not difficult to assume; and once they had passed Lamennais was able to accept the dogmas of his faith not merely in full sincerity but with some surprise that he had ever doubted them.[23] But that early hesitation is important, because it shows that his attachment to Catholicism was never unthinking. If, at the behest of his brother, he plunged into the bottomless abyss of theological apologetics, he still, even at this time, had a deep affection for Plato and Malebranche, for Cicero and Montaigne. We know too little, indeed, of these early years to do more than vaguely guess at their intellectual nature.[24] Royalist he was, of course, by inheritance. Catholic he could not fail to be in the sense that he accepted it as superior to all other religions. Yet there is no trace of fanaticism in his attitude, and the one certain passion which these years evoked was a hatred of the University in no degree traceable to any save personal causes.[25] The real starting-point of his religious adventure came in 1807 when he went with his brother to the little house at La Chênaie which was their joint inheritance. Jean Lamennais had only one object in life, the service of his church; and his indefatigable energy spurred on the undertaking of a common task. The result was the appearance, in 1808, of a joint-work on the condition of the Church. That is the true beginning of his career as a servant of ultramontanism.

We do not, of course, know how much of this early work is

[21] Cf. Spuller, *op. cit.*, p. 35.

[22] The story of these early difficulties is fully traced in Maréchal, "La Jeunesse de Lamennais," pp. 31-87.

[23] Cf. Laveille, "Vie de J. M. de Lamennais," I, 47-8.

[24] One cannot help feeling that M. Maréchal's fine book is marred exactly by this assumption of a logical sequence in Lamennais's ideas.

[25] Spuller, *op. cit.*, p. 67.

the product of Lamennais' own thought. That it enshrines much hard work on the part of his brother is clearly unquestionable; and in the fact that Lamennais himself refused it a place in his collected works,[26] is perhaps evidence that he did not regard himself as its principal author.[27] Certain it is, however, that it contains no doctrine which he would in his Catholic days have disavowed. Already its one clear effort is for the advancement of the church. Already he has a vivid sense of its corporate independence. Just as the experience of political pressure led Newman to the passionate denunciation of Erastianism,[28] so does Lamennais' dislike of ecclesiastical subjection lead him to demand an extensive cleric freedom. He stands at the outset as the avowed champion of its extreme claims, and he seems to enter the list as a knight who will encounter all adversaries with gladness. It is not a book of criticism but of assertion. It does not argue; it only pretends to refute. It is simply a statement of principles made on the assumption that they are axiomatic in character. It attacks the heresies from which the church has suffered. It paints in vehement colours the evils of liberty of thought.[29] It derides, almost with passion, the incompetence of the human mind. The whole achievement of the eighteenth century is dismissed with bitter contempt. The church is pictured as standing where it stood after the civil wars of the sixteenth century. What is needed is a new effort after freedom. The church must be released from the meddling of Jansenist magistrates.[30] There must be an end of the deadly egoism of the philosophers.[31] What can be hoped where the Revolution has spoiled, and the Directory persecuted.[32] If with Napoleon the Concordat has come that is the beginning and not the end of virtue.[33] Not until the church is restored to the fullness of omnicompetent power is

[26] "Correspondence" (ed. Forgues), i, 10.
[27] This would seem the net result of M. Maréchal's laborious researches. Cf. his "Jeunesse de Lamennais," Bk II, Ch. 1,
[28] Cf. my "Problem of Sovereignty," Ch. III.
[29] "Réflexions," p. 49.
[30] Ibid., p. 59 f.
[31] Ibid., 46-59.
[32] Ibid., 67-90.
[33] Ibid., 95-100.

there real hope for its future. What is needed is a regenerated
clergy which, now that the storm shows signs of passing, can
attempt the work of reconstruction. The life of the church
must be renewed in all its richness. The corporate vigour of
its institutions must be restored.[34] In scholarship and in
education it must resume its leadership and its control.[35] The
enemies are indifference and atheism, and without knowledge
they cannot be combated.[36] The book is clearly a programme;
and it is interesting to note how admirably it fits into the effort
of his liberal years. But it is also, on the whole, a moderate
book, nor does it, save by implication, attack the Napoleonic
settlement. Rather does it, not without much shrewdness,
suggest the inevitable lines upon which that settlement must
develop. Congregations are to be increased, missions are to
be multiplied, the faith more stoutly avowed. He was proposing, in fact, a church that should be worthy of the empire.
But that innovation must have been unacceptable to the imperial plans; for the book was confiscated by the police immediately on its appearance. The Pope had just hurled his
excommunication at the empire, and it was no time to think
of Catholic freedom.[37]

It is probably from that confiscation that Lamennais' hatred
of Gallicanism is perhaps most certainly to be traced. It
suggested to him that a strong church was not desirable to the
emperor. Napoleon desired to keep it in its chains; and he
boasted of their connection with the national tradition.[38] Lamennais could then but draw the conclusion that the result of
Gallicanism was the subjection of the church, and that only in
its abandonment could freedom be found. There is not, it is
true, anything in the "Réfléxions" directly incompatible with
Gallican doctrine. But the events of Napoleon's last years
were to force Lamennais to the conviction that a free church
must henceforth mean a Roman church, and he did not hesitate to draw the inference. It is in the light of this attitude

[34] *Ibid.*, 116-34.
[35] *Ibid.*, 134-42.
[36] *Ibid.*, 142-50.
[37] Debidour, *op. cit.* 263.
[38] *Ibid.*, 275.

that the study of episcopal origins is probably to be explained. The difficulties over the papal confirmation of Napoleon's nominees to the vacant bishoprics[39] gave to such an effort a peculiar importance. For to show the direct dependence of the bishops upon Christ is to argue, even if tacitly, that imperial interference is without justification. Apostolic succession involves apostolic independence; and Lamennais can urge that when the edifice of freedom is threatened, the time is not ripe for concession to the civil power.[40] The church must revolve on her own axis, and that the more proudly because of her divine origin. The two works, though they excited but little comment—Lamennais himself complains of the indifference with which they were received[41]—nevertheless are important in that they reveal a thought that is already formed. They did not, indeed, bring him reputation; nor did they still the tormenting doubt of his vocation which still caused him deep concern.[42] But they gave him a sense of his powers and were to prove the stimulus to further effort.

He had, already, in 1809, been received into minor orders, but he found no comfort in the thought of his priesthood. Already his letters are full of that bitter sadness from which he never obtained release.[43] "*Il n'y a plus pour moi,*" he wrote,[44] "*d'autre saison que la saison des tempêtes;*" and the thought was truer than he could then have conceived. He was uncertain of his career. Moments of confidence were succeeded by long periods of hesitation in which thinking and reading were alike impossible.[45] The earnest efforts of his friends could bring no peace to his agitated mind. In 1812, he seemed decided that the final step must be taken;[46] but he could not bring himself to act upon it. Meanwhile he continued to write. In 1814, he published, just before the Hundred days a passion-

[39] *Ibid.*, 265-8.
[40] Cf. Blaize, "Oeuvres Inédites de Lamennais," I, 108.
[41] Spuller, *op. cit.*, p. 55.
[42] Blaize, *op. cit.* I, 106.
[43] Cf. the pathetic letter printed in Roussel, "Lamennais," I, 22 f.
[44] Blaize, *op. cit.*, I, 107.
[45] *Ibid.*, I, 89.
[46] Forgues, "Correspond." I, xvi.

ate attack on the university as a servile instrument of the state. He re-edited the "Tradition de l'Eglise" and made it the occasion of a vehement attack upon the emperor.[47] He dreamed of a journal which should support the papal cause.[48] He thought of spending his days with his brother in perpetual collaboration.[49] But the mood soon passed. Even the Restoration gave him no pleasure; it was but the exchange of a strong tyrant for a feeble despot.[50] He disliked the antagonism of the Gallican bishops to Rome.[51] Ultramontanism seemed to him the one sure means of restoring Catholicism to its rightful position in France. So he re-edited his "Réflexions" in such a manner as to make more evident its Roman bias. A clergy with its own means of subsistence obeying only the sovereign and infallible pontiff seems to him now the one sure means of success.[52] It was the begining of that tremendous assault which sought to rewin for Rome the ancient dominion she had lost.

But the dream was not to last. Napoleon suddenly returned from Elba, and Lamennais, convinced that he was in personal danger, fled to England. He found little consolation there. His friendship with the abbé Carron, indeed, strengthened his resolution to enter the priesthood,[53] and he seems even to have thought of a missionary enterprise in America. But Napoleon's effort was broken into pieces at Waterloo; and Lamennais' return to France made his path inevitable.

But it was with a bitter heart that he strengthened himself for the last step. There is in his letters no sign of any gladness, no admission of any satisfaction. Rather does it seem to have been a response to the urgency of his friends. If it caused him anguish, they seemed even happy that he should be thus given so splendid an opportunity of self-sacrifice.[54] He was almost dragged to the altar by his brother and the abbé Carron; and

[47] See esp. "Tradit.," II, 306-8. M. Maréchal places their composition in 1813. "Jeunesse de Lamennais," p. 423.

[48] Blaize, i, 136.

[49] Blaize, I, 168.

[50] *Ibid.*, I, 150.

[51] *Ibid.*, 1, 170.

[52] "Réfléxions" (ed. of 1814), p. 96.

[53] Blaize, *op. cit.*, I, 215.

[54] *Ibid.*, I, 259.

there is no single fact to contradict the view that his decision was in truth wrung from him against his will.[55] Nor is it less certain that for him the step seemed to end all prospect of his happiness.[56] But it was, at any rate, a decision, and from the knowledge that it was irrevocable he may have derived some comfort. Henceforth, he was dedicated to the church and it was his function to do honour to her service. It was partly to drown the memory of his pain, partly, perhaps, that he might by work convince himself, that he took up with vigour his old polemic. A new era had dawned for France; and it might be that he could shape it to his purposes.

III. EARLY ULTRAMONTANISM.

IF the Bourbon restoration seemed a triumph for the Catholic Church, it was, in truth, a victory to which the facts themselves had set conditions. It was true that everywhere the union of throne and altar seemed the indispensable condition of national safety.[57] Nor was it likely thát men who had suffered so pitiable an exile would allow the ideals of the Revolution to obtain political or religious expression. But two fundamental facts stood in the way of a restoration of the *ancien régime.* The Charter was a guarantee of religious toleration; without it Louis XVIII could never have returned to the French throne. Whatever privileges the Catholic Church might, in the future, receive, it could not, as in the past, be the religious body to which the French State extended a unique protection. It would be compelled to endure the criticism of other religious societies which were no longer excluded from political existence. Nor was this all. The Charter had pledged Louis to the irrevocability of the sale of those national possessions in large part derived from ecclesiastical confiscation; and if this meant anything it meant that the restoration of church wealth would depend upon the doubtful generosity of an almost bankrupt state.

Nor was it a united church which returned to power. While

[55] Cf. Spuller, *op. cit.*, p. 87.

[56] Cf. the tragic letter in Blaize, *op. cit.*, I, 263.

[57] See, for instance, the remarks of the Bishop of Troyes in "L'Ami de la religion," I, 101.

men like Lamennais urged that ultramontanism had been justified by the experience of the Revolution, there were not wanting
able and influential men who insisted on the rectitude of Gallican
theories.   The French clergy, as a body, would admit neither
papal absolutism nor papal infallibility.[58]   They relied on the
generosity of the crown as the bulwark of their future.   They
had no sympathy with the Romanising tendencies of de Maistre
and of Bonald.   They were satisfied with the régime of a charter
which, whatever its defects, had declared Catholicism the religion of the state.   They were content to believe that historic
necessity would result in the restoration of what the Revolution
had destroyed.   They had none of the intractability of the
Petite Eglise; they lacked the deep sense of corporate independence by which the Ultramontanes were distinguished.   Where
they erred was in their failure to perceive that the promises of
the Charter were a fundamental stumbling-block in the path-
way of their dreams.   Whatever they might in substance a-
chieve—and of concessions they were to have a plethora—the
formal recognition of their desires had become impossible.
Louis XVIII might love to call himself the eldest son of the
Church,[59] but he was a son who by no means recognised the
patria potestas.   The spirit of criticism had gone too far to make
it possible for their ideas to obtain acceptance.   Their ambition
was bound up with an age that was past.   The future of the
Church lay with newer conceptions.

It was the signal merit of Lamennais to have perceived, even
before the Restoration, that it did not, in fact, promise real
hope for the church.[60]   The Revolution had taught him the
futility of placing confidence in the state.   He suspected its
motives, and he felt that it was guilty of a silence upon ecclesiastical problems which, indicated its lack of identity with
the interests of Catholicism.[61]   The fundamental problem was
the general indifference to religious matters which characterised the age.   If the temper of the people remained profoundly

[58] Cf. Frayssinous, "Les Vrais Principes de l'Eglise Gallicane" (ed.
of 1826), p. 89.
[59] Debidour, *op. cit.*, p. 332.
[60] Cf. Blaize, *op. cit.*, I, 152, 159, 170, 177.
[61] Blaize, *op. cit.*, i, 201.

Catholic, it did not find expression in dogmatic channels.   The essential task was to analyse the conditions of such an attitude and to attempt their remedy.   Chateaubriand had, indeed, sketched in magic prose the glories of Christianity; but he had conveyed an emotion rather than resolved a problem.[62] What Lamennais desired was to indicate the means whereby the Catholic church might regain its institutional integrity. It was without reference to the state that he desired to write. He would consider men as members of his church, and discuss the terms upon which its empire might be restored.   The "Essay on Indifference in Matters of Religion" was published at the end of 1817, and its result was to make Lamennais the first theologian in France.   Forty thousand copies were sold in a few months.[63]   The veteran de Maistre wrote of it with passionate enthusiasm,[64] nor were Chateaubriand and Bonald less generous in their praise.[65]   If there were some who detected grounds for theological suspicion, most men, as Lacordaire has told us,[66] looked upon its author as a new Bossuet.   Henceforward he was the uncontested chief of the Ultramontane party; and the government itself was anxious to win the adherence of one who had thus, in a single day, attained so notable a fame.[67]

The plan of the book is simple in the extreme.   It is an attempt to show that social salvation depends upon the supremacy of Catholicism, and it demands intolerance as the price of that victory.   It is the work of a man disturbed by the bewildering lack of unity in his time.   Everywhere there is indifference to fundamental dogma; everywhere men have erected their system of private alternatives.   On all sides there is an evident neglect of spiritual truth.   Reason and the senses fight once again their eternal combat.   But the fight against reason is the fight against order;[68] and the result has been the

[62] Cf. Spuller, *op. cit.*, p. 92.

[63] Boutard, "Lamennais," I, 152.

[64] "Oeuvres," XIV, 224.

[65] Boutard, *op. cit.*, I, 152-4.

[66] "Considerations sur le système philosophique de M. de Lamennais," Ch. I.

[67] Blaize, *op. cit.*, I, 285.

[68] "Essai," I, 9 (ed. Gannier).

pitiful lack of moral and political certitude. He does not, indeed, claim that this is a novel situation. Christianity— which for him is the combination of the spiritual truths thus far known to man—has struggled continuously to secure the paramountcy of reason.[69] It fought the selfish interests of imperial Rome; it triumphed over the persecutions of the decadent pagans; the attacks of protestant sects revealed the unbreakable strength of its foundations. Deism, atheism, philosophy—all these have left it unmoved.[70]

But the age in which he lives differs from its predecessors in the contempt for all belief by which it is characterised. Lamennais insists on the danger of this attitude. Action is the consequence of opinion, and when we know the faith of men we can predict their conduct.[71] Every idea reacts upon the social structure.[72] But every doctrine, being as it is either right or wrong, is therefore, of necessity, dangerous or beneficial to the well-being of society. The essential basis of an adequate social order Christianity had, at any rate before the Reformation, been able to supply. It had given a sanction to obedience. It had purified the customs of men. From its fountain the law had drawn its strength.[73] But with the Reformation there came a change. It was no longer admitted that authority was the basis of faith, and intellectual libertinism had replaced it. The Divine reason had been compelled to abdicate, and the human mind had not shrunk from the sacrilege of replacement.[74] Each man had become intellectual emperor over himself, and the spirit of independence erected anarchy into a social principle. It is obvious that society cannot acquiesce in its virtual annihilation.

The indifference he castigates so passionately has taken different forms in the life about him. Some deny religion for themselves, but admit its political value. They regard it as an admirable means of popular restraint.[75] But Lamennais

[69] *Ibid.*, p. 11.
[70] *Ibid.*, p. 12-18.
[71] *Ibid.*, p. 30.
[72] *Ibid.*, p. 31.
[73] *Ibid.*, p. 33.
[74] *Ibid.*, p. 35.
[75] *Ibid.*, Ch. II.

has no patience with this atheism. It cannot, so he claims, account for religious origins. It cannot explain the universal basis of society in religion.[76] It cannot explain the strength of the religious sanction not less in politics than in law.[77] He insists on the evil of the hypocrisy that would force upon men a faith in fact untrue.[78] Nor will he admit the natural religion of Rousseau. Humanity, he urges, has never been content with deism which is, in fact, only the vestibule of atheism.[79] It is no more satisfactory in its social result, and he cannot resist from heaping contumely upon its foremost representative. He does not, moreover, find Protestantism any less unsatisfactory.[80] It is the apotheosis of religious individualism. It destroys the unity of the church.[81] It has no answer to those who, like itself, take their stand upon the teaching of scripture.[82] It cannot have fundamental articles—whether sentiment or unanimity, or the admission of decisive significance.[83] It in fact denies the inspiration of God by substituting for his guidance the results of human interpretation. But, as a consequence, it leads in the end to atheism; for both claim to speak in the name of reason, and they are alike confounded by its social inadequacy.[84]

He had thus, in substance, denied the logic of any attitude distinct from that of Catholicism. What he had next to attempt was the constructive demonstration of its necessity. He had to show that religion was socially invaluable, and that by religion could only be understood the position he himself maintained. The end of man is happiness; but the condition of happiness is repose. Here is the first reason of religious utility for without it there is no contentment.[85] Surely the

[76] "Oeuvres" (ed. of 1834), i, 32.
[77] *Ibid.*, 34.
[78] *Ibid.*, 35-8.
[79] *Ibid.*, Ch. IV and V.
[80] *Ibid.*, Ch. VI and VII.
[81] *Ibid.*, I, 62 f.
[82] "Oeuvres," I, 60.
[83] *Ibid.*, I, 65 f.
[84] *Ibid.*, I, 73 f.
[85] *Ibid.*, I, 82.

cause of such a pronouncement is to be found in Lamennais'
own troubled soul. He had gone into the church that he
might find peace. It was then but natural that he should insist upon its splendour. But repose can come only when man
has discovered the laws of his being. Without them men cannot
realise their end. But those laws are religion and it is thus
that without religion men cannot attain their end. Philosophy
is useless for that purpose. What it does is to make of man a
God, and thus to destroy the bonds of social existence.[86] That
is an attitude socially impossible. All that we are, all truth
that we can know, comes in its origin from God.[87] We have
to put trust in him simply because from nowhere else is to be
derived the certitude and faith which are the conditions of
existence.[88] The result of religion is thus to put man in a
right relation to his environment. It assures that order and
fixity he so passionately desired. It centralises his life, and the
great object of human endeavour must be the discovery of
unity. That, indeed, is, for him, the whole object of order.[89]
To see life in terms of a single principle was to see it in the one
context that is socially adequate.

But unity demands its conditions. It can only be established by a system of relations. It necessitates the abolition
of interstices. The structure of society must be monistic.[90]
Lamennais has little difficulty in showing that this demands
an hierarchical organisation. The individual must be sacrificed simply because he has no interest except in relation to
the larger whole. The real unit, in fact, is society itself and man
becomes no more than a fragmentary moment of its existence.[91]
But the equilibrium must be maintained and power is its instrument. It is, indeed, the fatal error of philosophy that it
destroys that power; for when it proclaims the self-mastery
of men it in fact removes the foundation of authority. No

[86] *Ibid.*, I, 85.
[87] *Ibid.*, I, 90.
[88] *Ibid.*, I, 91.
[89] *Ibid.*, I, 97.
[90] *Ibid.*, I, 98.
[91] *Ibid.*

one will, he urges,[92] has any real right to assert its superiority over another. That is the flaw in Rousseau's social contract.[93] To make will the basis of society is at once to admit anarchy. But to derive society from God, to coerce its elements into oneness by the force of religion is to find a basis for the beliefs he cherished so deeply. It is then not difficult to urge that man exists for the glory of God and that the perfect and eternal society is that in which the glory of God is most amply pursued.[94] The littleness of the individual beside so infinite an end is clear; and Lamennais can take comfort in the pain that he has suffered by the thought that he in fact ministers to a harmony to which his very pain contributes.

It is here, moreover, that the church emerges; for man has to relate himself to God, and it was through Christ that the mediation was accomplished. But the fundamental achievement of Christ was the foundation of his church,[95] and we have then the text of the whole argument, For the church was clearly founded that Christ might preserve those rules of social order he had revealed in his gospel. When he confided their preservation to the church he in fact entrusted it with the government of society. He made it the vital link in that system of relations which Lamennais had postulated as fundamental. That is why the denial of Catholic sovereignty is a crime;[96] for it is the denial through human pride of an order established by God. All power, in its origin, must then be derived from the church. It is the guardian of social relationships. But the church means Rome, and Rome, as Lamennais was soon to argue, means the Pope. So it was that he went back to Rome that he might discover there the lordship of the world.

IV. THE GLORIFICATION OF ROME

It is not difficult to trace the origin of the first section of his essay.[97] To Bossuet and Pascal but, above all, to Bonald, it

[92] *Ibid.*, I, 99.
[93] *Ibid.*, I, 99.
[94] *Ibid.*, I, 134.
[95] *Ibid.*, I. 137.
[96] *Ibid.*, I, 139.
[97] Cf. M. Maréchal's fine analysis, *op. cit.*, 577-634.

is immensely indebted.[98]   It reflects the general reaction from
individualism so characteristic of his age.   Its exaltation of
authority, its insistence on philosophy as socially disruptive,
its translation of man into an entirely religious context—these
are the terms upon which Bonald and de Maistre had proposed
to rebuild the world.   Like them, even if by implication only,[99]
it was to Rome that he was driven back for his answer.   But
the book is everywhere distinguished by the magnificent originality of its spirit.   No one save Lamennais could have
written it simply because it bears in every line the intense
expression of the bitter struggle through which he had lived.
His denial of the importance of the individual is simply the
self-knowledge that he must sacrifice his ambition to the demand of his friends.   His picture of the evils of philosophy is
the angry farewell to one of the delights of his youth, the
attempt to convince himself that the sacrifice has been worth
the making.   The book, in fact, is essentially a personal docu-
ment.   But it is also more than that.   Its implications are far
more significant than the results it expressly declares.   Lamennais is laying the foundation of an argument of which the conclusion is an ecclesiastical imperialism based upon independence
of the state.   He is, in truth, insisting that for centuries the
centre of world-importance—a centre, moreover, distinguished
in his eyes by the divinity of its origin—has been Rome.   In
that aspect it is but a step to the demonstration that the
ecclesiastical federalism in which the Gallicans put their trust[100]
has no root in historical reality.   It subjugates the church to
the state.   For if power is Roman in its derivation, there was
good ground for the tremendous claims of Gregory VII, and
the minimising efforts of 1682 are so much error.   Such an
attitude, moreover, has even deeper immediate significance for

[98] Lamennais, indeed, speaks with immense admiration for the latter
throughout his work.

[99] It is to be noted that it was only later final attack on Gallicanism in
1825 and the following years that Lamennais expressly drew the obvious
conclusions from the "Essay on Indifference".

[100] A federalism, of course, which goes back to the conciliar movement.
Cf. Dr. Figgis' classic analysis in "From Gerson to Grotius" passim, but
especially pp. 16, 92.

the France of his time. It condemns the Revolution out of
hand. It is the text-book of intolerance, for it proclaims the
importance of orthodoxy in its liberal meaning of correct doctrine. That is, perhaps, in some sort due to Lamennais' own
character. Whatever he believed, it was essential for him to
believe wholeheartedly. He was above all things a great pam-
phleteer, and it was thus fundamental to his work that he
should be capable, granted his passionate temperament, of
seeing but a single side of any problem. The vivid eloquence
of the book gives it, even after a hundred years, a sense of
burning life which but little literature of its character possesses.
"Ce livre," wrote de Maistre,[101] "ce livre est un coup de
tonerre sous un ciel de plomb." But that thunderclap was,
in truth, no more than the vague herald of the storm.

For a decade after the publication of the first part of the
"Essai" Lamennais, while he was never friendly to the French
state, was at any rate not in active opposition to it. Nor is
the reason far to seek. If the Bourbons did not yield to the
enormous pretensions of the church there was always hope of
their surrender. The history of the Restoration, indeed, is
little more than a continuous effort of the church to capture
the political machinery of France. If too much was not to be
expected from Louis XVIII—after all a good-humoured sceptic
of the eighteenth century[102]—it was known that his heir dreamed
of nothing save a return to the golden days of the *ancien régime.*
And even Louis was willing to do much to efface the results
of the Revolution. The Concordat of 1817, whatever the
defects of its application was, after all, a great victory for the
church. An extensive attack was launched against the university—in a sense not the least fundamental of all Revolutionary institutions.[103] The Jesuits came out of their hiding-
places and made of the Rue du Bac a seat of government which
challenged comparison with that of the crown.[104] Missions

[101] Boutard, *op. cit.,* I, 152.

[102] Cf. Debidour, *op. cit.,* p. 331.

[103] It is indeed possible to make the struggle for educational control
between church and state the central thread in the history of France since
the Revolution. Cf. the admirable book of Grimaud, "Histoire de la
liberté d'enseignement" (1898).

[104] Cf. G. de Grandmaison, "La Congregation," *passim.*

and congregations multiplied with extraordinary rapidity. Members who sat on the Parliamentary Commission which examined the Concordat of 1817, did not hesitate, as a duty, to inform the Pope of its proceedings.[105] When it became clear that the project, in its original form, did not meet with the approval of the Chamber, its amelioration was effected by an act of grace from Rome and, even then, not through the ordinary diplomatic channels, but by a representation to the French government by the Grand Almoner of the French church.[106] When the Concordat of 1817 was finally abrogated, the clergy did not hesitate to stigmatize a ministry of which, from its own point of view, the sole fault was surely no more than weakness, as atheist in character.[107] Men like Bonald even affirmed that the creation of new bishoprics—in part, at least, a financial matter—depended not at all upon the wishes of the Chamber, but entirely upon negotiation between Louis and Rome.[108] When Richelieu resigned in 1821, it was permissible to doubt whether the state had not been reduced to the police department of the church.

It was as a journalist fighting for these ends that Lamennais is remarkable in these years. But he was clearly dissatisfied with the hesitations of the government.[109] He seems to have considered that the end of its weakness must be a new and more terrible revolution. So that he was not illogical in giving his support to those who were fighting for the most extreme claims the church could put forward.[110] But association with Villète and Chateaubriand inevitably meant the confusion of religious with political ends, and upon the latter Lamennais had no opinions. It is clear, moreover, that Lamennais disliked the use of religion as a political weapon. The extreme Right had, after all, ends to serve which made the religious question only a single aspect of its policy; nor was he certain that in those

[105] Debidour, *op. cit.*, 353.

[106] *Ibid.*, 355.

[107] *Ibid.*, 357.

[108] *Ibid.*, 361.

[109] Cf. the letter of November 10, 1819, to Benoit D'Azy Laveille, *op. cit.* p. 83.

[110] Cf. Boutard, I, 170.

other aspects he agreed with its aims. He had already come to regard opposition to the political results of the Revolution as impossible.[111] His own thought was almost exclusively occupied with very different things.

What, obviously, he was trying to do was to work out the principles upon which the French church could be regarded as itself a state—or rather part of the Roman Catholic state— of which the French government must not diminish the sovereign rights. He denies, for example, the right of the Minister of the Interior to ask for account of its charitable donations;[112] that is simply, for him, the irrelevance of unnecessary despotism. He insists that Gallican doctrine is subversive of the government of the church; and to postulate the inferiority of the Pope to the canon law he identifies with a spirit of license and rebellion.[113] He admits that the exercise of the clerical function is essential to the welfare of the state; but he is anxious for the church to build up, by means of foundations, its own revenues rather than depend upon official subvention.[114] He wishes to free the sacrament of marriage from its connexion with the civil law; for the marriage of Catholics concerns only the church which does not extend the admission of legitimacy to any other act of union.[115] He seeks to free the observance of Sunday from any reasons that are not purely religious in character.[116] When a Protestant is prosecuted for his failure to place a carpet before his house on the occasion of a religious procession, Lamennais agrees with the accused that the extension of toleration under the charter releases the state from any attempt to assist the church.[117] The state, he insists, is now non-religious in character, and where there is not complete fusion it is necessary that there should be the recognition of complete independence. So the civil authority may not force upon the church the burial of those who have violated its laws.[118]

[111] Laveille, *op. cit.*, p. 94, letter of March 2, 1820.
[112] "Oeuvres," I, 604.
[113] "Oeuvres," I, 606.
[114] "Oeuvres," I, 614.
[115] "Oeuvres," I, 616-23.
[116] *Ibid.*, I, 625.
[117] *Ibid.*, I, 626.
[118] *Ibid.*, I, 618.

The church has its own code of legislation and its self-sufficiency must be recognised.[119] From the principles of religious freedom that the charter has consecrated he draws the inference that the right to form associations is fundamental; for without them the Catholic church cannot prosper.[120] Because man belongs to two societies, the religious and the civil, his education is the function of both alike;[121] but he denies that government can in any sense act as the controlling agent in the process. The real decision must rest with the family, whose rights in this aspect no government may invade.[122] Clearly he is seeking to make of the allegiance of men to his church a thing in nowise distinct from that which the state may demand.

Nor is other proof of this attitude lacking. His interpretation of the Concordat of 1817 casts a special illumination upon his doctrines. The royal nomination to the bishoprics it established he looks upon as the concession made of grace by one sovereign to another.[123] It would, in his view, be impossible for the Chamber to create bishoprics or to define their functions. "Un pareil pouvoir," he declared,[124] " . . . . serait une sacrilège véritable de l'autorité spirituelle." He goes even further. He denies that the Chamber had the right to deal with the Concordat at all. In his view, the virtual withdrawal of that agreement was due not to its refusal by the representatives of the people, but by their unwillingness to provide the funds for its application. The Concordat itself he regards as no more than a piece of private legislation for the Roman church which the Pope, out of courtesy, had communicated to the king of France. Certain relations between the two required a readjustment of financial arrangements, but that was all. The analogy between this conception and the Catholic interpretation of Wiseman's famous pastoral of 1851,[125] is of course

[119] It is interesting to compare this situation with the similar controversy in England over the Deceased Wives' Sisters Act. Cf. my "Problem of Sovereignty," p. 118 n: 23.

[120] *Ibid.*, I, 629 f.

[121] *Ibid.* I, 649.

[122] *Ibid.*, I, 656.

[123] "Oeuvres," II, 123.

[124] *Ibid.*

[125] Cf. my "Problem of Sovereignty," p. 145 f.

clear. Each looks upon the church as containing within itself
all the essential elements of a state. That the field of territorial action is the same as that of the state proper it regards as
unessential; for the content of its regulation is purely mental
in character. But insofar as men give allegiance to the papal
crown it has the right to exercise a sovereignty over them.
"Le Christianisme," he wrote,[126] "est une société . . . . mais
point de société sans pouvoirs et sans devoirs, sans commande-
ment et sans obéissance; donc il existe un pouvoir et des devoirs spirituels, une autorité ayant droit de commander aux
esprits, qui sont tenus de lui obéir . . . . qui n'admit pas
un pouvoir souverain, perpétuel et permanent, ou ne s'entend
pas, ou nie l'Eglise." Obviously, such a conception of the
church leaves no room for secular interference. Rather does
it almost challenge it by the infinite power to which it lays
claim. And that was the more inevitable since Lamennais
makes continual insistence of the necessity of religion to the
state. At the same time to deny the state the right to suggest conditions upon which that relation may be established
is virtually to deny the right of the state to settle the terms
upon which it may exist.

Not even from that conclusion did Lamennais shrink. The
state has to decide between atheism and religion. If it chooses
to admit the latter it must not attempt the control of its associations. It must submit, where the influence of the church
is concerned, to the discipline it demands.[127] That is, in effect,
to submit to the Pope; for he accepts with eager gladness the
conclusion of de Maistre that the power of the sovereign pontiff
is illimitable.[128] To put one's confidence in councils is not
merely heretical, but even destructive of the basic conception
of the church. For the church above all things is an unity, and
to suggest a power above, or concurrent with, that of the Pope
is to destroy that unity.[129] So he does not hesitate to define
religious liberty as obedience to the civil power and to argue

[126] "Oeuvres," II, 129. The article is particularly important as it is an
enthusiastic review of de Maistre's "Du Pape" which had then just appeared.
[127] "Oeuvres," II, 156 ff.
[128] *Ibid.*, II, 135.
[129] *Ibid.*, II, 134.

that liberty is greatest where that obedience is most complete.[130]
To free man from religious obedience seems to him not different
from his erection into God; for from whom does power originate
if not from God?[131] He denies the sovereignty of the people
because its consequence is the subversion of all social order,
and a doctrine cannot be true of which the results are so disastrous.[132] So, too, tolerance becomes impossible; for it makes
of power the plaything of ambitious pride, and thereby destroys
at once its object and its function.[133]

It is a powerful assault against both individualism and the
foundations of the modern state. But what it lacked was the
demonstration—which neither Bonald nor de Maistre provided—that individualism is as a fact defective in its philosophic foundations. It was easy to dismiss the right of free
enquiry as the basis of belief; but the real necessity was to
show wherein its error consisted. It was to that task that
Lamennais addressed himself in the second part of the "Essai
sur l'indifférence" which he published in 1821. The volume,
indeed, made nothing like the sensation of the earlier portion;
and so careful a judge as Barante seems to have found it
tiresome.[134] But the book has an important place in the intellectual history of Lamennais since the theory by which he
sought to refute individualism, is, in fact, that which contributes most singularly to the destruction of his ultramontane
ideas. It is in reality Cartesianism that he is attacking. The
philosophic analogue of protestantism, it is the parent of social
disorganisation. So immense was the authority of Descartes
that practically unaided he had given a passport to rationalism
in theology.[135] What Lamennais strove to show was the bankruptcy of philosophy, its inability to solve the central problems
by which man is faced. He urges that the core of life is, in
fact, not doubt but certainty and that the basis of this certainty

[130] *Ibid.*, II, 165.
[131] *Ibid.*, II, 186.
[132] *Ibid.*, II, 188. In this he agrees with the famous speech of Chateaubriand, *Journel Officiel*, 25 February, 1823.
[133] *Ibid.*, II, 193.
[134] "Souvenirs," Vol. III, p. 126. Cf. p. 28.
[135] "Essai," Pt. II, Ch. 1.

is the unanimous testimony of men. In such an aspect, truth
is easily obtainable. It is no more, but no less, than the generality of men believes. It is not a system that he expounds.
What he does is to take those dogmas most necessary to his
system and to proclaim their truth by the demonstration of
their common acceptance.[136] Men have faith in God, and
therefore God exists.[137] The religion which rests on the broadest basis of visible authority is the Roman Catholic which therefore is the most incontestably true.[138] But if it is true it must
be revealed from God;[139] and that is to give it the authority
it had claimed for its principles in the earlier portion of his
essay.

Of the philosophic weakness of such an argument it is not
necessary here to speak.[140] It occasioned the most vehement
controversy, and there were not a few who regarded it as heretical.[141] The fundamental point was the fact that it left open the
road to liberalism. For Lamennais, after all, had only to convince himself that the majority of men disbelieved in ecclesiastical conservatism to be able to urge its untruth. At the moment
he might be the defender of ultramontane doctrine, but it was
the defence of a passionate individualist who thought that most
men believed it was right simply because he did so himself.
Rome, indeed, gave a tacit admission of the theological rectitude of his doctrines by permitting the appearance of an Italian
translation.[142] Whatever Rome may lack, she has the virtue
of abundant patience; and she was content to tolerate the un-
certainties of theological novelty where the political consequences were at the moment so beneficial.

Meanwhile, the political situation was giving new determination to the extreme royalists while it made the radicals more

[136] "Works," I, 177 f.

[137] *Ibid.*, I, 186 f.

[138] *Ibid.*, I, 229 f.

[139] *Ibid.*, I. 237 f.

[140] Cf. Janet, "La philosophie de Lamennais," p. 26 f, and Ferraz, *op. cit.*,
II, 180-210.

[141] Cf. Laveille, *op. cit.*, p. 121. Letter of November 9, 1821, and Boutard, *op. cit.*, Vol. I, Ch. XIV.

[142] "Correspond" (ed. Forgues), I, 41 f, and Cf. Boutard, I, 217, for a list
of distinguished Catholics who accepted it.

desperate. The seeds of the Revolution would have their harvest and if the retirement of Decazes meant the surrender of the king to the Right, it was evident enough that the intransigeance of that party was leading to disaster. Lamennais, certainly, did not deceive himself. The violence of the ministry seemed to him to be no less threatening than that of the Revolutionaries;[143] and he found their theory of a state-religion in every sense embarrassing. Between political atheism amd spoliation he was not anxious to make a choice.[144] The only sure remedy was the frank adoption of Christianity as the basis of society, and for that step the government lacked the necessary courage.[145] It was impossible, as he urged,[146] to give any sanction to authority without the establishment of a régime almost antithetic to that of the Restoration. He saw fear and jealousy as the guardians of national policy.[147] The principles of the Holy alliance seemed to him worthless; and already he foretold the onset of a new revolution.[148] The dislike of the Jesuits seemed to render impossible a genuinely religious policy such as he desired.[149] When men like Courier and Béranger were willing to undergo prosecution for their cause the unity he cherished was clearly far-off. The press might be controlled; but the passionate opposition of the liberals showed that patience would have its limits.[150] It was easy to attack such papers as showed a contempt for the State religion, and to deliver up the university to the priests. But each step that was taken only showed more clearly how utterly the old régime had passed. Guizot and Cousin might cease to lecture;[151] but it was impossible permanently to silence such men. Nor did the Spanish policy of the ministry prove as efficacious as might have been desired. The restoration of absolutism might be preached as a crusade, but

[143] "Corresp. entre Lamennais et Vitrolles," p. 86. I cite this volume as Vitrolles.

[144] "Vitrolles," p. 93.

[145] Ibid., 99.

[146] Ibid., 100.

[147] Ibid., 120.

[148] Ibid., p. 125, letter of Jan. 1, 123 cf., p. 132.

[149] Laveille, op. cit. 164, letter of Jan. 24, 123.

[150] Debidour, op. cit. 369.

[151] "Bardoux Guizot," p. 34.

the war was everywhere realised to be a disastrous failure which served only to make more evident the impossibility of royalist extremism. Lamennais might justify the Inquisition;[152] but he knew in his heart the folly of such efforts.[153] So high did passion run that the minister of the interior actually invited the clergy to preach Gallican doctrines, and particularly the articles of 1682, in the vain hope of assuaging men's anger.[154] When Charles X mounted the throne in the autumn of 1824 the clerical party may have obtained the king it desired; but it was the tragedy of his accession that his ideas made a successful reign impossible. For Charles was still the Count d'Artois and he was incapable of understanding the age in which he was to rule. The man of Coblentz could not govern a France which had tasted the sweets of Revolution.

The demands of the clerical party, in fact, were inconsistent with the charter which had been the express condition of the Bourbon restoration. What churchmen like Clermont-Tonnerre desired was simply the absorption of the state by the church; and if his audacious programme resulted in his prosecution, it was symptomatic of the temper of his party.[155] Charles' ministers might draw up new projects of a code of sacrilege in the manner of the middle ages;[156] but in the long run they could not meet the arguments of men like Constant and Royer-Collard.[157] The king might be given power to authorise by ordinance the establishment of new congregations.[158] But this in fact, was not a church-policy to which Lamennais could give his adhesion. It was Gallican to the core since it emphasised by its very nature the dependence of the church on the goodwill of the king. Villèle with his law of sacrilege seemed to him like the serpent tempting Eve in Paradise.[159] It seemed less like

[152] "Works," I, 193.

[153] As the whole of his correspondence with Vitrolles from 1822-4 makes evident.

[154] Debidour, op. cit. 376.

[155] *Ibid.*

[156] *Ibid.*, 379.

[157] See his great speech in Barante, Royer-Collard, II, 242 f, and the following essay.

[158] Debidour, op. cit. 383.

[159] "Correspond" (ed. Forgues), I, 191, March 13, 25.

service to the church than an act of devotion to the crown.[160]
"On pousse de toutes parts" he wrote,[161]"à une rupture avec
Rome et l'établissement d'une Eglise national, d'une Eglise
representative." What he desired was an opportunity for the
church to live freely its own life. One may imagine that he felt
this the more keenly since his reception at Rome in the previous
year had been all that his heart could have desired; the man
who found in the workroom of the Pope no other decoration
save the image of the Virgin and his own portrait[162] was not
likely to belittle the value of Roman influence, and that at a
time when Rome was more than suspicious of the Gallicanism
of French ecclesiastical policy.[163]

Nor, from his own standpoint, was he wrong in his suspicions.
The Gallican church had embraced the cause of royalism with
a fervour which suggested nothing so much as Anglican enthusiasm for the house of Stuart. Their bishops no less than their
priests seem to have convinced themselves that in the establishment of a royal despotism they would find the means of
ecclesiastical triumph. It is true that they did not hesitate to
make their victory the condition of their support; and it is
even possible to argue that many of them went further in their
demands than Lamennais himself would have done.[164] But the
fundamental fact remained that they were satisfied to work out
their own salvation through the state. What they wanted was
the exclusive establishment of the *ancien régime*; and they in
no sense realised that they were separated from their ideal by
the flaming sword of the Revolution. Lamennais saw more
deeply and more truly. He was far from certain that the cause
of monarchy was destined to triumph;[165] and he was unwilling
to prejudice the church by alliance with an institution which,

[160] *Ibid.*, I, 195, April 30, 25.

[161] *Ibid.*, I, 208, October 12, 25.

[162] Boutard, op. cit. I, Ch. XVI. It is impossible to know how much
credence may be attached to the famous story that Leo XII made Lamennais a cardinal *in petto*.

[163] Artaud, "Hist. de Leon XII," I, Ch. 20.

[164] Cf. the judgment of Viel-Castel, "Hist. de la Restauration," Vol.
XIV, p. 29.

[165] "Corresp." (ed. Forgues), I, 208, October 13, 25.

after all, would profit more than it would confer benefit by the alliance. He was acutely conscious of the important dissensions within the ranks of those who were eager to rebuild the ecclesiastical edifice. Clermont-Tonnerre might demand an ultramontanism expressed in terms of state-control; but there were men who, like Montlosier,[166] while earnest supporters of a church as the Jansenists conceived it, were yet bitter in their reproaches of a government which, as they urged, had surrendered itself to the clergy.[167] In any case, he did not like the idea of state-dependence. What he was convinced of was the power of the church to stand on its own foundations. It could reach the minds of men without the intervention of secular government. It was to the demonstration of that fundamental belief that he turned his energies.

V. THE ATTACK ON THE SECULAR STATE

WHAT, clearly, Lamennais feared was the sovereignty of the state; and it was to avoid its control over religious affairs that he elaborated in his discussion of the relations between religion and politics the basis of that theocracy which reached its inevitable culmination in the decrees of the Vatican Council.[168] He submits every sort and kind of question to the authority of the church, and the judgment of the church he equates with the papal judgment. The whole work, in fact, is a passionate protest against the implicit federalism of 1682. He does not, like de Maistre, attempt a historic justification of the ultramontane theory. Rather does he assert the simple doctrine that only, as a practical question, in the unified sovereignty of Rome can relief be found from the dangers by which the church is confronted. Every idea which tends to discredit the necessity of its unique control is, as he insists, a fatal blow at the whole ecclesiastical structure. What, of course, he is attacking is essentially the principles of liberalism. He attempts to dis-

---

[166] See Bardoux's able monograph, "Montlosier et le Gallicanisme."

[167] "Corresp." (ed. Forgues), I, 209.

[168] The "De la Religion Considerée dans ses rapports avec Hordre politique et civil" was originally published in two parts, the first four chapters as a volume in 1825 and the last set in 1826. I have discussed them as a single work.

credit them by proof that they are the logical precursor of anarchy. He denies the adequacy of any system which does not base itself and its rights upon the authoritative pronouncement of a single and supreme power. Without a centralised government he believes that every safeguard of orthodoxy is open to destruction. And since religion is the safeguard of the whole social edifice, it is clear that upon the acceptance of ultramontanism the salvation of society itself may without difficulty be made to depend.[169]

Lamennais, at any rate, so makes it; and it is interesting to reflect that when his own change of attitude was so near at hand the starting-point of his attitude should have been a distrust of democracy. The régime of the time he regarded as already—it seems incredible enough—no more than a representative republic,[170] and it was with a grim picture of its defects that he began his survey. The existence of the chamber he insisted was already the division of the sovereignty of the state.[171] The king was no more than a great memory of the past. His functions had passed from him to a ministry dependent upon Parliament. But that Parliament itself derived its powers from the people, so that France was already that democracy which is the source of political illusion.[172] But democracy lacks stability. It has no principles and it is irresistibly in a condition of perpetual agitation. You cannot teach it. It is contemptuous of authority and it trusts no one of superior talent. Those who attain its favours are always the mediocre, and they win their position by servility and dishonest adroitness. Democracy destroys christianity; for the latter centres itself round the idea of a single and supreme authority which is alien from the spirit of democratic government. And while christianity is conservative, democracy is by nature liberal so that there is already a fundamental incompatibility. It is thus that he explains the hostility of the Revolution to the church; for to strike at the guardian of orthodoxy is to prepare the way for that egalitaranism which he regards as no more than the parent of universal

[169] For a useful discussion of the whole work cf Janet op. cit. pp. 37-54.
[170] "Corresp." (ed. Forgues), Vol. I, p. 209.
[171] "Oeuvres," II, 15.
[172] *Ibid.*, II, 16.

confusion.[173]   There are, of course, minor confusions also,
corruption, the destruction of all sense of right, atheism and a
highly-flavoured type of despotic rule are sooner or later inevitable.[174] Legislation means no more than the triumph of special
interests, administration is the victory of caprice and incoher-
ence.[175] There is no longer room for virtue, and the multiplication of private speculation and invention results in the confusion of public prosperity with the progress of civilisation.[176]

Such an exordium does not promise well for particularisation.
When he applies these generalities to the France of the Restoration, it is at once clear to him that the state is atheist.[177] It is
true that the charter declares Catholicism to be the religion of
France, but these are words without meaning. It has become
essential to conciliate, and the real purpose of the charter can
no longer be maintained.[178] The result of this political atheism
has been to destroy the hold of religion on domestic society.
No one can now hope for a religious revival; indifference,
negligence, avowed disbelief are the characteristics of the time.[179]
Public instruction has become a political institution; and Bossuet's Defense of the articles of 1682 has become a text-book for
the young.[180] The law has come to look upon religion simply as
a political weapon; it is now a thing to be administered, a
public establishment which is recognised out of courtesy because
some millions of French men happen to believe in a certain form
of it.[181] It has thus become essential to regard Catholicism with
defiance, for alone of all religions does it pretend to set limits to
the sovereignty of such anarchic doctrines.[182] Protestantism is
in different case. Lacking as it does both dogma and discipline
it has no corporate bond. It is by its very nature destined to
dependence upon the civil power. But the duration of Cathol-

[173] *Ibid.*
[174] *Ibid.*, 17.
[175] *Ibid.*, 18.
[176] *Ibid.*, 19.
[177] *Ibid.*, Chap. II.
[178] *Ibid.*, 20-21.
[179] *Ibid.*, 25 f.
[180] *Ibid.*, 29.
[181] *Ibid.*, 33.
[182] *Ibid.*, 34.

icism would alone prove it to be the strongest of societies. It has, however, other and decisive virtues. It is divine in its institution and independent by its nature. It has its own hierarchy, its own laws, its inalienable sovereignty. It has remained unchanging from its origin. It has the noblest of missions. It teaches in the name of the greatest legislator of all. Whatever of stability the modern world possesses it owes to the Catholic church. Yet the exercise of its rights is hampered on every side by jealous men; and they seek to dissolve its unity as a corporate force. In such a situation the one object of men's efforts must be the preservation of its oneness that it may remain as the life-giving force of civilisation.[183]

What, then, he has to discuss are the conditions under which the existence of Catholicism is possible. He fastens at once upon its unity as the fundamental safeguard of its continuance. For him the whole motive force of the church has been Rome. It is he insists, [184] the constituting power of christianity. Only the name of Rome deters the enemies of social order from their fatal work. "*Point de pape, point d'Eglise,*" and that whether as a matter of history or of dogma. The church is a corporation in which true religion finds its resting place.[185] But, fundamentally, as it has been universal and perpetual, so it has been always one. But it could not be one unless it had a centre of unity, and that centre is to be found in the sovereign pontiff. So that if the pope is thus to be identified with the church—Ubi Petrus ibi ecclesia[186] —the consequences are clear. The Pope must be infallible and none must contest his authority. He is a supreme monarch, for once his decisions are called into question his sovereignty is worthless. But the syllogism is more tremendous even than its premiss. *Point d'Eglise, point de christianisme.* Idle dreamers have thought to revise the religion of Christ by reforming the church, but the result of their efforts has always been to destroy the principles of religion itself.[187] For to deny a single dogma is to destroy the structure of the whole; and what man cannot

[183] *Ibid.,* 85.
[184] *Ibid.,* 44. The phrase is De Maîstre's.
[185] *Ibid.,* 47.
[186] Ambrose's comment on Psalm XL.
[187] *Ibid.,* 48.

prove by his reason he must believe on faith.[188] So we are led to our conclusion. *Point de christianisme, point de religion . . . . et par conséquent point de société.* Once we declare ourselves independent of christianity duty is destroyed and vague sentiment takes its place.[189] Everyone, as in his own time, does as he pleases; the obligatory character of faith ceases to bind the conscience of men. But thus to loose the bonds of religion is to deprive society of the sanctions upon which its existence depends. So to attack the pope is a crime against society, an attempt at the destruction of the very principle of civilisation.[190] That we may be men, we must, in such an analysis, embrace ultramontane doctrine; and he will show from the examination of its antithesis how deadly are the effects of its rejection.

It is clear that in such an analysis whatever seems to diminish the strength of papalism is a severe blow at the roots of the church. Here is the real root of Lamennais' distrust of Gallican doctrine. It lays emphasis on the particular church instead of the universal. It fore-shadows a federal instead of a unitary organisation of its powers. What, above all, arouses his distrust is the fact that Gallicanism is not ecclesiastical but political in its origin.[191] It may demand "liberties" for the French church, but it asks them only that the state may the more completely destroy its independence. Gallicanism speaks of liberty; but the liberties of the church are rights that the pope concedes, and he would not concede the freedom of doctrine or of governance to a body which cannot meet save by secular permission.[192] But his objections go even deeper. The real effort of Gallicanism is summed up in two propositions each of which is fatal to Catholicism. It asserts the independence of temporal sovereignty. It assumes the superiority of a general council to the Pope. But he will admit neither of these conclusions. For to assert the independence of temporal power is at once to assert the duality of the world and thus to render impossible that reduc-

[188] *Ibid.*, 49.
[189] *Ibid.*, 50.
[190] *Ibid.*, 52.
[191] *Ibid.*, 53.
[192] *Ibid.*, 55.

tion to unity for which he was so anxious.   Moreover since the
church and the church only is the source of the divine law such a
doctrine assumes that a law made by men is to rank as of equal
worth with what comes directly from God.[193]   It does not even
admit that God's law must be supreme since it confers sovereign
power upon what is by definition non-religious in nature.   He
does not deny the existence of the two powers; but he insists
on the dogmatic and historical inferiority of the secular.[194]   Nor
will he admit that a council can control the papacy.   That is to
establish a collective sovereignty and thus to transform the
church from the monarchy it ideally is into a republic such as
Rome or Venice.[195]   But a collective sovereignty is no longer
unified, and to postulate it is thus to destroy the fundamental
fact that the church is one.[196]   Lamennais embarks upon a long
and acrimonious dissection of the tendencies towards church
nationalism so notably represented in his time by bishops like
Frayssinous and laymen like Montlosier.[197]   He denies that
popes can ever err.   He insists that the decrees of 1682 simply
deliver the clergy into the royal hands.[198]   But that is to weaken
the allegiance they owe to Rome, and to weaken that allegiance is
to destroy the corporate character of the church.   It is therefore
not merely uncatholic, but in its very nature it is the kind of
church that tends to dependence upon the good will of the
state.[199]   Even in the France of the Restoration, that good will
is apparent in the lack of fixity in the relations between the
church and the government.[200]   Today the church receives its
subvention, but no one knows the possibilities of the morrow.
The law passes an annual judgment upon the advisability of its
continuance; and its educational desires are frustrated by the
existence of the university.   The whole mechanism of church
government, in fact, is operated tentatively and with difficulty

[193] *Ibid.*, 57.
[194] *Ibid.*, 61.
[195] *Ibid.*, 65.
[196] *Ibid.*, 67.
[197] Cf. Frayssinous, "Les Vrais Principes de l'Eglise Gallicane" (1818);
Montlosier, "De la Monarchie Française au ler Janvier," 1824 (1824) and
Bardoux op. cit.
[198] "Oeuvres" II, 73.
[199] Cf. Chapter VIII, passim.
[200] *Ibid.*, 85.

when such continual account of the state has to be taken. It is only in complete independence that the terms of a satisfactory existence can be found.[201]

So he drives us back to the dreams of Hildebrand. There is but one pope and all kings are his subjects. The Pope must rule because, without his guidance there is no alternative but anarchy.[202] Where men erect themselves the judges of every social dogma, the fall of civilisation is certain. He deems that cataclysm already at hand; and it is to protect France against its onset that he proposes this pitiless solution. But, as with Bonald, Lamennais in nowise suggests the means by which that solution is to be applied to events. Nothing is more fatally easy than the diagnosis of social evils and their removal by heroic remedies. Lamennais lived at a time when the principle of authority could no longer command the widespread assent of men. If Royer-Collard and Guizot could find no comfort in his theories, it was assuredly not because they were hostile to the division of sovereign power. It was simply because an immense political experience had taught men that the safeguard against its abuse was its partition. Lamennais was striving to breathe new life into a loyalty that was already dead. The alliance of throne and altar no longer possessed the magic of the eighteenth century to support it; and he was profoundly right in his insistence that in such a partnership the throne would most greatly benefit. The dissolution of the alliance would, as he urged, give the church a new sense of freedom. She would cease to be chained to the wheels of the monarchic chariot. But the deduction from separation is not supremacy. It is one thing to believe that Rome is mistress of the world; but the fundamental fact remains that the greater part of men are unwilling to concede her right to dominion. He was right in his urgent assertion that Rome was a world-state and that the attempt to federalise her governance would be out of accord with her historic traditions. Rome has, since the Conciliar movement at least,[203] been consistently

[201] Cf. Chap. IX, passim.

[202] *Ibid.*, 93.

[203] Cf. Figgis," From Gerson to Grotius," Lect. II. N. Valois "Le Pape et le Concile" is a magnificent analysis of the whole attempt at, and failure of, the revolution in organisation.

Austinian in temper. She has set the model for centralised government, and not even the catastrophe of a Reformation or a Revolution could sway her in the direction of change. But she has been more and more compelled to surrender her position as a temporal power. She has been more and more compelled to confine her jurisdiction to the spiritual control of those who are willing to submit to her guidance. Even in Lamennais' own time she was losing that temporal expression of her penalties which, in the middle ages, had made what we now call the state, rank as no more than her constable. Luther had a final retort to her claims when he invented the divine right of kings.[204] Effective she still might be within her sphere —how effective the greatest of her advocates was himself within a decade to learn. But the effectiveness of her effort was no longer external; it had come to depend upon the consent of men. Membership of the state was no longer conditional upon baptism within her communion; and that, after all, was the final blow to her widest claims.[205] Her sovereignty, in fact, had been reduced from the universality of pre-Reformation times to a will, still, indeed, great, but now compelled to struggle not so much to advance, as actually to maintain its position. Men had freed themselves from the notion that power is justified by the mere fact of its existence. They had learned—and it is here that Rousseau has a claim on our gratitude that we have still to pay—that the fundamental problem in politics is not the description or maintenance of the organs of authority but the inquiry into their legitimacy.[206] In that light the claims of Lamennais were already obsolete.

Where, indeed, there was much to be said for his attitude was in his firm refusal to base his theory of social organisation upon no other consideration than that of public policy. Here, it is true, he was obviously medieval; for the abandonment of

[204] Of course it is much earlier in origin; but what Luther did was finally to make it effective as against Rome.

[205] Cf. for this view or in its most extreme form the "*Summa*" of Augustinus Triumphus (1473) XXVI, 5.

[206] Cf. the remarks on the distinction between Montesquieu's theories and his own in the fifth book of the Emile; and for his insistence that force gives no right the "Contrat Social" Bk. I, Chs. III and IV. I think T. H. Green accepted this view. Works II, 396 f.

the attempt to discover a natural order founded upon divine right is the chief political characteristic of the modern world. We have come to see that not the least significant criterion of any political structure is its expression in terms of the general happiness of common men. It is, perhaps, a more terrestrial standard than that which Lamennais adopts. He was above all anxious that men should be right; and he meant by right the acceptance of the extreme limits of Catholic doctrine. It is obvious, of course, that intolerance is implied in such an attitude and the modern rejection of intolerance seems based upon two assumptions of which Lamennais could take no account. We are too uncertain of the truth of any spiritual interpretation of life to give it the final sanction of complete authority; and we find that the historical results of intolerance in no sense justify its exercise. It is, in some sense, the banishment of God from politics; and in that sense we live in an anti-theocratic age. We have passed, as Mr. Figgis has finely pointed out,[207] "from the defence of rights to the realisation of right," and it is from actual experience that we give to right its modern connotation. What Lamennais did not realise was the historic fact that the multiplication of authority arose from exactly that process. Catholicism had abused its powers; and in the political no less than the religious sphere—he would, of course, have denied the legitimacy of such separation—new institutions arose to defend what men, if wrongly, at any rate sincerely, had come to regard as fundamental. The very existence of such diversity had relegated to the impossible the theory for which he stood. The old high-prerogative notion of sovereignty, three centuries of a history of which the Revolution was only a dramatic climax, had securely slain. His own theory of certitude by universal consent should surely have made him appreciate the significance of that diversity of opinion he so deeply regretted. But the time had not yet come when that realisation should be driven relentlessly into his soul.

VI. THE TRANSITION TO LIBERALISM

It was, at any rate, a striking protest; and if it met everywhere

[207] From "Gerson to Grotius," p. 17. The whole lecture is a very precious possession.

with a doubtful reception[208] it was yet a challenge which no weak government dare allow to pass unanswered. That was the more certainly the case since the very month before the publication of its second part the veteran Montlosier had charged the ministry with a cowardly surrender to the clerical party;[209] and even if the accusation were only in part the truth,[210] yet Lamennais' arraignment of the alliance between throne and altar seemed to give colour to his pretensions. The only step they deemed it possible to take was his prosecution; and his virtual acquittal,[211] after an argument in which his counsel, the great Berryer, denied that the decrees of 1682 were a part of French law, was in every sense a personal triumph.[212] But it was noteworthy that he had already arrayed against himself the episcopal powers of France. The bishops, headed by Frayssinous, addressed a declaration to the crown which was unexceptionally Gallican in sentiment;[213] and it was henceforth clear to Lamennais that neither from the crown nor from the episcopate was help to be expected.

That is the real source of his later liberalism. Disappointed by officialism in church and state, his only resource was the general mass of men. But, as yet, he had other hopes. He was still prepared to stake everything upon the action of Rome, and his letters show how much he built upon the accession of an energetic nuncio to the charge of French affairs.[214] Not that he concealed from himself the gravity of the situation. A long struggle was in front of him. From all sides there poured forth acrimonious criticism of his principles.[215] He believed, indeed, that the body of the clergy was well-disposed to him, and he still insisted on the glorious future of the church.[216] But that made him the more insistent on the need for a direc-

[208] Cf. Boutard, op. cit. I, 302-3.

[209] "Memoire à consulter sur un système," etc. (1826).

[210] It is denied, not without some interesting evidence by Grandmaison in his interesting work "La Congrégation."

[211] He was fined thirty francs.

[212] See Lamennais' own description of the trial in his "Corresp." (ed. Forgues), I, 246.

[213] Boutard I, 334 f.

[214] "Corresp." I, 241.

[215] See an account of these attacks in Boutard, I, 345 f.

[216] "Corresp." I, 253.

tion of their enthusiasm. "Tous les yeux," he wrote,[217] "sont fixés sur Rome . . . . qu'elle continue de se taire, qui osera, qui pourra, parler?"

He had ceased to expect aid from the state. His condemnation had completed in him a long process of disillusion. He could not interpret it otherwise than as a determination upon the part of government to use the church for its purposes. So that Rome only was left, and it was upon the issue of that confidence that his future depended. He seems to have thought highly of the Pope,[218] and though he declared that the idea of a national church was in everyone's mind, he did not doubt that once a frank word came from Rome, the loyalty of the provinces to the true conception of Catholicism would assert itself.[219] Rome, as he thought, could not long endure the supervision of its decrees by the government.[220] So great was the servility of the Gallican party that it had disgusted even the honest liberals. He was already prepared to believe that they would lend a new support to his cause if Rome would but do its duty. "Le monde a changé," he wrote to a friend,[221] "il cherche un maître: il est orphelin, il cherche un père. Le trouvera-t-il? Voilà la question." For, on all sides, the ultramontane position was menaced. Men who held his opinions were ruthlessly dismissed.[222] A society for the propagation of pious books was attacked because he supported it.[223] Orders of which the bishops did not approve were prevented from undertaking missions. People even went so far as to whisper that at Rome itself Lamennais' opinions were held in little esteem.[224] It is little wonder that he should have begun to feel a deep distrust of his opponents and that there should have crept into his writings that note of acrimony which made a distinguished Jesuit protest against his bitterness.[225] Even in the

[217] *Ibid.*, I, 257.
[218] *Ibid.*, I, 273.
[219] *Ibid.*, I, 274.
[220] *Ibid.*, I, 276.
[221] *Ibid.*, I, 288.
[222] *Ibid.*, I, 279.
[223] *Ibid.*, I, 270.
[224] *Ibid.*, I, 274. Cf. Boutard, op. cit. I, 350..
[225] *Ibid.*, I, 355.

Jesuits he had lost all confidence. Attacked as the society was on all sides, it had not ceased to intrigue with every party; and its declared ultramontane opinions were, for him, no excuse for the hatred it engendered in the minds of honest men.[226] The nuncio listed with politeness to his expositions of policy; but his responses seem to have been no more than diplomatic expressions of the papal difficulties.[227] If the ideas for which he stood sponsor were gaining widespread acceptance he still feared greatly the influence of authority against them.[228]

More and more he was driven to distrust the state. "Il faut d'avance," he said,[229] "poser les bases d'une nouvelle societé . . . . c'est folie de compter sur les gouvernements qui ne sont plus des gouvernements, qui ne peuvent plus le redevenir. Il s'agir de faire des peuples." It is a note which constantly recurs. Government might attempt the control of the press,[230] but he saw in it only a weapon by which ultramontanism might receive its deathblow. He was appalled at the incapacity of the clergy. Only a great reform could effect the requisite change.[231] More and more he feared that religion had ceased to exercise an influence over the minds of men. Europe had become simply a vast alliance of the strong against the weak and a system of principles gave way to a system of interests. Only when they regained their empire would it be possible to hope. Only one man could draw the attention of the peoples to their existence, and he was silent.[232]

That silence is the fundamental fact in Lamennais' transition to liberalism. Rome seemed to him too temporising in her attitude.[233] If she showed signs of compromise, that would be false to the future.[234] A new generation was arising which needed her direction. The progress of revolutionary ideas was evident on every hand. The government interfered with in-

[226] "Corresp." (ed. Forgues), I, 295.
[227] *Ibid.*, I, 298-9.
[228] *Ibid.*, I, 309.
[229] *Ibid.*, I, 310-1.
[230] Debidour, op. cit. 397 f.
[231] Vitrolles, p. 180.
[232] Spuller, op. cit. 144. "Corresp." (ed. Forgues), I, 348-9.
[233] *Ibid.*, I, 436.
[234] *Ibid.*, I, 466.

creasing enthusiasm in clerical affairs.   Speed, above everything, was necessary to the church's safety.   "Une immense
liberté," he wrote towards the close of 1828,[235] "est indispensable pour que les vérités qui sauveront le monde."   But that
liberty could come only when Rome should speak.   Lamennais
did not understand the thousand political considerations which
were the cause of her silence.   He was asking her to devote
herself to spiritual empire alone;   but that was to invite her
to surrender a faculty of temporal interference to which she
held firmly.   Nor did he yet understand that for Rome he was
himself less the guardian of a truth which meant everything
to her future than the head of a party within the French church
of which the success was more than doubtful.   Rome would
probably have agreed to many elements in his programme.
But she must have realised that what he demanded[236] she
would not attain without a struggle far more bitter than Lamennais can even have dreamed.   He was, after all, free;   and
he could follow his principles to their logical conclusion.   But
Rome had a hundred warring interests to conciliate and innumerable traditions to obey.   In the result, an abyss developed inevitably between their views.   His influence was growing and many of the younger generation were rallying to his
side.   The "Ecole Menaisienne" was already conceived at the
end of 1828.   Men like Gerbet and de Salinis were already
his firm friends.   Little by little he was coming to see that
authority, even in the church, may be poisoned at its source.
It was with this feeling already deeply rooted that he published, early in 1829, his "Progrès de la Révolution."

It is not so complete a rupture with his earlier views as he was
presently to make;   but the book marks in a real sense the
birth of liberal Catholicism and there are few of its doctrines
one may not implicitly find there.   In a society that is really
Christian, Lamennais points out, the unity of the people is
secured by spiritual ties;   as they submit to the prince so should
they submit to God.[237]   But from the time when Louis XIV

[235] *Ibid.*, I, 486.

[236] His programme is briefly summarised in the letter of Jan. 26, 1828.
"Corresp." (ed. Forgues), I, 416.

[237] "Oeuvres," II, 242.

proclaimed the destruction of the two powers the realisation of that ideal has become impossible. Two theories at least have arisen which aim at or result in its destruction.[238]   A liberalism so logical as that of the *Globe*,[239] must break every social bond; for while it denies sovereignty either to king or people, it replaces them only by individual opinion which is, in truth, to let loose the floodgates of anarchy. Nor is it favourable to liberty; for the condition of liberty is the existence of a legitimate power which shall act in accordance with the eternal principles of justice.[240] Nor is Gallicanism in better case. It is, in truth, a gloss for servitude. It does no more than free kings from the moral code and leads to their deification. It makes men think of religion as the natural ally of despotism and thus dissipates their affection for it. What is needed is a Christian order. After all, it is under the ægis of Catholicism that liberty was first born; and the guarantee of its continuance is the submission of the temporal power to the spiritual. If men turn once more to the church the destructive combat between liberalism and the Gallicans will cease.[241] With neither should the clergy ally itself. Rather should it proclaim its entire dissociation with all political life, and its connexion only with Rome. It must assert its ancient rights. The bishops must resuscitate the diocesan synods and the provincial councils. The mismanagement of the state in education and worship must cease. The clergy must free itself from the reproach of ignorance and take account of the march of knowledge.[242] The reign of the church will be the work of liberty; from freedom only can truth be born. Liberty of conscience, liberty of the press, liberty in education—these and not less than these are his demands.[243] "Sortez de la maison de servitude . . . . entrez en possession de la liberté." It is a cry that the church had not heard in two hundred years of her history.

[238] "Les Progrès," etc., Ch. II and III.

[239] The paper of Royer-Collard and the doctrinaire liberals. Cf. the admirable paper of Paul Janet in the *Revue de Deux Mondes* for 1879.

[240] "Oeuvres," II, 249.

[241] "Oeuvres," II, 251 f.

[242] "Oeuvres," II, 290 f.

[243] Cf. the preface to the Progrès de la Revolution.

The book is the logical consequence of his earlier work. Where, before, he had trusted kings, he now trusted the people; where before he had trusted Rome, he now puts his confidence in the collective power of the priesthood. He has seen that kingship has traditions which make its reconciliation, in any full sense, with Catholic ideals impossible. And if monarchy is thus held back in the state, his experience of Rome's hesitations suggested that the condition of the church is not different. To be driven back as he was to the general body of its members was to find its real meaning in the life that it led. It is surely this that explains the almost complete absence of dogmatic discussion from his enquiry. He is interested in Catholicism as a spirit which may become again the mistress of men's souls. Indeed, he is so far cognisant of the changing intellectual perspective that he insists on the necessity of the clergy being fully abreast of progress in scholarship. It is here, clearly, that the tenor of his liberalism is evident. That for which he is seeking is the conditions upon which the Christian church—for him that *societas perfecta* which seems destined eternally to haunt the minds of men—may develop unheeded. Doubtless he is still anxious that she may win the empire of the world. He is still—as he remained to the end—in the full sense of the word a theocrat. But he has already come to understand that the realms of church and state are by their nature distinct. He is already, even if, in some sort, unconsciously, admitting that authority cannot be single. He had hardly, as yet, worked out the implications of his admission. He perhaps did not then realise that he was thereby reducing the church to the condition of a voluntary society which, even if it had the features of a state, was nevertheless distinct from the territorial character of the secular organ. He no longer, as in 1818, spoke of government as all-powerful. He had not, indeed, as yet embraced liberalism in any full sense of the word. He appealed to it as men who are persecuted always make appeal to the principles of freedom. But he had come to understand that without it the guarantees of progress would be lacking. He disliked its vagueness; and he hoped to abrogate it by establishing his demand upon the basis of an acceptance of the Christian faith. He believed then, as he always believed, that only in the acceptance of the spirit of Christianity could Europe find its salvation. That was what he meant by saying that unity would be reborn in the struggle for freedom. That was why he welcomed the onset of the revolution he so clearly foresaw. Renovation must be the child of destruction; the tempest, as he said, would purify the air. But he did not yet know that he was speaking the language of revolutionary democracy as he was abandoning the ideal of papal Rome.

VII. THE FOUNDATION OF *L'AVENIR*

"When a certain number of men," Lamennais wrote early in 1829,[244] "keenly conscious of those truths which are the basis of social security shall unite among themselves, then we shall have the germ of a new order . . . . for that end two things are essential: we must enlighten men's minds by discussion, and we must strengthen their hearts by fighting. From that it follows that liberty, whether we have it, or whether we merely seek it, is today the first need of the people as it is the indispensable condition of our salvation." That is, in brief, the whole method and programme of Liberal Catholicism as Lamennais conceived it. The opposition to his attitude was passionate and strong. The Archbishop of Paris preached and wrote publicly against him;[245] the nuncio regretted the violence of his attitude.[246] His fierce determination was ascribed on every hand to pride and an overweening confidence in his own conclusions. Few realised, as did Lamennais himself,[247] the magnitude of the task he had undertaken. With the bishops unitedly against him, the silence of Rome was ever more exasperating; and the death of Leo XII deprived him of one who was perhaps his friend.[248] The church seemed to him as one given up in the arena to gladiators and wild beasts.[249] Not

[244] "Corresp." (ed. Forgues), Vol. II, p. 6.
[245] See his two letters in reply, "Oeuvres," II, 323 ff.
[246] Dudon, "Lamennais et le Saint-Siège," p. 76. Lambruschini himself seems not to have disagreed with his arguments.
[247] "Corresp." (ed. Forgues), II, 27.
[248] *Ibid.*, II, 15, and cf. his remarks on p. 18.
[249] *Ibid.*, p. 51.

even the Revolution of 1830 seems to have stirred him very deeply. He had long prophesied its coming; and he valued it only as a sign that his prevision was not mistaken;[250] nor did he conceal his view—nor his satisfaction—that the crisis must eventually end in a republic. The situation mainly interested him as a means to the greater freedom for which he was now so anxious. "Chacun," he wrote,[251] "chacun doit aujourd'hui chercher sa sûreté dans la sûreté de tous, c'est à dire dans une liberté commune. La liberté, c'est le droit et la faculté de se défendre contre toute volonté arbitraire et oppressive." The problem was the translation of that attitude into terms of Catholic life.

He did not embark upon its solution unprepared. His retreat at La Chênaie had for some time been a kind of communal retreat for those few close friends who, like Gerbet and Salinis, thought as he did upon the fundamental questions. As early as 1825 he had dreamed of opening there a kind of institute, where, with a few chosen comrades, he might work and think and pray. At Malestroit he had founded the little *Congregation of Saint Peter* which won the highest praise from Leo XII.[252] Its object was, above all, to harmonise the results of science and religion. "Lorsque l'Eglise tenoit entre ses mains le sceptre de la science," he wrote,[253] "c'etait une des causes de l'ascendant qu'elle avait sur les esprits." That was, perhaps, a somewhat chimerical ambition to anyone who had any historic sense of the Catholic church. But over his companions, as even a hostile witness like Wiseman bears testimony,[254] his ascendancy was amazing. It was under his aegis that Rohrbacher began that history of the church which, if its lustre be dim now, was for its time a mighty undertaking. Boré came there; the grim Lacordaire who came to doubt remained to bless; Sainte-Beuve felt its influence; and the letters of Maurice de Guérin bear witness to the joy that tender and graceful spirit

[250] *Ibid.*, II, 161.

[251] *Ibid.*, II, 160.

[252] Dudon, op. cit. p. 70. M. Dudon attributes this praise to mere politeness on the Pope's part; but when one considers the general relation between Leo and Lamennais that conclusion seems unduly sceptical.

[253] Spuller op. cit., p. 161.

[254] Cf. his "Four Last Popes," p. 301 f.

felt in the friendship of his master.   And a little later towards
the end of November, 1830, there came to his aid the ablest
and most renowned of his disciples in Montalembert.[255]   With
such men as these he could indeed face the future without fear.

If, at first, the Revolution of 1830 seemed hostile to the
Catholic forces, it soon became evident that this was in fact
a passing mood.[256]   The nation, as a whole, found its full satisfaction in having deposed the king who had broken the
Charter of 1814; and it was sufficiently Catholic in character
to indulge in no more than sporadic and momentary excesses.
Nor did the government show itself more inimical.   The new
dynasty was, after all, too frail to embark on the troubled seas
of religious persecution; and if the Charter of 1830 was more
liberal than its predecessor it in nowise deprived Catholicism
of its pre-eminence.   Lamennais did not disguise from himself
that difficult times lay ahead; but he believed that the support of the Orleans dynasty would lead to the protection of
those rights by which alone the existence of religion was possible.[257]   Almost immediately the means of active propaganda
were to hand in the foundation of that journal *L'Avenir* which
in its feverishly brilliant career, did nore, perhaps, than any
other weapon to fasten the roots of liberal doctrine deep down
in the soil of Catholicism.   "Son but," Lamennais told his
friends,[258] "(est) d'unir, sur la base de la liberté, les hommes
de toutes les opinions attachés à l'ordre."   At almost the same
time there was instituted a society for the defense of religious
liberty.[259]   It undertook to support every religious school.   It
protected the clergy from wrongful prosecution.   It safeguarded
the right of association.   It desired to act as the common link
by which all religious societies in France should be linked
together for mutual protection against all attacks on the liberty
of their faith.[260]   Both journal and society are simply Lamennais;
nowhere is there any thought in either of which he is not the

[255] The first volume of Lecanuet's admirable "Life of Montalembert"
details the history of their relations in full.
[256] Cf. Debidour, op. cit., p. 412.
[257] "Corresp." (ed. Forgues), II, 168 f.
[258] *Ibid.*, II, 173.
[259] *Ibid.*, II, 185, and Boutard, op. cit., II, 181 f.
[260] See their statutes summarised in Debidour, op. cit., 421.

directive inspiration. His letters take on a note of optimism by which, in general, they were rarely distinguished.[261] He seems clearly to have felt the greatness of the work he had undertaken; nor was he any longer possessed by the old terrors of its futility.

The *Avenir* lasted for a year, when the hostility of Rome compelled its suspension. Certainly no journal has ever more splendidly fulfilled its programme. Its very disappearance was important; for it marked the first of the three great defeats suffered by liberal Catholics in the first century of their existence.[262] Yet in the short period of its existence it was able to elaborate a political theory of which no one can as yet foretell the complete potentialities. Lamennais himself has told us the essence of the doctrines he therein preached. It started out from the assumption that the right to command, which he calls sovereignty, belongs to God alone;[263] every one is dependent upon Him and therefore no person can possess, in the strict sense, sovereign powers. As a consequence, all men are equal in their rights; for their rights are derived from their nature which come equally from God. Liberty is thus the essential condition of civil institutions. The power which is given to rulers is derived from the agreement of men to arrange for the protection of their liberties. Rulers, as a result, possess only that power which is judged by the citizens of a state necessary to the conservation of the law of their being.[264] Men have thus imprescriptible rights and it follows that liberalism must always be the basis of their existence. The Revolution and the Restoration alike denied these truths; it was by a policy of concerted violence that in their different ways each sought to govern. The monarchy of the Restoration, moreover, used religion as a political weapon and thereby brought it into discredit.[265] They

[261] e. g. "Corresp." (ed. Forgues), II, 177, and cf. Laveille, op. cit., 258.

[262] I suppose it would generally be admitted that the history of liberal Catholicism can reasonably be divided into the Lamennais period; that which culminates in their defeat at the Vatican council; and that which culminates in the issue of the encyclical *pascendi*. I have discussed the significance of the second episode in the fourth chapter of my "Problem of Sovereignty." The last is discussed below.

[263] Oeuvres, II, 362.

[264] *Ibid.*, II, 363.

[265] *Ibid.*, II, 366.

deprived it, in fact, of the character of a religion by taking from it its character of independence. They used it as a means against that democratic régime which is always incompatible with monarchy;[266] and they bought its compliance by the gift of money, of dignity and of power. But a struggle inevitably arose when the people came to realise that the state was being used for the interest of a privileged class. The people demanded their rights and they did not hesitate to take them. A new order was born; and it was to preserve Catholicism from the evils by which it was threatened that the *Avenir* came into being.[267] It is upon that foundation that its effort was made. It insisted upon the separation of religion and politics; a religion which is endowed by the state is no longer a religion but an establishment. It asked for the right to establish schools, the abolition of episcopal nomination, the complete independence of church and state. For the essence of their doctrine was to look upon Catholicism as in itself a sufficient way of life, bound not to earth but to God. So, by separating itself from the world, it secured the conditions of its freedom. So it became the mirror of that which it was destined to enshrine.[268]

There is no article in the *Avenir* throughout its history which is not faithful to this programme. It is difficult to do full justice to the eloquent passion with which it is throughout advocated. It is clear enough that Lamennais was happy in the work of propagation. His letters reveal a new faith in things which triumphs over the difficult physical conditions under which he laboured. He saw the work grow on every hand. The response to his charitable appeals was remarkable.[269] The demand for men of letters whom he could trust came from every part of France.[270] They gave active support to the Belgian Revolution and the Polish insurrection.[271] They followed the efforts of O'Connell in Ireland with eager enthusiasm.[272] They had feelings of deep sympathy for the kindred ideals of Görres

[266] *Ibid.*, II, 367.
[267] *Ibid.*, II, 368.
[268] *Ibid.*, II, 370.
[269] Cf. "Oeuvres," II, 368.
[270] "Corresp." (ed. Forgues), II, 193.
[271] *Avenir*, no. of Sept. 17, 31. "Corresp." (ed. Forgues), II, 189.
[272] Boutard, op. cit., II, 202.

and Dollinger.[273] They dreamed of a general union of Catholic forces throughout the world of which the end was to be the attainment of a general freedom for all peoples.[274] They protested against the enmity of science and religion; for Catholicism dare not fear truth otherwise it was not worthy of preservation. Nor is it difficult to see that in the process of work Lamennais became more and more convinced of the rightness of his attitude; certainly not even in the dark days of his suspension did his conviction for a moment falter.

It is not easy to mistake their system. On the morrow of a revolution they saw, as they deemed, but two things still firm amid the universal disorder: the action of providence and the need for liberty. It is with their integral reconciliation that they are, above all, concerned.[275] It is in effect, a demand that the spiritual future of the church be based upon an acceptance of what, in the most liberal estimate, the Revolution may be taken to mean; with the addition that where the Revolution misunderstood the significance of corporate freedom,[276] Lamennais insists upon its attainment. From that basis they make their judgments. Their connexion with Rome must be uninterrupted and direct; to attempt the control of such communication is an intolerable and oppressive surveillance. For it means that the papal power over the church is reduced to a nullity, and without that power the church can have no real existence.[277] They insist on the right of association. The holding of opinions implies the right to take means for their protection. Man is so pre-eminently a social being that without such right his life is deprived of half its meaning.[278] They demand liberty of instruction; for it is surely clear that without the opportunity to educate their children in Catholic principles they have no means of ensuring what they believe to be their salvation.[279] Nor does their demand end there. They recognise that religious liberty is the offspring of political liberty. That was why they rejoiced at the

[273] *Avenir*, Nov. 21, 30; Dec. 2, 30; May 11, 31.

[274] Boutard, op. cit., II, 213 f.

[275] *Avenir*, Oct. 16, 1830.

[276] Cf. the essay on "Administrative Syndicalism."

[277] *Avenir*, Oct. 26, 1830.

[278] *Avenir*, Oct. 30, 30.

[279] *Ibid.*, Nov. 26, 30.

Polish insurrection.[280]   That was why the power of government was by its very character an object of suspicion in their eyes. It was the very power of government which really lay at the bottom of their advocacy of separation. It was an historical deduction from their experience that a church so fettered cannot from the nature of things be free. Their desire for liberty of the press is only the implicit translation of liberty of thought into terms of action. Their insistence on such a form of election as will enable the suffrage to be exercised by the humblest men is a result of their desire to give power the broadest basis of consent; and it was for that reason that Lamennais declared himself opposed to the existence of an hereditary chamber.[281]   Nor was it less consistent with his theory of power that he should have demanded administrative decentralisation.   It was part of the natural right to self-government that he should desire to minimise the evil influence of the absorptive effect of the Napoleonic system. If we once admit the right of a people to look after its own affairs it becomes sufficiently obvious that federalism more nearly meets the needs of a complex society than the unitary state.[282]   Nor was he illogical in his view that only in the increasing application of intelligence to public questions, the continuous realisation that this is a changing world and that Catholicism must meet the implications of its changing perspective, could there be a victory for his principles.[283]   In the end, it is to that conception that all liberal Catholicism goes back.   The idea of a developing tradition was for him the simple deduction from the obvious fact that Catholicism was a living personality which, if true to itself, was surely destined to conquer the world.   If he states his belief, less in terms of a dissatisfaction with its narrow dogmas than of discontent with its narrow political outlook, that only means that he was the child of his age.   The need of the moment was political; the scientific criticism of Catholic dogmatics began to penetrate only a quarter of a century later. Yet his anxiety for a learned priesthood is sufficient evidence that he was not without some understanding of the need that one day would come.

[280] *Ibid.*, Sept. 17, 31.
[281] *Ibid.*, May 28, 31.
[282] *Ibid.*, June 28, 31.
[283] *Ibid.*, June 30, 31.

What, then, emerges from it all? The real problem by which he was confronted was the problem of government. He did not for one moment doubt the eternal truth of the fundamental maxims for which Christianity stands. But he had come to the stage where it was necessary to distinguish between the collective conscience of Christian society—the general will which lay buried beneath the appearance of evil and misunderstanding —and the consciously formulated practice of those who actually governed it. He had come to disbelieve that the church could be fully represented by her ministers. What she was, no one body of men could claim to be. She was essentially a brotherhood of a life to be lived on certain principles and the fundamental test of her worth was the regulation of her conduct in the terms of those principles. That was why he was prepared to reject the authority of the state. As a consistent Christian he could not regard himself as linked to what was in idea neither religious nor free. And that sense of antagonism to secular things made him anxious to insist in every particular upon the distinct and corporate life of the church—its self-sufficiency, its own right to freedom, to government, to development. It was for the expression of its personality that he above all cared; and he did not greatly mind that the sense of power a state-relation might add to it should be withdrawn. It did not greatly matter to him that he did not—perhaps could not—attempt the definition of Catholicism. For him the vital test was—as it is the vital test of every society—that he felt its meaning deeply enough to be able to share fully and richly in its life. He would never—certainly, at least, before 1834,—have denied that the church must actively organise her strength; his passionate defence of ultramontanism is the sufficient proof of that. But he was virtually claiming already a right to judge it, was reserving for himself the power to insist that, when the last order has been issued, it was, after all, a matter for his own judgment whether he would accept it. All his work had gone to show that he had, as much as any Catholic authority, a deep sense of the disintegrating effect of schism, a wish that there should be unity of purpose even if there were variety of effort. He had the deep and abiding sense of the church as an apostolic society of which the mission was the preparation of the city of God. But that is clearly a

Catholicism distinct in a fundamental sense from the sectarian orthodoxy of the schools or the political ambitions of Rome. It is, as the greatest of his successors said of the true Catholicism of his own time, "simply a spiritual society organised purely in the interests of religion and morality."[284]

Such an attitude, of course, involves the living of one's faith rather than the observance of its dogma or its ritual. Here, surely, is one of the keys to Lamennais' hatred of Gallicanism; for, as he interpreted it, it rendered impossible any full realisation of the Christian life. For Gallicanism, as it had developed under the Restoration,[285] had become an exclusive and intolerant search for power. It had lost sight of the significance of the spirit of the church, in the effort to re-assert a specialised and departmental control over a section of the thoughts of men; and it was not very careful as to the means it used to that end.[286] With such an attitude he had no sympathy. As an essay in the ideal church for which he lived it seemed to him abortive by the very fact that it trod the path of the state. The desires he cherished were different. A free church in a free state was reserved for other and greater destinies. It would link itself to the current of social change which was to fashion a new world. Science and liberty would be its comrades, and it would advance in kinship with the profoundest hopes of democracy.[287] If it rejected the sovereignty of kings, it was only that it might be true to itself. If it is suspicious of authority, it is only because it has experienced its evils. If he was prepared still to maintain *extra ecclesiasm salus nulla*, what he meant by the church was no longer obedience to a single power. He believed, it is true, in the unified governance of the church; but he believed in it

[284] Tyrrell, "A Much-abused Letter," p. 64. I do not think there is a sentence in this magnificent justification that Lamennais would have repudiated.

[285] One has to distinguish between different hands; that of Grégoire, or that which goes back to Porte-Royal, are very different from that of Frayssinous.

[286] It is interesting to note Macaulay's deep indignation against the church of the Restoration. On the margin of Paul-Louis Courier's pamphlet "Response aux Anonymes," No. 2 he wrote "Worthy of Demosthenes. It makes my blood boil against that accursed tyranny." Trevelyan, Life (Nelson ed.), II, 502.

[287] "Oeuvres," II, 372.

only so long as that governance was in accord with liberal doctrine. It is clear that he is already in the stage when in a choice between what Tyrrell called "the only absolute duty and the highest sort of conditional duty"[288] there could be no alternative. That is not to say he was a Protestant. His sense of the dangers of religious individualism were far too keen for that to be possible. It meant only that his sense of the church was such that he could give to her only the best that was in himself. The real problem was her attitude to his gift.

VIII. THE APPEAL TO ROME

HAD Lamennais been content with the composition of a hymn to liberty it is possible that his views, if they involved discussion, would yet have avoided condemnation. But, from the outset, both he and his disciples were anxious to promote their utilisation. Within a month of its first publication, Lacordaire urged the French bishops not to accept the nominations of Louis Philippe,[289] while Lamennais demanded the immediate abrogation of royal control. The result was a prosecution by the government in which both were acquitted.[290] If, as Lamennais himself thought, the verdict wrought immense good,[291] it was yet only the beginning of their difficulties. His own sense of their contingency is clear from his letter of a month later to Cardinal Weld. It assures him of their entire good will towards Rome, their humble dependence upon the papal commands.[292] He was soon repudiating calumnies which accused him—as falsely as intelligibly—of a desire to destroy the episcopate.[293] But more serious was the attack on their democratic principles from the Father-general of the Theatines, Ventura; not only was he a friend of Lamennais, but he was well acquainted with Roman opinion.[294] Lamennais, indeed, more than refuted his objections but the criticism, published as it was in the most intransigeant

[288] Tyrrell, op. cit. 99.
[289] *Avenir*, Nov. 25, 30.
[290] Boutard, op. cit., II, 216-223.
[291] "Corresp." (ed. Forgues), II, 197.
[292] *Ibid.*, II, 198, Feb. 27, 131.
[293] *Ibid.*, II, 199-202.
[294] Dudon, op. cit, p. 94.

of the Gallican journals, was full of significance.[295]   Bishops began to urge him to cease his propaganda.[296]   It was bruited abroad that the late nuncio had denounced him as one of the greatest enemies by which the church was confronted.[297]   The Jesuits began to cast subtle doubts upon the orthodoxy of his principles.[298]   Dupanloup, then on the threshold of his immense influence, had begun to intrigue for his condemnation.   Lamennais, he said,[299] "entraîne les jeunes prêtres dans l'indépendence politique et la rébellion religieuse."   Nor did Rome speak as he had hoped.   "Là on ne voit rien," he wrote of the papacy,[300] "on ne comprend rien encore; on est plongé, perdu dans les ténèbres exterieures des intérêts terrestres, qui ne laissent pénétrer aucun rayon de lumière."   Priests who were suspected of adhesion to his doctrines were attacked; and the clerical subscriptions to the *Avenir* suffered a forcible decline.[301]   They were threatened by interdict and intrigue, and Rome gave support to those accusations.   Their demand for encouragement from Rome met with no response.[302]   The note of sadness begins to reappear in his letters.   "Ce n'est pas le courage que je perds", he answered a friend who urged him not to lose hope,[303] "mais la voix; je prévois que bientôt elle nous manquera aucun moyen de résister à l' opposition épiscopale."   In October of 1831 he wrote to Montalembert that it was hopeless to continue in the face of such relentless antagonism.[304]   Lacordaire urged that they go to Rome to justify their attitude; and though Montalembert seems already to have feared condemnation, Lamennais himself insisted that it was impossible.[305]   On the 15th of November the *Avenir* was suspended, and the three friends set out, "as did

[295] Lamennais' reply is in the *Avenir* for Feb. 12, 31.   Ventura published his criticism as an open letter in the *Gazette de France*.

[296] "Correspondence," II, 214.

[297] *Ibid.*, II, 225.

[298] Dudon, op. cit., 95.

[299] Lagrange, "Dupanloup," I, 121.

[300] "Corresp." (ed. Forgues), II, 213.

[301] *Ibid.*, II, 227 f.

[302] *Ibid.*, II, 228.   This is doubtless a reference to the letter to Cardinal Weld.

[303] *Ibid.*, II, 230.

[304] "Lettres à Montalembert," pp. 6-7.

[305] Boutard, op. cit., II, 255.

the soldiers of Israel" to convince the papacy of the honesty of their intentions and the justice of their cause.[306]

The Roman adventure is to Lamennais what, three centuries before, the visit of Luther was to that greatest of schismatics. It is the real turning-point of his life. It brought to the final test his theory of the part that Rome was to play in the governance of the world. He had never denied the omnicompetence of the Pope. He had always insisted that the *plenitudo potestatis* was, in this realm, at least, justified by its exercise. At the distribution of religious power he had frankly scoffed. He had again and again been urgent as to the necessity of monarchical and unified direction by the church. Not even when he had come, by 1829, to realise the necessity of liberal principles had he changed his convictions in this regard. Nor did he doubt that Rome would welcome the opportunities that freedom offered. There is not a tithe of evidence that Lamennais expected an unfavourable reception; but the amazing dishonesty of his treatment completed in him a disillusion of which the first seeds were already sown. What he learned was the danger of unified authority even in the Catholic church. He was defeated by papal unwillingness to separate the spheres of temporal and spiritual. He found that, in thought, at any rate, the papal ideal was still the dream of a worldly dominion against which three centuries of reformers had uttered in vain their protest. He learned that the papacy regarded itself as a temporal power which had benefited by the possession of certain valuable spiritual weapons. The Rome of which he dreamed vanished the more speedily as he contemplated it in actuality. It was a Rome which was unwilling to regain a spiritual empire if secular dominion must be sacrificed.

It is, in fact, clear enough—even when the evidence arrayed against him by Rome itself is considered[307]—that the main grounds of his condemnation were not religious but political in character. Religious they could not be, for the sufficient reason that to the composition of his liberal Catholicism no element of

[306] "Oeuvres," II, 480. Cf. Corresp. (ed. Forgues), II, 231.
[307] Cf. Dudon, "Lamennais et le Saint-Siege" for the orthodox Roman interpretation of this time. It is such criticism as his that has led me to use Lamennais' "Affaires de Rome" only as a check upon the immediately contemporaneous documents.

dogma contributed. Gregory XVI sacrificed him to the fear
that the prolongation of his active career might embroil him
with the governments of Europe. The age was not liberal in
its outlook. The papal states themselves were the centre of
national disaffection. The English administration of Ireland
was rarely more harsh and never more unpopular. Russia was
breaking into pieces the men who dreamed of a reconstructed
Poland. Under the shadow of liberal phrases the Orleanist
monarchy was erecting a despotism not less ugly than the old.
In Prussia an omnicompetent bureaucracy was codifying the
maxims of Machiavelli upon the relations of religion to the state.
Austria seemed, under the oppressive reactionism of Metternich,
to confound the application of the penal code with that of the
Beatitudes. It was the antithesis of such doctrine that Lamennais came to urge; and what he offered to Rome was an alternative in which the nobler choice could have been taken only
by men who did not deem themselves bound by the ordinary
canons of secular diplomacy.

The powers themselves did not fail to urge Rome along this
course. Simultaneously with his arrival in Rome, the French
ambassador demanded his condemnation;[308] and he was able
to report to his government that the pope was as compliant as
he could desire.[309] The weight of Metternich's ·incomparable
authority was used to the same purpose. "Elle appartient," he
wrote of the *Avenir*,[310] "au désordre, comme les feuilles dé-
vouées au pur radicalisme." The Archbishop of Paris was
urgent in his request for immediate and adverse action, while
he skilfully mingled praise of intention with hostility to result.[311]
Even Russian influence was exercised for the same end.[312] The
commission appointed by the Pope to deal with Lamennais'
doctrines could by no possible fortune have been favourable
to him. Ventura had already published his suspicions. Lambruschini was, to say the least, distrustful of the whole tendency of which Lamennais was representative. Soglia had, towards the end of 1830, written to Lamennais urging him to

[308] Dudon, op. cit., 110 f.
[309] *Ibid.*, 113.
[310] *Ibid.*, 118.
[311] *Ibid.*, 122.
[312] *Ibid.*, 129.

retrace his steps.[313] Means were taken to prevent direct access to the Pope; and if they were allowed to present a memorial in which their position was defended, still Lamennais began to feel the amazing falsity of his position. What, after all, could Gregory do, a simple monk caught, as they were caught, in the meshes of a labyrinthine system?[314] The sense of embarrassment on both sides was very painful. "Notre démarche," wrote Montalembert,[315] "si catholique et si simple, a jeté la cour de Rome dans un embarras qu'elle ne nous a pas pardonné; uniquement occupés de leurs intêrets temporels, qui se trouvent dans la position du plus critique, les cardinaux et les prélats qui entourent le saint-père voient avec le plus grand mécontentemènt les efforts que nous avons faits pour détacher la réligion et l'Eglise de la causes des rois qui sont, a leurs yeux, la Providence vivante de ce monde." It was no more than the simple truth.

On every side, indeed, the situation conspired against them. If the pope was uniquely sovereign he still had need of his delegates and he was compelled, in some degree, to give ear to their complaints. So, even before any decisive action was taken, he accused Lamennais of sowing discontent among the French clergy,[316] and to rid himself of a troublesome visitor, he foreshadowed a long examination of doctrine which made his continued stay in Rome inadvisable. The fact of the matter was, as Lamennais began to realise,[317] that Rome had a choice between the liberalism of her original inception and the temporal interests resultant on her massive organisation, and she was not prepared to sacrifice substantial material possessions. Before the pilgrims separated, they were allowed to see the Pope; but discourse on the weather and the sardonic offer of snuff stifled from the outset all effort at discussion.[318] Lacordaire returned to France, Montalembert set out for Germany. Lamennais himself, for the moment, remained in Rome. His stay there was only serving the more firmly to convince him that it was essential to continue his work. He began with almost feverish

---

[313] *Ibid.*, 135.
[314] Blaize, op. cit., II, 92.
[315] Dudon, op. cit., 151.
[316] *Ibid.*, 154.
[317] Blaize, op. cit., II, 99.
[318] See Montalembert's account of the interview in Lecanuet's life, I, 228.

energy to draw up programmes of detailed future activity.[319]
He began to write a treatise on the ills by which the church was
oppressed.   Meanwhile the French ambassador was able to
inform his government that Rome was set firmly against all
such liberalising innovation.[320]   The revolt that simultaneously broke out in the papal states was not without its lesson.
If liberalism involved the occupation of Ancona by an Austrian
garrison—a step which seemed likely to embroil Gregory with
the rest of Europe[321]—he would have none of it.   The French
bishops gave him all the help he could desire.   Lamennais'
enemies, to the papal satisfaction, drew up a formidable list of
his suggested heresies.[322]   Upon their basis Lambruschini reported in favour of action.   The sacred Congregation at last
settled down to the final stage and recommended formally that
his programme should be condemned.[323]

It meant the rejection of a church which should pursue a
religious avocation.   It meant insistence upon the belief that
Rome, whatever her interests in the other world, has a very
definite connexion with the secular problems of the present.   No
one who reads the correspondence of Lamennais in Italy can
doubt that this was the foremost impression defeat would make
upon his mind.   Rome already seemed to him, morally, a desert
where none could breathe.[324]   He did not in any sense blame the
Pope for his silence; but he regarded him as the tool of corrupt
and ambitious men.[325]   It is certain that at this time at any rate
he had no other thought than obedience to the church.[326]   But
he would have been less than human if he had not felt bitterly
the intrigues against him.   Yet some hope he must have retained almost to the end, since he was insistent that funds should
be obtained for the continuance of the *Avenir*.[327]   How should
he not who had boasted so long of the splendour of Rome, and

[319] Blaize, op. cit., II, 115, 122.
[320] Dudon, op. cit., 163.
[321] Nielsen, op. cit., II, 60 f.
[322] Dudon, op. cit., 168 f.
[323] *Ibid.*, 177.
[324] "Corresp." (ed. Forgues), II, 235.
[325] *Ibid.*, II, 236.
[326] *Ibid.*, II, 238.
[327] "Lettres à Montalembert," p. 9.

could not but feel certain of the rightness of his cause? He was, indeed, saddened by the self-effacement of the papacy, its general deafness to popular desire, the ambition of the cardinals, and their absorption in secular interests. It was, to him, humiliating to find Rome completely dependent upon the good will of the European concert, painfully without answer for the new problems that confronted men. He could not avoid the thought that its preoccupation with politics was the root cause of its blindness to a new world. Nor did its internal condition make for betterment. The secular ecclesiastics were too ignorant, the very means of instruction were uselessly difficult of access. Rome was suffering from intellectual deterioration, and her attempt at the control of new opinion resulted in oppression.[328] He drew a striking picture of the suspicion with which the papacy was everywhere regarded.[329] He insisted again that only in the assertion of her permanent alliance with the forces of freedom could she restore her ascendency over the world, But he was asking too much of an institution so securely wedded to her past traditions, and he realised that it was useless to linger. He left Italy, and, with Montalembert, who joined him at Florence, he set out for Munich. There he met Görres and Dollinger, and found in their ideas a fine kinship with his own.[330] It was that same Dollinger who, a quarter of a century later, was to bring the whole weight of his incomparable learning and magnificent honesty to the service of ecclesiastical liberalism. There is a dramatic fitness in his presence at Lamennais' side when the news of the latter's condemnation was published to the world.

IX. THE CONDEMNATION

THE encyclical *Mirari Vos*,[331] is the first step on the road which led, first through the Syllabus of 1864 and the definition of papal infallability,[332] and later through the condemnation of modernism in the *Pascendi*, to the proclamation of war on the basis of mod-

[328] "Oeuvres," II, 573 f.

[329] *Ibid.*, II, 378.

[330] Boutard, op. cit., II, 325.

[331] See the text of the encyclical in Lamennais, "Oeuvres," II, 603 ff, or Dudon, op. cit., 389-400.

[332] I have tried to point out the significance of these in my "Problem of Sovereignty," pp. 176 f.

ern society by Rome. To Lamennais' plea that the cause of the
church and the cause of society are one, it virtually replied that
while that was undoubtedly true, the church would only permit
the triumph of the social cause upon its own terms. But those
terms were themselves the hard-won creed of a democratic time;
and by their rejection the papacy declared its determination to
stand aside from modern progress as we generally conceive it.[333]
No one will deny the greatness of that defiance. What, in fact,
it has involved, is a claim to a complete lordship over the minds
of men. Pius X only completed, on the dogmatic side, what
Gregory XVI outlined on the political. In that aspect the work
of de Maistre, and of Lamennais before 1830, has borne its due
fruit. The papacy has given birth to a political and intellectual
system of which the broad outlines are perfectly clear. The
Roman Catholic church has become a centralized and, for its
members, an infallible despotism. It has insisted that the life of
the world must be written in religious terms; which is virtually to
pronounce that the pope is its sovereign since to him has been
confined the control of religious destinies. Gregory XVI, at the
very outset of his encyclical, repudiated as noxious the notion
that the church was in need of regeneration.[334] He lightly casti-
gated those who attacked the celibacy of the clergy and the
indissolubility of marriage.[335] But the great evil of the time was
indifferentism, and from that every species of intellectual de-
lirium is born.[336] Liberty of conscience is impossible; in result
it is an invitation to erroneous opinion. It leads to a contempt
for sacred things and for laws that demand respect. It is the
root of all social evil. Nothing has so much contributed to the
decay of great empires than such immoderate freedom of opinion.[337] It of course follows that the liberty of the press is like-
wise condemned; it is no more than the instrument which
secures the expansion of monstrous errors.[338] He insists on the

[333] It is interesting to compare Tyrrell's judgment on this episode at the
time when his orthodoxy was unquestioned. See his, " Faith of the Millions,"
Vol. II, p. 86 f.

[334] Lamennais "Oeuvres," II, 604.

[335] Ibid, II, 608.

[336] Ibid., II, 609.

[337] Ibid., II, 610.

[338] Ibid.

necessity of submission to princes. To deny their right to authority is to deny the divinity of power. Nor must men preach the desirability of separating church from state. That union results in benefit to both and only the partisans of a boundless license can deny its virtue.[339]   He attacks the association of catholics with men of other religions;   it results only in the demand for impossible liberties and the destruction of worthy authority.[340]   Such doctrines he condemns as the reasoning of an insolent pride, the confidence of men in a reason that by its nature is weak and broken. Perhaps the most significant clause in the encyclical is its ending. That which Lamennais had demanded was, above all, the freedom of the church from secular interference, its independence from all external institutions by the very fact that it was a church. Of all this Gregory makes not merely abstraction but denial. It is upon the princes, whom he calls his children, that he lays the task of executing his theories. They have their authority not less for the protection of the church. It is in them that he puts his trust.[341]

Not even Metternich could have desired a more complete condemnation. The direction which Lamennais had endeavoured to give to the forces of Catholicism was repulsed to the minutest detail. He was offered a clear alternative. Either he must continue his work outside the church or he must submit to a catholicism in which he had ceased to find spiritual consolation. He could not take refuge in the propagation of his political ideas; for the religious implications of catholicism were so defined in the encyclical as clearly to include the whole field of political inquiry. That doctrine of the two kingdoms which, in reality, lay at the bottom of the philosophy of the *Avenir* could draw no sustenance from the papal pronouncement. He did not conceal its significance from himself. "Les princes et le pape," he wrote,[342] "ont crut qu'en s'unissant, ils arrêteraient le mouvement des peuples et les maintiendraient sous le joug. Grégoire XVI, comme vous avez vu, vient de proclamer cette grande alliance, et de condamner par là les catholiques à l'in-

[339] *Ibid.*, II, 612.
[340] *Ibid.*, II, 613.
[341] *Ibid.*, II, 613-4.
[342] "Corresp." (ed. Forgues), II, 245.

action. Ils ne peuvent pas défendre l'Eglise contre la volonté de son chef; nous nous tairons donc." The *Avenir* and the *Agence Générale* were suppressed with perfect submission to the papal authority;[343] and the pope had written in approving acceptance.[344] Not, indeed, that he had surrendered any of his opinions. He had simply agreed to silence because one who had the right to command him had so ordered. He was not less fearful for the future of catholicism than before; the tempest he had descried would yet shake Christianity to its foundations.[345] Meanwhile he asked only for peace.

But it was exactly peace that his opponents were not willing he should enjoy. Vague whispers began to be bruited abroad which were calculated to do him harm at Rome. It was suggested that his submission had been merely formal and that he did not mean it. Men pointed out that he had made no formal abjuration of his principles. It was the hounding of the wounded lion to his lair. He was reduced to the utmost poverty;[346] the pope had condemned him; the bishops still treated him as their enemy. He had, of course, a gigantic problem before him. If an infallible pope condemned a liberalism he believed to be essential what must be his attitude?[347] It was simple enough for him to say that infallibility came only when the papal voice was that of the whole church,[348] but who was to judge the occasion? He seemed himself uncertain. "Laissons aller," he wrote to Montalembert,[349] "le pape et les évêques . . . . il n'y a rien à faire par le clergé, ni avec le clergé," and there are surely few who cannot pardon that weariness of spirit.

μ The event which seems to have precipitated the catastrophe was the publication by Montalembert, early in 1833, of his translation of Mickiéwicz's hymn to Polish liberty in which he passionately defended the late insurrection. Since Rome had approved its suppression, the enemies of Lamennais did not hesitate to draw the conclusion that they were contemptu-

[343] Boutard, op. cit., II, 340.
[344] *Ibid.*, II, 346.
[345] "Corresp." (ed. Forgues), II, 250.
[346] "Corresp." (ed. Forgues), II, 264.
[347] Cf. the letter to Count Kzewuski. "Corresp." (ed. Forgues), II, 270.
[348] *Ibid.*, II, 272.
[349] "Lettres à Montalembert," p. 43.

ous of papal authority.[350]   Accusations were scattered broadcast that he was guilty of insincerity; and Gregory himself made protestations to the Archbishops of Toulouse.[351]   All his friends begged him to be silent and to submit once more.   He was willing enough where religion alone was concerned.   But outside the church he demanded an absolute freedom.   "In purely temporal affairs," he declared,[352] "particularly where France is concerned, I recognise no authority with the right either to impose opinions upon me or to dictate my conduct. I say boldly that in this sphere—which is unconnected with the spiritual power—I will never abdicate the independence that comes to me in virtue of my humanity, and that alike in thought and action I will take counsel only of my conscience and my reason."

It was undoubtedly a defiance of Roman sovereignty, an assertion of the supremacy of that last inwardness of the human mind which resists all authority save its own conviction of rectitude.   He wrote to Rome that so far as the church was concerned no speech or writing of his would discuss it; and he asseverated his acceptance of papal control in faith and morals.[353]   He insisted that all he had promised in the Munich declaration had been fulfilled and more than fulfilled.[354]   He resigned the headship of the Congregation of St. Peter and the little society of La Chesnaie was dissolved.   But the pope was not satisfied.   He insisted that a new submission was essential when the affront of Montalembert was borne in mind.[355]   The letter was written privately to the Bishop of Rennes who promptly published it with some comments which were simply calumnies.[356]   Lamennais replied by another appeal to the pope in which he emphasised his submission in all that religion demands as well as his eagerness to please him so far as his conscience would allow; but he insisted on his right to freedom

[350] Boutard, op. cit., II, 366.
[351] "Corresp." (ed. Forgues), II, 306-7.   Boutard, op. cit., II, 368.
[352] "Corresp." (ed. Forgues), II, 307.
[353] Ibid., II, 309.
[354] Ibid., II, 312-4.   The letter is clearly written to a Roman Cardinal.
[355] Boutard, op. cit., II, 378.
[356] Ibid., II, 379.

in purely temporal affairs.[357]   "I have defended the rights of God and of the church," he wrote to a friend,[358] "I will not insult God by deserting those of humanity;" and he insisted that to proclaim the twofold sovereignty of Rome would be to surrender men to an insupportable tyranny.   Nor could the urgency of his most intimate associates move him from that position.   "My conscience will not allow me," he told Montalembert,[359] "to abandon the traditional doctrine of two societies, each distinct in its own sphere, and I will make no declaration which suggests even my implicit abandonment of it."   To Rome such a limitation seemed entirely unsatisfactory.[360] Lamennais has told us himself that at this juncture he began to feel uncertain as to the very basis of Catholic authority. He wished only for peace and he would sign any declaration they chose to exact from him.[361]   A plenary submission was exacted and Rome congratulated itself on a magnificent victory.[362]

But Lamennais' own mind was still tortured by doubt.   He was distressed at the abuse Rome would make of such power as she claimed when she came to exert it over temporal interests.[363]   He had signed the declaration because he desired, above all, not to be regarded as a rebel and a schismatic.   He saw in the situation simply the necessity of peace, and to that end he would, as he bitterly said,[364] have been willing to identify the Pope with God.   What the event had impressed upon him was the urgent necessity of distinguishing between the divine and human elements in the church that the confusion of their demands might be avoided.   For himself he was determined to avoid for the future all contact with ecclesiastical affairs.[365] He was beginning to make plainer to himself that distinction

[357] "Oeuvres," II, 555.

[358] Laveille, op. cit., p. 303.

[359] See the fundamental statement of his position in the letter to Montalembert of Nov. 25., 33.   "Lettres à M.," p. 219 f.

[360] "Oeuvres," II, 558-9.

[361] *Ibid.*, II, 561.

[362] Dudon, op. cit., 292 f.

[363] "Lettres à Montalembert," p. 229.

[364] *Ibid.*, p. 231.

[365] "Corresp." (ed. Forgues), II, 351, 353.

between Catholicism and Christianity which had for some
time impressed him.[366] He angrily repulsed some curious attempts to attract him to Rome.[367] But even in this difficult
position his antagonists did not cease to annoy him. The
Archbishop of Paris was insistent that he should thank the
Pope for the acceptance of his submission. A priest of Saint-
Sulpice published an acrimonious attack against him to which,
by the nature of his agreement, he could make no reply.[368] His
health was broken, and so generous a soul as Maurice de
Guérin was moved to indignation by his sufferings.[369] He
needed something that would restore his self-confidence and
make him feel that he had not deserted his ideals. After all,
he was certain of their truth; and peace at the price at which
he bought it was not worth the purchase.[370] He was deeply
moved by the cruelty with which the Lyons insurrection was
suppressed;[371] and that seems to have been the last pain he
could bear. He was not a man to whom silence came easily
and where he felt profoundly his thought took expression in
his pen. By the end of April, 1834, the "Paroles d'un Croyant"
was ready for the press. He seems to have had no illusions as
to the bitterness it would arouse; but the time had come when
he could contain himself no longer. "I have seen," he wrote,[372]
"the tears which becloud the eyes of the people; I hear their
cries of pain, and my heart yearns to comfort them." He did
not doubt that he would be attacked. Men would tell him
that he ought to have kept silence. The simple answer was
that he could not. "How could I be silent," he asked,[373] "surrounded, as we are, by such iniquity, such tyranny, such pain,
such want? I have felt that deeply; I have said my say.
Could I consent to allow future generations to lay to my

[366] "Lettres à Montalembert," p. 124.

[367] "Corresp." (ed. Forgues), II, 351.

[368] Boutard, op. cit., II, 403.

[369] "Lettres," Jan. 10, Feb. 1, May 10, '34.

[370] This feeling comes out very clearly in his letter of March 29, '34, to
the Archbishops of Paris, "Corresp." (ed. Forgues), II, 360.

[371] *Ibid.*, II, 362-4.

[372] *Ibid.*, II, 367.

[373] *Ibid.*, II, 369.

memory's account one of those iniquitous silences which harm not less, and often more, than direct connivance at wrong?" He felt this the more keenly since his thought had now reached a point where he looked for salvation in purely political propaganda. He reported to Montalembert—still faithful to him when Lacordaire had already deserted his ideals—a rumour that the Russian ambassador had accused him of desiring to make Catholicism a power once more, an effort which Russia would never permit. "I am glad," he said,[374] "that he will not permit it. That way we shall find no solution."

Only those who read day by day the letters to his closest friends can realise what the decision must have cost him. He did not hide from himself that he was burning the bridges behind him. To write a hymn to the splendour of democracy was indeed, after all that had passed, to hurl defiance at Rome. It is useless to blame him. It is too fatally easy to ascribe his determination to pride, to self-confidence, to an overweening sense of his own rightness for such analysis to be satisfactory. The issue is far more complex. Rome had extorted from him the admission of dogmas to which, in his heart, he could give no assent. If, like Tyrrell, like Dollinger, he strove hard to stand by the ancient ways, to make himself one with what he believed to be the real splendour of a Catholicism that enshrouded itself in an appearance of evil, there came at last the realisation that, in any final examination, he must take for truth and right conduct that which his conscience told him he might identify with truth and right conduct. Rome, he admitted freely, had the power to demand obedience from him; but the power to exact it she did not possess. It was the simple fact that in the last resort only his own conscience could be sovereign that he asserted. Wrong remained to him wrong however much his masters might proclaim its rectitude. He counted the cost of measuring his forces against the greatest of ecclesiastical institutions. It might bend him; certainly if he remained subject to its strength it would absorb his forces as the rivers are absorbed in the endless sea. But he was too confident of his own soul thus to mangle it. What Rome called a submissive sacrifice he branded as an unrighteous desertion. What she called the

[374] "Lettres à Montalembert," p. 254.

victory of her collective wisdom he denounced as the blindness of her past. So he took the privilege of every human being to think out for himself the conditions of his intellectual striving.

X. THE RED CAP ON THE CROSS

WHERE even the magic of Sainte-Beuve has failed to give adequately the significance of the "Paroles d'un Croyant," none else may attempt its analysis. It is a lyrical version of the "Communist Manifesto." It denies the legitimacy of all authority that is not based upon the widest liberty and heralds in its destruction the onset of a brighter dawn. It is written in a style that has a splendour and elevation not merely unique in Lamennais' own work, but in the whole range of French literature. It is instinct with a passionate generosity, and its flaming mysticism has in it much of the exquisite character of à Kempis. Sainte-Beuve has told us how the workmen responsible for its composition could hardly continue for their excitement.[375] New editions could hardly keep pace with the demand. Lamennais himself has written how workingmen contributed from their savings to buy a copy that they might read together at night; and how it was read aloud in the workshops.[376] Students declaimed its finest passages in the Gardens of the Luxembourg; and even the members of the Chamber of Deputies forgot the pressure of public business in their anxiety to feel the throb of its eloquence.[377]

But no one can attack the foundations of an existing order without waking the slumbering vigilance of property.[378] "It is the apocalypse of Satan," wrote his friend, the Baron de Vitrolles.[379] "It is the red cap of liberty upon a cross." The Duchesse de Dino was amazed at his Jacobinism.[380] A distinguished journalist denounced him as the herald of insurrec-

[375] "Nouveaux Lundis," Vol. I, p. 39 f.

[376] "Lettres à Montalembert," 316.

[377] *Ibid.*, 270.

[378] Mr. Gladstone has an interesting reflection on this attitude. Morley, "Life," III. 352.

[379] "Vitrolles," p. 248.

[380] "Souvenirs de Barante," Vol. V, p. 137.

tion.[381] Guizot has left us a curious and involved expression
of horror at Lamennais' tergiversations.[382] De Rigny, the
minister of foreign affairs, wrote to Rome at the universal
astonishment that such ideas should emanate from a priest.[383]
The *Gazette d'Augsburg* declared that if the devil visited the
world, he would come with the "Paroles" in his hand.[384] There
was no question of defence, nor did Lamennais desire it. He
had written, as he said, to salve his conscience and to cleanse
his soul from its association with an insupportable tyranny.[385]
Refutations poured in on every side. The book was speedily
prohibited at Rome, though Lamennais at first thought it
doubtful whether the pope would pronounce officially against
it.[386] Lacordaire, with a cruelly indecent haste, had signalised
it as the end of the Menasien school,[387] and his own brother
did not dare to read it.[388] If there were favourable voices they
were nowhere those of authority. It is clear enough that this
adverse opinion failed to move Lamennais from the certainty
that he had done right. Once he was certain of that, he cared
little for their praise or blame.[389]

Rome, as always, moved slowly. The reports that came to
Lamennais seemed, on the whole, to suggest that she would
keep silent.[390] But it was, in reality, impossible for the papacy
not to pronounce its judgment. The encyclical "Mirari Vos"
was hardly two years old; and its plea for political obedience
was implicitly set at naught by Lamennais' work. The French
government itself was in a quandary. Had it prosecuted Lamennais for sedition it was more than doubtful if a jury could
have been persuaded to convict him, and it dare not risk the
chance of failure. Metternich, indeed, did what the French
ministry did not feel able to do, and sent a passionate denun-

[381] S. M. Girardin, "Souveniers," p. 270.

[382] Cf. his "Memoirs" (Eng. trans.), Vol. III, Ch. III, passim.

[383] Boutard, op. cit., III, 39.

[384] *Ibid.*, III, 43.

[385] "Corresp." (ed. Forgues), I, 115.

[386] *Ibid.*, II, 380.

[387] "Considérations sur le système philosophique de M. de La Mennais."

[388] Boutard, III, 51.

[389] "Lettres à Montalembert," p. 260.

[390] *Ibid.*, 287., Lavalle, op. cit., 324.

ciation of the book to Rome, and Russia also made its protest.[391] It is doubtful enough if Gregory needed such persuasion. His secretary of state, Bernetti, looked already upon Lamennais as a Catholic Luther.[392] The Pope himself spoke freely of the pain the book had caused him; and in the encyclical "Singulari nos" of June 25, 1834 the condemnation was published. It rightly recalls that Lamennais had agreed to obey the teachings of the "Mirari vos" and that the "Paroles" was a defiance of its letter and its spirit. It excited disobedience to kings, contempt for law and order, destruction as well of religious as of political power. Its attitude to authority was denounced as an outrage to the civil and ecclesiastical hierarchy—a mere cloak for the attainment of freedom of conscience and the press. It attacked Lamennais' call to the peoples of the world to unite, its justification of tyrannicide, the astute temerity with which it had cited scripture to its purpose. "Its propositions," said the Encyclical,[393] "are false, calumnies, rash, conducive to anarchy, contrary to the word of God, impious, scandalous, erroneous and already condemned by the church in such heresies as those of the Waldenses, the Wyclifites and the followers of Hus." It was, in fact, a doctrine totally out of accord with the political direction that Gregory had finally chosen.[394] The historical relation of Lamennais' teaching is, after all, mere verbiage; his democracy had as much connexion with the doubtful communism of Wyclif as with the antagonistic safeguard of the Fourteenth Amendment; though Lamennais, like the great English heretic, did sever the action of the church from that of the world by reason of his deep sense of its unearthly dignity.[395] If it is a sin to love the church so greatly as to be fearful of its degradation, assuredly no one will question the rightness of the papal condemnation.

If Lamennais was surprised, the blow seems to have hurt him less for himself than for his friends.[396] He did, indeed, feel

[391] Boutard, op. cit., III, 76-8.
[392] *Ibid.*, 82.
[393] See the integral text in Dudon, Op. cit. 427 f.
[394] Cf. Nielsen, Op. cit. 11, 64 f.
[395] Cf. Mr. Poole's comments, "Illustrations of the History of Medieval Thought," p. 302 f.
[396] "Lettres à Montalembert," p. 306.

deeply indignant that a power he had served so well and so deeply loved should speak of him as the basest of men. He hated the low intrigues which had led to his fall. He objected to the condemnation of a book in terms so vague as never to specify wherein its error consisted. He did not for a moment believe that the blow could at all arrest the onrush of forces which were working towards the destruction of an intolerable régime.[397] He was, indeed, unfortunate in his attempt to distinguish between the voice of Gregory the pope, and that of Gregory the man; Rome has given us no criterion for making such delicate distinctions.[398] His complaint that Lamartine and Chateaubriand spoke as he did and yet escaped condemnation misses the point that they were not, after all, priests, and the measure of authority that could be exacted from them was therefore different. It was useless to hope that peace could be made. The fact was that so long as 'Lamennais made his conscience the supreme arbiter of his faith there was no place for him in the church unless his doctrine coincided with that of Rome. He saw in the fight the same old struggle of medieval time;[399] and not even the most earnest solicitations of Montalembert could induce him to withdraw from his position. At the end of 1834 even Montalembert deserted him so that the last of his disciples was gone.[400] He was now alone and there remained only the task of completing the defence of his ideas. The "Affaires de Rome", which he published towards the end of 1836, was the narrative of his difficulties with the Papacy. It is a magnificent piece of dispassionate analysis, unanswerable as it has gone practically unchallenged. Only at the end does he permit himself reflections and it is then only to prophesy that since the victory of democratic principles is certain, Rome must embrace liberalism or perish. But Rome had chosen another path and the break between them was final. Henceforth he devoted himself entirely to the cause of the people. There is a certain dramatic irony in the thought that, almost simultaneously, Newman had entered upon that

[397] "Corresp.," II, 386.
[398] "Lettres à Montalembert," p. 307.
[399] *Ibid.*, 324.
[400] Boutard, op. cit., III, 103.

struggle against dogmatic liberalism which ended in his adoption of the Catholic faith.[401]

XI. IMPLICATIONS

IT is an astounding evolution. Yet it is an evolution conditioned at every stage by the logic of a bitter experience. Lamennais started out with a firm belief in royalism and the church. He was the envenomed antagonist of the Revolution, and few have drawn up, from his standpoint, an abler indictment of its tendencies. He distrusted the people and he found no comfort in the dogmas of individualism. He came, in the end, to see that all for which he had previously contended was a tissue of error. Nor is clarity wanting to the basis of his change. He saw the church used as no more than a political instrument, and, like Chalmers and Newman, he made insistence upon its corporate independence. It was here that he found the means of a sympathetic acquaintance with liberal doctrine. But he soon found that ecclesiastical liberalism is only part of a larger whole. He discovered that, when the government of men is despotic, religion is too valuable an instrument in the security of servitude to be left untrammelled. So he was led to the examination of the political basis of despotic government and thence to its rejection. He came to understand that a free state was the condition of a free church, that he had, in fact, allies exactly in that party for which he had earlier professed the deepest hostility. He urged upon the church an adventure in liberalism. Let it once make the people free and its own triumph must inevitably follow. If Rome would abandon the pursuit of earthly power and devote herself to the liberation of those who loved her most deeply, she could save herself from the contamination that came from alliance with the apostles of political tyranny.

He did not, at the outset, doubt that such an appeal must win response. But he had totally mistaken the character of the church. He had himself been the protagonist in the definition of her Austinianism without, as it seems, understanding the real significance inherent in such power. For Rome could

[401] "Apologia" (ed. Ward), p. 150; and cf. my "Problem of Sovereignty," Chapter III.

not embrace the cause of the people and remain blind to her own condition. The men who directed her government were too deeply fond of power ever to submit to its partition. To make alliance with liberalism would be to condemn the church's past, to lessen the empire to which her greatest governors had for eight centuries laid claim. Herself rigidly authoritarian in temper, her natural affinity was with those powers which were struggling against the tidal wave of democratic advance. What, in truth, Lamennais asked was that she should be untrue to her special ethos. Of dogma, indeed, he might make entire abstraction; but to ask the church to concern herself with the discoveries of modern civilisation was to demand her admission that there was a truth of which she was not the appointed guardian from the dawn of her history. She would not suffer such diminution of her sovereignty. If the choice was between a claim to the widest powers and an alliance with the unknown future, she would take her stand by that past which had given her those powers. Her situation was consistent. Lamennais would have made a newer and a different Rome. He would have turned a state into a church. For Rome is the one fundamental institution of medieval times which has retained the indicia of her universal dominion. Today, perhaps, they are no more than a magnificent gesture, but they bear witness to the tenacity of her memory.

Her expulsion of Lamennais was the registration of her sovereign power. Yet, by that very exercise, she demonstrated her impotence. Even the mightiest prince, as Hume pointed out in a famous essay, is dependent upon his ability to lead men by their opinion. It was herein that Rome failed. For while she possessed the external sanction, she could not exact passive obedience. She might command, but she lacked any security that she would be obeyed. She demonstrated once more not, perhaps, so much for herself as for the world outside, that a final control of opinion rests always with each individual member of an association, and that whatever the penalties attached to its adoption. Nor was this all. The rejection of Lamennais from a society he so deeply loved is, when the last criticism of him has been made, still a tremendous tragedy, and it is well to enquire into its conditions. For what, basically, was he condemned? He had no faith in any creed except Catholicism. No man of his generation had more eloquently repelled the seductions of alternative creeds. He was unequalled, save by de Maistre, in the unlimited hope he placed in the benefits of papal sovereignty. It is, as an acute observer noted at the critical epoch of Lamennais' life, little less than astounding that it should have repulsed the one man of genius who then lent it the service of his powers.[402]

The answer involves the most gigantic problem by which we are confronted: the nature of corporate personality. Wherein that personality consists is sufficiently matter of strenuous debate. The claim of Lamennais was that the real basis of the church was not its doctrines but its life. He saw in it a living society which, even in change, remains true to itself and not a mass of individuals united by a chance agreement upon certain formulæ.[403] The conception of Rome was far more akin to the legal interpretation of the English courts. The members of the church were to it simply an associated body of beneficiaries who profited by the commands enjoined by a governing court. In such an aspect, the withdrawal of Lamennais was inevitable. If he could not obey the commands, he could not profit therefrom. If he was out of sympathy with its dogma, he was out of accord with its principles. Yet no one who reads what Lamennais has written can deny his essential sympathy with the broad aims of Catholicism. If Lamennais had lived in the time of Leo XIII his condemnation would have been extremely dubious; but that, to say the least, is to assert that there is an integral part of the Catholic church with which he was at one. To deny the validity of dissent is to prohibit the growth of corporate opinion, to insist on changelessness as the basis of the church. Yet it is impossible to deny that the church has changed, impossible, at any rate till answer has been made

[402] Cf. the very interesting comments of d'Herbelot, "Lettres à Montalembert," pp. 88-9, 146. These were written as early as 1829.

[403] I have discussed this question partly in my paper on the "Personality of Associations," 29 *Harv. L. Rev.* 404, and partly in that on "the strict interpretation of ecclesiastical trusts" in 36 *Canadian L. T.* 190. The whole force of the distinction between the two views will be apparent to anyone who compares the judgments of Lords Halsbury and Macnaghten in the Free Church of Scotland case as published in Mr. Orr's verbatim report.

to its own historian's account of its councils, or to the masterly polemic of Dollinger. Newman's "Doctrine of Development" is not yet on the *Index;* and it is simply a plea for the recognition in dogma of that which Lamennais demanded in politics.

For, after all, he was asking no more than the opportunity to convince the church of the superiority of one way of life to another—as Saint Francis made his plea for poverty, as, in another sphere, the Jesuits made demand for the dogmatisation of the Immaculate Conception. He did not ask it to change its personality, any more than Gerson did when he would have federalised its government, or Mariana when, contrary to the later teaching of Gregory XVI, he issued a justification of tyrannicide.[404] For, after all, the collective experience of the church, the sense of its collective experience, is a greater thing than its interpretation at any given moment of its history. Papal infallibility meant something very different to Newman from what it did to Manning; yet, somehow, the church was wide enough to include them both.[405] It is characteristic of any society, whether or no it be religious in its nature, that it should contain elements in some sort diverse. We cannot, in fact, avoid the incessant evolution of doctrine so long as man is a thinking animal. To each one of us the fact appears somehow different and, as a result, the interpretation can hardly coincide.[406]

It means, perhaps, that within every organisation, as within each individual, there must be a continuous struggle between life and tradition. In that sense, the career of Lamennais would be intelligible as the expression of a moment in which tradition was victorious. But the larger problem still remains. To ascribe the whole life of a society entirely to one element or the other is a dichotomy that is wanting in perspective. It is to mistake life for anatomy or physiology. The body cannot function without its background; and a skeleton is still dead

[404] Cf. Figgis,"From Gerson to Grotius," pp. 191-3. On all this his fourth lecture in "Churches in Modern State" is invaluable. See also a very good little book by Mr. Richard Roberts, "The Church in the Commonwealth."

[405] Cf. My "Problem of Sovereignty," Chapter IV.

[406] On all this the reader will find invaluable assistance in the two famous books of M. Loisy, "Autour d'un petit livre" and "Quelques Réflexions."

matter, even if it have living form. The principles of any society are not and can not be an expression of the totality of
motives by which men bind themselves into a community. For
community is like friendship in that it lies too deep for words.
Its relations do not end with their formal utterance, and it
subsists even where majority and minority conflict. The fundamental thing is to remain true to the life of the society. It has,
indeed, principles so fundamental that their violation involves
the rejection of that life. One could not deny the historic
existence of Christ, and yet remain a member of the Catholic
church. If the basis of Lamennais' condemnation be found
here, then it would be argued that the alliance of Catholicism
and the political system of the French Restoration is fundamental to membership of the church; but it is evident that
this is not the case. That, indeed, is the weakness of Lamennais'
ultramontane teaching. He equated the church with its head,
and he found himself, in the result, compelled to deny the truth
of his infallibility. From the standpoint of organisation he
discovered that while it might have its conveniences it was not
free from grave difficulty. For, once admit the fact of variety,
and the "tradizione son io" of Pius IX may be heresy in a
coming generation. It is the distinction which Rousseau makes
between the "general" will and the will of all. The "general"
will, in this aspect, is the will that is true to the social life not
at any given moment, but in the broad perspective of its history and its prospects. The "will of all" is the will that, at
a given moment, gets itself obeyed. In an Austinian system
like that of Rome the "will of all" becomes concentrated in
the person of the pope. We judge its identity with the will
of the church in the light of the years that lie ahead.

The quarrel of Lamennais with Rome, in fact, goes back to
one of the decisive moments of the fifteenth century. The defeat of the federalising efforts of Gerson and Nicholas of Cusa
at the great council of Basle in 1449 resulted in the erection
of a papal absolutism. It is the decisive step on a road that lead
logically to the definition of papal infallibility in 1870. But
the result was to give to Rome exactly those powers against
which Lamennais made complaint in the modern state. When
the Reformation split Europe into a collection of diverse sover-

eignties each state inherited the shattered fragments of the Roman imperium. It was in that sense that the obsequious Parliament of Henry VIII declared the realm of England to be an empire. But the history of the ensuing three centuries is the record of a transference of sovereign power from a single head to the general body of the state. By Rome alone, in Western Europe, was this tendency successfully resisted; and by Rome alone has the maintenance of absolutism been consistently secured. The knowledge of her vast pretensions was, throughout the nineteenth century, a fertile source of diplomatic difficulty. It was from those pretensions that, little by little, the states of Europe were compelled to build up what is essentially an alternative scheme of civic life. It was those pretensions which made of toleration the ultimate dogma of modern politics. It was those pretensions which resulted in the stern control of Catholic life. The Roman church was nowhere free. Her claim to statehood was on all sides met by the response that her competing system of allegiance was incompatible with the sovereignty of the state. It was against the assumption that the sovereignty of the state must be unique that Lamennais made his first protest in the name of liberalism. It was a claim made in the face of an external power. It did not discuss the conditions of an interior life within the church itself. It sought only to show, as de Maistre had attempted to demonstrate, that in her corporate freedom Rome will find such means of dominion as will enable her to govern the world. But corporate freedom was not a synthesis in which a system of which Metternich was the symbol could find comfort or hope.

From the protest against external bonds Lamennais turned to the internal life of the church. But here, too, he found himself confronted by a similar problem. The virtual apotheosis of the Roman pontiff stifled on every side the initiative of the individual. There was no limit set to the bounds of papal authority, and, as a consequence, there was no room in the church for any save those who agreed with the expressed declaration of its will. Loyalty was interpreted to mean not faith in the future of the church, not belief in the principles of its creeds, but acceptance of the political principles by which its sovereign chose to be guided. Of course such a sovereignty must, in practice, have been limited by the obvious facts of life. But where, as in Lamennais' own case, the individual was forced to dissent from the conclusions of authority, no choice was offered between obedience and expulsion. He felt that the Roman theory was false. The liberalism he had applied to the external relations of the church he endeavoured to insist must be true of her internal relations also. To be a true church her will must be the will of her whole personality and not of a part of it. It must synthesise the whole, and not a part, of her purpose. It must, in actual terms, be something more than the voice of a feeble old man dominated by an ambitious and grasping bureaucracy. They substituted their private advantage for the public need, and the church paid the penalty of such prostitution of its purposes.

He learned, in fact, what has been one of the fundamental lessons in the history of the modern state. Disguise it how we will, the sovereignty of the state will mean, in the long run, the sovereignty of the rulers who govern it.[407] On occasion, indeed, the exercise of power by those who misrepresent the general will may result in their dethronement; but history is sufficiently uncatastrophic to make revolution the exception rather than the rule of political life. Lamennais might protest that the sense of the church was against the decision of Gregory; but the only defence he could make was an appeal to the future. That, for the most part, is the defect of any distinction between the will of the state and of those who govern it. The latter, at any given moment, possesses the formal attributes of sovereign power. There is no means of questioning it save the means of patience. But, after all, the counsel that truth will eventually prevail is a maxim for eternity rather than for mortal men. Lamennais found that the concentration of power in the hands of the papal government deprived him of every normal means of protest and of argument. In the result, there is every cause to understand why the protagonist of ultramontanism should have become the tribune of the people.

Nor was his second discovery less important. He had him-

[407] I have discussed in detail this contention in the first chapter of this book.

self suggested that the centralised system of French civil administration neglected the welfare of the provinces. He found that the centralisation of the Roman church was not less unfortunate. Here, again, it is to the conciliar movement that the main thread of his ideas goes back. He confronted, intellectually, exactly the situation that the Europe of the fifteenth century confronted in matters of organisation. An England that had passed its statutes of Provisors and Præmunire knew the dangers of a unitary government. The plea of Gerson was frankly utilitarian and he argued that "solus populi suprema lex" cannot safely be interpreted in terms of centralisation.[408] So, too, did Nicholas of Cusa speak in the name of Germany when he made his striking plea against the reduction of a Christian community to papal serfdom. The difficulties of the sixteenth century were material difficulties—problems of finance, of jurisdiction, of place. Those of the nineteenth century by which Lamennais was confronted were spiritual in character, but it is to the same source that they are to be traced. So long as the powers of the constituent parts of the Roman church were derivative and not original it was useless to contend against the papal will. The Roman bureaucracy had everything on its side. It was useless to appeal to history or to tradition for of these the Pope was the appointed interpreter. It was unmeaning to accuse him of error, for he had been made the church and the church had been dignified by infallibility. It was useless to protest that, after all, the Pope was a man and thus subject to error. It was the future to decide whether he had spoken with the Jovian thunder of an *ex-cathedra* decision. The whole problem was but one instance of the fundamental truth upon which Dr. Figgis has insisted that "wherever blind obedience is preached, there is danger of moral corruption."[409] The institution, in fact, which can safely deny the necessity of criticism, the value of dissent from its conclusions, the resultant good of a re-examination of its foundations, is thus far unknown to human history. The claim of perfection is a common error among societies, but it is never

---

[408] Cf. Figgis, "From Gerson to Grotius," p. 64 f; and for the whole problem of Valois, "Le Pape et le Concile," Vol. I, Ch. II-III.

[409] Figgis, "Churches in the Modern State," p. 154.

made save where there is evidence of decay.   The omnipotent autocracy of Rome revealed its ignorance of the real conditions of social existence when it made that claim.   For the totality of influences, spiritual, intellectual, historic, that go to the building of a community are not to be resumed in the dicta of authority.   There is no loyalty compelling enough to absorb the affections of men.   All that we can hope is so effectually to exclude the possibility that its demands may be rejected as to minimise the dangers of anarchy.   But that is only to urge that the basis of our institutions must be liberty.

XII. THE INHERITANCE

ONCE again in her history Rome was given the opportunity to make her peace with modern life.   The modernist movement was, of course, for the most part, and directly, a theological movement.   But, indirectly at least, the problems it raised were not theological questions at all, but governmental questions, and it was a discussion as to the nature of a particular form of community that was in reality the main issue.   The critical work of men like Loisy may have provided the movement with its intellectual penumbra.   He doubtless expressed its yearnings after a more adequate scholarship with an ability that has made him one of the most striking figures of our time. But the thinker most representative of the modernist spirit was not Loisy but Tyrrell.[410]   For it was Tyrrell, above all, who realised from the outset that what was in fact in debate was the nature of communal authority.   He never denied the fundamental necessity of order in a state; where he was insistent was upon the limits that may be set to its demands. He was not a scholar; and the technical details of M. Loisy's researches he doubtless would have been willing to concede as beyond his purview.   What he essentially urged was the fact that Catholicism was a life, and that the only unchanging principle of life is the fact of change.   Like Lamennais, the

[410] Miss Petre's biography is our main authority. His most important works are (1) "A Much-abused Letter;" (2) "Through Scylla and Charybdis;" (3) 'Medievalism;" (4) "Lex Credendi." The reader will also find much of importance in the two volumes of essays collected under the title "The Faith of the Millions."

fundamental burden of his protest was a regret that the end
of Catholicism should have perished in pursuit of means.[411]
A member of the most ultramontane of ecclesiastical foundations, he had an unique opportunity to study its objects and
to test its purposes. It was by the deliberate choice of conscience
that he took the road which led eventually to his excommunication. But in his travelling he had evolved a theory of social
structure which is one of the most precious possessions of our
time.

The real problem that confronted him was the place of
liberty in organised life. With unlimited individualism he had
no sort of sympathy; for the rights of one man must inevitably
conflict with the claims of another and order is essential to
the maintenance of a just equilibrium. So he saw that the
Catholic church is not a group of men who can believe anything they please. "As to dogmas and Catholic truths," he
wrote,[412] "all loyal sons of the church are bound to accept
them." That is no more than to say that the Catholic church
has a certain personality loyalty to which is essential to membership. But he saw also that loyalty to the Catholic life was
not the same thing as loyalty to its government. Where that
government seemed to him false to the church he was bound,
as Newman held himself bound, to proceed by the light of his
conscience.[413] "I am driven on," he wrote,[414] "by a fatality
to follow the dominant influence of my life even if it should
break the heart of all the world," and thereby he proclaimed
the truth which lies at the bottom of every scheme of social
arrangement. Rome seemed to him to be suffering from a
feverish worship of authority, and to demand as a consequence
an uncritical and unquestioning obedience from Catholics which
it is not in human nature to give.[415] The problem then confronted him as to whether he should obey those who had the
technical right to demand his submission, or follow what he
believed to be the truth. Like Lamennais, he came to see
clearly that in such a choice there was in fact no real alternative.

[411] "Life," II, 74.
[412] "Life," II, 129.
[413] *Ibid.*, II, 141.
[414] *Ibid.*, II, 142.
[415] *Ibid.*, II, 146.

What baffled him was the unqualified absolutism of Rome. She was not amenable, as he deemed,[416] to the arguments of truth and justice. The seal of orthodoxy was set upon views which virtually denied all personality to the church as a whole to concentrate it in the Pope alone.[417] But such a view, as Dollinger had long before shown, was totally out of accord with the history of the church. "It is in the collective mind of the church," he says,[418] "not in the separate mind of the Pontiff that the truth is elaborated . . . . so the Pope cannot be conceived to speak *excathedra* except when he professedly investigates the ecumenical mind." Infallibility, in fact, is reserved for those occasions where the papal will interprets the "real" will of the church. Obedience then becomes due not to the Pope as a person, but to the Pope as the registering centre of a general consensus of opinion. But, it is clear enough, such a consensus would take account of minds like Loisy and Tyrrell and their direct condemnation would be thus impossible. So that he can draw a distinction, often, indeed, an antithesis, between obedience to authority and obedience to the church, precisely as Lamennais had done when he urged that Rome only was against him. Moreover such an absolutism was obviously bound to result in stagnation. "A creed and a theology," he wrote,[419] "ought to have been merely and only the product of her spiritual life and its exigencies." But in such an aspect it would be necessary for dogma to undergo continuous adaptation to the varying needs of each age. The difficulty with Rome was exactly her use of sovereign power to prevent the exercise of that adaptive faculty. She claimed to project her decisions without the category of time; and by claiming an immediately eternal character for her pronouncements she misunderstood the nature of society. For the "only adequate organ of religious development" was to him "the recognition of the entire Christian people as the true and immediate Vicarius Christi."[420]

The distinction, of course, is fundamental; it is the distinc-

416 *Ibid.*, II, 149.
417 *Ibid.*, II, 156.
418 *Ibid.*, II, 156.
419 *Ibid.*, II, 185.
420 *Ibid.*, II, 191.

tion between autocracy and democratic government. The "consciously formulated mind and will of the governing body of the church" could not obtain his final allegiance just because in his view, it mistook its class interest for the interest of the whole.[421] That governing body was endeavouring to make the life of the church run into channels which were, in fact, not wide enough to contain it. To him the unconscious self of the church was, equally with the conscious, the personality to which he owed his allegiance.[422] The fault of Rome was to neglect that deeper life and it had thus far failed in its work of the improvement of civilisation. To Rome, then, he would owe no duty save that of doing what in him lay of bringing her back to a sense of her greater mission. Nor was he confounded by the obvious difficulty that if the government of the church had failed no one could officially record her nature. "When authority," he wrote,[423] "is dumb or stultifies itself, private conviction resumes its previous rights and liberties." For authority is based upon trust and the violation of trust is duly resultant in its dissolution.

Such a distinction between clericalism and Catholicism[424] is obviously fundamental enough. The weakness of individualism is admitted, and the purpose of submission to collective organisation is to remedy it. "Our courage and hope and confidence," he said in a noble passage,[425] "are measured by our sense of the strength of the army to which we belong, of the history of her past victories." But the victories must be the victories of truth and the strength the strength of virtue. To share in a collective experience is not to be assured of salvation effortlessly. The soldier upon whom there is borne in a sense of purpose so wrong that the whole personality of the army becomes for him an evil thing has no alternative save to lay down his sword. That does not mean that his original membership was wrong. "On their spiritual side," he said of societies in general,[426] "and in so far as they are freely self-

---

[421] "A Much-abused Letter," p. 58.
[422] Cf. the very beautiful passage in *Ibid.*, p. 52 f.
[423] *Ibid.*, 47.
[424] *Ibid.*, 66.
[425] *Ibid.*, 83.
[426] "Through Scylla and Charybdis," p. 13.

forming, their future evades all prediction since it is not contained in or predetermined by their present . . . . spiritual development is not a process of passive unfolding, of which each step is vigorously determined by the preceding; but a process of active reconstruction, conditioned by the chance materials furnished by the quite incalculable succession of experiences." Life, in fact, refuses the categories of a formal syllogism, just as Lamennais' ultramontanism broadened, by actual contact with chance experience, into a liberal doctrine so wide that his theology was absorbed into its expanse. So Tyrrell understood, as Lamennais came to see, that the vital fact in membership of any society was not the actual bond but that of which the bond was symbol. He was compelled by his standards of right not merely to be a member of his fellowship, but also to stand outside and judge it.

Nor was that dualism insignificant since it formed the basis of the society's authority. "It is not their red robes," he said,[427] "but my own judgment about them that gives the pack of cardinals any title to distinction. Like Elizabeth, it has frocked them, and can unfrock them. It is they who are in peril, not we." The ability to withstand such a judgment is surely not the test of social worth. It is obvious enough, in religion above all things, that the judgment will not be made save in the most decisive conflicts of interpretation; and the only criterion of adequate compromise is the conveyance, on one side or the other, of genuine conviction. Nor does it matter where the problem of conflict shall arise. We too little realise that the fundamental principles are so important as inevitably to challenge an incessant discussion. Nor is it less inevitable that the existence of variety in temperament should result in diversity of interpretation. Newman and Manning could never have agreed in the meaning they attached to the dogmas of the church any more than it would have been possible for Cromwell to make his peace with Charles I. What is required on both sides is a willingness, not, at the final conflict, to use the bludgeon of authority instead of the rapier of argument. It was exactly the lack of that willingness on the part of Rome which resulted in her mistaken conception of authority. So

[427] "Life," II, 196.

long as she held that her governmental interpretation of dogma was not a phase but eternal, she could not, as Tyrrell saw, but be hostile to intellectual liberty.   Partly, of course, her hostility was the result of her belief in the divinity of her mission; but even when the temperamental consequences of that attitude are admitted grave difficulties remain.   For even if it be granted that the Roman church is an eternal society, it has had periods in its history which are not the expression of a golden age.   Did she not forget, as Tyrrell asked,[428] "that development means death and decay as well as growth, that it means continuity only by way of reproduction in a new generation?"   Even if Rome expelled from her principles the idea of development she could not destroy it; for even she must be bound by the laws of nature.

The problem Tyrrell thus confronted in the church he found not less acute within the Society of Jesus itself.   In the whole range of theological literature there are few analyses more incomparable at once in their subtlety and their simplicity than the account he penned of his relations with the Society.[429] Nothing of the splendour of Newman's own *Apologia* seems wanting to it; and it has the additional merit of being written from an impersonal attitude that only adds the greater weight to its authority.   It begins by a refutation of the ordinary charges against the Jesuit order.   "I do not see in the Society of Jesus a monstrous and deliberate conspiracy against liberty and progress in religion and civilisation."[430]   What he attacks is the attitude of those within the order who object to criticism on the ground of disloyalty.   One who loves the society to which he belongs must inevitably work for it; what he found was that to work for the interests of Catholicism, as he understood them, was to invoke the hostility of his superiors.   To defend liberalism, as he defended it, was to be the upholder of a cause to the destruction of which the whole forces of the Society were devoted.   Nor could he change its purpose.   "The alterations needed to adapt it to our days," he wrote,[431] "were

[428] *Ibid.*, II, 220.
[429] *Ibid.*, II, Ch. XII, and the letter to Father Martin printed as Appendix III.
[430] *Ibid.*, II, 272.
[431] *Ibid.*, 277-8.

too radical to be ever recognised or carried out by a body whose supreme government was vested in the rare assembly of a senate of men . . . . of whom only about one-eighth represented the living and progressive nationalities of the world. Unable to progress with its environment, the Society could only hope to live and to retain its ascendency in the church by keeping its environment unchanged." He did not blame it completely. "Corporations and crowds are non-moral agencies, and, judged by the standard of individual ethics, seem to commit atrocious crimes which, in fact, are no more crimes than the ravages of sea and storm, or of brute passion, or of other natural forces."[432] He rather dissented from the whole idea for which it had come to stand.[433] He objected to its exaction of "a slavish, unintelligent military obedience" which destroyed the whole purpose of the true submission to society.[434] He regards it as importation from state to church and as "wedded to principles subversive of . . . . social order and progress."[435] It has become less a zeal for progress than an enthusiasm for mechanical uniformity. It has abandoned its trust in unity of spirit to replace it by a juridical compulsion.[436] It has neglected the manysidedness of personality. "Even a soldier," he finely says,[437] "has a life outside his barracks in which he is a man and not merely an instrument . . . . he does not, like the Jesuit, deliberately, as a matter of religion and principle, merge his whole life in his profession, nor of set purpose disown his personality and rights as a free spiritual individual." Yet it is to this obedience that society drives its members. It sets as the correlative of its autocracy an obedience that is blind and uncriticising. Such a method "is the worst and most profoundly immoral forms of government that the world has yet known. For the essence of all vice and immorality is the destruction of spiritual liberty."[438]

[432] *Ibid.*, II, 279. Cf. his essay on the Corporate Mind in "Through Scylla and Charybdis."
[433] "Life," II, 465.
[434] *Ibid.*, II, 467.
[435] *Ibid.*, II, 469.
[436] *Ibid.*, II, 476.
[437] *Ibid.*, II, 479 f.
[438] *Ibid.*, II, 481.

He does not, it has been pointed out, blame the society as he would blame a man. "So far," he writes,[439] "as a society has a self at all, it must be self-assertive, self-complacent, proud, egotistical;" but it is just because of its inherent openness to these dangers that the loyalty of its members dare not be unlimited. "A sane and healthy loyalty, far from blinding a man, will make him keenly critical of his regiment and observant of its defects and weakness, and will check any sort of dangerous complacency and optimism." He insisted on the significance of the influence exerted by the corporate action of the society upon the character of its members. He denounced its corporate complacency. "The first condition of progress and improvement," he said,[440] "is a confession of fault or of fallibility." But this the society virtually refused to admit since it would have been an invitation to thought upon the part of its members. But thought was incompatible with passivity, and it was that deadly negation of personality which, above all, the society desired.

What was the result? "I see in Jesuitism," he wrote,[441] ". . . . just the counter-extravagance of Protestantism; on this side liberty misinterpreted as the contempt of authority; on that, authority misinterpreted as the contempt of liberty. The Society's boast is to have stayed the spread of Protestantism and to have saved half Europe to the church. Its success has been its ruin; its action has been met with reaction; in buttressing, it has crushed liberty and established Absolutism . . . . The true synthesis of liberty and authority is still to seek." Assuredly, Tyrrell himself did not pretend to supply it. But where he insisted upon the extravagance of absolute power he was surely correct in his assertions. His own case is the clearest proof of the dangers of a system which regards itself as immune from attack. The fact is that Nature expresses herself less in absolutes than in compromises. It may be true, as a distinguished French thinker has argued,[442] that only in the

[439] *Ibid.*, II, 482.

[440] *Ibid.*, II, 485.

[441] *Ibid.*, II, 497.

[442] Cf. M. Sorel's preface, p. 12, to M. Berth's "Les Méfaits des Intellectuals."

absolute affirmative can the seeds of progress be discovered; yet the penalty of such formulation is the inability to supply more than a temporary need. Such lack of elasticity is surely in itself evidence of an unfitness to survive in an environment where the true criterion of worth is an adaptability to a changing environment.

Nor is this all. No discussion of social organisation is satisfactory which does not take account of the inherently plural character of human personality. That was what Tyrrell meant by his urgent insistence upon freedom. For however rich may be the genius of a man for fellowship he has also an inwardness of perception which no association can absorb. Few men have been more passionately at one with the church than was Lamennais before 1829; yet even amidst the fever of a passionate activity he remained a brooding and lonely being. It is the existence of that intimate and precious arcanum of the soul which makes loyalty, in the last analysis, in every case a matter of the private judgment of each of us. Organisation may attempt, as Tyrrell urged that the Society of Jesus attempted, to root out the recesses. Doubtless a long training in subjection to despotism is more powerful than the individual will. Yet the experience of nations seems to suggest that the effect is one rather to be stamped afresh upon each generation than to be inherited by the memory of a people. Excessive authoritarianism breeds less affection for, than suspicion of, a government. For it is guilty of one of the gravest fallacies in the business of administration by its effort to treat men as uniform machines. No government is secure which fails to remember the uniqueness of the individual. Practical legislation may take the greatest common measure of consent or of desire, but where men are driven back to first principles it is only moral unanimity that is, as the fathers of the church were wise enough to realise, in the full sense effective. Every Ireland will have its Ulster[443] where fundamental human emotion is at stake and no theory of society that neglects it will be adequate because it will be then no more than a theory of coercion. A papal condemnation may drive a Montalembert and a Hefele into acceptance of ideals to which they have been a stranger; but a Lamennais and a

[443] This must not be taken to indicate a belief that Ulster has been right.

Dollinger will remain unmoved, and it is the protest that will live rather than the acquiescence.

In the last instance, then, the individual can make his appeal beyond that tribunal which, for practical purposes, is clothed with sovereign power. "Above the constitutional headship," wrote Tyrrell,[444] "there is the pre-constitutional, which is a necessary fact and not a doctrine. It cannot be denied that in the life of that formless church which underlies the hierarchic organisation, God's spirit exercises a silent but sovereign criticism; that his resistlessly effectual judgment is made known, not in the precise language of definition and decree, but in the slow manifestation of practical results; in the survival of what has proved itself life-giving; in the decay and oblivion of all whose value was but relative and temporary." It is, perhaps, an appeal to the future; but it is an appeal to which judgment must be rendered, since it takes its stand upon the basic character of the institution involved. It means, of course, ultimately, a refusal on the part of men to accept the reduction of social form to unity; for such reduction implies, as we have learned, the destruction of what is living and vigorously individual to be replaced by a meaningless uniformity. A Lamennais who surrendered his liberalism otherwise than by the slow arrival of a conviction of its error would be no longer, in any real sense, the Lamennais we know. That is why, despite its practical efficiency as a working instrument, authority must, at every stage of its activity submit to the closest scrutiny. It must not so exert itself as to involve treason on the part of its members to their consciences. From some, doubtless, that treason will not be difficult to secure; but there will always be those who, like Lamennais and Tyrrell, feel themselves bound to show "that resistance was still a contingency to be reckoned with . . . . that Rome was trading on the assumption that the idea of actual obedience had so triumphed that she might say or do anything, however reckless."[445] The choice has its difficulties and, as Tyrrell finely said,[446] "the deliverers of the crowd will be stoned and crucified by the crowd . . . . (but

[444] "Through Scylla and Charybdis," p. 381
[445] "Life," II, 340.
[446] *Ibid.*, II, 347.

when) . . . . the religion of the crowd is corrupted . . . . there we cannot be with the crowd." Both of them saw that Rome had gone beyond the boundaries of her real purpose, that she was asking·from her children an allegiance to ends in fact unconcerned with the true ethos of catholicism. To Lamennais she was the ally of despotism as to Tyrrell she was the assailant of civilisation and each saw the fatal prospects of her effort. "Rome," wrote Tyrrell in a letter that might have been Lamennais',[447] "Rome cares nothing for religion—only for power . . . . *Hinc illae lacrimae!* she will never yield willingly. But her power will soon be broken to pieces by the pressure of modern governments—weary of her turbulence and sedition; and then perhaps she may have no reason to oppose modernism and may remember her true *raison d'être*." But until that return had been made obedience was impossible. "I rightly or wrongly hold," Tyrrell said to one who consulted him in distress,[448] "there is a limit to ecclesiastical as to civil authority—a time when resistance is duty and submission treason. If I believe the captain is unawares steering for the rocks I will not obey him. I am not infallible; he may be right; but I must go by my own moral certainties." That is still the watchword of the deepest freedom.

Yet there is one weakness in Tyrrell's attitude upon which it is worth while for a moment to insist. There are few things more dangerous than the effort to evolve for corporate personality a standard of judgment different from the criterion by which we judge of the conduct of men. It is, of course, true enough that the unity of corporate life is less strong, in the sense that it is less tangible, than that of individual personality. Yet it is clear enough that in law, in politics, in economics, at the present time, the emphasis of our needs is driving us to an insistence upon vicarious liability. We are forced more and more to recognise that while, in the last resort, a corporate relation is, basically, a relation of individuals, nevertheless, for most practical purposes, it is of the fact of their unity that we must take notice. How Rome is built up matters, to outsiders, but little; but the influence of the Rome so built upon modern

[447] *Ibid.*, II, 355.
[448] *Ibid.*, II, 405.

life matters to all of us very greatly. A modern corporation acts as an individual would act in a similar situation; that is to say by agents and servants. Surely, if that be the case, an adequate interpretation of their activities must take account of the real unity whence they derive.[449]

It is not an adequate reply to answer as certainly Tyrrell, perhaps Lamennais also, would have answered, that the "real" will of an institution may differ from that of those who operate it, that the will of the Roman Church is not the will of its sovereign pontiff. The will upon which our judgment must be expressed is surely the will that is promulgated and obeyed. The dumb and enforced acquiescence of a people may be tragedy enough; but if the cohesive force of their acquiescence is bent to the corporate purpose it is difficult to see how the separation of their acts from its own may be made. For, after all, it is precisely the fact of their acquiescence which permits the registration of wrong. The only course is active dissent from the conclusions of authority, as both Lamennais and Tyrrell implicitly admitted when they withdrew from the Roman Communion rather than follow it in paths they deemed mistaken. Lamennais could easily have urged that it was folly to pit his strength against Rome and have acquiesced in the condemnation of democracy. Tyrrell could similarly have insisted that his single effort would not avail to teach Rome the inevitability of modernist doctrine. Yet they would not have been Lamennais and Tyrrell if they had been silent even where they loved so greatly.

For the fact is that to argue, as Tyrrell argued, that a social will is by its nature more liable to egoism than an individual will means surely no more than the answer that we must then be more vigorous in the application of our standards. Our judgment that corporate sin is more easily to be excused is probably no more than an inference from the separation Machiavelli effected between politics and ethics. How fatal that step has been Lord Acton has magistrally demonstrated in a famous argument.[450] It is, in short, a simple excuse for wrong-

[449] Cf. my papers in 29 *Harv. L. Rev.* 404 and 26 *Yale Law Journal* 122 f.

[450] Cf. the great inaugural lecture, reprinted in his "Lectures in Modern History" with the introduction to Mr. Burd's edition of "The Prince."

ful conduct. Because, as in the famous *Taff Vale* case, men will
do things for their trade union which they would hesitate to do
in private life, that is no reason to excuse an institution of which
the nature demands illegal activities from its agents. Because
the church of Rome was anxious to discredit the efforts of the
French republic, that does not justify the activities which
culminated in the curious tissue of falsehood and corruption
revealed by the publication of the nuncio's dispatches.[451] If we
are definitely wedded to a complex scheme of group-loyalties,
the only method of moral safety is to demand from each group
the standards exacted from its individual member. The argument so often and so unthinkingly made about the non-existence
of corporate mind misses the point completely. We are dealing
with unified action and we cannot mistake the real character
of its personality. We have too recently had demonstration of
the tragic evil which comes from elevating it without the moral
law, to be willing to allow it release from the penalty of its corporate offences.

Such an attitude, indeed, would serve to strengthen the position of Lamennais. It is no more than the affirmation that
what, above all, we need is the democratic interpretation of the
principles of authority. We refuse to reduce the individual to a
nullity simply because he is a human being. The basis of our
social organisation is living and not mechanical; it is founded
upon the consciences of men. It does not conceal from itself
the dangers to which it lies open. Consciously, it is a threat
against order. Consciously, it offers a loophole to what may
well resolve itself into revolution. But that is only because we
are certain that the supreme thing in the modern world is the
love of what men deem to be right. A society which is able to
admit the protest of its members has already safeguarded itself
against the shock of disruption. If the principle of its life be
the exclusion of fundamental dissent, that life is already poisoned
at its source. That was why Tyrrell flung abroad his flaming
protest against the evil of absolutism. The individual doubtless, will often be mistaken just as authority itself has never
been free from error. Yet in the clash of ideas we shall

[451] Cf. the collection of documents published as "Les Fiches Pontificales
de Monsignor Montagnini" (Paris, 1908).

find the means of truth.   There is no other safeguard of progress.

XIII. CONCLUSION

LAMENNAIS never returned to the Catholic church.   He lived and died and suffered with those for whom he had chosen the path of exile.   His ideas grew more and more liberal until, towards the end, he found himself in close kinship with the apostles of communism.   Of the love the common people bore him there is evidence enough; and his pen was ceaselessly employed in the task of their liberation.   He found new friends who, in some measure, at least, healed the wounds that had been caused by the defection of the old.   The church made divers efforts to secure his conversion but always without success.   His death seems to have meant but little to a democracy that was being fed on the dangerous fruits of imperial adventure.   Yet even as it was, so great was the honour of his name that the government of Louis Napoleon compelled his interment in the earlier hours of dawn.   He was buried, as he had wished, without any religious ceremonial; and it was by his request that Auguste Barbet refused the usual offer of a cross.   That was perhaps less an epitaph than a prophecy.

CHAPTER FOUR

THE POLITICAL THEORY OF ROYER-COLLARD[1]

I. THE SIGNIFICANCE OF THE RESTORATION

T HE restoration of the Bourbon House created more problems than it solved. It was intended by the allies less as a consecration of political doctrine than as the refutation of the Napoleonic idea. It had, indeed, the merit of preserving, to some extent, the self-respect of the French nation by returning to it a ruler supported by every historic tradition in France anterior to the Revolution. But it was exactly therein that its error is to be found; for to make abstraction of the Revolution had already become impossible. The new system, in fact, was, from the outset, incapable even of understanding the problems with which it was called upon to deal. Those who had returned with Louis from exile in nowise perceived that new and acceptable dogmas had already replaced the prejudiced privileges of the *ancien régime.* They came not to fulfil but to destroy. They did not realise that even the despotic system of Napoleon had taken due account of the revolutionary spirit. They were, above all things, eager to restore the social and political edifice of the eighteenth century. They did not understand that their principles, no less than their methods, were already obsolete.

For the Revolution, despite its excesses, had been a fruitful epoch in political thought. It had been an incredible experience in the formation of political habits. Those who had

[1] The fundamental authority is the life of de Barante which collects the text of Royer's speeches. M. Faguet has a brilliant study of him in the first volume of his " Politiques et Moralistes" to which I am much indebted. There is a useful little life by Spuller; and M. Nismes-Desmarets has recently published a laborious and exhaustive analysis of his political doctrines. The essay by Scherer in the first volume of his "Etudes" and that by C. de Rémusat in the second of his collected papers are both of much value.

tasted the sweets of national sovereignty were not willing to resign their power because Napoleon had been beaten upon the battlefield. From the thousand strands of the complex web of the Revolution, a certain order and meaning had eventually emerged. The idea of privilege had suffered a final shock. The sovereignty of the state had been transferred from king to people. The *Declaration of Rights* had embodied an enthusiastic belief in the dignity of human personality which suggested the potentialities of a new and profitable organization of society. The idea of toleration, if it had been bent by the oppression of Napoleon and the unclean craftiness of Fouché, was far from broken. The third estate had arrived at manhood; from being nothing it had come, as in Sieyès' superb prophecy, to demand all. If it was a serious limitation upon democratic growth that the workers should have been excluded from power still, when nobility and bourgeoisie stood face to face, the prospects of advance were fortunate. For no one could doubt where the victory must one day lie.

Little enough, indeed, of all this was perceived by those whom the downfall of Napoleon had swept into power. What rather is remarkable is the rapidity with which the old order was established again. The reaction was as thorough-going as the Revolution; and even if the essential work of the Revolution had penetrated too subtly into the structure of the social fabric to be overthrown at all speedily, signs are not wanting that it was not for lack of ill-will towards it. The Restoration divides itself clearly into three periods; and only in one brief moment was there the faint hope that a compromise with liberalism might be effected. No justification save that of revenge can ever be found for the pitiless extravagance of the reaction which followed the Hundred days;[2] not even the combined efforts of a king and government which alike took no satisfaction in persecution were able to withstand the brutality of its effort. From 1816, when the moderation of M. Decazes stayed for a period of four years the desire of royalism to come to death-grips with the remaining factions which clung to the ideas of 1793, there was hope of peace. But the period was

[2] M. Viviani has finely described it in his contribution to Jaurés' "Histoire Socialiste." See Vol. VII p. 99, 103.

full of troubles and dissension; and the assassination of the
Duc de Berri persuaded Louis that a compromise with liberalism was an invitation to disaster. Henceforth, as M. Scherer
has finely said,[3] it was already Charles X who ruled. The
system that the charter had endeavored to inaugurate was
struck at its foundations. The reactionary efforts of the Royalists only spurred their opponents to greater violence. It was
the old antagonism between the émigrés and the Revolution
in which the former had learned that the methods of parliamentary government can be used to effect an administrative
despotism. Henceforth they had no other object; and the barricades of 1830 were the one possible answer to their pretensions.

It was an assault upon individualism that they attempted;
and thinkers were not lacking who were willing to invent a
theory upon which to embroider the necessity of oppression.
Nor is the passion by which they were inspired unintelligible
to a generation which has felt the shock of an European catastrophe. They proclaimed the superiority of society to the individual and drew therefrom the inference that their own self-
interest might be equated therewith. To the revolutionary insistence that only by his own efforts could man create an adequate civilisation, they retorted that the only true creation
could come from the hands of God. Where the Revolution
had asserted the significance of novelty they affirmed the supreme value of tradition. They sought out the true principles
of social order and discovered them in the antithesis of revolutionary doctrine. Whether their interest was in politics, as
with Bonald, or in religion, as with Lamennais, it was always
the secret of unity for which they were searching. They were
convinced that the source of the Revolution had been the
weakness of authority and they sought to re-establish it upon
an unshakeable foundation. They had no experience of a
world in which power might be safeguarded by its dispersion.
All they could understand was its expression in the ancient
terms. They considered the problem of the relation of the individual to the state and answered unhesitatingly that he must
be absorbed by it. It is the beatification of the *status quo* and
it is very intelligible. Their fundamental desire was to safe-

[3] "Etudes," I, 68.

guard a system which they believed essential for social salvation. That it happened to coincide with their retention of the control of the state was perhaps rather accidental than the result of set purpose. For they were, in some sort, empirical in their outlook. They had a real sense of the growth of institutions.[4] They set themselves firmly against a political theory which should fit its facts to an *a priori* system. But their empiricism was essentially emotional and, in reality, it signified no more than the translation into facts of their political desires. Their sense of development was limited to their respect for certain well-worn and traditional avenues of growth. They were almost amazingly unable to understand that the Revolution was a fact no less than a tragedy; and their effort to ignore its meaning was only evidence of their intellectual limitation.

The truth simply is that they were in no real sense seekers of truth. Political ideas for them were essentially offensive weapons. They held themselves at liberty to misinterpret ideas, to falsify conclusions, to distort purposes. Their view of human nature was uniformly low and they were never logical enough to admit that their vilification must apply equally to themselves. They seized upon a single fact in the political history of France and made of it a gospel of defiance. Power was theirs, and the efforts of philosophers and evil men had hurled them from what was rightly their own. What, then, they had to do was to search out the conditions upon which the maintenance of its restoration might be possible. Of the obvious change in social perspective they took no account. That commercial growth and intellectual discovery was rendering obsolete the paternal system for which they stood sponsor they had no shadow of perception. That the source of authority in anything so complex as a political society can never in fact be single they did not in the least degree understand. They wished the people well; but the possession of will they restricted to themselves. They did not grasp the basic fact that the state is in truth no more than a will-organisation and that if, on occasion, that will may result in unified activity that gives no guarantee of permanent unity. They misunderstood the conditions of state-life. They did not perceive that

[4] Cf. H. Michel, "L'Idée de l'Etat," p. 167 f.

there are always limits to the exercise of power. They were so nicely tender of their own consciences that they did not admit the existence of conscience outside their own order. They were so satisfied with their manipulation of the state that they mistook their private good for the general welfare and Paris retorted in its usual fashion to that error.

Their theocracy, in brief, was as violent as the passionate democracy they so virulently condemned. Yet it is important to remember that their ideas were not confined to France. The war of liberation resulted in England in seventeen abortive years of stagnation and distress. The very poets who had written hymns to liberty found excuses for the deferment of its application. The typical English statesman of the age was Eldon; and the toryism he represented was not less profound than that of France. The English bishops adopted an attitude to Catholic emancipation which suggested nothing so much as a belief that England was the private appanage of the English church.[5] The Duke of Wellington was little more able to appreciate the drift of opinion than the Prince de Polignac. If England avoided a theoretical revolution, the Reform Act of 1832 was symbolical of a new era in the history of political structure. It was the admission that Toryism was dead, and when Sir Robert Peel became Prime Minister his first act was to recognize that a revolution had been silently effected.

Nor was the reaction less marked in Germany.[6] The effort of Savigny was toward nothing so much as the dethronement of the rationalism by which the eighteenth century had been distinguished. "Law," he said in effect, "cannot be made at the behest of men;" and if he was justified in his emphasis on the thousand forces that go to its construction he was yet as surely transforming the doctrine of evolution into a defence of conservatism. His theory of legislative function is so precisely the antithesis of that of Rousseau as naturally to occasion the

[5] Cf. my "Problem of Sovereignty," p. 123. The intellectual current of time is finely analysed in Professor Dicey's classic "Law and Public Opinion," Lect. V.

[6] The really admirable essay of R. Haym "Die Romantische Schule" is a mine of wisdom upon this problem.

suspicion that he was answering the latter. His sacrifice of the individual to the state, his insistence upon the superiority of its life to that of its constituent parts[7] could be used, in the hands of Hegel, as the high road to a thoroughgoing absolutism. Herder and Schelling could find sufficient beauty in the romance of Rome to disguise the direction in which its ideals were bending. Fichte did not hesitate to absorb the individual in the state.[8] In such an analysis personality becomes no more than the opportunity to become part of an immense organism in which no interstices are to be found. But such negation of the individual mind is, in fact, no more in its results than a theocracy in which God has been replaced by the King of Prussia. Germany, in fact, threw off the bonds of Roman despotism only to demonstrate that the root of her objection was less to the despotism than to its foreign character. So she, too, could forge the weapons which, in Bismarck's hands, were to stimulate the ideal of a world reduced to an unity expressed in terms of German dominion.

Liberalism, in such an attitude, was clearly difficult enough. Much of this distrust of freedom was, of course, intelligible. It was a dictum of Sir Henry Maine's that progress is the exception in history; and certainly in each epoch of novel ideas the universal tendency of those who hold the reins of power has been to insist upon the virtue of traditional system. They feared so greatly the movement of liberal ideas that it seems never to have occurred to them that they might be harnessed to government. They met the proclamation of belief with an emphatic defiance; and demonstrated once more the danger that is inherent in the very fact of power. Those who stood by the cause of freedom in these difficult years had much obloquy to undergo. To accept the fact of the Revolution was held to be synonymous with a justification of its excesses. To put the individual outside the state, to deny his absorption by the various loyalties by which he was bound, was regarded as giving a handle to every sort and kind of dangerous ambition. Anyone who reads the long list of legis-

---

[7] Cf. his "Heutige System das Röm. Rechts," Bk. I, Ch. II, Sec. 9.

[8] His "Geschlossene Handelstaat" (1800) is a striking example of this attitude.

lative efforts during the Bourbon Restoration can make no mistake as to its nature. Control of the judiciary, censorship of the press, restriction upon the right of association, laws of exception, limitation upon the right of franchise, a system of military privilege[9]—by these on every hand we are confronted. The idea of toleration seems almost dead. The generous enthusiasm of 1789 is hardly to be perceived. It is a cynical generation, mistrustful, wearied, without conviction of progress, without courage to experiment. It is a generation that has seen its parents gamble for their lives and conceived a natural distaste for adventure. Yet it is also a generation redeemed from unrelieved suspicion of men by the devoted eagerness of some few of its most distinguished figures. A generation in which Guizot learned the principles of representative government and in which Royer-Collard united to ethics the politics from which it had been too long divorced, is not entirely without its fascination. It serves, at any rate, to enforce the lesson that even the most vicious of political systems contains within itself the germs of self-destruction.

II. THE THEORY OF THE CHARTER

THERE is little or no dramatic interest in the life of Royer-Collard. He was a typical member of the bourgeosie whom one at least of his opponents did not hesitate to characterise as jealous of the ancient nobility.[10] He sat in the National Assembly, and his deep opposition to the Jacobin policy resulted in a narrow escape from the guillotine.[11] With the coming of more moderate days he sat in the Council of Five Hundred and was, for a time, the cherished adviser of the exiled Bourbons. In the Napoleonic régime he withdrew from political life and occupied himself with the study of philosophy as a lecturer at the Sorbonne. With the return of Louis XVIII he took a distinguished place in the lower house of the Chamber of Deputies and remained there almost to his death. Apart from a place on the Council of State, a directorship in the council of

[9] Cf. the speech of Royer-Collard, Barante, 1, 371 f.
[10] Villèle, "Mémoires," I, 346.
[11] See the splendid story of his escape in the Life by Spuller, p. 29-30.

Public Instruction and a brief Presidency of the Chamber, he held no political office. He was in sympathy with no administration save at a single moment in his career. Save for his association with Guizot, De Serre and Camille Jordan, it is not untrue to suggest that he never belonged to a political party in the sense of merging his convictions with those of a group of men. His authority came from the power of his eloquence, the impressive distinction of his personality, the substantial splendour of his convictions. He was, indeed, a difficult colleague. He had a sufficient sense of his power to make others realise a little acutely his awareness of it.[12] He was regarded for so long as infallible by a group of admiring friends that he came, in the end, almost to share their convictions upon that question.[13] His spirit was difficult alike from his mistrust of power and of its exercise,[14] as from his persistent and disdainful refusal of office.[15] Whether Villèle is right in his suspicion that his aloofness came from a pride that had been hurt by the ingratitude of Louis XVIII[16] the fact remains that while he was willing to disturb ministers he was never eager to construct them. Of his private life we know little or nothing; and though his love of Pascal is evidence enough of his sincere attachment for the somewhat mellowed jansenism amidst which he was educated, we have little enough evidence whereby to estimate its influence upon his opinions. All that can be said of the man himself is that he was sincere, that he was honest, and that he was deservedly eminent. There have been few men in history whose life is so completely to be sought in the doctrines that he preached.

The name that has become attached to his school is, in truth, in no small degree misleading. We tend to think of the Doctrinaires as a body of men who applied arid principles to circumstances for which they are unsuited. It is much more accurate to compare them to that Fourth Party which rendered so great a service to English politics in the last century. Different as

---

[12] Cf. Vitrolles, "Memoires," III, 73.
[13] Cf. remarks of the Duchess de Broglie in Barante, "Memoires, "II, 374.
[14] Cf. Guizot "Memoires" (Eng. trans.), I, 117.
[15] Spuller. op. cit. 154
[16] Villèle op. cit. II, 46.

were their constituent personalities, the four men in each were invaluable alike from the independence as from the ability of their criticism. Each continually drove back government upon the principles from which it took its vise, principles too often so implicit in the business of deliberation as to be forgotten by those whom they inspire. Not that the Doctrinaires were any clearer than Lord Randolph Churchill in their ultimate meta-physic. What surrounds them is less a theory than an atmos-phere, so that M. Michel could without injustice claim that what they attempted was simply the analysis and justification of a certain interpretation of circumstances.[17] Yet the assertion is perhaps less true of Royer-Collard than it is of his colleagues. Anyone who compares the political theory of Guizot with his policy as minister will not be inclined to doubt the grotesque flexibility of his ideas. Royer-Collard's attitude was in every situation consistent. If he seemed to be effecting a compromise between the *ancien régime* and the Revolution, he would probably have explained his effort by justifying it. The whole of his life was spent in the insistence that government depends upon rational principles of compromise. He was alike opposed to the gloomy extravagances of royalism as to the democratic pre-tensions of the disappointed heirs of the Revolution. Each signified for him the party of a despotism and he endeavored to search out the philosophy of a *juste milieu*. It was thus that he was led, as Guizot has aptly remarked,[18] to the maintenance of interests rather than the affirmation of rights. That was why he equally condemned the Chambre Introuvable and the ideas of 1793. For he believed that the true analysis of political structure renders impossible any conception of national inter-ests which suggests their unified nature. He on the contrary insisted that the state is composed of interests often antag-onistic between which an equilibrium must be maintained by compromise. The maintenance of that balance was the busi-ness of government and it was in that very absence of unity that he therefore discovered merit; for, by its very nature, it set, as he deemed, a limit to the abuse of power.

What, in fact, is the keynote of his whole doctrine is the

[17] Michel, "L'Idée de L'Etat," p. 291.
[18] Guziot, "Memoires" (Eng. trans.), I, 154.

denial of the existence of sovereignty. He admitted the existence of power, but he was always, as Guizot remarked,[19] a mor-
alist who was suspicious of its exercise. The result was his
insistence that its necessary limitations should be discovered
and it was to that search that he devoted himself.[20] The peculiar expression of policy for which he stood was embodied in the
charter. To him the charter was not so much a compromise
as a solution. He never seems to have realised how unwillingly
it had been drawn from the restored king. He did not feel,
with so many of his contemporaries, its lack of clarity. He did
not understand their refusal to believe in its certainties. "For
all of us," Barante has said,[21] "it was simply a formality exacted
by circumstances and destined to perish with them. The Liberals saw with what repugnance and, consequently, with how
little good faith, submission had been made to the necessities of
the Revolution." Royer-Collard did not regard it in this way.
Sceptical of all things he may have been by nature;[22] but in the
virtues of the charter he put complete confidence. It was for
him a touchstone by which the rightness of all action might be
tested. He looked upon it as the crystallised experience of the
whole of French history.

It was the expression of such limitations upon the exercise
of power as the past seemed to suggest. Sovereignty of king
and people it alike rejected. The one presupposed a despotism
and the other a republic. But France by her political nature
was a monarchy in which the king governed by means of his
ministers. He chose his ministers and his will was law. But
upon his action a vital check was laid. The Chamber of Deputies was a deliberative council resort to which gave government
the means of realising wisdom in legislation.[23] Since the object
of royalty was to translate into action the balance of interests
within the Chamber the result was to limit the possibility of
despotic government. Neither king nor Parliament was therefore
sovereign for the simple reason that the power of each was lim-

[19] "Memoires," 1, 117.
[20] Barante, "Life," II, 130.
[21] "Memoires," Vol. I, p. 385.
[22] *Ibid.*, III, 20.
[23] Barante, I, 219.

ited, either in practice or in theory. To each was assigned functions which, while they might involve the exercise of will, never admitted the possibility of a will without control. The king was government, and government might involve the exercise of force; but the problem was always the extent of force to be used and the test was the principles of the Charter. Nor did he admit an uncontrolled right in the people. They represented only the brute mass of men and he would not admit that the mere agglomeration of numbers would justify the exercise of sovereign powers. The despotism of many was for him still a despotism, and he rejected it.[24] He would no more admit that principles so fundamental can be contradicted by tradition or number than he would have admitted the justice of extravagance.

The psychological background of this attitude it is not difficult to discover. The abuse of sovereignty under the *ancien régime* had resulted in the despotism of the Convention. In each case the claim of uncontrolled power had resulted in the destruction of liberty. It did not matter that in one case that lack of limitation could give itself historic background. It was unimportant that in the other men were tasting, for the first time, a right which they had been too long denied. He saw clearly that some system of checks and balances was essential if order and peace were to be safeguarded. That safeguard he discovered in the Charter. It was the connective tissue of the body-politic. It represented the principles upon which the state could with security lead its life. To say that the charter was the source of law was to say that any specific exercise of power was in accord with the tradition of France.[25] And the charter divided power. If it gave the king the power of government, it gave power of criticism, of suggestion, of grievance to the aristocracy and the delegates of the people. So complex is its scheme of contribution to law-making that when the act is on the statute-book none can in reality say whence, exactly, it is derived. But that is to show that the charter is successful. It is to admit that varying interests have combined in a result which, because limited by all, is acceptable to all.

[24] *Ibid.*, II, 152, 463.
[25] Cf. Faguet, op. cit., I, 263.

It is the whole history of France that he finds in the charter.[26] Long centuries have gone to its painful elaboration. It was needful that he should urge the accuracy of this fiction in order thereby that he might counterbalance the strength of royalism. For, clearly, that upon which he was engaged was the substitution of a rule of law for a rule of force. Unless he could gain the admission that the strength of a law is not the chance acquiescence of a majority behind it the administration of power would be therein deprived of its moral significance. But, to that end, it was essential that he should not have to struggle against the past and he prevented that catastrophe by annexing it. He saw quite clearly that two powers stood face to face. The monarchy had elaborated the dogma of personal sovereignty; the Revolution had transferred it to the nation. If he could emphasise the legitimacy of the one, by which he meant its full accord with the national tradition, he could then insist upon the significance of the other. He could point out that the decline of royal absolutism was only the growth of a condition already inherent in the *ancien régime*. France was the synthesis of many sovereignties which need not always claim a royal origin.[27] They had lived together; and that was to say that the conception of a balance of internal powers was already old. What the Revolution had done was to abolish those sovereignties and to leave the individual face to face with the state. "Nous ne sommes pas citoyens," he said in an effective phrase,[28] "nous sommes des administrés," and the problem was to prevent the submergence of the individual that had been effected by the centralisation of power.

That, in effect, was the object of the charter. The path from the despotism of the *ancien régime* to the new despotism of the Revolution was largely accidental but equally dangerous. "La démocratie," he said in a famous sentence, "coule à pleins bords"[29] and there was for him no need to suspect it of needing safeguards any more inherent than the ancient monarchy had possessed. What then it clearly became necessary to do was to put certain states of fact beyond the reach of ordinary adminis-

[26] *Ibid.*
[27] Barante, II, 13.
[28] *Ibid.*, II, 131.
[29] *Ibid.*, II, 134.

tration.   France had become egalitarian and centralised.   The
pressure of its parts must not overwhelm certain principles that
safeguard the fullness of life.   These principles are rights in the
possession of which the individual will find protection against
absorption.[30]   These rights will be general in character; Jacques
Bonhomme has been made the center of the French state by the
Revolution.   They will be private rights in the sense that they
attach to individual personality.   But they will be general in
that unlike the rights of the *ancien régime* they will not be exceptional in character.   They will replace the old privileges that
the flood-tide of 1789 had borne away upon its eddies.   They
will be a centre of inviolability and thus a limitation upon power.
Therein he finds of course, the main source of their virtue.

III. NECESSARY FREEDOMS

BROADLY speaking, the liberties which lie at the base of his
system were four in number.   Liberty of the press he would
perhaps have regarded as most fundamental.   It was, for him,
not merely a condition of political liberty, but, even more, its
very foundation.[31]   That it might result in abuse he would certainly not have denied any more than he would have refused to
punish the violation of the right to publication.[32]   The problem
for him was to find the conditions under which the right could
be most wisely exercised.   It was wrong to dispair of a solution.
It was wrong because the result of so desperate a conclusion must
result either in an anarchy or in despotism.[33]   But it was only
by means of the press that the ideas of the mass of men might
become known.   Such knowledge clearly must set limits to the
exercise of power.   It is a safeguard; for it is from popular
silence that, above all, the idea of despotism draws its richest
nourishment.   "Power," he said in a striking sentence,[34] "like
the individual, has its temperament, its manner, its natural
instinct."   But that is to say that it is capable of being influenced, and freedom of the press was a valuable weapon to that

[30] *Ibid.*, I, 298.
[31] *Ibid.*, I, 340.
[32] Barante, II, 500.
[33] *Ibid.*, I, 341.
[34] *Ibid.*, I, 349.

end. Its inconvenience to government he in no sense denied; but he attributed that inconvenience less to the inherent nature of thought than to the absorptiveness of power. So long as a desire for arbitrary action is checked at every point of its advance by those whose business it is to examine its justification, its translation in fact is sufficiently remote to ensure the general security.[35] That in practice it will become the possession of a few he knew. But he was unwilling to leave at the mercy of government the surest method of criticising it. It was a barrier against absolution. In his eyes it needed no further justification.

It was, indeed, for him the replacement of those old checks on the abuse of monarchy which had characterised the *ancien régime*. Just as the independent magistracies of ancient France had limited the full exercise of sovereignty for the common good, so is freedom of the press a political institution which safeguards the rule of law. "The day on which it perishes," he said,[36] "is the day on which we shall return to servitude." He insisted, moreover, upon its necessity for another reason. The democracy of France was full of spirit and energy. It was possible to direct, it was impossible to destroy its progress. What it meant was the admission of an ever greater number of men to the full benefits of civilisation.[37] Nothing so surely prevented the growth of wrongheaded thinking in a changing society as the free interchange of thought. Democracy had power; and nothing was more useless than the failure to recognise that the possession of power meant influence in the work of government. The whole problem by which they were confronted was the instruments by which that power should be exerted. To deprive the people of a liberty which had taken such deep root in France was to destroy the surest guarantee of peace. It was to drive underground ideas which must then translate themselves into action without the purifying influence of criticism and of correction.[38] It was to offer no alternative between conquest and resolution. It resulted in the profanation of Justice. "The only remedy for liberty," he said in a magnificent speech,[39]

[35] *Ibid.*, II, 132.
[36] Barante, II, 133.
[37] *Ibid.*, II, 134.
[38] *Ibid.*, II, 138.
[39] *Ibid.*, II, 293.

"is prison, the only remedy for intelligence is ignorance." But upon both of these it is only the most dishonourable of governments that takes its stand.

In similar fashion he demanded freedom of religious belief. Every church was a power in the state and its danger to the body politic could only be mitigated by the admission of its freedom.[40] That was why a privileged church resulted in discontent as it was why a theocracy was the most dangerous form of absolute rule.[41] For to add to political power the sanction of religion was to make captive the intelligence of men. That was why a church to which freedom had been guaranteed was a perpetual pledge of private liberty.[42] It was the admission that there is no institution so vast as to absorb the complete allegiance of man. It made him conscious of his duty to his intelligence which, in fact, is his duty to his humanity. It results in the freedom of his soul. It insists upon the development of his conscience. It enables him to refuse submission to wrong by the creation of a criterion of right which is not merely the judgment of the state. It is a powerful safeguard of originality because, by reminding the citizen of the perpetual duty of political judgment, it guards that individualism which makes him adamant against the assault of absolute power.

Nor is he less insistent upon the influence of religious freedom on the church itself. Where the church is free it is an association of consciences and at once a moral element is introduced into its composition.[43] It is a republic within the state, an association which sets limits to the demand the state may make upon its members. But once its freedom is changed into state-union the conditions of value disappear. Inevitably it becomes officialised. Inevitably those who direct it are compelled to subvert it to their purposes from the very temptations it offers. It lives on the bounty of the state and the price of its maintenance is at least its silence and in general its support. It brings to the centralised power a source of authority of which the possession is fraught with danger. It gives a religious sanction to state-de-

---

[40] Barante, II, 99.
[41] II, 103.
[42] *Ibid.*, II, 100.
[43] *Ibid.*

cisions which are in fact entirely without relation to ecclesiastical purposes. It aggravates the possibility of despotism by
tinging government with the suspicious colours of theocracy.
It offers temptation in another direction. It asks, inevitably,
for privileges.[44] It desires to exalt itself at the cost of its com-
petitors. It ceases to regard any conscience other than its own.
It puts itself under the protection of the political police. It submits the choice of its rulers to government.[45] It meddles in the
appanage of temporal power. What it may gain in dignity it
loses in independence. It becomes a social magistracy, and the
basic purpose of its existence is diverted to temporal ends. He
cannot resist the comparison between the simplicity and effectiveness of the catholic church in England and the stately gran-
deur of the Anglican Church.[46] The latter he regarded rightly
as no more than the creature of the civil power. It had ceased
to be a church and had been debased into an establishment.
"Let a religious organisation," he said,[47] "be exclusive or ever
dominant and one may rest assured that its ministers will be
rich and important in political life, that they will exercise a vast
dominion and intervene without cessation in civil life to bring
it under their own control." No one who reads the history of
the Church of England in the first half of the nineteenth century
can doubt that it is an illustration of this general principle. No
one who is acquainted with the history of the Catholic Church
in France under the *ancien régime* can mistake the fact that it
was exactly from these vices that it suffered. It was nonsense,
in his eyes, to argue that a state which does not profess some
definite religious belief is already atheist.[48] The choice is not
between infidelity and theocracy. The choice is between the
use of an illegitimate weapon for wrongful purposes and the
admission that the function of religion does not enter into the
field of politics. The charter, as he insisted, had recognised its
value by giving it the means of independence. It offered them
the protection of the law; but it realised so far the danger of

[44] Barante, I, 321.
[45] *Ibid.*, II, 101.
[46] *Ibid.*, II, 100.
[47] *Ibid.*, II, 101.
[48] Barante, II, 250.

choosing out some form of faith for especial favour that it preferred the loneliness of a complete impartiality between them.[49]

The recognition of literary freedom and religious independence is the admission of impalpable influence. Both result less in the control of practical power than in the creation of an atmosphere in which it may be suitably restrained. The one throws the full glare of public criticism on governmental activity. The other, by its refusal to admit the entire absorption of the individual in the state, gives him a certain externality which quickens the public conscience by its insistence on the significance of the elements which go to the constitution of the whole. But more than that is required. Power that is uncontrolled in practical affairs can hardly be limited by theoretical criticism. It is only when opposition becomes materialised into a legal barrier that we have real safeguards against absolutism. Such a safeguard he believed to exist in the immovability of the magistrate. Just as the admission of freedom of conscience puts a conscience outside the state that account may be taken of its actions, so does the permanent tenure of judicial office involve the admission that not even the state can transgress the principles of justice. It is the guarantee of impartiality in the fundamental process of the state. The judge is the guardian of all the natural and social rights of man.[50] It is upon his integrity alone that they depend. The whole existence of society is dependent upon the satisfactory administration of his office. But even a judge is human and he needs protection against his frailties. If the fear of dismissal is before his mind he must inevitably be affected in his decisions by the result they will exercise upon his career. He is given permanent tenure in order that he shall be free from such a possibility. He is immovable because he is then in a position to protect the principles of the charter even against those who appointed him to office.[51] His immovability simply connotes his independence. It is a recognition of the fallibility of the state. It sets a limit to the temptations of power. Undoubtedly, he is a functionary of the state; but he is a functionary

[49] *Ibid.*, II, 252.
[50] Barante, I, 171.
[51] *Ibid.*, I, 172.

appointed for the express purpose of protecting society against itself.[52]   It is the guarantee of those privileges that reason demonstrates to be necessary to social welfare.

Yet all these liberties he counts as nothing compared to the supreme privilege of parliamentary government. This, above all, is the final check upon absolutism. This, above all, provides the mass of men with the material means of guaranteeing a régime of liberty. For what, in the last analysis, is meant by parliamentary government? The right of self-determination in finance and of its supervision when the vote has been made.[53] Liberty, at bottom, is a matter of hard purchase. You keep the government in the path of right conduct by the potential refusal of the means of its subsistence. Should its foreign policy displease you can refuse the funds for its support. If its domestic administration is unjust, you may keep your hands in your pockets. It is, perhaps, somewhat rude as a governmental method; yet, of all, it is the most efficacious. It effects a practical revolution without the destruction of a single life.

Of course it is itself a power that has its dangers; and few have sketched more vividly than Royer-Collard the inherently sinister potentialities of a parliamentary system. It tends, by its nature, to absorb the very power it limits.[54]   Instead of making laws, of applying the principles of the Charter to the political situations which may arise, it desires to invade the executive function and to undertake the actual work of administration. That is, of course, simply a manifestation of the thirst for power which is common to every person and institution. But when a parliament attempts it, it steps outside its proper sphere. Government requires rapid decision, secret determination, continuous resolve.[55]   It must in the last resort be unified action, the action of, at the most, a small group so single in thought as to act as one will. With a modern parliament he denies that such action is possible. It is responsible to the nation and, by its very nature, it must discover the will of the nation before it can act. A deputy is thinking less of

[52] Barante, I, 172.
[53] *Ibid.*, I, 22.
[54] *Ibid.*, I, 219.
[55] Barante, II, 132.

the governmental decision that has to be made than of the verdict that will be passed upon his decision by his constituency at the next election. He cannot work swiftly and silently. What he is demands at once deliberation and prominence. But that is to say that his business is the elaboration of general principles which is in no sense the business of administration.

Royer-Collard is naturally led to examine the roots whence this theory of usurpation takes its origin. It starts out from the assumption of the sovereignty of the people. It suggests that the Chamber of Deputies as the representatives of the sovereign people is the recipient by delegation of their sovereignty. But that is to assume the identity of parliamentary government with representative government and he hotly denied the equation.[56] The deputies do not represent the nation. They represent the interests of the nation, and he insists upon the vital character of the distinction.[57] Were they to represent the nation no form of government save a republic would be possible. To represent the nation is to represent man, an eager, passionate thinking being, who possesses in himself an atom of power. But you cannot, so Royer-Collard argues, delegate that power.[58] It rests where it originates and each can only exert it for himself. Representative government is, he sees clearly enough, majority government and power goes to the party whom the greater part of the citizen-body supports. But that is already direct government which is not the government of France. The deputies depend for their existence not upon the people but upon the charter.[59] The charter conferred rights upon the people but it did not give them representation. What it did was to create a body of men who should represent in the constitution of the state the divers interests of the nation. To represent the historic unity of France it gave the government to the King. To represent the upper classes it created the House of Peers. But from each of these there is a distinct interest—that of the people and the charter represented that interest in the Chamber of Deputies.[60]

[56] *Ibid.*, I, 228.
[57] *Ibid.*, I, 229.
[58] This is the whole tenour of the speeches on electoral reform.
[59] Barante, II, 20.
[60] *Ibid.*, I, 230.

It was careful to insist upon indirect representation for the very reason that it is from the charter that the Chamber derives; had it been intended to create representative government only universal suffrage would have been logically defensible.[61] In such an analysis the chamber is simply a function of the state. It is not coeval with it. It cannot pretend to override the two checks upon the exercise of its powers.

For Royer-Collard saw clearly that the effort of the popular chamber was aimed at the possession of sovereignty. If that sovereignty did not exist, it was clear enough that its effort was vain. It is clear that it was not intended from the mere fact that there are two chambers. There are two chambers because there are two interests and neither of them can uniquely be sovereign.[62] He emphasises that conclusion the more vehemently because of every aspirant to supreme power it is of parliament that he is most suspicious. It hides itself behind its corporate personality and thus lacks the responsibility of actual office.[63] It is the maker of laws and so continually encroaching upon authority that is not its own by very reason of that favourable situation. It can obtain control of the executive, as it can break the independence of the judicial power. It can destroy the external guarantees of freedom by curbing alike thought and conscience. That is why limits have been placed to its activity. That is why, for example, the charter did not establish single-chamber government. Had it done so, it might equally have established a plébiscite. But each alike is the manifestation of a supposed popular sovereignty and of its existence he has already made denial. For whatever sovereignty we recognise is a depositary of force and from it will originate law. Since his effort is to trace the origin of law to a reasonable interpretation of conditions in the light of certain fundamental principles of justice, it is obvious that he cannot admit that conclusion.

What then, he asked himself, is the people? He had no doubt of the reply. The people, like the King and like the aristocracy, is simply the depositary of a function in the state.[64]

[61] *Ibid.*, I, 222 f.
[62] Barante, II, 18-20.
[63] *Ibid.*, I, 472.
[64] Barante, I, 212.

It has to set a limit to absolutism. But it has, simultaneously, to be prevented from usurping that power which it has itself come to limit. That is why it is counterbalanced by king and nobles. That is why it cannot vote at pleasure but only as the fundamental law may permit it.[65] That is why the charter did not recognise universal suffrage. That is why the chamber is only partly renewed at a general election; for a total renewal would be a plébiscite, and the force behind a plébiscite would, whether for good or for evil, be too massive to make effective resistance possible.[66] It would then engender the creation of a sovereignty, and in that creation would be involved the denial of the charter. It would be an ochlocracy of the most dangerous kind, and it is with vehemence that he repudiates its consecration.

IV. IMPLICATIONS

M. FAGUET has insisted that the political system of Royer-Collard is in no sense a metaphysic and there is certainly a sense in which this is entirely true.[67] For what it clearly desires to do is to effect the canonization of one fundamental truth derived from his own experience. He had learned alike from history and his own share in the Revolution that the use of power is poisonous to those who exert it. That for which he was anxious was the prevention of its exertion for dangerous ends. He did not care greatly whether the wielder of it were one or many. What he desired was to prevent the recurrence of a time when the personality of men should be stifled by the authority of the state. That does not mean to say that he was in any sense anarchistic in outlook. Again and again in his career he accepted the necessity of repressive legislation when occasion for its passage seemed to him evident. But for the normal state he was clear that political life would be intolerable unless certain limitations of power were postulated as fundamental. The individual must have certain liberties no matter what inconvenience may flow from their possession. He must

[65] *Ibid.*, 211, 298.
[66] II, 32 f.
[67] Faguet, op. cit., I, 285.

have certain liberties because once their possession is denied the result is either Louis XIV or the Convention. That is what he meant by his famous doctrine that liberties are the capacities to resist.[68] It is an opportunity to deny the validity of encroachment. It is a chance to insist upon the submission of any given situation to the analysis of reason. It was, on the whole, a simple and practical attitude, intelligible enough when one reads it in the light of his time. For he was witnessing, after all, a gigantic struggle between two parties anxious on the one hand to maintain, on the other to destroy, the work of the Revolution. He saw clearly enough that their collision must inevitably be violent. What he sought to outline was a political method under which an orderly progress became possible. He had no sympathy for those who, like Villèle, regarded the work of government as the privileged possession of king and nobles. His defence of legitimacy shows how little he appreciated the spirit of democracy in his time. His philosophy was one of checks and balances, derived, perhaps, from an admiration of the way in which the British constitution had preserved the equipoise of interests without a revolution.

Not that he desired to see France governed upon the English model. Few of his speeches are more admirable than that in which he insists on the specialist character of a national tradition.[69] France cannot import the English constitution simply because she is France; to do so would be to reverse the significance of a thousand years of history. His mind was essentially compromising in its outlook and the rigidity with which he is usually credited comes not from his enunciation of a system of dogmas as from his constant search for the conditions under which a compromise may be effected. When there was hope of a moderate liberalism under Decazes he did not object to the grant of extraordinary powers; it was under the oppressive absolutism of Charles X that his insistence upon the value of liberty found its full strength.

The influence of Montesquieu upon his mind is, of course, obvious enough. That separation of powers upon which the former insisted as the key to liberty became in Royer-Collard's

[68] Cf. Faguet, op. cit., I, 291.
[69] Barante, I, 216 f.

hands the corner-stone of his political edifice.[70]   But in his
hands it also underwent a vast extension.   He desired not so
much the separation of powers as the separation of power.
What he wanted was to prevent the supreme force of the
state from being concentrated at any single point within it.
So long as the possibility of effective resistance had to be considered there was a reasonable certainty that power would not
be abused.   His insistence that sovereignty is no more than
a peculiar synthesis of power is immensely valuable.   It prevents the attribution to the state of any mystical rights or
functions.   He saw that while the state as a whole has, from
the nature of things, the theoretical possession of all power,
actually that power is always distributed among its constituent
elements.   The sovereignty of the state then comes to mean in
actual practice the amount of power that is exerted by the
governing body of the state.   What Royer-Collard emphasised
was the danger of permitting that power to become so great
as to override all possible expression of difference within the
community.   What you have to do is not to strangle opinion
but to persuade it.   Hence, for example, his postulation of
liberty of the press as fundamental.   A government that is
continuously subjected to the raking fire of criticism is in fact
a limited government; it cannot become a despotism save by
the real consent of its subjects—which is to say that it cannot
become a despotism.[71]   For, to its subjects, two appeals are
already addressed and the question of obedience becomes a
problem of how far the decision of authority outweighs in the
strength of its appeal the moral force of organized opposition
to it.

It is difficult to deny the validity of such an argument.
The separation of powers is admittedly a cumbersome conception.   Translated into the practical expression of the American
Constitution it may result, as an acute observer has emphasised,
simply in the confusion of powers.[72]   But that is simply because
in its orthodox form it forces a natural assumption into an unnatural classification.   The threefold division of governmental

[70] Barante, I, 207 f.
[71] Cf. Barante, II, 15 f.
[72] Cf. Mr. Lippmann's remarks, *The New Republic*, Vol. X, p. 151.

power into executive, legislative and judicial, is only the rough apportionment of convenience and does not exist in the nature of things. Indeed the profoundest student of the American Constitution has recently and expressly emphasised the conclusion that the logic of judicial review involves *ipso facto* the exercise of legislative power.[73] But what Royer-Collard saw clearly is that our inability to force so muddle-headed a classification upon government is not equivalent to the conference upon it of absolutism. What on the contrary it suggests is the need of setting limits to its power by the admission that without it there exist rights which, on occasion, will call its activity into serious question. Admittedly those rights are only vaguely defined. Admittedly, he did not lay down the conditions under which they may justifiably be exercised.[74] But that only means that he refused to prophecy the future. It only means that he recognized how difficult it is to forecast the precise manner in which events will shape themselves. He laid down the general principles upon which the conduct of authority must be judged in each situation; but his own career as a member of the chamber revealed how clearly he understood the compulsion of circumstance. He knew that the France of the Restoration must confront its problems differently from the France of 1789.[75] The exact nuance of the change he dare not have predicted. What he saw was that so long as the existence of the state was not threatened there must be an eternal conflict between its constituent parts. Events have not thus far contradicted the general correctness of his interpretation.

In such an analysis, of course, the conception of an unitary state must disappear. Where there is sentient existence, there will be judgment; wherever there is personality there will be power. The state then becomes multicellular in character. It develops features traditionally associated with what we term federal organisation. The vast claims of legal theory for any single organ of the state begin to lose their substantiality. Not, indeed, that they lose their legal correctness. No court

[73] See the dissent of Holmes, J. in *Southern Pacific v. Jenien*, 244 U. S. 221.
[74] Barante, II, 237, 309.
[75] This is indeed the whole essence of the Doctrinaires' position.

will question the legal right of parliament to work its will in whatever way may to itself seem most necessary.[76] Our doubts of its authority must obtain a sanction in every case extra-judicial. Yet it is surely clear that a theory so little connected with the reality of political life is unsatisfactory enough. That is where the force of Royer-Collard's analysis becomes obvious. The rights he demanded as the guarantee against absolutism are rights which, sooner or later, no state can afford to disregard. He may, indeed, have been vague enough in his conception of liberty; though here it might justly be argued that those who have been most precise in its defini-tion have usually been unable to make their concept stand the test of analysis. The simple fact is, as he seems to have perceived, that liberty is less a tangible substance than an atmosphere.[77] We know what it is less by its presence than by its absence. It is the sense of a cramped personality, the arrest for spiritual development, that signifies encroachment upon its necessities. To Royer-Collard certain rights might be defined which would prevent the onset of despotism. He defined those rights; and their fundamental object was to prevent the con-centration of power at any isolated centre of the state. That, surely, is the fundamental characteristic of federal government.

He insisted upon its value less for the reasons we should today assign to it than for the single cause that it prevented the absolutist tendency of government to have its sway. But it is of interest to note that the milieu in which he sketched the nature of power should have swung so exactly upon the lines he suggested. He lived in a period of developing parlia-mentary power. It was the Chamber of Deputies which over-threw the government of the Restoration just as, in England, the fortunes of the ministry depended upon the goodwill of the House of Commons. But there has been an interesting divergence at this point between the experiences of France and of England. Right down to our own day the great fact in French administrative history has been the increasing power of the Chamber of Deputies; and the demand for administra-

[76] l. e. What Professor Dicey calls "legal sovereignty;" my whole point is that this is an entirely unnatural conception as a separate fact.

[77] Cf. the eloquent remarks of Mr. Philipps, "Europe Unbound," Chap. II.

tive autonomy on the part of the fonctionnaire is simply the effort to restore a balance of power that has been regrettably lost.[78] The instinct of tyranny which is so nourished by acquaintance with power has led in France to an impossible situation.[79] Today, as a consequence, the rights that the civil servant is claiming are exactly calculated to take from the Chamber of Deputies all power save that regulation by the proclamation of general principles which, fundamentally, was Royer-Collard's conception of its function.[80]

In England the evolution has been in an almost antithetic direction. Where Bagehot could note the overwhelming supremacy of Parliament the fact which confronts the modern observer is the even greater power of the executive body.[81] The House of Commons has come to depend upon the cabinet; and as yet, at any rate, we have discovered no means of restoring an effective balance of power. Yet here, too, the result has been exactly what one who accepts the general analysis for which Royer-Collard stood sponsor might have predicted. More and more the executive organ has attempted to free itself from the trammels of the rule of law. The development of a specialised administrative code was probably inevitable; and certainly French experience suggests that its growth can well harmonise with the simultaneous acceptance of the idea of responsibility. The fact still remains that, as yet, the increasing power of the bureaucratic side of English government has not brought with it its compensations in the safeguarding of general liberty.[82] It is more than absurd to talk thus early of a transition to the servile state. Yet it is difficult not to analyse the latest fruits of English legislation in terms of a movement from contract to status.[83] Synchronously, indeed, may be observed the appearance, in half-articulate fashion of

[78] Cf. Lefas, "L'Etat et les Fonctionnaires."

[79] As is admirably pointed out by M. Leroy in his "Transformations de puissance publique."

[80] Barante, II, 193 f.

[81] Cf. Low, "The Governance of England," passim.

[82] Cf. Dicey, "The Growth of Administrative Law," in the Law Quarterly Review for 1916. There is some interesting material in a curious volume by E. S. P. Haynes. "The Decline of Liberty in England."

[83] Cf. Pound in Harvard Law Review for January, 1917.

the attitude which the French call solidarist—the attempt to interpret political life in terms of function instead of terms of property. The growing distrust of étatisme is, doubtless, significant enough in this regard; and it is worth while suggesting that it is in the conception of a fundamental social interdependence which an étatiste régime obscures that we shall regain the synthesis we require.[84]

Nor must the significant moment of American development be disregarded. Of the conflict between centralised and local authority it is not necessary here to speak. But due attention must be paid by any observer who would grasp the real nature of sovereignty to the process of American government at the present time. Observers have long insisted that the traditional institutions of 1787 would prove unequal to the strain of crisis; and if the Civil War seemed, in some degree, to negative that conclusion, it is emphatically accurate at the present time. The original suspicion of executive authority threw the burden of power into the hands of Congress, and so long as the ordinary conception of representative government reflected with accuracy the conditions of American life, the emphasis of authority began slowly to move away from that centre. It has become commonplace to assert that the President is today more powerful than at any time in American history. It is still more obvious that congressional debate has largely ceased to influence the character of public opinion. New instruments of opinion are everywhere in the making. The conventions of the American Constitution already merit examination. New administrative organs are already in process of construction. Much of what has come into being has no popular mandate for its rulings; it depends on what seems to have become the far more effective sanction of expert confidence. Congress, it is clear, would be chary enough of risking a total collision with its opinions. No one can estimate the future of these novelties except to feel dimly but decisively that they have a future. The individual congressman has undergone an eclipse as complete as that of the private member of the House of Commons. The Congressional committees have become less the moulders of legislation

[84] Cf. my introduction to Duguit's "Transformations du Droit Public" in its English form and his "Droit Social, Droit Individuel."

than its pathetic because grudging recipients. The key to the whole has come to lie in the president's hands and in the discernment of the few chosen councillors he has gathered about him. This is not, it is clear, the government envisaged by the constitution. Equally certainly, it is not a government which meets with the approval of Congress. In some sort issue has been joined between the two; but the fact that it is already a government which functions suggests the inevitable outcome.[85]

Observation, then, seems to tend in the direction of confirming the conclusion at which Royer-Collard arrived. It would seem to demonstrate that the legal theory of sovereignty is without root in actual existence. It would suggest that there exists rather a broad thing we call power and that sovereignty is simply its exercise in actual terms of life. Sovereignty, then, is simply an act of will. It depends upon the consent of the members of the state for its effectiveness. Generally speaking, what decisions the organ of sovereignty may make will obtain acceptance; and Royer-Collard most certainly would not have doubted that government is so vital a thing as to make the refusal of obedience the extreme marginal case. But the consecration of a region into which government may not normally enter is the guarantee of a reservoir of resistance which confirms his theory that no conception of power is adequate into which the element of morality does not enter; and that is already to say that no power can in any event be absolute.[86] What we do, then, is to remove the check upon the exercise of sovereignty from without the organ which exerts it. We insist upon the externality of the individual. We make of him a complete personality who, while he is a member of the state, and thereby contributes to the justification of its authority, is, at the same time, something more. It is an affirmation of political pluralism, the belief that while the state is responsible to itself, is a moral being from which self-judgment is expected, the nature of power demands also the retention of the safeguard that we, too, as beings with personality, are compelled

[85] There is no better comment on this change than Mr. Croly's articles in *The New Republic* from April to September, 1917.

[86] As Lord Bryce has noted, Cf. his essays on "Obedience and Sovereignty" in his "Studies in History and Jurisprudence."

not merely to passive reaction to its decisions but to active registration of our dissent therefrom. What, of course, it suggests is a type of government very different from anything we have thus far known. If the spirit of decentralisation is implicitly present in every state, it would seem an economy of organisation to give it distinct existence in form.

That problem, indeed, Royer-Collard did not face, for the sufficiently good reason that he was not confronted by it. Those who occupied themselves with the politics of the Restoration had a different task from our own. The nations of Europe had made holy alliance against democratic principles and the main problem for all who recognised, as did Royer-Collard, that the basic demand of the Revolution was right, were occupied in the affirmation of it. That involved a different and simpler struggle from our own. The distinction between the *ancien régime* and the Revolution was, after all, clear even to the least acute spectator of events. The whole problem was simply whether the basis of government should be the will of one or a generalised representation of the will of all. The Restoration answered that question in two antithetic ways. The Royalists proclaimed loudly that the intellectual teachings of the Revolution had produced such disastrous results as to be inacceptable to honest men. They desired for that cause the return to the conception of power by which the *ancien régime* had been governed. Those who may broadly be termed liberal in outlook suggested what was in effect a compromise. While they distrusted the dogmas of royalism they were a little sceptical of the full and logic consequences of its negation. What they sought was the synthesis of the potentialities of both; and it was by the limitation of authority in the recognition of individual rights that are, generally speaking, inviolable, that they sought to effect it. The solution, of course, was too simple. The ancient institutions of France could not be at once idealised and modernised. The practical defect of Royer-Collard's own outlook was that he did not take sufficient account of the legacies of hatred that had been inherited. His own confidence in the charter was pathetically unique. To Charles X it was a subject of abhorrence; to Barante it was useless because it was operated without good will;[87] to Chateaubriand it was merely the material for an elegant, if capricious, pamphlet.[88] The charter did not, as Royer-Collard had hoped, reconcile the institutions it had established; it merely provided a basis for their more violent division. The fact was that it sought the unification of two permanently irreconcilable principles—an active monarchy and a democracy. Until the triumph of the one or the other had been secured, their collision was unavoidable.

V. ETHICS AND POLITICS

IF the main motive of this outlook is the effort to solve a fairly definite and practical problem, the answer has an ethical implication which it is worth while for a moment to examine. Royer-Collard was the philosophic disciple of Reid,[89] and, like the latter, his metaphysical work was really an attempt to find means of escape from the scepticism of Hume. That to which his analysis led him was an insistence on the worth of conscience. Few theorists of his time have so greatly emphasised the importance of what contribution each individual can make to the general fabric of state-thought. He had realised that the insistence the Revolution had laid upon the worth of human personality was in some sort its most vital work. For it immediately involves on the part of the state an effort to organise means whereby that personality may obtain expression. Here, clearly enough, emerges the real significance of the connotation he attached to freedom. Liberty, for him, is the hindrance of attack upon the development of personality. That is why he is so anxious to put beyond the area of ordinary interference certain rights without which personality is worthless. That was why, also, he was suspicious of authority. For where authority encroaches beyond the domain that circumstance will, in a rational analysis, ascribe to it, it negatives the meaning of personality. That was the defect of the *ancien régime*.

[87] "Mémoires," II, 180.

[88] "La Monarchie Selon la Charte." For the circumstances of its origin cf. Daudet, "Louis XVIII et Decazes," pp. 153-5, 169-70. Viel Castel, "Histoire," Vol. V, pp. 240-53.

[89] Barante, II, 70 f.

It confined humanity within certain bounds and the richness of which it was capable failed to obtain adequate recognition. Of course Royer-Collard had here the defects of his time. His perception of the value of the individual conscience did not go far enough to make him see the necessity of universalising its political expression. He was so wrapped up in his doctrine that what obtains representation is not will but interests that he failed to realise that interests are no more than the material expression of will. He did not push far enough his analysis of the basis of the state. Had he done so he would have grasped firmly what, in fact he only dimly perceived; that it is in actual life impossible to test the legitimacy of a will that clamors for expression merely by the discussion of its origin.[90] His own theory, indeed, was one of function; and he satisfied himself that the interests of the French people were sufficiently expressed in the power of the middle classes to which he himself belonged. The day of the workers had not yet dawned; and the attempt to explain the economic significance of class-distinction certain English thinkers had only begun to attempt. It is, of course, an inconsistency in his thought to have stopped at a point where the conference of political power would then have prevented the violence he hated so passionately. But his thought was always limited by the necessities he encountered; and he did not pursue its implications into the realm of abstract possibility.

Whatever that limitation, his insistence on the value of personality as the real source of political power is very important. It is difficult not to feel that it is derived, above all, from Kant. Henri Michel has pointed out how greatly Guizot, at any rate, was influenced by the German speculation of his time;[91] and what influenced Guizot would not have been unknown to Royer-Collard. His own spiritualist philosophy led him to attach great weight to the idea of the soul; and he realised early that it is an attitude favorable to liberty.[92] If, as he was never weary of insisting, man alone, of all creatures, is given the faculty of judgment, no state can be adequate in

[90] This, I think, is the real defect of his interpretation of the charter.
[91] Op. cit., 298.
[92] Ferraz, "Histoire de la Philosophie," III, 157.

which provision is not made for its exercise.[93]   Indeed, it is that faculty of judgment which in fact lies at the basis of society. What it demands is the recognition that certain ideal rights are inherent in the fact of individual existence.   The self cannot be itself unless it is given material upon which to pass judgment.   But the provision of that material is already the recognition of liberty of conscience.   It involves the conception of a personality that is more than the sum of its relations. It is not, of course, in any sense a legal conception.   That which, in any state, is the accepted organ of ultimate power may refuse the recognition in its code of such rights.   But there is set alongside the legal conception of right a moral claim of which it is difficult to make denial of the inherent superiority.   Actual law and ideal law may never coincide; but where they come into conflict there can hardly be doubt as to where the ultimate allegiance is due.   But such an analysis must surely mean that the claim of the state upon us is emphatically subjective, depends, for its validity, upon the moral appeal it makes to our conscience.   Where its policy seems to step beyond right, it becomes, as Royer-Collard realised in 1830, a moral duty to warn those who are exercising its control, that the acquiescence of its constituent wills has become at least matter of doubt.[94]   And, in the last resort, the refusal of obedience is inevitable.   That refusal, indeed, may involve pain to him who thus makes his challenge; and, indeed, as Mr. Barker has argued,[95] it may well be that the presumption is against us.

Yet the duty surely remains.   There are few rights more precious than the right to be wrong.   For once we accept the idea of the state as not merely the whole of ourselves, but a thing without us of which we are compelled to take ceaseless account, it is clear that we can accept no doctrine that would derive our rights from the state and condition than by the decisions of its will.   That is, in fact, to postulate for the state a kind of centralised infallibility of which we have thus far

[93] Barante, II, 293.
[94] Cf. Barante, II, 419.
[95] "English Political Thought," p. 60.   The whole chapter is immensely valuable.

had no experience. It is difficult to conceive of its decisions as having in any sense "a final moral value," for that is to confer upon ourselves too vast a relief from thought. Here, surely, is the real meaning of the new form given by Kant to the fundamental principle of law.[96] Before his time law had attempted no more than the preservation of order. The condition of society had rendered peace the vital social interest. Dissent then clearly becomes an attitude contrary to law; for dissent is nothing if it is not the disturbance of peace. So there comes a strife between the interest of the individual who would make his protest and that of the state which would prevent him. What Kant did was to insist that the problem we have to solve is the reconciliation of government with liberty. Justice, for him, was simply the opportunity for the good-will to obtain its fullest development in action; and he sought to find wherein the balance of individual interest and social interest might be discovered. Our own problem is in nowise different. If our greatest need is, at the moment, organisation, that does not in any sense lessen, rather does it increase, the value of individual responsibility.[97] A state in which the liability of its members is shifted to the shoulders of government is not likely long to remain free. Organization may, indeed, leave room for initiative; but the very condition of its preservation is in the understanding of individualism. It would, indeed, be a simple world if all of us could be swept into the vortex of an all-embracing personality like the state. But a truer analysis seems to suggest that, as James said, "every smallest bit of experience is a *multum in parvo* plurally related."[98] Because experience is many and not one the individual personality can not engulf itself in a single expression of one of its aspects. When, that is to say, you have described man as a member of the state you have not exhausted his nature. He refuses that reduction to unity. He refuses it for the simple reason that it does not represent the facts. He is not merely a member of the state. His capacity for fellowship

[96] Cf. Janet, "Science Politique," II, 576 f.

[97] Cf. the suggestive paper of Dean Pound in the *American Journal of Sociology* for May, 1917.

[98] "A Pluralistic Universe," p. 321.

is not so meagrely exhausted. Above all, there are moments when the Athanasius element in his nature must have its way. But that is to admit already breakage and ignorance in the world, to postulate a discontinuity which impels decision as to where the leap shall be taken.

Here, surely, is the moral background of the liberty that Royer-Collard envisaged. It is the one certain guarantee against absolutism. It denies perfection by the very fact of its insistence that the object of individual judgment is to secure moral progress. It does not deny personality to the state. On the contrary, it is the ascription of moral purpose to the state which it deduces from the fact of personality. But it realises that, like the individual, the will of the state is not a simple effort after good. It would, perhaps, be simple if we could base our activity upon such an analysis. But the will of any being may be perverted to wrong ends; and exactly as the state will judge us for the use we make of our personality, so, reciprocally, we must judge the state. For, after all, our own will is swept into the strength of its decisions; and where we deem it wrong only the active registration of dissent can excuse us from participation in its crimes. Royer-Collard had experience enough of a state that wrought its own purposes without the hindrance of dissent. He realised the uselessness of any doctrine that, merely for the sake of survival, would confuse pacific conduct with good conduct. It is, indeed, clear that a state in which the only effective will is that which at the moment of expression has to be taken for the general will can never be a democratic state. For the very condition of democratic organisation lies in the realisation that self-government means something more than to contribute one's mite of personal agreement to the vast whole of which one is part, and, in this aspect, it is surely significant of much that what time the democratic state seemed to waste in the effort to attain unity of action in fact gave to that action a moral strength denied to unthinking acquiescence.[99]

But, in such a conception, it is clear that the object we ascribe to the state is something more than survival. It is to that end only that acquiescence is directed. A freedom of conscientious

[99] Even the most zealous advocates of state-unity seem to have admitted this, cf. *London Times*, May 17, 1917, p. 231.

objection such as Poland knew, may have been the inevitable precursor of partition. We may have, as Royer-Collard realised, to sacrifice the rigidity of our theory to the changing perspective of events.[100] But that simply involves our realisation that the cost of survival may be too great; to perish, as he once bitterly remarked,[101] may also be a solution. A state may, as Machiavelli said, go to work against good and charity, but assuredly the result of its effort will be written deeply in the life it will thenceforth lead. That was the point of Huxley's oft-misinterpreted dictum that the cosmic process is opposed to the ethical. For all that the state is primarily concerned to do is to secure survival and that means fitting its methods to a non-moral end. But if the environment be bad, the ethical process suffers as a consequence. In a world of murderers the survival of any one man does not guarantee an ethical superiority. That was surely the meaning of Aristotle's distinction between the good man and the good citizen. Herr von Bethmann-Hollweg may have saved his state when he agreed to hack his way through Belgium; but he himself admitted that it was a crime. The state was working its end through him; but most of us are agreed that its end was not a moral end. It is interesting to speculate as to our judgment of one who, in such a crisis, should fearlessly challenge the state-decision. In our own time, certainly, it seems to have profited it but little to aim at the conquest of the world at the cost of its soul.

This does not mean that the ethic of the state must be distinct from that of the individual. Anyone who studies the historical consequence of such a difference will be convinced of its impossibility. It means rather that we must reject the test of state-life which insists on its quantitative expansion and look rather to its qualitative intensity. In that aspect we are compelled to stand outside the state and judge it. There will come to us clearly the knowledge that there is an end greater than its survival and perpetuation. Most of us would rather have perished with Leonidas at Thermopylæ than have survived with the Persian tyrant; but Persia survived. Was the end its sur-

[100] Barante, I, 302.

[101] The dilemma is in reality worth more consideration than is usually given to it; but the instinct of state-life is very strong.

vival served more ethical than the end that would have been
served by its downfall? Most of us would doubt it. And it
then becomes surely arguable that one of the results of recent
evolution has been to make the individual bi-partite—no less
himself an end than contributory to the end of the state. The
test of value in an institution may be rather its advantage to
the state than to the individual, but who is to judge its value if
not ourselves?[102] An individual may decide on a course which
enables justice to be done even though the state perish in the
doing of it. From the standpoint of survival that may not serve
the state. But that only leads to the insistence that even if the
ethical process be the derivative of the cosmic it is not one with
it, any more than a man is one with the father from whom he derives. "The simple truth has to be told," says Meredith of
Nevil Beauchamp, "how he loved his country, and for another
and a broader love growing out of his first passion, fought it."

It is at least a conceivable attitude, even if it is rare. Undeniably, of course, it is an attitude fraught with elements of
danger to the body politic. The state-life cannot be lived if its
members may make rebellion against its authority. But the
rarity of their dissent is a factor of vital consequence. No one
could have predicted that the Royer-Collard of 1814 would, in
1830, have acquiesced in the overthrow of legitimism; yet the
sequence of events drove him to an opposition upon which he
entered with grave distrust.[103] The fact is that the business of
the state is the service of men, and where her defection from that
course imperils the rightness of her conduct somewhere or other
the protest will be made. And it may then be urged that a state
which is in fear of revolution by reason of its policy is less likely
to be wrong than a state whose citizens have ceased to aim their
consciences against it. Ambition, tyranny, selfishness, these
men will fight in whatever guise they may be discovered; and
it is in their willingness so to do battle that the real safeguard of
morals is to be found. A conception of the relationship between
rulers and ruled which does not include the possibility of

[102] This, as I conceive, is the real defect of such idealistic interpretations
of the state as that of Mr. Bosanquet. Cf. the first chapter of this volume
and the first essay in my "Problem of Sovereignty."
[103] Cf. Barante, II, 34 f.

renouncing the relation is always incomplete; for it is demanding a measure of loyalty and unselfishness from subjects far greater than is sought from their governor.

The difficulty of anarchy must, of course, be faced;[104] and no consideration of politics would be adequate which failed to take account of its dangers. No one was more convinced then Royer-Collard that government is necessary; no one, assuredly, would have more willinging admitted the vastness of the problem. If Luther may take upon himself the purgation of the world-church, how shall she retain the splendor of her empire? Yet the problem is, in fact less simple. It is important to remember that creative opposition has come, less from those either fatally certain of their opinion, or eager to play the martyr, than from those who, with Luther, can simply retort that they cannot do otherwise. Yet such wholehearted antagonism will not come to a state which seeks the path of justice. It is when a fundamental choice must be made between right and wrong that men like Luther grow daring enough to shake the world. It is when, as in 1830, warning has been neglected and principle trampled underfoot that men like Royer-Collard, fitted by nature for the part of order rather than that of change, will be content to remake the institutions of the state. The danger of anarchy intervenes when wrong has become unendurable. It remains where the path of right conduct is yet uncertain. It is useless to hope that such moments will never come. None can say where the supreme twinge of conscience may be felt. A supreme issue may be clothed in the garb of an army-officer accused of espionage;[105] it may be found in the exaction of an educational tax. Yet few can read the long history of protest against state-policy without feeling that, on the whole, the fact of its existence has been productive of good. The Lamennais of the nineteenth century may vainly choose the path of exile; but he will inspire the victorious Lamennais of a later age as he will instruct the institution which cast him forth. Great events such as this become so intimate and vital a part of the state-tradition that none can measure the efficacy of their result. We shall not write in the future the his-

[104] This is the difficulty felt by my able reviewer in the *Times Literary Supplement*, May 17, 1917.

[105] Cf. Halévy, "Apologie pour notre passé" (1910).

tory of a second Galileo. The state, no less than the church, must learn that is not paramount in the realm of ideas. Few things are more fatal than the triumph of authority over truth.[106]

The great fact that Royer-Collard perceived was that in the denial of infallibility to authority we may prevent that disastrous victory.[107] When we insist that, in the last analysis, only the individual is sovereign over himself, we make it possible for him to contribute his best to the sum of social life. But his best, assuredly, is not blind obedience. His best is the utmost insight of which his judgment is capable. Compared to that, the chance of disorder is relatively unimportant. For the probability is that a view which men will so embrace as to ask the final test of its survival is a view that responds to some inherent need of nature. Christianity, in its early history, was exactly a danger of this kind to the empire it was slowly permeating. The christian had choice between his civic obedience and his religious loyalty. He saw, on the one hand, the vast authority of an empire so great that its very limits were hardly conceivable by him. He saw on the other a little fellowship of souls driven underground, testifying its faith only at the cost of suffering, suspected on all sides of crimes the mere thought of which was a stain upon their reputation and their opinions. In the perspective of time the weight of authority as against what the christian deemed to have been truth seems almost unutterably large; to have cast his handful of incense was so pitifully easy a thing. Yet, also in the perspective of time, it is impossible to doubt that the christian did service to civilisation when he counted the empire of authority without meaning as against the empire of what to him was truth. "The worth of a state," Mill finely said,[108] "in the long run is the worth of the individuals composing it; and a state which pospones the interests of *their* mental expansion and elevation to a little more administrative skill, or of that semblance of it which practice of it gives, in the details of business; a state which dwarfs its men, in order that they may

[106] As Lamennais and Tyrrell saw in their sphere.

[107] This is the whole point of Lord Acton's fine protest. "History of Freedom," p. 151.

[108] "Liberty" (Everyman's ed.), p. 170.

be more docile instruments in its hands even for beneficial purposes, will find that with small men no great thing can really be accomplished; and that the perfection of machinery to which it has sacrificed everything will in the end avail it nothing, for want of the vital power which, in order that the machine might work more smoothly, it has preferred to banish."

We dare not, in brief, surrender the individual conscience. Only upon its continuous exercise can our state be securely founded. Only therein can we discover the essential compromise between fundamental principles which is the real nature of public policy. Here, surely, lies the greatness of Royer-Collard's doctrine. For he came to importance in public life at a time when two antithetic systems of political organisation stood face to face. He was able to understand that neither was of itself strong enough to triumph. He was quick to perceive that the unlimited victory of either would be in no sense an unmitigated benefit. He opposed the theory of the royalists because it made the state the privileged possession of a single interest. He opposed the theory of democracy because, as he conceived, France was not ready to accept pretensions alien to what had thus far been the historic system of her institutions. But in each he perceived a truth which might, in combination, work for good. The value of royalism lay in its insistence upon continuity. Royer-Collard himself admitted that no rational interpretation of national existence can ever be catastrophic and he accepted the fact of monarchy as the basis of the state. But he simultaneously realised that the danger of monarchical government lies in its natural tendency to absolution. The apocryphal equation of Louis XIV had become already an anachronism. What was needed was the impetus of a doctrine which should take account of the personality of each member of the state, and give to that personality the opportunity for self-expression. He saw that so limited, no monarch can aim at absolute power without invoking disaster. Yet he saw, too, that a personality of which the exercise was at every stage limited by the will of the state was in no real sense capable of activity. So it was that while he admitted that the idea of national survival was fundamental, he insisted also that the individual by reason of his humanity has certain rights no state may contravene. He defined those rights; and he pointed out wherein they tend to the guarantee of liberty. It was a noble effort nobly sustained.

That it had defects and inconsistencies is undeniable. It is too often the speculation rather of an orator than of a philosopher. It is the speculation of a man of affairs in that it limited itself to the analysis of situations which actually confronted the chamber of Deputies. It is a system rather by implication than by statement. It had not the coherent prevision of the possibilities of labour, or, if it suspected its advent, it was curiously suspicious of the result. It tended too often to express itself in terms of a mathematical balance from which the facts are in the real life remote. But it remains, even when these defects have been noted, a constructive advance upon the ideas of his age. It is not a mere collection of unreasoned prejudices like the attitude of Villèle; t is more than the uncritical opportunism of Guizot. It was based upon an immense experience, and it was an experience that had been deeply felt and carefully understood. It was an experience which taught him that however valuable may be the benefits of order, they are useless so long as they stifle the spontaneity of the human mind. It led him to insist that tradition is of today as well as of the centuries that are past. He tried to free a generation that had suffered from the ills that had been inherited. He sketched the foundations of a state that should base its order upon freedom. There are few higher claims to the enduring gratitude of men.

CHAPTER FIVE

ADMINISTRATIVE SYNDICALISM IN FRANCE[1]

I. THE RIGHT OF ASSOCIATION

FRENCH tradition has not been favourable to the growth of associations.[2] Man may be, even in France, a community-building animal, but the state has watched narrowly his efforts at construction. It is only within the last thirty years that the bonds of a restraining vigilance have been finally relaxed. The right of association was, before the Revolution, strictly dependent upon the monarchical will. The royal sovereignty towered above all, so that even the natural tendency to labor organisation became nothing so much as a vast secret society living less by governmental benison than by defiance of it. It seems clear enough that what associations, whether religious or secular, were able to exist, were the offspring of a privilege tardily given and illiberally exercised. For to exert even the legislative powers implied in the concession of recognised personality seemed to the jurist no less than to the political theorist to involve a derogation from state-power. The king must be master of his estate; and he will not hesitate to teach his subjects that sovereignty knows no limits save his good pleasure. The *ancien régime* implied a monistic state; and when for the crown was substituted the nation, the worship of a unified indivisibility underwent no change. Rather did it increase in intensity; for the associations of that period which the Revolution made at a stroke antiquity were the symbols of a hated privilege. So it was that Le Chapelier could take to heart the teaching of Rousseau;[3] and when corporate freedom

[1] For a very complete bibliography cf. P. Harmignie "L'Etat et Ses Agents" (1911) and M. Leroy. "Syndicats et Services Publics" (1909) to both of which I am greatly indebted.

[2] For a history of the right of association in France from 1789-1901, see the very able doctor's thesis of M. Faget de Casteljau (1908).

[3] "Contrat Social," Bk., II, Ch. III. Faget de Casteljau, op. cit., III f.

interposed a loyalty between state and individual, it could not avoid destruction.

It was hardly a generous outlook even if, in the event, it has its explanation. For where the state attempts the absorption of the loyalties of men, what it effects is either to drive them under ground or to transfer their energies to a sphere where the restraint is mitigated. The law might forbid the Jesuits to preform their religious functions in the state; but the historian has no difficulty in discovering their presence under a variety of different forms.[4] Nor is it unmeaning to suggest that the division of French parties into a plethora of groups owes its origin less to any inherent naturalness or to a proved benefit in the performance of party-functions than to the possibility such division affords for the erection of a system of loyalties external to that of the state. Certainly no such phenomenon has been seen in Anglo-Saxon countries where, on the whole, the right of association has found but little legal hindrance;[5] and it is surely notable in this connection that when de Tocqueville visited America, within half a century of the foundation of the Republic, what should, above all, have impressed him was the astounding wealth of American group-life.[6]

Such suppression was, in fact, no more than a decadent inheritance from the Roman conception of the state.[7] It might be necessary when the restored Bourbons were aiming at the destruction of the Revolutionary ideals. It had its value when the effort of Guizot was towards the erection of a quasi-despotism under democratic forms. The brief history of the second republic shows an immediate restoration to men of the forms under which their natural instincts may obtain the satisfaction of unconcealed gregariousness.[8] But the plébiscite which enabled Louis Napoleon to renew the system of his great ancestor involved the adoption of that ancestor's attitude to all loyalties which might stand between him and his subjects. The third

[4] Cf. Debidour, "L'Eglise et L'Etat de 1879 à 1870," p. 329 f.
[5] Cf. M. H. E. Barrault's very able thesis, "Le Droit d'association en Angleterre."
[6] "Democracy in America," Part II, Bk. II, Ch. V.
[7] Cf. Duguit, "Les Transformations du Droit Public," Ch. I.
[8] Constitution of 1848, Art. 8.

republic, in its early history at least, was too precariously established to venture on a freedom which, in the result, might well have proved too costly. It was not until 1884 that M. Waldeck-Rousseau took his courage in his hands and allowed what was virtually freedom of professional association. It was not until seventeen years later that the ideals of 1848 were at last fulfilled and a general right of association established. Yet, even today, the significant limitations that exist bear testimony to the stubborn persistence of the older ideas.

Into one branch of the state the idea of a freedom of association penetrated with even greater difficulty. A civil servant was, in the *ancien régime*, above all a servant of the king; and in that centralised system which de Tocqueville has so magistrally shown to be anterior to the Revolution, the idea of a reciprocal relation between master and servant seems not to have entered. For down to the very eve of 1789 the government of France possesses, at least to an external observer, many of the characteristics of the king's household.[9] The king cannot have about him servants displeasing to his majesty. He may, indeed, like a fourteenth century king, announce that he will look not to the man but to the office;[10] but when sovereignty is no more than the royal pleasure this is but a counsel of perfection. It does not, at any rate, seem to have been enforced, and the principles of administration were left unchanged by the Revolution save that the genius of Napoleon secured an efficiency before unknown.[11]

It is not until the later years of the nineteenth century that signs of a change could be observed.[12] Whatever breach in hierarchical systems the tidal wave of democratic advance may have made, in the administrative régime it did not progress. Divine right may have been overthrown. A new and more fruitful conception of the state may have forced its way to general acceptance.[13] The irresponsibility of public power may

[9] Flach, "Origines de l'ancienne France," III, 504.

[10] Quoted from G. Demartial, "Le Statut des Fonctionnaires.' The remark is from a royal edict of 1356.

[11] Cf. Leroy, "Les Transformations de la Puissance Publique," p. 143 f.

[12] Lefas, "L'Etat et les Fonctionnaires," Introduction.

[13] Cf. the first chapter of this work.

have been at last reduced to the admission of limitations; but behind the veil of the internal processes of governmental activity no force could penetrate. The picture drawn by Balzac in the third decade of the nineteenth century was as true, in all its essential details, at the beginning of the twentieth.[14] A complete and arbitrary control over the details of administration was, after all, an idea that had behind it the weight of a long, if not an honourable tradition. It had survived, within a century, no less than seven régimes—which seemed at least a progmatically adequate test of its efficacy. Nor was it a system which might be expected to arouse much popular interest. Mr. Graham Wallas has made it a commonplace to observe that a democracy is but rarely interested in the processes of administration. What compels its attention is not so much methods as results. Where it is, largely speaking, indifferent even to the more dramatic aspects of its own political adventure,[15] it could hardly be expected to concentrate its mind on the mechanical routine in which, from day to day, the civil servant is engaged. So long as the services of government were performed with what seemed an adequate efficiency, the sovereign elector was content to allow his sovereignty to go by default. It is a political maxim of some import that what is unseen does not exist. Public attention was not concentrated upon the problem of administration simply because its existence as a problem went unrealised. It was only when it became obvious that the transformation of the state had affected no less its organization than its functioning, that it became clear that a new administrative synthesis was being in fact effected.

It was an inevitable synthesis to anyone who had observed at all accurately the evolution of the state. Its sovereignty might go unquestioned so long as the functions it endeavored to perform were hardly related to the positive side of national existence. A state which limited its services to the provision of police, defence and justice had hardly need of new conceptions. But with the advent of what Professor Dicey has called

[14] Scènes de la Vie Parisienne, "Les Employés" (1836).

[15] For two very different demonstrations of the difficulty of obtaining a really public opinion cf. Lowell."Public Opinion and Popular Government" with Mr. Wallas' "Human Nature in Politics."

the collectivist age the infallibility of public power was no longer acceptable. The state itself became an industrial instrument; and it was inevitable that those who worked for it should be unable to regard it differently from any other employer. Just as the private entrepreneur was being more and more subjected to a new legislative status,[16] so did the worker desire that the state should recognize the superiority of law to itself. Nor was this all. On all sides, pressure upon the political mechanisms of the state assumed almost alarming proportions. Parliaments seemed, often enough, little more than bodies which registered the will of a successful combatant in a conflict where it had no voice.[17] Fiction might declare its will national and sovereign; but that lighthearted sacrifice to tradition was not in fact deceptive. The life of the state, in fact, had overflowed the boundaries in which political organisation would have encased it, with the natural result that voluntary effort of every kind began at once to enforce and to supplement political action. It was impossible even for French tradition to resist the impulse implied in these changes; and the *loi des associations* of M. Waldeck-Rousseau did no more than enshrine popular aspiration in legislative form.

In actual fact, it was simply logical that the growth of associations should change the perspective of the life of the state. Once new loyalties had been established they became for their members sovereign within the limit to which they fulfilled the purposes with which they sympathised. It became clear, for example, that in a choice between loyalty to his fellow-workers in a trade, and loyalty to a state which aimed at preventing those workers from attaining certain ends they deemed good, there was no inherent certainty that the average trade-unionist would feel a deeper claim on the part of the state. *Raison d'état* lost its magic exactly at the point where the variety of group-life made it clear that the will of the state is operated by its agents and that those agents, whom the dissentient worker might himself help both to choose and dismiss, could

[16] Cf. my "Basis of Vicarious Liability" in the *Yale Law Journal* for Nov. 1916, for a discussion of the nature of this change.

[17] As was very strikingly evinced in America in the railway crisis which resulted in the Adamson Law.

lay no claim to infallibility. Indeed, where they came from a class with which, mistakenly or no, he believed himself in permanent conflict, he might even cease to believe that the state had any claim upon his loyalty at all. It would become, for him, the instrument of men with whom he was at war, and his effort would be directed towards its destruction.[18]

It is in the light of such a development that the growth of a demand for autonomy in the French public services must be understood. When the old notion of sovereignty showed signs of decay, it was inevitable that those most greatly affected by its control should seek release from its trammels. With the growth of state-enterprise in industry it was even more inevitable that the state-proletariat thus brought into being should refuse the surrender of privileges it had fought so hard to win outside the public service. And in an age when the notion of authority itself was, in its old acceptance, assailed on every hand, to the servants of the state there seemed little enough reason to abstain from additional criticism. It might be true that the entrance of these revolutionary ideals into the civil service was hardly perceived by the mass of men. The democratisation of institutions had become so general that it is doubtful if men were aware of the retention of despotic ideals in the internal organisation of government. Where, indeed, it did, it was easy for statesmen to lull the awakening suspicion by depicting revolt as an attack upon that process upon which the life of the state depended. Government was democratic in its origins. Its birth might thus be used to throw a cloak of saintliness about it. So that even if the administration of France remained arbitrary in method and hierarchical in structure it had some sort of popular sanction for its retention of an antique custom. A far more radical effort was needed if public opinion was to realise the significance of administrative corporateness.

II. THE COMPLAINTS OF THE CIVIL SERVICE

THE claim of the civil servant of the right to association has raised legal and political problems of a magnitude so immense

[18] Cf. the very able essay of M. Berth, "Marchands, Intellectuels, et Politiciens" in the *Mouvement Socialiste* for 1907–8.

that it is almost impossible to set limits to their implication. They have been very variously regarded. To some the herald of release[19] from a state dangerous because it is as inefficient and arbitrary as it is unintelligent and all-powerful, to others[20] it is little less than an invitation to anarchy. If the civil servant claim the right to defy the state from whom can obedience be expected? Yet, in fact, the problem is less simple than such statement seems to make it. The effort of the civil servant is less towards defiance of the state than towards the discovery of means whereby the challenge may be rendered unnecessary. In that aspect the movement is less towards anarchy than towards order. And a demand so widespread must, after all, have had its causes. The claim put forward by those who advocate the right to association is simple. It is that the abuses from which they have suffered are inherent in the present system. It is impossible, in their view, at all effectively to mend the civil service. What has become essential is its complete reconstruction. It is a technical ideal they have in view— an insistence that administration is a professional service so expert in character as to demand a regulation beyond political control of the ordinary kind.[21] But their critics see in their cause no more than an effort which may well paralyse the national life. They urge that what is demanded is derived less from an enthusiasm for administrative efficiency than from the ordinary phenomena of corporate selfishness. Nor is public opinion more sympathetic. A people which sees on every hand great increase both in the number of civil servants and in the budget they entail, has not the patience, even if it had the time, to examine those demands in detail. The civil service seems to the average man the most comfortable of existences. The salary is fixed and certain. There is no fear of unemployment. Economic crises leave it unaffected. Provision is made against both accident and old age. In a period of growing

[19] Cf. Leroy, "Syndicates et Services Publics," Ch. III.

[20] F. Faure in *Revue Politique et Parlementaire* 1907, "Les Syndicats des Fonctionnaires et le projet du Governement." I have discussed these various attitudes below.

[21] Cf. Book IX of M. Leroy's really noble book, "La Coutume Ouvrière" (1913).

taxation what he tends to see is less the grievance than the privilege of such labour. He remembers not the services he has secured from public administration so much as the ills he has suffered from its suspension. What impresses him is less the result of uninterrupted routine than the disasters which may attend such dislocation as the famous postal strike of 1909. He knows that there are close upon a million civil servants in France, and Guy de Maupassant has with genial irony convinced him that they have causes for other sentiment than grievance.[22] Complaints are for him no more than the unusual accompaniments of a process in which he has no interest. They represent the failure of services which he pays taxes in order to guarantee. They thus defeat for him the end of the state; and he finds it difficult to understand, much less to condone, the ambitions they imply.

Yet the problem cannot be thus easily dismissed. More than a thousand societies testify to the determination of the civil service to protect its interest against abuses. They constitute essentially trade-unions, and, like trade-unions, they aim above all at the defence of the economic interests of their members. They have, too, the additional object of safeguarding professional standards, exactly as similar organizations among lawyers and doctors. Nor can it be denied that their grievances are real. Not, indeed, that they have developed in any special degree in the last ten years. Rather it is that during the last ten years there has come an increasing consciousness of the way in which they may best be removed. So long as the sovereignty of the state went virtually without challenge, it was hardly conceivable that where others were silent, its own servants would resist. It was only with the visible transformation of the very nature of public power that a realisation came of what weapons lay in their hands.[23]

The main abuse of which the civil service complains is naturally favouritism. Positions of trust are at the mercy of the

[22] On the numbers and salaries of the Civil Service cf. Lefas, "L'Etat et les Fonctionnaires," Chap. II.

[23] For the number of associations and their growth see the official report to the Chamber of M. Jeanneney (Hachette, 1908), p. 230 f. But he does not count the societies formed prior to 1901 and suppressed by authority.

government. Partisanship is the test of public advancement; and even so distinguished a statesman as M. Waldeck-Rousseau did not hesitate to assert that confidence could be given only to those of whose political views the government had the assurance implied in support.[24] Irregularities of every kind are committed, so that the very rules by which the different departments of the civil service are governed become in fact worthless. An official may be nominated to the police service without passing the necessary examination. A distinguished historian like M. Delisle can be dismissed from a lifelong post at the Archives to make room for a young political nominee ignorant of even the rudiments of his profession. An inspector in the ministry of education is almost at the mercy of a deputy who can not only destroy his career, but that of the teachers with whose supervision he is charged.[25] Similar complaints come from the post-office, the government arsenals, even the magistracies.[26] France has what has been in England unnecessary since 1870, its Black Book of political nepotism.[27] In a single year, M. Simyan, the under-secretary of state for posts and telegraphs, received more than one hundred thousand letters recommending candidates for office almost entirely on political grounds.[28] M. Steeg has given numerous instances in the Chamber of Deputies itself of nominations that have been granted in every part of the civil service for reasons other than merit, and without regard to the regulations involved.[29] Against the political power a deputy can exert the fact is clear that few officials dare hope to compete. They cannot make headway against the influence of a man upon whose vote the government is counting for its very existence, and that the more certainly in a country where, as in France, the executive

[24] See the famous Toulouse speech of Oct. 28, 1900. For an almost exactly similar American utterance of the speech cf. Mr. Johnson, a congressman for Kentucky, in the *Congressional Record* for Oct. 10, 1913.

[25] Leyret, "La République et Les Politiciens," p. 29 f.

[26] On this last evil of the very able speech cf. M. Louis Martin in the Chamber, *Journal Officiel*, Nov. 10, 1905.

[27] Cf. "Le Livre d'or Des Fils à Papa."

[28] M. Thibault, "Les Syndicats de Fonctionnaires" (1909).

[29] *Journal Officiel*, May 9, 1907.

has not yet made itself master of the legislature. It is surely clear that the civil servant is literally driven to combine against the minister to preserve the very regulations by which the department is supposed to be governed.

The private opinions of the civil servant are subject to a degrading surveillance. "The state," says M. Leroy-Beaulieu with graphic emphasis,[30] "strangles its personnel." It seems, indeed, to imagine that it has the right completely to control the personal life of its officials in every particular. M. Briand's ministry, at the time of the Separation, refused even to guarantee officials freedom of religious worship.[31] A teacher was dismissed for visiting the curé of his commune, and not even the unanimous petition of its inhabitants could secure his reinstatement.[32] A postmistress was transferred on the ground of reactionary opinions because one of her sons was a priest, and the other employed by a notorious conservative.[33] An inspector was dismissed for refusing to answer political letters of recommendation.[34] And one distinguished politician, M. Clémenceau, does not seem to doubt that what the governments pays for is intellectual servitude.[35] "The government," said M. Dubief, a former minister of commerce,[36] "will not surrender the right to know the attitude of its servants to the republic."

It of course follows that if private opinions are so carefully scrutinised their public expression is rigidly suppressed.[37] Liberty of action is necessarily denied if private opinion is to be controlled. Teachers have been dismissed for making pacifist speeches.[38] Officials who take a leading part in the work of professional organisation find themselves interrogated, sus-

---

[30] P. Leroy-Beaulieu, "L'Etat Moderne et Ses Fonctions," p. 81.

[31] *Journal Officiel*, Nov. 20, 1905.

[32] *Journal Officiel*, Jan. 31, 1909.

[33] P. Harmignie, "L'Etat et Ses Agents," p. 31.

[34] *Réforme Social*, April 1, 1909, p. 417.

[35] *Ibid.*

[36] *Journal Officiel*, Feb. 8, 1905.

[37] On this problem in England cf. the Report of the Royal Commission. Parl. Papers, 1914, Vol. XVI, p. 95.

[38] Guiraud, "L'Ecole et La Famille," p. 103.

pended, even dismissed.[39] A teacher was dismissed for attacking the prefect of his department in the press. The maritime prefect of Toulon refused to admit into the arsenal the trade paper of the Marine Workers' Federation. A clerk who prophesied in the journal of his association that conditions in the local treasury must eventually result in a strike was dismissed for so doing. Discipline, it was argued in all these cases, is impossible if the right to criticise anything relating to government is assumed. Yet when the administrative means of individual protest are deemed inadequate it is difficult to see how, on the one hand, the technical journal of a profession can avoid the discussion of a technical problem, or why it is more inappropriate for a civil servant to have opinions on pacifism than it is for Mr. Disraeli to make epigrams about Darwin.

Problems such as these are the most complex the administrative issue affords, for their solution involves the regulation of parliamentary government in a way that has thus far been unknown.[40] The questions raised by the material situation of the civil servant are far less complex in character. It is natural enough that all kinds of grievances should exist in relation to the physical conditions of service. Wages are often low; the hours of labour are deemed over-long; vacations do not come at a time when they can be adequately profitable. Not, indeed, that the civil service has not involved a constantly-increasing expenditure. In the post-office, for example, where the intensity of grievance has on two occasions led to a serious strike, the expenses have increased in ten years from 177 to 297 million francs, and the receipts have not risen proportionately.[41] The same is true, in some degree, of every government department,[42] and that at a time when it is claimed by M. Clémenceau that they are all overstaffed.[43] The problem of pensions is no more than a variation upon a similar theme.

[39] *Revue Socialiste*, 1909, p. 388.

[40] Except at England where they have largely been met. But for a recrudescence of the evils of patronage see an article in the *Civilian* for Nov. 23, '12.

[41] Cf. the Report to the Chamber on the Budget des Postes of M. Noulens, in 1908.

[42] *Bulletin de Statistique du Ministère des Finances*, July, 1905.

[43] *Journal Officiel*, May 15, 1907.

The problem of administrative discipline and promotion is far more complex, and the report of every commission that has discussed the subject shows that it has nowhere been satisfactorily solved. The right to discipline a civil servant has as its aim the repression of such conduct as may hurt the condition of the public service. That, after all, is simple and obvious enough; but the way in which the repression is to be exercised involves immense difficulties. Is it action taken by the minister in the name of the state? Does he therein occupy the position of an employer who settles at his pleasure how he will deal with an inefficient workman? Is it action taken by the minister in the name of the state, as the head, for instance, of a railway company may act as the representative of the corporate person? Or is it, as the civil servants claim, action taken still, indeed, by the minister, but acting as the head of a professional and technical service temporarily placed under his control? The tendency of ministers themselves is to act upon the first hypothesis; it is only natural, when the evolution of the idea of public service is borne in mind, that this should be the case. Every minister is in theory charged with the compilation of rules to deal with the officials in his department. It is not, then, difficult for him to assume that if he can make and unmake them at his will, his power is autocratic. The hierarchical structure of French administration[44] tends, in any case, to identify order with a somewhat arbitrary exercise of power. Discipline, it has been argued, is impossible if democratic cooperation on the part of the civil service is admitted. That autocracy is naturally a matter of grave suspicion to the official. He desires to replace it by a method which will enable him to share in the determination of punishments. He has, indeed, already a certain share in the councils of discipline; but this is always minority representation and rarely elective.[45] He is anxious, moreover, that official control should be strictly limited to acts done in the course of public employment. If M. Nègre, for example, displays a poster containing an open letter

[44] For a brilliant analysis cf. Duguit, "L'Etat," Vol. I, p. 475 f, and the caustic analysis of M. Leroy in the third chapter of his "Transformations de la Puissance Publique."

[45] Cf. Bonnard, "De la Repression des Fautes."

to the Prime Minister of a somewhat critical character, he ought not to be penalised for an act obviously done, so it is claimed, in his capacity as a citizen.[46] The civil servant demands the replacement of such arbitrary power by a system of guarantees. The entrance to public employment should be so regulated as to put it beyond the reach of ordinary ministerial control. Fairness should be guaranteed by communicating to every civil servant the documents upon which his position depends. Punishments should no longer be arbitrary and accidental. They should be applied not secretly and from above, but openly, and from below. The council of discipline should cease to be a mere board of advice composed of the minister's nominees. It is only by the removal of these grievances that the civil service can recover its confidence in the goodwill of government.

And as with discipline, so with promotion. If there is perhaps a tendency among officials to lay too great emphasis on length of service—the natural tendency of the expert to confuse antiquity with experience—some safeguard is surely needed against the abuse of favouritism. Unless a bulwark is erected against promotion at pleasure, the deputy, as now, will pick out his candidates for promotion. There are numerous instances of the acceleration of advancement for purely political reasons. At present there is too little guarantee that a meritorious continuity of service may count at all. No precautions are taken to see that those whose names are accepted for promotion are really worthy of it. A vacancy in a higher position is filled in the most arbitrary fashion. Where seniority counts, it counts absolutely instead of relatively, so that no precaution can be taken to see that it is coupled with efficiency. No system exists which regulates the transference of officials from one department to another. If a civil servant advances, as he thinks, too slowly in one department, he uses political influence to obtain a position two or three grades higher in another. It is obvious enough that thus to remain at the mercy of what is practically the minister's whim should make the official demand the security of professional standards organised under a charter of independence.[47]

[46] "Libres Entretiens," 4th series (1907-8), p. 230 f.

[47] Cf. Demartial "Les Statut des Fonctionnaires" (1909) and Georgin. "Les Statut des Fonctionnaires." (1911). I have discussed below the significance of these claims.

No one can doubt the broad conclusion implied in these grievances. Each of them is too vast to make individual effort in any probable sense productive. Each of them demands concerted action if speedy redress is to be obtained. That is why the last decade has seen the immense growth of trade-unionism among the civil servants. That growth was itself the effect of an intolerable situation, and without it the crisis would never have occurred. But it is one thing to form associations and another to secure their recognition. The law of 1884 admitted association for the purpose of safeguarding professional interests; but it is absolutely clear that its extension to the civil service was at no moment intended.[48] The law of 1901 permits the formation of societies for any general purpose not contrary to public well-being; but it lacks the professional and economic connotation that attaches to the law of 1884.[49] It is the benefit of the first law that the civil servants demand. Without it, and all that it implies, the right of association would be fruitless. For ministers have been prodigal in their promises; and it is sufficiently clear that the mere formation of amiable and well-intentioned groups who have neither threats to make, nor the weapons with which to fulfil them can prove at all effective.[50]

The result has been to drive the lower grades of the civil service more and more in the direction of the syndicalist movement. Teachers, postal workers, hospital warders, have formed trade-unions despite the legal prohibition that seems to exist. They attempt to join the Bourses de Travail.[51] The more eager spirits do not hesitate to claim, and sometimes to secure, affiliation with the Confédération Générale du Travail; and thus to make proclaim of their eager desire to overthrow the bourgeois state.[52] Prohibitions and dismissals have made little difference. Dismissals can always be recalled by pressure in the chamber, and since they are the only means by which the

[48] Cf. below.

[49] Paul-Boncour, "Les Syndicats de Fonctionnaires," p. 15.

[50] Alibert, "Les Syndicats de Fonctionnaires," p. 84.

[51] Cf. the prohibitive decree of August 11, 1905.

[52] Cf. the Open Letter to M. Clémenceau reprinted by Leroy in "Syndicats et Services Publics."

prohibition can be enforced it is not surprising that they remain ineffective.[53]   Nor are the different departments remaining distinct.   Federations and congresses, sometimes even international in character, testify to the community of feeling by which the civil service is penetrated.[54]

The implication of the demand to associate under the law of 1884 is, of course, perfectly clear.   When the association becomes a recognised trade-union it possesses the right to strike; and certainly there are few among the more advanced fonctionnaires who deny their appreciation of this weapon.   If it is answered that the strike is not only brutal but often ineffective, the civil servant makes reply, just as the syndicalist, that nothing is so likely to give his colleagues their proper sense of class-consciousness.   Indeed, the emphasis on the law of 1884 is, above all, an emphasis of sentiment.[55]   The humble fonctionnaire cannot help feeling that to call him a member of the governing classes is an absurd mis-application of terms.   Relative to the government, his situation is exactly the situation of an ordinary member of the working-classes and the equation of position demands, in his view, the equation of methods.[56] Arguments derived from legal theory rather naturally leave him a little cold.   When he is told by so sympathetic an observer as M. Duguit[57] that a strike in the civil service is subversive of its very nature he is not likely, until his grievances have received their fundamental remedy, to be overwhelmed with a sense of shame.   He will say quite simply that he is immediately interested not in the functioning of a service for ends of which he does not approve by methods from which he suffers, but in taking the shortest route to a transformation of the whole system.   He has technical ideals without doubt; but one cannot have technical ideals until an adequate milieu for their application has been obtained.

[53] Cf. *Journal Officiel*, July 11, 1906, March 10, 1908, June 22, 1909.

[54] Beaubois, *Mouvement Socialiste*, April, 1909, p. 291.

[55] Bouglé, "Syndicats de Fonctionnaires," *Revue Metaphysique et Morale*. 1907, p. 671.

[56] Fournière "Les Fonctions de L'Etat," *Revue Socialiste*, 1907, p. 40.

[57] "Droit Social, Droit Individuel," pp. 134-7.

III. THE CLAIMS OF THE CIVIL SERVICE

WHAT, obviously enough, is important in all this is the end it has in view. It is not so much a revolt as a revolution, and it it at the heart of the unified state that it is aimed. The reality of the grievances under which the civil service has laboured is unquestionable; but the sentiment to which they have given rise is no longer to be assuaged by their amendment. For the real problem that has been created is not a doubt of the end to which the state is directed, but a doubt whether the present mechanisms of government can in fact attain that end.[58] The need of authority is undoubted; but challenge is issued to that authority simply because the fonctionnaire no longer believes that its autocratic exercise can achieve the purposes for which, theoretically, it exists. The fact that authority depends on its acceptance by those over whom it is exerted no longer needs demonstration. Here, as elsewhere, the capital fact is demonstrated that the fundamental problem of political science is not how power originated, but how it can be justified.[59] What the theorists of this movement have done is to divide the state into rulers and subjects and to proclaim to the latter that the object of the state cannot, in the present synthesis, be fulfilled. So that they are compelled by conviction to join hands with the revolutionary elements of modern society that, from their joint efforts, a new state may be born.

Even so barely stated, the argument is far-reaching enough; but the method of its detailed presentation gives it a strength that is even more striking. Unquestionably, of course, the movement contains men of moderate opinions who did not sympathise with the active enmity to the state displayed in the postal strike and desire no more than an improvement in their position.[60] Undoubtedly also, as in every great movement, the opinion of the associations has, for the most part, been guided by the ability and energy of a few. But, equally clearly, it is this active minority that has formulated the accepted principles of

[58] Cf. Berth, "Marchands, Intellectuels, Politiciens," in *Mouvement Socialiste*," 1907-8.

[59] As Rousseau and T. H. Green clearly perceived. I have discussed the problem in the first chapter of this book.

[60] Pouget, "Les Bases du Syndicalisme," p. 21.

the movement, and their leadership is responsible both for the direction it has taken and the successes it has attained.[61] Their attitude is simply that of the militant proletariat. They look upon the administrative world as basically akin to that of industry. The class-struggle is no less real there. The humbler civil-servant there, as in industry can free himself only by his own efforts. His triumph will come only from the strength and power of his associations which must more and more attempt the domination of the services to which he belongs. By the strength of those groups he can attain the desired reforms, if not peaceably, then by the accepted methods of direct action. The result will be the transformation of the state.

It is an arresting analogy that is not without its fascination. The humbler fonctionnaires seem, undoubledly, to constitute an administrative proletariat. The hierarchical control exercised over them by their technical superiors is in no sense likely to produce any real sentiment of co-operation. The attitude adopted to them by the parliamentarians is in every sense lamentable. It is only at a crisis that they obtain a hearing; but the promises so prodigally made are rarely, if ever, fulfilled. The statesmen are too occupied with the mechanisms of politics to care for the processes by which their decisions are fulfilled. And within the administration itself there is a hierarchy of classes which corresponds to that of the general social organisation.[62] The division between the privileged few who are well-paid and the mass whose salary is inadequate is very marked. The average civil-servant cannot hope to arrive at those posts; and where promotion is secure, it applies only to the central administration and not to the provinces.[63] There is, in fact, a general disproportion between labour and reward exactly as in private industry.[64] And if the higher fonctionnaires thus reap the profit of their subordinates' work, the state itself is for the mass of civil servants simply an employer. That is, of course, clear

[61] Cf. Harmignie, op. cit., p. 145, *Journal Officiel*, May 14, 1907 (M. Briand).

[62] Cf. Fournière, *Revue Socialiste*, 1907, p. 40.

[63] Cf. *Economiste Français*, Nov. 18, 1905, p. 737 (a civil-servant's letter).

[64] Leroy, "Transformations de La Puissance Publique," p. 222.

when it makes matches or builds ships. It is not less an employer when it takes charge of public instruction. Its work of administration requires a manual and intellectual proletariat just like any business house. Even in its judicial aspect, so M. Leroy has claimed,[65] the reality of this character is apparent. Clearly, if the state is an employer its servants are wage-earners, and they cannot, through the accidental choice of employment, deprive themselves of means which will prevent their exploitation. Their position, as M. Millerand has said,[66] is no more than a particular instance of a general industrial problem. The fight is a struggle against privileges, whether, as in industry, those of the rich, or as in politics, those of the government.[67]

If they are a proletariat, they must, like the workers, accomplish their own salvation. To that end a sense of unity is vital and nothing can be gained until it has been created. So the fonctionnaires have not only formed what correspond to craft-unions, but also federations of workers in the different departments. They have seen that an injury to one may affect the strength of the whole; and they have not hesitated to make corporate protest against individual injustice.[68] They have supported one another at times of crisis. They have held congresses where assurances of fraternity have been exchanged. And their feeling of identity with the working-classes has led to an important rapprochement between them. Its basis, indeed, was already prepared in the existence of an undeniable proletariat in the state-monopolies;[69] and the steps thence to civil servants who in the technical sense are associated with the administration was not a great one. The teachers were the first to take action. Not only did they attempt to join the Bourses de Travail—despite ministerial prohibition[70]—but they have gone so far as to seek affiliation with the Confédération Générale du Travail which is avowedly revolutionary in purpose. Undoubtedly, indeed, that action has failed to secure unanimous

[65] "Syndicats et Services Publics," p. 187.
[66] See Le Temps, Feb. 25, 1906.
[67] Revue Hebdomadaire, August 3, 1907, p. 13.
[68] Harmignie, op. cit., 91.
[69] Cf. Beaubois, Mouvement Socialiste, Jan. 1909.
[70] Decree of August 11, 1905.

support. But what is important is the fact that it should have
won any support at all. "We shall march by its side," said
M. Nègre, the outstanding person in the movement,[71] "to work
together for the emancipation of the industrial and intellectual
proletariat." M. Nègre is a teacher, and his attitude is the more
striking in that the intellectual position of the teacher in France
would seem to relate him to the middle class; but the avowed
exponents of official syndicalism have at length accepted their
adhesion.[72]

Nor is there any distinction of method between the militant
fonctionnaire and the militant proletariat. The whole purpose
of their desire to benefit rather from the law of 1884 than from
that of 1901 is the ability the former affords of using the weapon
of the strike. "The collective suspension of work," says M.
Briquet,[73] "is the indispensable aim of every labour-group which
desires effectively to promote the collective interests of its members." Indeed, a simple association, the Association of Postal
Workers, has not hesitated to disregard the technical distinction
between the two laws. It is for them simply a sterile discussion
of doctrine with which they have no concern.[74] The police of
Lyons did not hesitate to go on strike, and, after the face of the
government had been saved, it appears that they were successful.[75] The teachers, indeed, in some respects the most advanced
of all the fonctionnaires, have not proceeded so far; for it is
clear that in their case the temporary suspension of a public
service that would be involved, does not relate with sufficient
intimacy to the necessary conduct of the national life. If these
strikes have not had the large results of which their leaders
dreamed, they have at any rate shown the powerlessness of law
to prevent them. They have demonstrated the all-important
fact that a challenge can be issued to government. They have
suggested, since the movement is only at its beginning, that it is
a challenge to which there may one day be no possible reply.

It is, then, essentially a revolutionary spirit with which the

[71] Harmignie, op. cit., p. 105.
[72] Beaubois *Mouvement Socialiste*, 1905, p. 505.
[73] *Mouvement Socialiste*, 1903, p. 147.
[74] Though it has discussed.
[75] *Journal Officiel*, May 23, 1905. cf. the London police strike of 1918.

government is called upon to deal.   Exactly as the ultimate aim
of the industrial movement is an attempt to create an industrial
democracy, so do the fonctionnaires aim at the creation of an
administrative democracy.   They are compelled, therefore, to be
suspicious of power.   The state is to them, as it is to the workers,
the real citadel to assault.   To attack the government is to sap
the foundations of an authority the basic purpose of which seems
to them illegitimate.[76]   The present system of administrative
organisation seems to them unsatisfactory simply because its
underlying principles are inconsistent with the aims they have
in view.   So long as the hierarchy is maintained, the democratisation of administrative power is impossible.   So long as the
present division exists between the higher civil service and the
humbler fonctionnaires, the former, whose position is, for the
most part, secure, are bound to gravitate towards the deputies
and make the civil service political instead of technical in character.   That is why the fonctionnaire refuses his confidence to
the Chamber.   Its object is too different to be compatible with
his own.   It is, so to speak, itself a trade-union and its administrative exertions are only one of the ways in which it promotes
the interests of its members.   It also, then, uses a kind of direct
action for its purposes;   and the gesture of the civil service is
thus not distinct in quality from that of the politician.   This
discontent with authority expresses itself in many ways—open
contempt for administrative regulations,[77] vituperation of the
Parliament,[78] distrust even of the republic itself.   "We no
longer believe in words," said an able representative of this
attitude,[79] "we demand realities;   we have lost our attachment
for forms.   We calculate their worth and measure their productivity.   We no longer sacrifice ourselves for sentiment, we con-
sult our interests.   The heroic times have passed away;   the hour
of practical effort has arrived."

The civil service, indeed, has not stopped its effort at the mere
criticism of the administrative system.   It has been compelled
to realise that the administrative system is, in fact, but the re-

[76] Cf. M. Jaurés in *L' Humanité*, May 1, 1908.
[77] Cf. citations in "Harmignie," op. cit., p. 126.
[78] *Ibid.*, p. 128.
[79] And cf. Ch. Dupuy in *Le Soleil*, April 5, 1909.

flex of a larger whole. There are other institutions within the state which equally constitute its stalwart defences. Its military organisation is essentially a reservoir of state-power. To become a soldier is so it is argued, to lose contact with the working-class, and to destroy a system which thus uses that class against itself is clearly fundamental. A congress of teachers has pledged itself to pacifism, and some of them have suffered dismissal for the violence of their antimilitarist propaganda.[80] As is usually the case, the offspring of pacifist doctrine has been internationalism, and at any rate before 1914, many members of the civil service had gone far towards its adoption.

The fonctionnaires, in fact, do not conceal from themselves that it is nothing less than an entire social reconstruction at which they are aiming. That they can effect it alone, they do not for a moment profess to believe; but they urge that government normally disposes of so great a power that without their assistance a successful revolution can be hardly accomplished. Nor, given the conditions, is that an exaggerated assumption. Each group of them, moreover, has its function in the task. It is the duty of the teacher to begin in childhood the revolutionary education of the people; while those actually concerned with the technical work of administration can overthrow the whole machine at the critical moment of its functioning. M. Jaurés, indeed, was in nowise disturbed by the character of the movement. "The affiliation," he said,[81] of civil servants to the labour movement, to the class-struggle, is a revolutionary fact. It is not less than a revolution when the servants of the state work to reconstruct the basis of that social order of which the state is the expression and the guardian." It is a movement which has penetrated every section of the civil service. It is ably organized and its propaganda is conducted with relentless energy. It has a brilliant literature, and a press of its own. It has definite ends to pursue, and it is evolving means by which those ends may be attained. It is a movement which at every stage of its progress, has been marked by the courageous termination of its leaders. Certain it is that one who is at all interested in the

[80] *Journal Officiel*, June 27, 1908, Guiraud, "L'Ecole et La Famille," p. 111.

[81] *Journal Officiel*, May 15, 1907.

development of political processes dare neglect the richness of its possibilities.

For, after all, no social movement is unique in its age. Political change has links with the past so strict and so far-reaching that it is rarely possible to ascribe novelty to what the heralds of an idea themselves deem striking innovation. Certainly this is the case with administrative syndicalism. It represents a crisis for which there has been long and careful preparation. It is part of a larger federal synthesis which has ramifications throughout the industrial world. The very solutions it proposes have intellectual ancestors which were themselves the product of their time. This is not, indeed, to argue that administrative syndicalism is a phenomenon so ordinary that it can with safety be neglected. It draws a special importance from a situation which has of necessity tended to throw it into striking relief. It has succeeded simply because the evolution it summarises is beginning at last to translate itself into terms of practical achievement. It is a variation upon the theme of economic federation which is itself the offspring of a breakdown in the machinery of capitalist organisation. It represents in relation to the state simply what the large aspects of syndicalism represent in industrial change. It gives a new connotation to sovereignty. It federalises the will of the state. The lines, indeed, of its evolution can not yet with any certainty be drawn. We can use descriptive terms, suggest tendencies, discover signs of change. In the elements of opposition are to be discovered the means of more intimate analysis. From whatever source they are derived, it is a crisis that the facts suggest. The tidal wave of democratic advance has at last reached the inmost recesses of the imperial state. Our task is the measurement of the energy it conveys.

IV. IMPLICATIONS

It is usual to distinguish three different systems of administrative organisation.[82] What has been called the monarchical solution would leave the civil service at the mercy of the executive power. The present régime, that is to say, might be altered in its accidentals, but its fundamental features would

[82] Salaun, *Revue Politique et Parliamentaire*, Jan. 10, 1908, p. 148 seq.

remain unchanged. Such a method, it is clear, would leave the main cause of the present unrest entirely unsolved. It would involve a patent contradiction between a democratically organised political system and an autocratic administrative system. It would withdraw a whole field of social activity from the dominant influences of the time. It would look, not to the organisation that is to be, but to the past history of the state. It could be maintained only by violence, and probably at the sacrifice of administrative efficiency. The second means is its direct antithesis. It proposes to hand over to the civil service the control of administrative functions. The political head of a department would state his demands, and his orders would be fulfilled by the fonctionnaires themselves. The department would be in every way autonomous, so that there would be no room left for the grievances by which the service is oppressed. This, clearly enough, is the organisation which meets with most favour among the civil servants themselves. It transforms them into a technical profession, and it leaves no opportunity for personal causes external to the service to interfere with its functioning. The third solution is midway between the two others. It envisages a statutory organisation of the civil service. The minister will remain in control, but it will be a legally conditioned control. Every step of his policy will be conditioned by statute. The method of promotion, the redress of grievance, administrative responsibility, the mechanism of suggestion, will be at every stage controlled by legal regulations. The vise of the monarchical system will thus disappear while the danger of administrative independence of the national life is sufficiently safeguarded. The justice of the complaints urged against the monarchical system is admitted, but it is not felt that they justify so great an innovation as administrative syndicalism would entail.

Very clearly, the starting-point of any enquiry must discuss the origins of modern centralisation. That is in nowise doubtful. We need not agree with Taine's theory that the Revolution resulted in the deterioration of human nature[83] to agree that the general chaos prevented the employment of the mechanisms of liberalism. Where the very existence of power was

[83] "Régime Moderne," Bk. II, Ch. I.

threatened, it was only by its concentration that it could survive. What Napoleon did was to synthesise that power within himself; and the equality that remained was the equality of a common subjection to his will. He realised that action in the modern state must be as certainly unified as deliberation must be multiple. He demanded from the civil service an absolute abandonment of their personality.[84] It was the fulfilment of Sièyes' prevision. "Power," he had said,[85] "will come from above; from below there will be simply confidence," and that was no more than a simple statement of fact. And certainly his administrative system was not his least durable work. The country was satisfied with an administration that was at any rate efficient; and the reaction upon it of political democracy was as yet too novel to be at all impressive. So that Napoleon's successors could not only use his system but even extend it. "Ce sont des administrés," writes M. Chardon,[86] "qui de propos délibérés, étendent chaque jour l'empire de l'administration," and, indeed the fact is obvious enough; for not the least important result of the extension of collectivism has been the general expectation that government not only can, but must, meet every conceivable emergency.[87]

But while administrative power was thus extended, its exercise underwent no democratic percolation. The executive power retained its imperial purple. Nothing in the whole path of the nineteenth century seemed able to influence its organisation. Government, as in the time of Napoleon, is the representative of the sovereign people, and to confide power to those who are not elected would be to create a state within a state and destroy the unity of the whole. That is why Taine's brilliant description of the Napoleonic prefect remains not less true today than of the time of which he wrote.[88] The civil servant is not an actor in the events of which he is the administrator. He is a kind of perpetual secretary; and M. Chardon

[84] See Tarne's impressive remarks, "Régime Moderne," Vol. I, p. 170.

[85] *Ibid.*, I, 168.

[86] "L'Administration de la France," p. 2.

[87] This was very strikingly evinced in the food crisis of 1917 which led to Mr. Hoover's appointment as administrator.

[88] "Régime Moderne," Vol. II, p. 240 f.

insists that there are able and competent men who never have a single decision to take throughout their career.[89]   The service is recruited in exactly the same way as at the Revolution; everything is controlled by the central power.   If France has no longer Napoleon, she has his ministers, and they are less successful in their psychology in the degree to which they lack his personal fascination.   Here, again, it was Taine who perceived the real crux of the problem.   "They do not," he said,[90] "look upon human association . . . as concerted initiative generated from below . . . but as a hierarchy of authorities imposed from above."   Where the fundamental change in the modern state is an evolution almost directly antithetic to this attitude, it has left untouched the civil service.   Not even the admission of corporate freedom has penetrated within the executive realm.[91]

It is a persistence as difficult to justify as it is easy to understand.   It is difficult to justify because it is an apparent and, as it seems, unnecessary contradiction of democratic government.   It is surely an erroneous attitude to separate competence and responsibility; and that, in fact, is the result of the present system.   It is easy to understand because, from a long historical chain of events,[92] the average citizen in the modern democracy seems anxious, above all, to perform his political functions vicariously.   What he asks from the professional politician is orderly government and he rarely examines the means by which it is attained.   Whether M. Clémenceau ever really remarked that he could remain in office so long as he wanted,[93] the fact remains that he epitomized very neatly the

[89] "L'Administration de la France," p. 9.

[90] "Régime Moderne," Vol. I, p. 213.

[91] Cf. the admirable remarks of M. Seignobos, "Hist. of Cont. Europe," p. 222 f.

[92] They have been brilliantly analysed, psychologically, for England by Mr. Graham Wallas in his "Human Nature in Politics" and for American Society by Mr. Lippmann in his "Preface to Politics." In institutional terms of the magistral analysis of Ostrogorski, "Democracy and the Organisation of Political Parties." I do not know of any similar French work, but the syndicalist criticisms of the modern state, as M. Lagardelle's "Socialisme Ouvrier" esp., Part I, are very valuable on this point.

[93] Duguit, "Droit Social, Droit Individuel," p. 129.

typical governmental attitude to the civil service. Democracy seems to have considered that the security of its life depended on the retention of the hierarchical system.[94] That may, perhaps, have been true before the separation when the safety of the republic was still matter of debate. But with the assurance of its survival, the Napoleonic system is already obsolete.

That, indeed, is the real meaning of the growth of administrative syndicalism. It has come because there is now no reason to restrain it. Antiquity is not a reason; and democracy is, internally at least, in little danger of disappearance. The executive power can not make a plea for its autocratic exercise when the army is no longer a source of disloyalty, and the church has been reduced to a shadow of its former influence. The only reason for the retention of the present system is the power it places in the hands of statesmen. It enables them to corrupt both the civil service and the electorate. The one he can hold by the fear of dismissal, the other by the hope of office. But it is too obviously humiliating for the civil servant to remain subject both to public and private control. The only justification of arbitrary power is the impossibility of democratic power. That impossibility the civil servant denies. He maintains that it is based upon an entirely false conception of the implications of sovereignty. The theory that the state must, by its very definition, be irresponsible seems to him without root in political fact. He knows what that irresponsibility has meant in the past. He has weighed it and rejected it. The hour has come for new systems.

It is in some such fashion that the monarchical system is rejected, and, psychologically at least, there seems every reason for its rejection. No administrative system can be adequate in which power is concentrated and not disturbed. No service can attract ability where the influence it offers is hidden and potential, not real and responsible.[95] Nor are the syndicalists more enamoured of a status that is guaranteed by parliament. They are too suspicious of the state to feel secure at what emanates from its organs.[96] It is, after all, from the

[94] *Journal Officiel*, M. Clémenceau, Speech of March 13, 1908.

[95] Mr. Wallas' admirable remarks, "The Great Society," pp. 285-8, 290 f.

[96] For interesting evidence of a similar suspicion in England cf. *Bulletin of U. S. Bureau of Labor*, Vol. 5, p. 36.

Parliament above all that they have suffered; and it is largely by the manipulation of the civil service that the majority in the chamber retains its power. They do not believe in the modern state simply because theirs has been the most intimate experience of it. What laws have been suggested are all of them conservative in character. They attempt the compromise of two irreconcilable theories. The administration wants to exercise a final control where the civil service demands autonomy. Nor are they eager for a special position in the state. That suggestion is for them no more than an erroneous idea derived from the original irresponsibility of the sovereign state. It is a decaying theory,[97] and they will not found their relief upon it. Nor is it, in any case, destined very long to survive. Every day, the jurisprudence of the *Conseil d'Etat* makes one more inroad upon its life.[98] The dogma is already too seriously compromised to be capable any longer of valid application. It would still leave their relation to the state non-contractual in character to regulate their position by statute. What they desire is a service on equal terms, a right to make their situation a part of the common law. Nor are they—and this is of supreme importance—willing to enjoy a situation which would in fact break the bonds of their friendship with the industrial proletariat. For to attach themselves to the present state is to surrender the right to work for its transformation. It was exactly the need of that change they above all felt at the time of their original revolt against its excesses. Clearly, to accept a favour from its hands would be to desert not merely those who stood by them in their need, but also the original and avowed purpose of their movement. They will not share in so great a self-stultification.

So that for them there is no alternative save the monarchical and syndicalist solutions. They reject the first because an organization which deprives the workers of a voice in the determination of their labour is in fact psychologically and morally inadequate. The second alone is satisfactory because there only is there guarantee that the humanity of the administrative proletariat is recognised. There only can the method

[97] Cf. Duguit, "Le Droit Social, Le Droit Individual," p. 72.
[98] Cf. Duguit, "Les Transformations du Droit Public," pp. 65-73.

of action be in such fashion a fusion of wills that every
voice can find representation in the result,[99] can make administrative personality democratic in a corporate sense. They
believe, moreover, that institutional evolution is far more in accord with the position they have taken up than with the proposal of a statute. The parliamentary solution does not, after
all, depend upon an improvement in the condition of the people
as a whole. Thereby merely to base government upon number
is still to leave it open to the pathetic manipulation by which
it has been traduced during the nineteenth century,[100] for we
are less confident than before that majority-rule is a final
solution. They point to the increasing development—common
to the whole world—of a political life outside the ordinary
cadres of parliamentary systems.[101] Not only are they, as it
seems, determined to make the government inferior to law by
making it responsible, but also, by associations of every kind,
they bring pressure to bear upon the legislative process. It is
a new and striking effort to bring authority within the bounds
of popular control.[102] It makes it less likely to remain merely a
weapon in the hands of those who exercise it. Nor can the
significance of the elaboration of legislative projects by those
who have a professional relation to their functioning be under-
estimated.[103] What we are beginning to see is virtually law-
making by those over whom the particular statute will exercise
its empire. To say that the system is in its infancy is in nowise
to belittle its implications. It is a new source of legislative
power, even if it be an indirect one; and it clearly bears, in very

[99] Cf. the speech of M. Sembat at the Congress of the Agents des Postes,
June 5, 1905; and his paper in *Documents du Progrès,* May, 1909, p. 408.

[100] This dissatisfaction with the merely numerical solution is admirably
expressed by a publicist who cannot be accused of syndicalist ideas, M. Ch.
Benoist; cf. his "Crise de l'Etat Moderne."

[101] Cf. the very important remarks of M. Maxime Leroy, "Libres
Entretiens," 4me series, p. 385 f.

[102] Cf. M. Leroy, "La Loi," p. 346 f.

[103] This is not less true of America than of France. Cf. Leroy, "La Loi,"
p. 212 f, with the fact that men like Professors Williston and Brannan of
the Harvard Law School have been charged with the drafting of statutes
which political bodies pass into law. The influence of such professional
autonomy as that of doctors and lawyers is, of course, analogous.

decisive fashion upon the nature of parliamentary authority. For the preparation of law by the private initiative of experts is the preparation of law by men whose opinion it is difficult to neglect.[104] Public opinion may be a reserve power, but no one can mistake the ultimate control it can exert, and public opinion tends more and more to appreciate the evolution of this technical legislation. It almost seems, in fact, that a democracy which has been thwarted of its authority by its unification has found new means of its assertion by dividing the source of power.

In such an atmosphere, the attitude which regards the state as in any sense an institution of a special character can hardly survive. Once the equality of citizens before the law is postulated, it is evident that their internal relations must be democratically organised. We have passed, as M. Duguit has insisted, from a régime of subjective rights to a régime of objective duties. That, from those duties, rights may find a secondary justification does not alter the fact that the real defence of authority is to show the objective necessity of its exercise.[105] Let it be granted that the personality of the state is real, it yet does not follow that corporate personality begets rights superior to individual rights.[106] What each state-action must show is that the force it entails produces a result so valuable that the life of society would be the poorer for its absence. But that is to say that the real test of state-theory is not the principles upon which that theory is based so much as the manner in which they function. The principle, in fact, cannot be separated from the process; its teleology is, at bottom, inductive. Its intentions may be admirable; but judgment cannot be made until the intention is realised in conduct. Exactly where the modern state is being transformed is at the point where the judgment upon its action has led to new methods of political life. Since the only justification of government is the quality of life its policy secures, the members of the modern state are

[104] Cruet, "La Vie du Droit," pp. 289, 332.

[105] Cf. Chapter I, *supra*, on this point.

[106] M. Duguit has denied this; but, as I have elsewhere tried to show, on insufficient grounds.

seeking new centres of power. Administrative syndicalism is an effort towards their realisation.

It is thus a kind of decentralisation for which the fonctionnaire is anxious. But it is not merely the reconstruction of ancient territorial groupings for which he is concerned. It has, indeed, to some extent been tried already in France; and its connection with the *ancien régime* has led the monarchist party to lend it a somewhat eager support.[107] But territorial decentralisation does not touch the real root of the problem. The real question to be resolved is that of internal organisation within the different groups themselves. Decentralisation of a purely territorial kind is no guarantee of autonomy. Local control might be as difficult and static as centralised control. The desire of the syndicalist is different. He urges that the business of government has now become so complex that it cannot maintain at once unity of purpose and unity of method. The explanation that the interest of the state is single, does not, even if it be true, involve the need of unified administration. On the contrary, the administration of the state cannot be satisfactory so long as it is so organized. What is desired is to confide the operation of the different branches of the state to technical services acting under government control.

But that control would be a declaration of purpose and no more. Its actual execution would be the business of the department concerned. Administrative autonomy would thus become real and effective. The department would execute a law for government exactly as a contractor builds a ship for the admiralty. It would know what was required and take the necessary measures. But its life would be self-determined. Its method of response would be spontaneous and not automatic. It would realise the spirit Rousseau envisaged when he made the social contract binding because it was mutual.[108]

---

[107] Cf. above all J. Paul Boncour and Charles Maurras, "Un Nouveau Débat sur la Décentralisation" passim. A curious book by H. Cellerier, "La Politique Fédéraliste" has much of interest on this point. The short remarks of M. Duguit, Droit Social, Droit Individuel, p. 144 f, give the pith of the matter; and M. Charles Brun, "Le Régionalisme" is a useful summary of the whole attitude.

[108] "Contrat Social," II, IV.

For the worker who had a certain power of independent responsibility would obtain, in such a system, exactly that psychological situation which makes administration a human thing. He would take part in deliberation. He would have ample means of discussion, of suggestion, of experiment. His task would become democratic even while it remained professional, simply because the compulsion of a purpose to be fulfilled would not, by its method, obscure the possibility of a free co-operation in its fulfillment.[109]

It is natural enough that where the evolution that is thus envisaged is itself but on the threshold of its first dumb beginnings, detailed plans should be lacking. After all, this is not an evolution that will be accomplished in a moment of time. It is bound to proceed by stages, and to be temporarily determined by the fluctuations of its failures and successes. Whether, for example, promotion would be self-regulating, or a matter of internal choice, or of election by the members of the particular service, is not a matter for deliberate prophecy. Most of the leaders of the movement have been wisely careful to abstain from it. That upon which they have mainly laid insistence, from their standpoint assuredly with commonsense, is the fact of autonomy. What they have emphasised is the fact that this autonomy must act as the destroyer of what is unacceptable in the modern hierarchical system. Above all, they have pointed out that self-regulation is the only effective guarantee of equal opportunity. What has been admirably termed an inexorable subalternism is impossible where the administration is in fact a republic, imbued at every stage with the democratic spirit. The conduct of the service will be better simply because men will obey with greater willingness a chief whose position is itself the proof of competence than one of whose powers they have had no reasonable demonstration.

The aim is not the abolition of society. The syndicalist does not wish to make the administration a closed system impermeable to outside influence and outside control. To give the schools to the teachers, the postal service to the postal workers in full ownership is a solution that only a few of the more extreme enthusiasts have claimed. For they are suffi-

[109] Cf. Berthod, *Revue Politique et Parlementaire*, March 1906, p. 428.

ciently alive to Mr. Wallas' grave warning[110] not to desire a restoration of that feudal structure which sought to solve the problem of society by the unthinking and purposeless multiplication of groups. They recognize that society has its place in every human equation, and that, as a consequence, it has a right to an indirect control over everything that is related to a social function. The teachers, for example, have not hesitated to ask for the assistance of parents in the redaction of their educational programmes.[111] The very method of organisation adopted by the Confédération Générale du Travail is in fact a guarantee against the dangers of separatism.[112] Indeed, as M. Leroy has aptly pointed out,[113] the very situation of the workers makes a federal structure as necessary as the bourgeois organisation of society demands a centralised system. The complete independence of any department would be strictly limited to those problems which do not directly touch the business of any other. Where common problems arise, they must be settled by common decision. The state, in some form or other, must persist to protect the common interest, and it must retain a certain measure of power for that purpose. There are some, indeed, who would make wages and prices a matter for general control; and M. Thomas has lent the great weight of his authority to the suggestion that the interest of the consumer must obtain adequate representation at every stage of the new administrative process.[114]

The problem of the strike then remains. It is clear enough that the operation of a public service must be in the general

[110] "The Great Society," p. 324 f. On the place of the state in the most recent system of social reconstruction cf. Orage (ed.) "National Guilds," 150, 263, and Cole, "Self-government in Industry," esp., Ch. III.

[111] Resolution of the Lyons Congress, 1908. Cf. Laurier, "Les Instituteurs et Le Syndicalisme" (1908).

[112] The best account of its structure is in Leroy, "La Coutume Ouvrière," pp. 481-575. Cf. also A. Pawlowski, "La Confédération Générale du Travail." The real secret of the difference between American trade-unionism and that of France will be apparent to anyone who examines the structure and purpose of the kindred groups in either country.

[113] "Les Transformations de la Puissance Publique," pp. 272, 278.

[114] *Revue Socialiste*, Oct. 1905, cf. the very able article by M. Bourget, *Revue Politique et Parlementaire*, 1908, p. 365.

interest of society. If its care is entrusted to the members of that service is the suspension of work at all capable of justification? If the operation of the state is put into the hands of its servants is not that autonomy the correlative of a responsibility for which there must be adequate guarantees? It is difficult to avoid this conclusion. "It is simply elementary prudence," says M. Hauriou,[115] "that the relation with the public, above all upon the fundamental problem of responsibility, should not be broken." It is surely obvious that the privilege of autonomy logically implies the acceptance of the purpose for which that responsibility is given. Once the professional group is given the means of independent action, it must be fully and stringently responsible for the causes of its acts.[116] That syndicalists are but little inclined, at present, to admit the extension of the corporate responsibility of their groups does not touch the real point at issue. For the narrowness of their responsibility is, for the moment, simply a weapon forged to meet a special industrial situation. Once the cause for that narrowness is removed, there is no reason for such restriction to continue. The state could not confide the interests of society to men who would not accept the responsibilities of their trusteeship.

V. THE ATTACK OF THE JURISTS

It was inevitable that such an attitude should provoke a violent hostility. The dogmas it attacks are too consecrated by historic tradition to surrender at all easily to an opposition in part, at least, the product of an ideology. The changes it involves are too far-reaching to be accepted without criticism by the conservative forces of the state. And, after all, such antagonism is natural enough. For the dogmas that administrative syndicalism has endeavored to undermine have behind them this justification that they are the source from which the

[115] Cf. his note in *Sirey*, 1908, Vol. III, p. 83.

[116] Cf. Rolland, *Revue de Droit Public* 1909, p. 301. Duguit, "Droit Social, Droit Individuel," p. 147. M. Hauriou's remarks are very striking, "Principes de Droit Public" (ed. of 1916), p. 745 f. For the theoretic basis of vicarious liability see my papers in 29, *Harv. L. Rev.* 404 f, and 26, *Yale Law Journal*, 105 ff.

modern state has derived its strength. The two great theories
of sovereignty and the unitary state are, for the most part,
the offspring of the great controversy between church and
state, matured by the influence of the classical jurisprudence
of Rome.[117] They are the weapons whereby the state attained
its freedom from ecclesiastical trammels. And they are even
more than that. For, with the growing independence of the
civil power, it was possible to transfer the seat of sovereignty
from monarch to people. National sovereignty thus came to
mean something akin to the vindication of popular freedom.
To attack it was to imperil the progress for which the Revolution stood as the proof and symbol.

Nor was the history of the unitary state less striking. The
great danger from which, in its recent history, France has
suffered is the diverse allegiance of its citizens. There were
many whose membership of the nation did not seem to involve
them in loyalty to the Republic; and they did not hesitate to find,
sometimes in Rome, sometimes at the half-tragic court of some
barely remembered royal exile, the real dwelling-place of their
affection. There was thus a danger to be confronted external
to French society. Concentration of power might then, with
some show of reason, be deemed a vital thing. If a citizen
did not stand by the Republic, if the Republic did not possess
the power to make upon him the fullest demand, its survival
was, to say the least, uncertain. Its sovereignty was strikingly
asserted; the fact of unity was at every point displayed. It
was not, therefore, difficult to charge administrative syndicalism
with a purpose that might well destroy the state. It would
render vain the whole purpose of the nineteenth century. It
was the coronation of anarchic effort; and compromise with so
sinister a movement was thus almost logically deemed fruitless.

Such, for the most part, has been the spirit in which administrative syndicalism has been met. It is an opposition that
is rarely constructive in character. It tends to take its stand
less upon the analysis of future possibilities than upon the
adequacy of the present inheritance. But, in sober truth, that
is to say no more than that it at no point fully meets the effort
of the fonctionnaire towards the transformation of the modern

[117] Cf. my "Problem of Sovereignty," pp. 27-9.

state. What it has rather tried to do is to demonstrate that such purpose is illegal and unpractical. It is held illegal by the lawyer because the categories of nineteenth century jurisprudence have no place for so novel an effort. It is held unpractical by the· statesman because it is a problem he has never before confronted. To the central principles it enunciates, they unite to return an unqualified negative.

There are, of course, both in law and in politics, exceptions to this general rule. There are some who have been able to see that the present conception of the state is in no sense permanent, and it is, for them, natural to expect that the development of its jurisprudence will be coeval with its political evolution. There are statesmen who have been able to realise that administrative conservatism is already obsolete. The crisis of the public services has gone too deeply to the root of the body politic to be solved by an uncompromising denial. The more timid spirits have, as is natural, suggested the wisdom of compromise. And, in the sense that reforms will do much to remove the bitterness that has been manifested on both sides during the past ten years, reform has a merit that is undeniable. But the claims, both of one side and the other, are too divergent to admit of compromise. There is no half-way house effectively to be occupied between the present administrative control and the full independence demanded by the civil service. The criticisms, indeed, are important; for they show, alike from the standpoints of legal and political philosophy, the defences of modern authoritarianism. And while they are in essence distinct, they both have the merit of an obvious simplicity. They thus serve to throw into a clearer light the significance of the competing claims.

The juristic attack upon administrative syndicalism originates in the attempt to find a legal basis for the claims of the civil service. There are some who have not hesitated to assert that the movement is in no sense opposed to the existing law. On the whole, the lawyers have united to reject that assertion. While they are unanimous in their agreement that the law of 1901 provides a clear path of association which the civil servant may take, they are almost equally unanimous that the law of 1884 applies to a type of professional association with which the civil service can have no connection. Their fundamental criticism is based on an interpretation of the nature of the state on the one hand, and the relation to it of the civil servant on the other. They insist that the régime of administration can at no single point, except one, be approximated to the modern system of industrial organisation. It of course logically follows that the position of the civil servant is in no sense similar to that of the worker. The attempt is made to show that once we are in the domain of state-activity we are in the presence of special facts to which the ordinary formulae of private law are inapplicable. From jurisprudence, therefore, administrative syndicalism has nothing to expect.

It seems legally unquestionable that so far as the relation of the laws of 1884 and 1901 really affects the fundamental issue, the legal critics are absolutely in the right. There is not a shred of evidence that it was ever intended to apply the law of 1884 to members of the civil service; rather, on the contrary, does it seem to have been the express intention of the legislature to exclude them from it.[118] The law of 1884 was simply an effort to equalise the bargaining power of labour to that of capital; and those who passed it no more dreamed of its application to the problems of the state than did Mr. Justice Holmes when he enunciated a similar proposition.[119] Indeed, the syndicalists themselves have admitted, on occasion, that the civil service has a privileged position.[120] Not, indeed, that the argument which denies that the state can be equated with the private employer has been very vigorously supported. For, if it is true that the minister is limited by his dependence upon the legislature, that is more and more coming to be the case with the private employer, especially in those industries where the public interest is most directly concerned;[121] and the result

[118] Cf. Mermeix, "Le Syndicalisme contre le Socialisme," p. 83.

[119] *Coppage v. Kansas*, 236 U. S. I, 26.

[120] Cf. Beaubois, *Mouvement Socialiste*, 1905, p. 430, and Montbruneaud in *ibid.*, p. 295.

[121] The action of Congress in the passage of the Adamson Law is, of course, a very striking example of this. On the theoretic issues involved cf. for Anglo-Saxon countries, the remarkable paper of Mr. E. A. Adler in 28 and 29, *Harv. L. Rev.*

of a ministerial regulation in regard to the civil service, is not very different, whatever its nature, from the collective agreement that is coming to be characteristic of modern business. Nor does M. Briand's insistence that the state does not possess the elasticity of initiative by which private industry is distinguished in any way destroy the validity of the comparison.[122]

Not, indeed, that the analogy is in any sense fundamental to this issue. The main fact, after all, is that the Penal Code still makes it a criminal offence for civil servants to plan a strike;[123] and this has been more than once ratified by the courts;[124] nor have they hesitated to declare illegal the formation of such trade-unions in the civil service as they have had occasion to judge.[125] Nor is parliamentary opinion less clear. The two efforts that have been made to give teachers a right to form unions have not even been discussed.[126] A similar proposal in regard to the medical profession made in 1894 was expressly negatived, at the urgent request of M. Loubet, then President of the Council, on the specific ground that doctors are continually performing services which bring them into relation with government. Where permission has been given, as in the case of the state-railways, and the state tobacco monopoly, it is simply because, in that aspect, the state has definitely undertaken the functions usually performed by a private employer.[127] M. Waldeck-Rousseau, the author of the law of 1884, has expressly declared that he did not have the civil service in view when he proposed it,[128] and M. Clémenceau, one of its leading advocates, has equally insisted that it had in view only those whose wages are subject to the variations of economic law.[129]

There remains the law of 1901; and, despite the criticisms

[122] *Journal Officiel*, May 14, 1907.

[123] Code Pénale. art, 126.

[124] Duguit, "Traité de Droit Constitutionel," I, 519 f.

[125] Cf. *Gazette des Tribunaux*, July 9, 1903, *Revue des Grands Procés Contemporains*, 1909, no. II, contains a full report of the leading case.

[126] *Journal Officiel*, March 24, 1886, *Ibid*, 1890, p. 1533.

[127] Cf. M. Ramel in *Journal Officiel*, May 23, 1894.

[128] Cf. *Mouvement Socialiste*, March, 1905, p. 320.

[129] Cf. his reply to the teachers' manifesto cited above.

of M. Berthelémy,[130] it seems clear that it is sufficiently broad
to cover the associations formed within the civil service.[131]
The lawyers, moreover, have been eager to point out that there
is little or no juridical difference between the two systems of
coalition; for the one serious benefit the trade-union seems to
possess, the power to receive legacies and gifts, is hardly very
likely to be exercised by the civil servants;[132] and M. Saint-
Leon has shown that even this difficulty can be avoided.[133]
Yet the invalidity of the legal argument rests here precisely
on the fact that it remains merely legal. For the real question
involved is not legal at all, but psychological, and the main
advantage that the advocates of administrative syndicalism
seem to expect would be purely moral in character;[134] for, as
the great strike of 1909 made apparent, a mere matter of words
will not prevent the use of weapons deemed, for any reason,
desirable. For the real purpose of this insistence on the law
of 1884 is the advantage it would give of contact with the
working-class. It is one more proof of the fact that the movement has become far wider than a simple protest against particular abuses of a definite authority and has broadened into
an attempt to dethrone a whole system from its controlling
eminence. That is why the choice of methods will have more
than verbal results; for to admit that the civil servant can form
a trade-union is to give him increased opportunity of empha-
sising the relation of his demands to those of the workers.

The lawyers have not, of course, failed to perceive the burden of this manoeuvre, and it is in this aspect that they have
erected their ablest means of opposition to administrative syndicalism. For, juristically at any rate, the real problem involved is that of the legal status of the civil servant. If his
relation to the state is one of contract, it is clear that the
problem admits of an obvious solution; for once we are dealing

[130] *Revue de Paris*, Feb. 15, 1906, p. 883.

[131] Cf. M. Hauriou's admirable note, *Sirey*, 1909, 3, 17.

[132] Cf. *Revue Générale de l'Administration*, 1906, I, 203.

[133] Cf. his interesting comparison in "Annales du Musée Social," 1906,
p. 61, and the paper of M. Perrinjaquet in *Annales de Faculté droit
d'Aix* 1910, p. 133.

[134] Cf. Bougle, "Syndicalism et Démocratie," p. 27 f.

with contract it is legitimate to apply the ordinary rules of private law. If it is, on the contrary, a matter of public law, if it bears upon the nature of the sovereignty of the state, then it is clear that the position of the civil servant is specialised in character. Or, as has been urged, it may well be that the state is only in part a specialised institution in that aspect, it is only those who work within the area of its specialised activity who are subject to a special law.[135]

Naturally enough, the advocates of administrative syndicalism have insisted that the relation between the civil servant and the government is one of contract. His position would then be analogous to that of the worker in private industry and most of our difficulties would have been solved. But the question is, in fact, less simple. A civil servant cannot resign, or, at least, the government need not accept his resignation.[136] The civil servant who throws up his post to go on strike remains a civil servant despite himself until it should please the authorities to dismiss him.[137] If this is a contract, it is clearly contract of a kind unknown in private law. A contract ought to be the source of rights; and it is clear that against a government which can change his position, his salary, his work, or even dismiss him at will, he is not protected in any contractual fashion. It is, of course, true that he has what may be called a mediately contractual position; that is to say the ministerial regulations are binding upon the parties concerned. But since they can be altered at will, that is no great guarantee. The will of the state as expressed by its ministers clearly predominates in the situation.

Nor is the problem made easy by distinguishing between different kinds of civil servants, as M. Berthelémy has urged us to do. Any one can see that the position of a judge is suffi-

[135] This is the well-known distinction of M. Berthelémy. "Droit Administratif" (5 ed.), p. 78, between fonctionnaires d'autorité and fonctionnaires de gestion. Cf. Nezard, "Théorie juridique de la fonction publique," p. 461; and for criticism of it see Duguit, "Traité de Droit Constitutionnel," I, 429 f, where, as I think, its impossibility is effectively demonstrated.

[136] Rolland, "Revue de Droit Publique," 1907, p. 722. The analogous position of a member of the House of Commons is, of course, suggestive.

[137] Cf. the note of M. Hauriou in *Sirey*, 1909, 3, 145.

ciently different from that of a worker in a state match-factory
as to give each different rights and duties; but to draw a broad
line between the two becomes impossible immediately we take
certain critical instances. A prefect, for example, is a civil
servant who is charged by delegation with the exercise of certain sovereign powers; but he is also the recipient of orders which
it is his duty unquestioningly to fulfil. Mining engineers are,
for the most part, technical experts who have no connection
with the semi-political problems of the service; but where they
draw up notes on the contravention of government rules in the
mines, their position is immediately changed. Nor is it possible
to obtain any large measure of agreement as to where technical
service ends and the detention of a part of public power begins.
M. Hauriou does not doubt that teachers and postmen are
fonctionnaires d'autorité; M. Fontaine hotly denies it.[138] One
government official seems to imagine that any civil servant
who reports infractions of the law is a holder of some delegated
portion of sovereign authority.[139] The distinction is thus obviously too difficult to make its application as helpful as is suggested by its external simplicity.

If the legal assumptions are admitted, they constitute, then,
a complete refutation of the syndicalist thesis. They imply
the satisfactory proof that the relation is not in any real sense
contractual. The lawyers, however, have been, perhaps, somewhat less happy in the theories by which they attempt to
replace the notion of contract. No one—at least in France[140]
—now accepts the principle of Rousseau that the citizen, having surrendered all his rights to the state, must undertake at
its behest whatever functions it should choose to ordain.[141]
M. Hauriou has suggested what is, in reality, a feudal notion of
this relationship. He regards the tenure of office as a kind of
fragment of the public domain, and he suggests that the true

[138] *Sirey*, 1907, 3, 49.

[139] Cf. the report of M. Malepeyre, D.P., 1905, I, 259 "(L'Affaire
Belloche)."

[140] But it is accepted by many very reputable German authorities, cf.
Perthes, "Die Staatsdienst in Preussen," p. 55, and the authorities there
cited.

[141] "Contrat Social," Bk. II, Ch. IV.

analogy is that of the feudal lord, investing his vassal with a fief.[142] That public office was, in medieval times, essentially a property-right is a fact which admits of little denial;[143] but it does not fit the facts of the modern situation. The hereditary butler was, after all, a household servant of the crown, and the concept of property is, in that aspect, intelligible enough. But the modern civil servant owes service to the head of the state in his official" and not his personal" capacity. The feudal lord gave to his tenant a portion of sovereignty; and certainly where, as in modern French law, the inalienability of sovereignty has been, since the Revolution, little less than a religious dogma, such indivisibility cannot be equated with a property-concept.[144] Nor is M. Larnaude's theory that the situation is entirely specialised and can be explained, like the bond created by naturalisation, by a presumption of *lex specialis*.[145] For lex implies statute, and the idea of a statute is the merest fiction. Nor is the analogy of naturalisation very happy; for if ever there was a legal relation in which contract was implied, it is surely the relation created by the adoption of citizenship. To explain the problem by insisting that it is exceptional is, in reality to urge that it cannot be explained at all. Such a mystery might well account for the advent of administrative syndicalism, but it would hardly meet its problems.

M. Duguit explains the situation in a fashion which, while analogous, at the same time attempts to meet the difficulties involved in the hypothesis of exceptionality.[146] In his view, the whole field of administration is settled by statute or by general ministerial regulations which are akin by nature to

[142] *Sirey*, 1899, 3, 6.

[143] My friend Prof. McIlwain will shortly publish a paper in which this fact is demonstrated for the whole of medieval English history. He has already hinted at it in his paper on judicial tenure in the *American Pol. Sci. Rev.* for May, 1913.

[144] Cf. Duguit, "L'Etat, les Gouvernants et les Agents," p. 392, for a very complete criticism.

[145] *Revue Pénitentiaire*, 1906, p. 830.

[146] Duguit, "L'Etat, les Gouvernants et les Agents," p. 4, 13 ff. Cf. "Berthelémy, Revue de Droit Public," 1904, p. 20 f, and Jèze, *ibid.*, p. 517, esp. the latter for a very clear exposition of this attitude.

statute. We have, in fact, a purely objective law which settles the whole relationship with regard to the general end that administration is to serve. Nomination is a power of bringing some citizen within the purview of this law in order that he may fulfil its purposes. The act of nomination derives its whole force therefrom; and the acceptance of nomination simply completes the process. Yet it must surely be admitted that the theory is far less satisfactory than appears on the surface. If the nominee may reject the preferred position it is surely therein implied that whatever takes place has about it a contractual nature. The nominee is agreeing to submit himself to the regulations of the service in return for the enjoyment of a position he desires. He may not have named the conditions of his employment. The contract, that is to say, may be unilateral in character. But it still remains a contract; and it is difficult to see how this element can, in the circumstances be explained away.

For the simple fact is that all these legal theories are, from the standpoint of administrative syndicalism, vitiated by one grave defect. They are all built exactly upon that conception of the state against which the fonctionnaire has made his vehement protest. They do not take account of the psychological fact that if the situation of the civil servant has a certain specialised character, it is yet a character from which the conception of a contract can hardly be excluded. The state may say that it makes no contract; but if it fails to provide what its servants deem reasonable conditions of labour they will not work for it. It may theoretically demonstrate that its will dominates the situation, but the fact will still remain that the will of its servants is not less relevant. For while they identify themselves in a special sense with the state, they do not so finally merge their personalities with its own as to be incapable of active opposition to it. The state may make its laws for their governance; but if it finds that they refuse obedience to its laws they will prove of no avail. It may proclaim its sovereignty; but a sovereignty that cannot win the assent of those who are to be the subjects of its control is not impressive.

And the change in the status of the civil servant is surely indicative of an important innovation. More and more the status is coming to be settled as the result of discussion and bargaining in which the civil servant takes his full share. The French Railways are governed by an agreement which is the result of joint deliberation between the political and administrative personnel.[147] That is the beginning of an evolution of which the end may well be the erection of self-government within each department. It is perfectly true that the status so determined must receive the official sanction either of the minister or of Parliament. It draws its sustenance from an enabling statute. But that enabling statute is itself based upon a prior agreement. It does not create so much as registrate. A sovereignty that merely accepts what has been agreed upon outside of itself is, it may be suggested, a sovereignty that has been deprived of its sting.[148]

The truth is that the character which the lawyers attempted to attach to the state dates from a time anterior to the advent of democracy. It is impotent in the face of administrative coalescence. It might work when the right of association had not yet so far advanced as to give the civil servant the opportunity to organise his corporate interests. But immediately he had discovered what had been released by the law of 1901, the concept of a sovereign state which determined his situation without reference to his wishes and without the recognition that he had rights it could not infringe became impossible. It was exacting from him the surrender of exactly that which he had combined in order to attain. The sanction of law is not its existence but its ability to secure assent.[149] The civil servant refuses to admit the vast authority which is claimed by the state simply because he has suffered too greatly from the effects of its exercise. He finds himself in a position to bargain with the government. Whether the result of their joint deliberation affects him only, or involves also the rest of the com-

[147] Cf. Duguit, "Les Transformations du Droit Public," p. 114. The system of self-government instituted in 1896 for the French universities is full of fascinating suggestion in this regard. Cf. Hauriou, "Principes de Droit Public" (ed. of 1916), p. 745 f.

[148] The similar relation of Congress to the railway situation of 1916 is of interest.

[149] Cf. my "Problem of Sovereignty," p. 12 f.

munity, the relation that is slowly being established is, clearly enough, no longer unilateral. Certain states of fact are arrived at by agreement. They are deferred in regulations. If in theory the state retains the power to alter those regulations in practice that power is as valuable as the sovereignty of the English king. It is a tribute to a great tradition rather than an admission of its present operation.

And that, after all, is only to say that the legal theory which rejects the notion of contract is, by that definition, an inadequate theory. Law cannot persistently neglect the psychology of those it endeavours to control. So long as the fonctionnaire refuses to be at the mercy of the government, it is useless for jurisprudence to evolve a theory which implies his subjection. Nor does it matter in what kind of subtleties that subjection is concealed. We may talk of an objective law that is removed from the clash of personalities and securely grounded in the facts themselves.[150] But that, in the end, is to do no more than transfer the discussion to the nature of the objective law. Anyone, for instance, who reads the history of the postal strike of 1909 will not doubt that M. Simyan's conception of the objective law by which the service should be governed would differ very markedly from that of M. Pouget. Whether we found our demands on the desire or the duty that lies before us, we cannot escape the problem of rights. The civil servant very clearly feels that he can make certain demands which the state ought not to refuse. In the eighteenth century they were a deductive claim; today they are an induction from the experience of a bitter illusion. But the fact still remains that they are rights and, as such, they evade the categories in which authority would enshrine them. No legal argument against the claims of administrative syndicalism can therefore be valid that is based upon the theory of the state as it presents itself in the orthodox currency of today. For, in the first place, the syndicalist would deny its validity, and, in the second, it is clearly a theory that is passing away. The task that confronts the jurist is still the same. He has still to reconcile administrative autonomy with a state of which the authority is made subject to the strictest limitations. He has to show how law

[150] Cf. my note on M. Duguit in the *Harvard Law Review* for Nov., 1917.

can maintain responsibility while it admits a reasonable independence. But it is with new weapons that he must come to his task.

VI. THE ATTACK OF THE POLITICIANS

It was hardly to be expected that so novel a phenomenon as administrative syndicalism could meet with approval from the politicians. It was, in the first place, too alien from their traditional theories of politics to be acceptable. The very grievances of which it made complaint were the outcome of the parliamentary system. Their approval of it would have involved self-condemnation; it would have been the tacit admission that the criticisms passed upon the system of which they are at once the founders and protectors, were firmly rooted in reality. Yet a curious distinction is to be noted in the political attitude. In principle, it has proved adamant against the introduction of novelty. When the resources of argument were exhausted, resort was had to the copious reservoir of rhetoric; and there have been few more brilliant debates in the chamber than those in which MM. Clémenceau and Briand have vindicated the sovereign state from the pitiful assault of its anarchist detractors. Yet alongside this immovable determination in theory, there has gone a consistent pliability in practice. The statesmen of France have never dealt with fonctionnarisme; but they have always been careful to reckon with it. They have been consistently gentle at election-times; and their earnest eagerness to find a basis for compromise with principles they have steadfastly declared impossible has not been without its pathos. It is a noteworthy distinction; for it is the expression of a genuine effort on the part of the state to find ways and means of admitting in practice the advent of a fundamental transformation in its nature even while the terminology of the past is preserved. How far it is likely to prove a successful effort is dubious matter for the most dangerous kind of prophecy. The war intervened exactly at the point where it was beginning to be possible to catch the first clear signs of the new evolution; and the clouds have not yet sufficiently drifted to make again visible the rays of the political sun.

Yet the theory upon which this political antagonism has been founded is, throughout its history, unmistakably clear. The nation, in their view, enjoys a sovereignty which is complete and in no degree subject to limitation. Its personality is at every point superior to that of its constituent members. The nation, in its political expression, is the state; and thus, obviously enough, upon the institutional organs of the state, the majesty of the national sovereignty descends by delegation. To threaten the state, is thus to strike at the heart of the national existence. And this is even more truly the case with the civil servant whose very powers are derived from his position as a state-instrument. He negatives the whole purpose of his existence once he rebels against that from which he derive all that makes him different from the ordinary citizen. Administrative syndicalism thus becomes a particularly reprehensible variation upon an anarchic theme. To make concessions to it is to derogate from the national power. A refusal to bargain with it thus becomes the preservation of all that makes the nation a self-governing instrument. Once concede internal autonomy and the national unity is at a stroke destroyed.

It is a simple theory, upon which every conceivable variation has been made. It seems to have been born in 1887 with M. Spuller who, in a famous circular,[151] insisted that it was inconceivable that a group of public officials could enjoy a corporate personality outside their membership of the state. Twenty years later the argument is in nowise different. "Officials," said M. Rouvier,[152] then Prime Minister, "who exercise any portion of sovereign power, are members only of one corporation—the state; and the state is the nation itself." M. Briand drew the obvious inference from that attitude. "What," he asked,[153] "is the democratic state? . . . Is it the government? . . . That cannot be because government is only an agent which executes orders. . . . The civil service has against it the national representatives, that is to say the nation itself." M. Clémenceau has pointed what he regards

[151] Cf. Cahen, "Les Fonctionnaires," p. 59., M. Spuller was then Minister of Public Instruction.

[152] *Journal Officiel*, May 23, 1905.

[153] *Journal Officiel*, May 12, 1907.

as the moral of the argument. "Government," he said,[154] "is under the control of the chamber; the chamber is controlled by universal suffrage; but neither government nor the chamber is under the control of the civil service." The great postal strike of 1909 did not suggest any new synthesis to M. Barthou, the minister most concerned. "The postmen," he told the chamber,[155] "are in revolt against you, gentlemen, against the entire nation, . . . what we have to determine is whether a government which represents the sovereign nation can abandon the care of general interests before a rebellious civil service." M. Ribot has insisted that while the ordinary citizen can plan the transformation of the state, the duty of the public official is at all costs to defend its present organisation.[156] M. Deschanel seems to regard the civil servant as the delegate of the nation for the performance of certain functions; clearly, therefore, anything that does not involve their performance is a transgression of his powers.[157] And M. Poincaré has again and again uttered the warning that a new power, irresponsible in its nature, confronts the sovereign nation. He seems to consider its advent as nothing less than an attack on the life of the French republic.[158]

All this, of course, is a purely theoretical argument. It simply insists that the authority of the state is final without at any point examining the basis upon which that insistence is founded. It does not, therefore, meet the argument of administrative syndicalism; what it rather does is to lay down certain counter-assumptions of which the truth is still debateable. It does not seem to have realised that the fonctionnariste movement is nothing if not a challenge to these conceptions; and it is not, to say the least, particularly helpful to have the whole discussion shelved in this facile manner. Far more important is the argument derived from the needs of practical administration. Here, at least, the politicians have had a real case to urge and they have put it with no small skill.

[154] *Ibid.*, March 13, 1908.
[155] *Ibid.*, March 19, 1909.
[156] *Ibid.*, May 14, 1907.
[157] *Ibid.*, May 12, 1907.
[158] Speech of April 27, 1907.

This, they point out, is pre-eminently a period in which the functions of the state are undergoing continuous extension. More and more it is coming, if not to take actual charge, at least to regulate, the conduct of great departments of public life.   In that aspect, the main problem by which it is confronted is to ensure to its constituents the regular and continuous operation of the services under its control.   Whether it purveys railway or postal facilities, whether it sells matches or procures an adequate police, obviously the one thing the public has a right to demand is their efficient operation.   For where these services are managed as public utilities by companies or individuals working for gain a special system of law is instituted of which the cardinal point is the guarantee of continuity.

It is at least partly in the light of this attitude that the political opposition must be interpreted.   "I am here to affirm," said M. Sarrien,[159] "that no government, even if it were formed of the very persons who now beg us to permit freedom of association to teachers, to postal officials, and other civil servants, could possibly consent without committing suicide, without imperilling the very existence not merely of the Republic, but any regular and normal political régime."   M. Clémenceau has again and again insisted that the first task of a minister is to compel the civil servant to accomplish his duty to the state.[160]   M. Briand has affirmed that the operation of government does not permit the constitution of a privileged nation within the ranks of the nation itself.[161]   Their attitude was the more interesting since both they, and some of their colleagues had, before taking office, urgently upheld the right of the fonctionnaire to enjoy the benefit of the law of 1884.[162] But it is to be assumed that the experience of office has dissipated these idle dreams.

The real difficulty in the analysis of this argument is to know exactly where a beginning of criticism should be made.   It im-

[159] *Journal Officiel*, Nov. 8, 1905.

[160] *Ibid.*, March 14, 1906.

[161] *Ibid.*, July 12, 1906.

[162] Cf. the speech of M. Willm, in *Ibid.*, May 11, 1909, and of M. Sembat, May 14, 1909.

plies that there is a golden rule of administration which succes-
sive governments have laboured earnestly to follow; and the
cardinal principle in that rule would seem to be the refusal of any
minister to permit for one moment the organisation of the civil
service within his department. Yet, in fact, no such policy has
ever been followed. M. Benöist has justifiably complained of
the alternation of strength and weakness in the governmental
attitude.[163] It is a matter of common notoriety that the defiant
challenge to administrative syndicalism undergoes a sensible
diminution at election time. What is legitimate in the Ministry
of Public Works is fraught with grave danger in the Ministry of
Public Instruction.[164] The ministers dismiss civil servants in
order to emphasise their authority, but, sooner or later, they
always take the vast majority back. And it is difficult to discover whether this high degree of control is necessary to maintain the service as it now is; or, on the other hand, whether it is
the basis of a future improvement. If the first hypothesis be
the correct one, it is difficult to reconcile with expert opinion
that the condition of the civil service is simply lamentable.[165]
If the second interpretation be correct, it is still more difficult
to see why the government should be preparing to abandon
that control in order to institute a general status which shall
put the majority of these problems beyond the reach of the
ministerial whim;[166] and it is not less hard to know why the
government is prepared to admit the jurisprudence of the Council of State which is more and more tending to give the civil servant and his associations protection against arbitrary treatment.[167]

But the greatest irony remains. Those who thus profess
themselves so anxious for the quality of the civil service are the
persons most responsible for its corruption. Even if it be true
that their responsibility is mainly weakness in the face of parlia-

[163] *Ibid.*, March 26, 1909.

[164] Cf. Paul-Boncour, "Syndicats de Fonctionnaires," p. 20 f.

[165] Cf. Cahen, "Les Fonctionnaires," Ch. IV.

[166] The government has several times introduced proposals towards this
end and the whole problem, seemingly with ministerial approval, has been
discussed often in the Chamber.

[167] Cf. Cahen, p. 317 f.

mentary pressure, the fact still remains that it was in their power to remedy these grievances and that they have deliberately abstained from so doing. No one denies that the business of govment must be carried on; but it is at least open to the gravest doubt whether the different ministers have ever tried so to organise the civil service as to assure the absence of the grievances which might, above all things, interrupt it. It is not a solution to take refuge in the necessity of a rigid authoritarianism. The position of the civil servant in the modern state may be a specialised one; but he does not surrender his human impulses in becoming a civil servant. That the grievances of which he complained were real the government tacitly admitted on the different occasions when it embarked upon the task of reform; but even when the difficulty of its accomplishment has been admitted, no impartial observer can doubt that there has never been any genuine intention to give effect to the reforms proposed. For the real doubt must remain whether, in the present situation of French parliamentarism, the reforms so postulated can in fact be achieved. Any system in which the executive is at the mercy of the legislature is, in the nature of things, bound to search for means whereby it can control its master. That is the secret of the corruption of English politics in the eighteenth century. Sir Robert Walpole only did more crudely what the average French minister is compelled to attempt in a more delicate fashion if his government is to remain in office. So long as no single party dominates the chamber it is necessary to buy the support of groups numerous enough to constitute a majority; and patronage is the obvious means to that end. So that, in practice, the real implication of the vast authority the minister tends to demand as essential, has, as its object, not the efficient operation of the public departments, but the retention of a convenient means to power. In that light, the anxiety for the regular conduct of public business appears a less noble aspiration. A minister naturally dislikes the dislocation that follows upon the assertion of grievances simply because its consequences in the Chamber are, as a rule, inconvenient. He can be certain at least of an interpellation; and of a French interpellation no one dare prophesy the outcome. But it is in the highest degree difficult to see that an analysis, not of governmental pretensions, but of the steps actually taken by government towards the amelioration of the actual state of affairs, could lead to the conclusion that control has as its purpose the end that rhetoric implies.

Nor, after all, is it possible to feel that the psychology of administrative control is so simple as governmental theory would make it. It is, of course, undeniable that the continuous functioning of the civil service is fundamental to the modern state. It is as obvious as can be that inefficiency in a government department, hardly less than actual dislocation of service itself, has evil consequences that reverberate throughout the body politic. Yet the doubt must remain whether the way in which the civil service in France is organised can secure the results that modern government must achieve. No one who reads the literature of the French fonctionnaires can doubt that the authority of the minister is too overshadowing. The motives it leaves to the official are simply not adequate. The reports that either no one ever sees, or that lie buried amid the official archives, do not call forth the best qualities of which the official is really capable. He does not come into contact with the chamber, or, if he does, it is only to persuade some friendly deputy to use his influence for his promotion. The whole effort is towards making thought a routine instead of an invention. There is too little certainty that effort will obtain its reward. There is too little opportunity for the exercise of those creative faculties which responsibility alone will call into play. There is too little chance that the official will be able, if not to decide, at any rate to deliberate, those great public questions which, from their very nature, must serve to quicken the imagination. Too much energy is occupied in the writing of minutes upon the minutes of other people, and too little upon the defence, in the verbal interchange of thought, of the ideas which those minutes contain. If the civil servant knew that to make himself an authority upon some public question was bound to result in bringing him into direct relationship with those who frame the answer to it, the general picture of the civil service would not be that which the curious can find in the novels of Balzac and de Maupassant. He can do none of these things simply because they in reality make him essentially an expert who must, because of his expertness, be given the right to at least a measure of independence. That independence, from the nature of his position, will tend to grow until it absorbs the group to which he belongs. But where that is once achieved, not only is the main demand of administrative syndicalism conceded, but at the same time, the future of parliamentary government in France becomes even more problematical than it is at the present time.

And this, in fact, is the real crux of the governmental attitude. Safety and permanence are not the distinguishing features of French ministries; but at any rate the minister knows the technique at present in vogue. To change it is virtually to set him out on an uncharted sea. He will have to discover new methods of manipulation in the Chamber. His relations to his department will undergo a total reconstruction. He will retain the direction of its activities. He will still be able to say what he wants, to determine the large outlines of policy. But he will suggest administration rather than actually operate it. It is a break with tradition so large that everyone can understand why he should feel suspicious of the readjustment. And he is moved by another consideration. At present he is responsible for his department. For whatever the humblest of his officials may do, he, and he only, must answer to the chamber. That, in his view, is not the least reason why he has the right to autocratic control. For if the policy of the department may result in his downfall, clearly he has the right to demand that, in, principle and in detail, it shall be his own policy. To make the civil service independent of him is to make him suffer for faults that will not be, even in theory, his own.

Certainly, to an Englishman who has been brought up to see the ample cloak of ministerial charity cast around the erring official on every occasion, there is much plausibility in such an attitude. But, equally certainly, it is a meritricious plausibility simply because it ignores the essential factors involved. There are obviously two kinds of fault of which the civil servant may be guilty. His fault may be due to the inherent nature of the work he is called upon to execute; or it may, on the other hand, be due simply to some blunder of his own. In the first case, it is clear that the minister is responsible. If a minister should order the police to tear down a Roman Catholic Church, the resultant noting is surely to be ascribed to the stupidity of the minister.

But it is not less clear that no one could hold the minister responsible for a personal blunder of an official. If, for instance, a teacher in a school should deliberately go out of his way to break the regulations which deal with educational neutrality upon religious questions, that would in no way affect the minister's position. It would, perhaps,[168] be his business to see that discussion of the teacher's act was made by the proper authorities concerned. But there his functions would end. Personal fault, that is to say, would involve on the part of a minister nothing more than the duty of seeing that the regular disciplinary procedure was at every point observed. Faults that are derived directly from a policy which the minister has conceived must be laid no less directly at his door. Now it is true that, again and again, difficulties will arise in interpretation, no classification can pretend even to be perfect. But, in such a division of responsibility as this, it is surely evident that an adequate safeguard exists for protecting ministerial interests. It is not difficult to imagine that the average statesman would even feel relieved if he did not bear the burden of every departmental care. Undeniably, the result of such a change upon parliamentary life would be far-reaching. Not less clearly, if ministerial responsibility is divided, means must be created for the adequate protection of the public against the faults of the official. That, however, is in no sense an impossible task.

In such an interpretation the political answer to administrative syndicalism is at no point an answer at all. What, undoubtedly, it has effectively done is to show the determination with which the upholders of the present system will maintain their defences. But there is an implication in the argument that is put forward that cannot be too strongly denied. "The state," writes M. Fernand Faure,[169] "cannot, ... in the measure of its functions, be too strong." It must act, that is to say, at every instant as a sovereign authority whose demands can brook no question. "The state alone," says M. Larnaude[170] "can re-

[168] "Perhaps," because it is possible to envisage an organisation of the civil service in which even this intervention is unnecessary.

[169] Cf. his long attack in the *Revue Politique et Parlementaire*, March, 1906.

[170] *Revue Penitentiare*, 1906.

main master of the event," and M. Berthelémy seems[171] to regard the whole movement as nothing more than an unworthy effort, clearly deserving only of suppression, to exploit the state for private purposes. But, surely, in criticism such as this it is not really the state that is in question. What the civil servant attacks is the group of men who, at the moment, possess the fused power the state possesses. It is a revolt against government of which they are complaining. The transition from state to government, is, of course, a fatally easy one; but it is a transition of which each step demands the closest investigation. No one would object to a strong state if guarantees could be had that its strength would be used for the fulfilment of its theoretic purposes. The real problem involved is the suspicion of those who watch the actual operation of its instruments that they have been, in fact, diverted from the ends they were intended to serve. To admit the sovereignty of the state, in the sense in which statesmen understand that concept, is simply to give added power to the government. It is, that is to say, to mistake the private will of a constantly changing group whose interests are at no point identical with those of the nation, for the interests of the state as a whole. A strong state does not mean a state in which no one resists the declared will of government; or, if it does, we need new political terms. For, in that event, change would never be justified except insofar as it met with the approval of those who held the reins of power; and it is historically obvious that any general acceptance of such an attitude is entirely subversive of progress.

A state, after all, is no mysterious entity. It is only a territorial society into which, from a variety of historical causes, a distinction between rulers and subjects has been introduced.[172] The only justification for a claim by government of its obedience is the clear proof that it satisfies the material and moral claims of those over whom it exercises control. We

[171] *Revue de Paris*, Feb. 15, 1906.

[172] I owe this conception to M. Duguit, but I think that he has never emphasised sufficiently the territorial character of the state as opposed to other societies. I have tried to suggest the implications of this distinction in the first chapter of this book. It is impliedly present in the first chapter of my "Problem of Sovereignty."

cannot wander on blindly with self-shut eyes, merely because order is convenient and rebellion attended by the gravest dangers. The whole case for administrative syndicalism goes most clearly to show that government has not been able to give proofs of that satisfaction. So widespread a movement must have had causes more profound than the antagonism of its opponents would suggest. It is, above all, a problem in organisation. What it suggests is inherent error in the mechanism of the modern state. It suggests a redistribution of power. It indicates a conviction that certain of the demands now made by government are in fact unnecessary to the fulfilment of its purposes, cannot, further, be made if the purposes of government are to be fulfilled. It is in the highest degree difficult to understand what exactly is gained by the empty insistence that the state must be strong without giving the valid demonstration of the purpose for which that strength is to be used. Government is only a convention which men, on the whole, accept because of a general conviction that its effort is for good. Where the machine breaks down, where the purpose of those who drive it becomes to an important class sinister, it is humanly inevitable that an effort towards change should be made.

To those who hold the reins of power it was perhaps inevitable that such an effort should be regarded as the coronation of anarchy. To oppose the government is, for them, to destroy the state. But it is, in fact, anarchy only in the sense in which the replacement of the nobility as the governing power at the Revolution was anarchy. The seat of authority therein passed to the middle classes. But government remained at once a narrow and irresponsible power. It has been attacked at two points since that time. Economically, the workers show increasing sign of dissatisfaction with the fulfilment of its purposes; administratively, the civil service rejects the notion of its authority. The change that is implied in this impatience is not less profound than that of a century and a half ago. Whether the change that accompanies every great transformation in the seat of authority can be accomplished without violence is a problem to which the answer has still to be discovered. Certainly· there is no need to becloud the question by representing revolution as a rare exception in historical pro-

cedure. Aristotle realised that well enough when he devoted
a book of the "Politics" to its discussion. If we endeavour to
stand outside the historic process it is not difficult to see that
this, like so many of his general maxims, remains not the less
true two thousand three hundred years after his time.[173]

VII. THE MOVEMENT TOWARDS REFORM

OBVIOUSLY enough, a movement so widespread as this must
have swept some effort at reform into the eddies of its current,
and both in politics and in jurisprudence it is possible to find
signs of a changing temper towards the civil service. A serious
attempt was in process, at least before the outbreak of war, of
which the general purport was to limit the arbitrary character
of ministerial discretion. That, after all, is the fundamental
point; for ministerial discretion was essentially an inheritance
of the *ancien régime* which stamped the whole system with its
peculiar and vicious character. It was an assertion that the
minister, as an agent of the state, partook of its sovereign
nature; assault upon his powers was therefore *a priori* fruitless.

That attitude is already dying. The courts have shown
signs of an important eagerness to insist on regarding as *ultra
vires* any infraction of the departmental regulations. The
minister might make his own rules, but, until he changed them
he was at every point bound by the clear purpose they had in
view. The government itself was proposing perhaps, indeed,
with a heart less determined than the situation made desirable,
to bring the position of the civil servant within the scope of
statute within the civil service itself. The faint and fitful development of a new autonomy has not as yet been sufficiently
clear to be suggestive. It was, it is true, an auto-limitation.
It did not involve derogation from the sovereign power of the
state. No one was bound by the action that has been taken.

---

[173] "Politics," Bk. V. 1301 a. "All these forms of government have a kind
of justice, but tried by an absolute standard, they are faulty and therefore
both parties, whenever their share in the government, does not accord with
their preconceived ideas, stir up revolution." The plea of administrative
syndicalism would seem to be that the absolute standard of justice cannot
even be approached without a radical change in the distribution of the
share in government.

The effort that has been made is in every event indicative of the advent of a new epoch rather than the actual inauguration of it. But auto-limitation has an historical habit of giving way to an objective law. Administrative admission becomes administrative practice; sooner or later the convention becomes strong enough to resist the force of pressure. Those who have witnessed the substitution of rule for discretion will not easily go back to the chaos of an earlier time.

Parliament has discussed proposals which have endeavoured to give a definite status to the fonctionnaire. None, as yet, has reached the statute-book; but the mere fact of their proposal, and the wealth of superlative discussion they have evoked, are in themselves indicative of much. The two projects derived from government sources had not, indeed, high value. They were not based on adequate consultation with the fonctionnaires themselves; and the attempt to make the Council of State an advisory, but not a compulsive body, was a clearly hopeless one.[174] The denial of the right of federation meant the retention of the hierarchical system and of departmental separatism.[175] Defects like these struck at the root of any possible concord; and, in fact, they only produced the famous *Open Letter* to M. Clémenceau which brought clearly into the light the inability of his ministry to appreciate the real facts at issue. The government proposals aggravated a schism rather than healed it. They made clear the certainty that sooner or later the movement must be dealt with; but they made it also not less evident that it was already too strong to be deceived.

Far more serious in character, because far more comprehensive, have been the efforts of the chamber itself. The commission of which M. Jeanneney was the reporter has, at any rate, understood the significance of the movement. If its report was, on the whole, a somewhat unsatisfactory compromise,[176] that was less from the spirit it displayed than from the fact that between the aim of the government and the ideal of the fonctionnaire there is no possible compromise. No solution can be satisfactory which does not take account of the unity

---

[174] Cf. Leroy, "Syndicats et Services Publics," p. 267.

[175] Cf. M. Leroy's acute comment, *Ibid*, p. 269.

[176] It has been published separately by Hachette.

of the civil service; and from the fact of that unity alone, any attempt to insist on departmental separatism is doomed to failure.[177] No prohibition of the strike can be effective which does not envisage the cause of recourse to such a weapon. It is true enough, as M. Jeanneney reminds us,[178] that the object of the civil servant is to ensure the operation of the service with which he is charged; but equally fundamental is the condition under which he is to perform his duty. The Commission seems to have grasped this fact; and it was yet prevented from dealing firmly with the obvious implications of its admission by the fear of government opposition. The chamber, in any case, has not been able to take up the project, and later discussion, while it has clarified the problem, has not advanced the answer to it.

But it has served to make two things clear. It is obvious, in the first place, that the problem of the civil service is only part of the far wider problem of governmental reform. In every aspect, the instruments of the state are in need of reconstruction. Some of its mechanisms are expensive and outworn. Others demand autonomy or decentralisation for their adequate operation. The sovereign state, as M. Duguit has repeatedly emphasised, is becoming a great public service corporation; and its organs demand readjustment to the new purposes it is to serve. It is, moreover, clear, that, in such a perspective, the first demand to be made of government by its subjects will be the continuous and undisturbed performance of its functions. That, it can hardly be doubted, involves something in the nature of a status for those who are employed by government. They may see the element of contract in their situation; but the element of duty will be not less sharply defined.[179]

The problem, in such an aspect, becomes very largely a psychological one. It is the problem of translating a psychological satisfaction into definite legal terms. It will be useless to prohibit strikes by statute[180] so long as the mass of

[177] Rapport, p. 98.
[178] *Ibid*, p. 109.
[179] Cf. Duguit, "Tiansf. du Droit Public," p. 156 f.
[180] Or by injunction as, impliedly, in the Adamson decision.

the civil service feels itself sufficiently oppressed by its grievances to refuse obedience to the law.   The history of the last
few years has notably demonstrated the powerlessness of
statute in the face of great popular movements.[181]   That is
not because of any inherent or growing disrespect for law.[182]
It is simply that we are living in an age of change so vast that
administration can not keep pace with its demands.   Law follows popular sentiment rather than creates it; and the modern
disparity has been notably widened simply because our jurists
have been working with the instruments of an earlier time.
A theory of law which endeavours, in such a synthesis as this,
to frame its solution in the pragmatic terms of the conflicting
interests involved has alone the opportunity to make a convenient unity out of this multiplicity of principles.[183]   It will
start from the acceptance of what is, in theory at least, perhaps a fundamental novelty—the notion that the interests of
government are in no instance paramount.   It will not deceive
itself by the too-facile belief that the primary interest of law
is in the preservation of order.   There are times when the
business of law is not the maintenance of an old equilibrium
but the creation of a new one.   It is to that task that our
efforts must today be directed.

And what is here significant is the perception by the supreme
administrative tribunal of France of the implications of this
new orientation.   The time has already passed when administrative jurisdiction could be regarded as distinct from the ordinary judicial power, when it could be regarded as simply
executive justice by act of grace.   It is coming to be nothing
so much as an organ of protection for such non-governmental
interests as are affected by *ultra vires* acts.   It is coming to
insist on the responsibility of the state for its acts as a dogma
not less necessary to our own time than state-irresponsibility
could be regarded as essential by the nineteenth century.   It
is modifying, gradually, it is true, but also with a steady and

[181] Cf. my "Problem of Sovereignty," p. 27.

[182] As Professor Dicey seems to think, "Law of the Constitution" (8th
ed.), p. xxxvii.

[183] Cf. Pound, Address to the New Hampshire Bar Association, June 30,
1917, p. 14 f.

almost marvellous persistency, the relations of the state with its officials on the one hand and private citizens on the other. It is no longer possible for the state to defend its acts on the ground that they are clothed with the mystic power of sovereignty. Not only the form, but the contents also, of an act may be impugned. The state, in short, has become a private corporation which must act in accordance with its fundamental and general purpose on the one hand, and its special instructions for each immediate situation on the other. Its law, that is to say, is no longer the subjective command that issues from its sovereign will; it is an objective interpretation of necessity drawn from the study of the facts of each issue that may arise.[184]

This evolution is likely, within certain well-defined limits, completely to revise the time-honoured relation between the state and the fonctionnaire. It is not in any sense a final revision. So long as the power of regulating civil service conditions belongs to the minister as the head of his department it is a revision at each stage liable to reversal. The time, of course, will come when this auto-limitation will no longer be deemed adequate, and the minister will then, no less than his humblest official be subject to the rule of law. But, for temporary purposes, it is an advance; and it points the way to a time when the scope of sovereignty will be limited by a system less liable to interruption than the régime of whim and caprice. Since 1903, at any rate, it has been impossible to uphold an irregular nomination. So long as there are rules the Council of State will enforce them. It has been admitted that those who are technically qualified to fulfill certain functions have sufficient interest in appointment to them as to prevent men who are not qualified from nomination.[185] It was no more than a natural deduction from that advance to prevent

[184] On this general evolution cf. Duguit "Les Transformations du Droit Public," Chaps. V and VII, and for details, G. Teisser "La Responsabilité de la Puissance Publique." I have dealt with its implications in the first chapter of this book.

[185] Arrêt Lot et Molinier, II, Dec., 1903, cf. Duguit, "Traité de Droit Constitutionnel," I, 474.

irregular promotion and dismissal.[186] It was clearly wise to insist upon the observance of the rule that a civil servant must be informed of the grounds upon which any disciplinary measure is taken against him.[187] Before 1907, it was by individual action that these rights were guaranteed. Since that time a great step forward has been taken by the permission given to civil service associations to appear as parties in actions where they can prove that they are directly interested.[188] Nor is it without significance that one court at least should have been willing to receive the plea of a federation of teachers against an alleged libel of the Archbishop of Rheims;[189] and even where other courts have hesitated to admit such a plea the existence of corporate prejudice has been recognised.[190] English experience suggests that the further step is inevitable;[191] and it is hardly too much to say that these decisions mark an epoch in the history of administrative law.

Nor is the organisation of private citizens less important in its ultimate consequences. Alongside the growth of these producers' organisations we have an evolution of consumers' control. Its effort is directed towards almost every conceivable object of governmental activity. The subscribers to the national telephone system have organised a society which not only protects its members in their complaints against inadequate operation, but also insists that the government pay regard to the most modern scientific improvements. The Catholic church has welded into a formidable organisation the fathers of families who belong to that religion to insist upon the due observance of scholastic neutrality. The taxpayers have grouped themselves together with the object, among

[186]Arrêt Warnier, July 7, 1905, (promotion); Arrêt Fortin (Aug. 6, 1908) dismissal.

[187] Arrêt Vilar, Aug. 6, 1909.

[188] Arrêt of Dec. 11, 1908. "Association Professionnelle des Employés Civiles du ministère des colonies," *Sirey*, 1909, III, 17, with note of M. Haurion.

[189] Cf. Cahen, op. cit., p. 325.

[190] *Ibid.*, p. 326.

[191] Brown *v.* Thomson & Co. (1912) S. C. 359. Cf. my article in *Harvard Law Review* Vol. xxix p. 242f.

others, of insisting upon due economy in the performance of
governmental functions.   The League of the Rights of Man
undertakes the most laborious inquiries into alleged miscar-
riages of justice.   Nor is this all.   On every hand the government is beginning, tentatively, indeed, and without evident
understanding of its ultimate significance, to associate the private citizen with the business of administration.[192]   The Superior Council of Agriculture is a board of expert council.   The
Consultative Committee on Railways, instituted by the minister of public works, comprises within its membership representatives of most of the great industries by which the railways
profit.   It is a committee with genuine functions and a growing
power.   It speaks with a representative suggestiveness that is
far too powerful to be ignored.   Nor is this less true of commerce or of charity.   On all hands there are growing up associations of every kind which aim directly at supplementing the
work of parties on the one hand, and directly controlling the
business of administration on the other.[193]   They in nowise
supplant the ordinary mechanisms of party; but they are often
enough important in the direction they can give to the forces
of public opinion.   They are the beginning of what will eventually be the definite organisation of every interest that is affected by the action of the state.   They are the admission of
elements within the national life that refuse to find their ordinary satisfaction in the accepted methods of politics.   They
represent the growing emphasis upon the diverse elements that
go to make up citizenship, and, in particular, the insistence
upon the importance of function.   They are at the beginning
of their evolution and not at the end of it; for the definite
organisation of the consumer's interest in the state has a significance scarcely capable of exaggeration.[194]

Ultimately, indeed, what such a movement implies is the

[192] It is, of course, profoundly suggestive to compare this tendency with
the organisation of the Council of National Defence instituted by Congress
after the outbreak of war.

[193] On all this cf. Cahen, op. cit., pp. 266-95.

[194] Its beginnings in England and the United States in such organisations as the Navy League, the Housewives' League, etc., are of course,
well-known.

advent of a consumers' syndicalism—the organisation of the consumer's interest in the product of an industry exactly as there is today the organisation of the producers' interest. It is unquestionable that a public opinion so created would tend to assist the claims of the civil service. It would, in the first place, be obvious that the abuses of which the fonctionnaire complains are productive of waste and inefficiency. It is hardly less clear that the whole basis of good administration is the possession of a contented civil service. It is difficult to say whether a public opinion would today admit fonctionnariste autonomy; the probability is that a long process of education would be needed before that end could be achieved. But it is hardly possible to doubt that the organisation of opinion upon the problems of the civil service would lead to striking reform. Certainly this has been the lesson of English experience in this regard.[195] No large step could be taken which would not involve its freedom from the control of political interests; and that is likely to prove a first step on the road to the autonomous decentralisation that is claimed.

It is impossible to prophesy in the face of a cataclysm. What alone emerges as immediately certain is the growing importance of the administrative function. It is certain that for long to come the state must burden itself with a far fuller control of the social life than it has ever before assumed. Obviously enough, in such an analysis, the position of the civil service becomes one of the greatest significance. It will be fundamentally impossible to go back to the epoch before the outbreak of war; the only question will rather be what measure of satisfaction the fonctionnaire will obtain. Never before will the need of efficient administration have been so great; never before will the penalty of discontent have been so heavy. The evolution of administrative syndicalism in modern France connects itself logically with this outlook. For the task of government is likely to prove far too vast to make possible an efficient and centralised control. In administration, not less than in economics, a law of diminishing returns is applicable. There comes a point in the business of government when the

[195] Cf. the report of the Royal Commission on the Civil Service (1915), especially the separate memoranda signed by Mr. Graham Wallas.

further burdening of the central authority does not produce an adequate return for the outlay it involves. Decentralisation becomes at that point essential. It is the only way in which the congestion by which all unitary governments are oppressed can be relieved. It provides the only method by which the necessary attention can be given to special and local needs.[196] That is true not less of special occupations than of special areas. No one, for instance, can study the problem involved in the fixation of railroad rates without feeling at once the immense difficulties that are involved in the assumption of any necessary desirability in a uniform system.[197] We are on all hands faced by the questions of diversity and delimitation. The erection of distinct and autonomous authorities is the logical outcome of that recognition.

The mistake we have made in the past is to think of federal government in terms simply of area and of distance. Federations in the past have been so naturally the outcome either of vast size on the one hand or of the coalescence of historically separate communities on the other, that it has been difficult not to translate our federal thought immediately into spatial terms. We must learn to think differently. Even in America, the classic ground of federal experiment, it is a new federalism that is everywhere developing.[198] If, as with the districts of the Federal Reserve System, and of the Rural Credits Board, it is at least partly a matter of area, it is not less obvious that a federalism of functions is at hand—that is to say that exactly as in the past we attempted delimitation by area, so, today, we are attempting the delimitation of purposes. There is a clear tendency upon the part of industrial and professional groups to become self-governing. Legislation consecrates the solutions they evolve. They become sovereign in the sense— which, after all, is the only sense that matters—that the rules they draw up are recognized as the answer to the problems they have to meet. They are obtaining compulsory power

[196] Cf. my "Problem of Sovereignty," Appendix B.

[197] Cf. the remarkable evidence of Mr. Justice Brandeis before the interstate Commerce Commission of the U. S. Senate, Sixty-Second Congress, 1911-12, pp. 1267-72.

[198] Cf. Mr. Croly's article in the "The New Republic," Vol. IX, p. 170.

over their members; they demand their taxes; they exercise their discipline; they enforce their penal sanctions. They raise every question that the modern federal state has to meet and their experience is, governmentally, a valuable basis for national enterprise.[199]

But their assumption of sovereign powers is important in another aspect. To make the state omnicompetent is to leave it at the mercy of any group that is powerful enough to exploit it. That has been, indeed, one of the main historical causes of social unrest. It transforms every political struggle into an economic conflict. It inevitably introduces the bitterness of a fight between interests which, in such an aspect, dare not offer compromise with their antagonists. The only way out of such an impasse is the neutralisation of the state; and it cannot be neutralised saved by the division of the power that is today concentrated in its hands. For to proclaim, to take a single example, the supreme interest of the state in preserving order in times of strikes, is already to make it take sides. The supreme interest of the state is in justice, and it does not necessarily follow that justice and order are in perfect correlation. No one who has studied the relation between the state's interest in the preservation of order and the exploitation of that interest in Colorado will find room for serious doubt in this regard. To make the state universal and paramount is to make it the creature of those who can possess themselves of its instruments. What obviously must be done is to secure the limitation of its activities, on the one hand, and the independence of its instruments on the other. But the functions so delimited demand, in their turn, their organisation and we are thus driven back to federal government.[200]

It is in such an aspect as this that the movement towards administrative syndicalism must be interpreted. It is not a revolt against society but against the state. It is not a revolt against authority but against a theory of it which

---

[199] Not the least powerful argument against direct government, for example, is the experience from early trade-union history, cf. Webb, "Industrial Democracy," pp. 1-71.

[200] On all this M. Paul-Boncour's "Fédéralisme Economique" is an admirable mine of information.

is, in fact, equivalent to servitude. For the obvious fact is that men will not peacefully endure a situation they deem intolerable; and any theory of politics which denounces their action out of hand at once stamps itself as inadequate. The truth obviously is that the state must organize itself on lines which admit to the full the opportunity for the realisation of personal and corporate initiative; and it is simply an induction from the experience of the last century that a sovereign state can be driven so to organize itself only by compulsion. That is the real importance of the theory of this movement. The federalism and the decentralisation it implies[201] are, in fact, the basis upon which the state of the future can be erected. They are the sign-posts of its new orientation. They take account of the obvious fact that the sovereignty of the state is a power to will; but they insist upon the limitations of that power. For a study of the processes of the state convincingly demonstrates that without such limitation there is no real security for liberty. The purpose of the state may be good; but more important than the doctrine that it inculcates is the actual life that it leads. It is the experience of its life, the contact with its personality, that has made the fonctionnaire refuse absorption by it. He is unwilling, even in theory, to leave it as Leviathan. For sovereignty, it cannot too often be emphasised, implies the possession of legal rights; and by its legal rights—in theory limitless—the state will define its moral powers.[202] The individual gets caught in a complex web of rights and duties where morality is confounded by the ambiguity of terms. To limit state-power is to suggest at once that its action is capable of judgment. It is to exalt the importance of individual personality and thus to give to citizenship a profounder value. It is to make the use of power at every moment a moral question by demanding enquiry into the end it is to serve. It is, in Mr. Figgis' phrase, to replace the study of rights by the study of right; and if that attitude is frankly medieval, it is none the worse for that.[203]

[201] Though related they are different things, cf. Duguit, "Manuel de Droit Constitutionnel," p. 77 ff.

[202] Cf. my "Problem of Sovereignty," p. 20.

[203] Figgis, "From Gerson to Grotius," p. 153.

For authority, after all, must depend upon internal roots if it is to be of any avail. We too rarely consider how difficult is the decision to combat the state. The presumption in general opinion is, for the most part, on its side. Order is the accustomed mode of life, and to betray it seems like enough to social treason. There is probably no epoch in social history where organised resistance to state-decision has not its root is some deep grievance honestly conceived. It was so in 1381; it was so in 1642; in 1688 and in 1789. "Reform that you may preserve" is, as Macaulay said,[204] "the voice of great events." The state has barely heeded that constant warning; and the beatification of the *status quo* is ever its main source of danger. Administrative syndicalism is simply a step towards translating into effective terms the programme of democratic government. It is its statement as a process instead of as a claim. Above all, it has realised that to preserve the play of mind, whether in the government of the state or of more private enterprise, its active exercise is the one sure path of safety. The real danger in any society is lest decision on great events secure only the passive concurrence of the mass of men. It is only by intensifying the active participation of men in the business of government that liberty can be made secure. For there is a poison in power against which even the greatest of nations must be upon its guard. The temptation demands resistances; and the solution is to deprive the state of any priority not fully won by performance. That is what is implied in the fonctionnaire's demand. He can, as he thinks, make the state a fuller and richer thing by the dispersion of its sovereignty. He can preserve his own respect by securing an effective voice in the determination of events. He can prevent the exploitation of the administrative services by making their processes objective in character. It is a movement that is as yet but at its beginning; and it is as dangerous as it is fascinating to depict its end. Of this only we may be certain, that there is no phase of social life in which its motives are not, however dimly manifestly penetrating; and it will one day mean, perhaps for the first time, a state wherein the basis of citizenship will be the active intelligence of enlightened men.

[204] "Trevelyan's Life," I, 149 n.

NOTE ON THE BIBLIOGRAPHY OF LAMENNAIS

Any full list of the books on Lamennais would itself make a small volume. All I propose to do here is to suggest the most valuable sources for the period covered by the preceding essay (A). For his actual works I have used the quarto edition in two volumes published just after his excommunication. This contains everything of importance up to that time, including his articles in *L'Avenir*. Hardly less important is the correspondence of which there are several volumes. (I) Those edited by M. Forgues. (II) Those edited by his nephew, A. Blaize. (III) The "Letters to the Baron de Vitrolles" ed. Forgues. (IV) The "Letters to Montalembert" ed. Forgues. (V) "Un Lamennais inconnu." ed. Laveille; (the letters to Benoit d'Azy.) (VI) "Lamennais d'après des documents inédits" ed. Roussel, contains many unpublished letters, but the commentary by their collector is ignorant and prejudiced. (VII) "Lettres à la baronne Cottu" ed. d'Haussonville. Those volumes edited by M.Forgues are by far the most valuable, though the correspondence edited by Blaize has much significance for the early years; the rest of what has been published has, except for odd letters, mostly a literary or psychological interest (B). The most complete life of Lamennais is that by the Abbé Charles Boutard in three volumes (1913). It is, however, severely hampered, as a critical study by the necessary theological limitations. The life by Eugene Spuller (1892) errs almost as much on the side of anti-clericalism, but it is the best brief study we have. On the early years the full study by M. Charles Maréchal is admirable. On the conflict with Rome I have used the essay by Père Dudon, "Lamennais et la Sainte Siège," as it collects all the relevant documents, but its polemical object is obvious throughout. The best philosophic criticism is still that of Janet, "La Philosophie de Lamennais" (1890), but there are good studies by M. Faguet in the second volume of his " Politiques et Moralistes," and by M. Ferraz in the second volume of his "Histoire de la Philosophie en France." That by Renan, in his "Essais de Morale et de Critique" is by far the most sympathetic psychological analysis; though the more famous essay of Sainte-Beuve in the *Revue des Deux Mondes* for May 1834 was one of the first to seize the real significance of his life; see also the essay reprinted in *Portraits Contemporains*. I have seen no adequate study in English, though there exists a book by the Hon. W. Gibson on "Lamennais and Liberal Catholicism" which I have been unable to procure.

INDEX

A

Acton (Lord), on states-general, 39; definition of liberty, 55; nature of good in politics, 121.

Aristotle, sets the perspective of political science, 19; on the purpose of the state, 20; on separation of powers, 70; value of his definition of citizenship, 73; on secret of happiness, 89.

Arnold (Dr.), on Jewish emancipation, 38.

Authority, justification of, 32 f.; limitations of, 42 f.; perversions of, 49 f.; problem of, often unknown to government, 51; must be divided, 69 f.; judged by purposes, 74; danger of, where centralised, 78 f.; should be divided for sake of ethical achievement, 107 f.; Bonald derives from God, 141; necessary in Bonald's theory, 148; division of rejected by Bonald, 150; not justified by mere existence, 224; cannot have implicit obedience, 266; mistaken use of, by Rome, 271 f.; relation to liberty, 274; must be democratically interpreted, 279; must be widespread, 305; derives from individual personality, 311; dependent on popular acceptance, 336.

B

Bacon (Francis), definition of trust quoted, 102.

Bagehot (Walter), on danger of labor combination in politics, 36; criticism of reform, 40.

Bentham (Jeremy), sneers at natural rights, 63.

Béranger, prosecution of, 214.

Berryer, denies that the articles of 1682 are a part of French law, 226.

Bismarck, failure of his attack on Roman Catholic church, 45; his canons of conduct, 69.

Blackstone, on sovereignty, 24; attitude to corporations, 84.

Bodin, on sovereignty, 24; on separation of powers, 70.

Bonald, character, 128 f.; theories derived from 17th century, 130; his political theory, 130 f.; attack on individualism, 136 f.; implications of his attack, 143 f; his religious philosophy, 147 f.; on danger of discussion, 151 f.; on importance of religion in state, 157 f.; criticism of his views, 161 f.; later influence, 166 f.; debt of Lamennais to, 205.

Bossuet, the inspiration of Bonald, 130-1; his attack on the reformation, 143.

Bourget (P.), a reincarnation of Bonald, 170; his traditionalism, 177 f.; conception of aristocracy, 180; attack on parliamentary régime, 183; wants a monarchy in France, 185.